# THE RISE AND FALL OF GERMANY'S
## COLONIAL EMPIRE
### 1884 - 1918

# The
# Rise and Fall of Germany's Colonial Empire
## 1884-1918

BY

MARY EVELYN TOWNSEND

WITH AN INTRODUCTION BY
CARLTON J. H. HAYES

NEW YORK

Howard Fertig

1966

First published in 1930 by
The Macmillan Company


Howard Fertig, Inc. edition 1966

Library of Congress Catalog Card Number: 66-24356

PRINTED IN THE UNITED STATES OF AMERICA
BY NOBLE OFFSET PRINTERS

# INTRODUCTION

It has long been customary to find high adventure and stimulating romance in the record of the rise and fall of the French colonial empire of the eighteenth century. Years ago Francis Parkman immortalized that empire, and a host of subsequent writers have added many details to the memory of it: its building by a gallant succession of explorers, missionaries, adventurers, trappers, traders, settlers, soldiers; its sweeping expansion from the mouth of the St. Lawrence to the delta of the Mississippi; its epic conflicts with the English; and its tragic end in the fatal duel of Montcalm and Wolfe.

History never exactly repeats itself, for no two personalities are ever identical, and material conditions and circumstances are always changing. But there are parallels in history. There are recurring human dramas that present striking similarities of character and scene. Everybody recognizes—sometimes too easily—such parallels, such similarities, especially if these are associated with the distant past which historians have explored and popularized. Usually it is more difficult for a contemporary generation, unaided by the imaginative genius of historians, to perceive in its own seemingly prosaic age any deeds that can be compared, or even contrasted, with those splendid far-off dramas of which it has read.

The very generation which is now passing away has

hardly comprehended that it was spectator of, or participant in, the rise and fall of a colonial empire, which as sheer drama promises eventually to rival, if not to surpass in human interest and significance, the romantic story of the rise and fall of the old French colonial empire. For the German colonial empire of our day was builded more rapidly, expanded more distantly, experienced more kaleidoscopic changes, and came to a more abrupt end, in a far vaster cataclysm, than that old empire of the French. In 1878 Germany possessed not a square foot of colonial domain. Twenty years later she owned huge areas in Africa, East, South West, Central, and West, and spacious islands and whole archipelagoes in the Pacific, and was looking forward to the rôle of residuary legatee to the colonial estate of Spain and Portugal. Ten years more, she ranked third among the Powers of the world in the extent, population, resources, and strength of her oversea holdings, and second in those by-products of imperialism—navy, merchant marine, commerce, and tariff protectionism: she was indeed Imperial Germany. Another ten years, and the curtain had fallen on the last act far more dramatically than it had risen on the first: *Weltmacht* had been succeeded by *Niedergang;* Germany's merchant vessels were vanished, her warships were at the bottom of the sea, her flag was flying only in Europe; and not a square inch of colonial domain did she possess: she was, in fact, Shorn Germany.

This latest story of the rise and fall of a colonial empire deserves a telling, and in the present volume Dr. Townsend has told it from start to finish. Hers is the labor of the pioneer. She is the first person to study intensively the whole range of Germany's colonial experiences and to relate it within the covers of a book. For the first time it is now possible for the reader to obtain a general survey, and much detailed knowledge, of a most impressive and significant development of recent times.

Dr. Townsend's pioneer work is competent. She herself is a trained historian, long interested in Germany and familiar with the source-materials of modern German history. Some years ago she published a scholarly essay on *The Origins of Modern German Colonialism,* and during the past ten years—ever since the conclusion of the World War —she has been assembling data and preparing manuscript for the present volume.

The present volume should interest a large audience. In the first place, it is a specific discussion of general problems of imperialism which nowadays concern all good citizens in every industrialized country. It shows in detail how a national state may drift almost accidentally and quite suddenly into imperialism; how a few seekers of fame, fortune, fun, or heathen souls may cooperate wittingly or unwittingly to arouse a nation to colonial endeavor; how a national government, in defense of the "rights" and "interests" of some of its citizens, may be led to establish and extend an oversea dominion; how, once a colonial empire is founded, problems multiply for "backward" natives and "forward" settlers, novel international difficulties arise, and the mother-country, while seeking to conciliate foreign rivals, must prepare to fight them. It also shows how the end may come terribly swift and definite. It should appeal to all those who would know the complexities and perils of imperialism, and its responsibilities.

Secondly, the book should serve to correct numerous popular misconceptions concerning the German colonies. A considerable part of the propaganda, which emanated from Allied countries during the World War, consisted of allegations against German colonial administration, with the pur-

# INTRODUCTION

pose of proving that Germany had misused her colonies and
mistreated the natives and that therefore, "in the interests
of civilization," she should be obliged to surrender her
colonial empire to the Allies. Now, ten years after the
war, it is possible for Dr. Townsend to view matters more
objectively and to do fuller justice to Germany. She holds
no brief for or against any country, but by a strict adherence
to facts she presents ample evidence for her belief that Germany's colonial administration was neither better nor worse
than that of any other colonial Power similarly circum-
stanced. Her evidence should be welcomed by all persons
who desire to free themselves from war myths.

Finally, Dr. Townsend has conveniently assembled a
factual record in which the more imaginative among us can
readily perceive the high adventure and stimulating romance
that have characterized our own days as well as those of
Champlain, Marquette, and Frontenac. To all such, this
book is especially commended.

CARLTON J. H. HAYES.

Columbia University,
November 11, 1929.

viii

# PREFACE

A CONTEMPORARY historian has said:

There are few chapters in the history of the world at once so important, so small in compass, so complete in themselves and so rich in political lessons. A whole oversea empire was won and lost by Germany in a single generation.

A. P. NEWTON, The Sea Commonwealth<br>(London, 1919), p. 33.

The present book is an attempt to relate this chapter. Here the reader may find the pioneers, the "Trader Horns," the groups responsible for the German colonial empire of our own day. He may read a description of its African provinces and its South Sea Islands; the value of their palm trees, their cocoa plantations or their phosphate beds; the amount of their trade and the administration of their native blacks. Here also he may discern, if he will, the relationship of these suddenly and tardily acquired colonies to Germany's own expanding life between the years 1871 and 1914: to her vigorous material growth, to her lively party politics and to her drive for world power.

At the same time the narrative aims to present Germany's modern colonial movement in its contemporary setting formed by the imperialistic activities of the other Great Powers and their mutual relations: to show its connection with British and French rivalry in Africa, with British and Russian competition in the Near East, and with the strife for empire in the Pacific. In short, the discussion is designed to insert one more section into that vari-colored picture puzzle of world politics which immediately preceded the Great War.

## PREFACE

In the main, the study has been prompted by the fact that there exists nothing in English which provides a connected colonial history of one of the most important Great Powers before 1914. Consequently, it is hoped that the book will supply the missing chapter, and furnish a handy manual for college students and others engaged in the study of late nineteenth and twentieth century imperialism and international politics.

The author makes no claim to any extensive original investigation prior to the year 1871. The *Introduction* which surveys German colonial traditions before the nineteenth century is based with few exceptions upon secondary works. On the other hand, the material embracing the period 1871-1914 has been drawn almost entirely from first-hand sources, of which there exists a great wealth, especially for the Bismarckian era. These consist for the most part of the *Reichstag Debates, White Books,* government documents, records and letters of Bismarck, official publications of colonial and other commercial societies as well as propaganda literature, programs of political parties, periodicals, newspapers, histories of trading and banking companies. Recently, "of the making of books there has been no end" in the field of international relations immediately prior to the Great War, so voluminous is the mass of published *Archives, Documents, Correspondence,* as well as the numerous *Memoirs, Autobiographies, Lebenserinnerungen,* and *Confessions* of the chief actors of the period. All such material illumines directly or indirectly Germany's colonial history especially in its connection with that of the other Powers, ofttimes correcting in a startling manner what prove to have been well-rooted misconceptions. No one more than the author, however, is aware of the inadequacy of the present work in reflecting the results of a complete examination of this literature.

Nor is the author insensible to the many and varied obligations owing to all those who have so generously aided in the preparation of this volume but heartily welcomes an opportunity to acknowledge them with sincere gratitude: to Professor Carlton J. H. Hayes of the department of History, Columbia University, for the original impetus to the study, itself a continuation of the graduate research once pursued under his stimulating direction; to Professor William R. Shepherd of the department of History and to Professor Parker T. Moon of the department of Public Law, Columbia University, for their encouragement and expert criticism; to Professor Joseph V. Fuller of the Division of Publications, Department of State, Washington (Diplomatic History), author of *Bismarck's Diplomacy at Its Zenith,* for his helpful reading of the chapters on Bismarck; to Professor James T. Shotwell of the Carnegie Endowment of International Peace, to Professor Frederick Heuser of the department of Germanic Languages, Columbia University, as well as to the *Institute of International Education* and others for their facilitation of valuable contacts in Germany; and to Dr. Mildred S. Wertheimer of the Research Department of the *Foreign Policy Association* for her critical reading of the manuscript.

In addition, the author wishes to thank those many German scholars and officials whose generous courtesy and cooperation made possible the use of indispensable materials. Among them are: Dr. Eduard Rosenbaum of the *Commerz-bibliothek* in Hamburg; *Regierungsrat* Hans Zache and others of the *Kolonial Institut* in Hamburg; Dr. Gustav Wahl, Director of the University Library, Hamburg; Professor Rein of the University of Hamburg; Professor Arthur

Salz of the University of Heidelberg; Dr. Heinrich Schnee, ex-Governor of German East Africa; Dr. Seitz, President of the *Kolonialverein;* Dr. Hans Ziemann, ex-Staff Physician of South West Africa and Professor in the University of Berlin; Professor Hobohm, Professor of History, University of Berlin; Dr. Bernhard Dernburg, ex-Colonial Secretary; General Rochus Schmidt, veteran of the early colonial wars; the officials of the German Foreign Office, of the valuable library of the *Kolonialverein* in Berlin and of the *Kolonialschule* in Witzenhausen.

Finally, for their generous permission to reproduce maps and graphic illustrations, grateful acknowledgment is accorded to Professor Max Eckert, author of *Wirtschafts atlas der Deutschen Kolonieen* (Dietrich Reimer, Berlin), and to *Regierungsrat* von Jastrow and Dr. Dannert, authors of *Deutschland Braucht Kolonieen* (Berlin, 1924).

MARY E. TOWNSEND.

Washington, Connecticut
September 15, 1928

# CONTENTS

xiii

# CONTENTS

# CONTENTS

# CONTENTS

# CONTENTS

# CONTENTS

# MAPS

# GRAPHIC ILLUSTRATIONS

# TABLES

# THE RISE AND FALL OF GERMANY'S
# COLONIAL EMPIRE
## 1884 - 1918

# THE RISE AND FALL OF GERMANY'S COLONIAL EMPIRE 1884-1918

## CHAPTER I

### GERMANY'S LACK OF A COLONIAL EMPIRE

#### PRESENT POVERTY AND PAST TRADITION

##### *Introduction*

TODAY Germany stands alone, the only Great Power without a colony. The German Republic possesses no single square mile of oversea territory, no naval base, no sphere of influence. For the Treaty of Versailles demanded that Germany renounce to the Allies "all rights and titles to her oversea possessions," all special rights and privileges in China, Siam, Liberia, Morocco, and Egypt,[1] and thus, at one stroke, entirely swept away the German colonial empire.

Since 1918 the Allies have partitioned these lands among themselves, and hold them today as mandates under the League of Nations. Great Britain administers most of German East Africa, now the Tanganyika Territory, one-sixth of Kamerun, one-third of Togoland, and the phosphate island of Nauru in the South Seas; Australia is the Mandatary for the Bismarck Archipelago and Kaiser Wilhelms-land in the South Seas, New Zealand for German Samoa, and the British Union of South Africa for the neighboring territory of German South West Africa; France holds two-thirds of Togoland and five-sixths of Kamerun and Belgium

1

a small part of German East Africa known as Ruanda Urundi; while Japan, having restored Kiao-Chow to China, retains the Marshall Islands.

Although Germany's late colonial empire appears large when broken up into so many pieces and separately enumerated, it actually amounted to only 1,027,000 square miles all told; an astonishingly meager total when considered in relation to the size and position of the mother country. Before the war, among the seven colonial nations of Europe, Germany had the largest home population and the smallest ratio to it of oversea empire; today, the Peace Settlement has still further increased the difference between her position and that of the other colonial Powers. For instance, Belgium, with a population of seven and a quarter millions, has a colonial empire of nearly a million square miles; Portugal, with a population of six millions, has an empire of equal extent; France, with thirty-nine millions, has an empire of nearly five million square miles; Great Britain, with forty-four millions of inhabitants at home, has an empire of thirteen million, six hundred and sixteen thousand square miles;[2] while Germany, the third greatest industrial Power, stands outside the ranks of colonial nations.

Additional evidence of Germany's conspicuous backwardness in the acquisition of colonial territories is the striking fact that her entire oversea dominion as it existed in 1914 had all been won within the span of a single generation: prior to the year 1884 not a square mile of it belonged to her. For Germany had been as much of a late-comer in entering the field of expansion as she had been in achieving her national unity and in joining the family of nations in Western Europe. So late was she in fact that she found all of the desirable lands oversea for the most part already occupied either as a result of the colonial activity of the sixteenth and seventeenth centuries, in which she had only a small and insignificant share, or because of the imperialist movement of the nineteenth century in which she had participated somewhat tardily, handicapped by youth and inexperience.

## Germany's Rich Colonial Tradition

Seeking some explanation of this backwardness, this apparent "arrested development," one is led to inquire whether Germany was deficient in colonial initiative. But even the most superficial search into her historical background shows the exact opposite to be the case. Such an examination reveals that the country possesses one of the oldest and the richest colonial traditions; that the urge for expansion, in fact, has been a constant factor in her history, no period of which has failed to give it some expression.

It must be remembered in this connection that the word "colonization" is employed here in its broadest, most comprehensive sense rather than in its modern, restricted meaning. For the term is used to include migrations into neighboring or contiguous territory and not to refer only to the acquisition of lands, economic concessions and spheres of influence oversea. It must be recalled, in other words, that "colonization" before the fifteenth century meant expansion in Europe or on the shores of the Mediterranean, the Black and the Baltic Seas, the establishment of agricultural or trading colonies, or the cultivation and settlement of desert lands; and only from the second half of the fifteenth century did modern "colonization," best expressed today, perhaps, as economic imperialism, begin.

But, no matter which of these interpretations be attached to the word "colonization," German history can provide an

3

illustration of each. If it is migration that is meant, we have but to observe the geographical situation of Germany which has always fostered expansion, for, unlike many other countries, Germany has never possessed any natural boundaries. The Germans, therefore, have always been unrestrained by barriers and, being a prolific folk, have literally "sprawled over Central, Western and Eastern Europe, whether, in their long history, their land has been called Germany, the Holy Roman Empire, Austria-Hungary, Brandenburg-Prussia, or the German Empire." Unlike France, for example, a territorially fixed unit and therefore static, Germany has no material, clear-cut frontiers and has therefore always been dynamic.

## Early and Medieval Migrations

During the period of migrations from the fifth to the eighth centuries, German tribes penetrated and overran every part of Western Europe. The one constant factor in that confused and chaotic epoch was the ubiquity of the Teutons: they spread from Northern Africa to the British Isles and Scandinavia; from the home of the Franks to the Balkan Peninsula. But Teuton supremacy endured in these lands only from two to three hundred years at the utmost. Ultimately succumbing to a more advanced civilization, the conquerors became assimilated and maintained German dominance only where the Romans were in the minority, that is, in "Old Germany" itself, the country on the right of the Danube, in Bavaria and on the right bank of the Rhine.

As concentrated peoples emerged in the Middle Ages, notably the Franks, German colonization turned back to the East from whence it had originally come, and, because the range had narrowed, especially after the Treaty of Verdun (814), became much more intensive and focused toward

4

certain well-defined areas. Thus, a distinct wave of expansion, eastward, or rather a series of waves, characterized the years from the eighth to the twelfth centuries.[3] Fraught with historical significance to Western Europe, the movement deserves some description here, although owing to the limits of this discussion, it cannot receive the detail which its importance and interest merit.

While the Teutons had been pressing westward in the general migration prior to 800 their neighbors, the Slavs, had followed closely at their heels occupying, permanently to all appearances, the original home-lands of the Germans. The year 800, therefore, found the Slav world of huge extent, stretching roughly from the mouth of the Elbe to the head of the Adriatic, and thus confining the Germans approximately to the valleys of the Rhine and upper Danube, to Bavaria, and to Thuringia and Saxony. On the other hand, the increasing dominance of the Franks and their political separation from the Germans after the break-up of Charlemagne's empire created a wall which effectually blocked any further westward expansion of the Teutons. Moreover, the increasing economic stability of the West, which was crystallizing into the feudal system, drove the Germans out. Indeed, this agrarian revolution was largely responsible for the eastward drift, which reveals itself as a definite trend in the ninth century. The small German landowner and free farmer fled before the encroachments and increasing extension of the manorial régime and before the "grasping character of the Frankish Grandees." Furthermore, ecclesiastical and commercial interests, those ever-present forerunners of colonization, had prepared the way for German expansion eastward: monkish missionaries had been active among the Slavs; Rhine merchants had been importing grain from the Slav-tilled fields; and at the market of Naumburg the Wend exchanged wares with the German.

Animated, then, by the colonial motives of every age, race supremacy, religion, language, trade, customs and most of all, land hunger—and inspired by Charlemagne's conquest of Saxony during the last quarter of the eighth century—the German *Drang nach Osten* was well under way by the year 900 and resolved itself into three movements more or less parallel or overlapping each other. The first one, chronologically, advanced southeast, sweeping through Bavaria, Austria, Hungary, Silesia and parts of Poland. It was a great popular, peaceful migration, pushed from the rear by the rapidly growing populations of Saxony and the Rhine valley, as well as by the Dutch dispossessed of their territory by the sea; and stimulated from the front by invitations from the non-German princes who desired German industry and skill in settling their unoccupied soil. "Not the sword of the knight but the plough of the peasant developed the land," ⁴ whose pioneers were missionaries, merchants and princes.

The second movement concerned itself mainly with reclaiming and settling the fertile plains of the Elbe and Oder rivers, regarded by the Germans as their "home-lands," and with the acquisition of Nordalbingia, Schwerin and Ratzeburg. After long and fierce struggles with the Slavs, it culminated in 1134 when Albrecht the Bear gained Brandenburg, and in 1157 when Henry the Lion occupied Lübeck. And the third and last movement, building upon the second, spread northeast along the Baltic coast into Kurland, Esthonia and Prussia under the leadership of the Brothers of the Sword and of the Teutonic Knights. These monks and crusaders succeeded in colonizing for Germany the territory halfway round the Baltic Bight; while the

German merchant landing in Livland from the trading post at Wisby completed the semi-circle and thus laid the foundations for the brilliant rise of the Hanseatic League. All three movements united in forcing back the Slavs and their net result represents a displacement of Slav political domination, Slav economic, religious and cultural civilization by German, a displacement which still remains a matter of dispute in our own day.

## The Hanseatic League

On the other hand, if it is the purely economic sense that is attached to the word "colonization," meaning the establishment of trading colonies, the winning of spheres of commercial influence oversea, then, before all other countries, Germany can produce the best example in the famous Hanseatic League. For of all the individual forces responsible for German expansion in the Middle Ages, the Hansa merchants were the most effective. They carried German goods and German customs throughout North and Northeastern Europe, and made German commercial power second only to Italian in the commerce of Western Europe. Although they founded their settlements and far-flung Factories in the interests of trade alone and not for colonial settlement, strictly defined, still they imparted a stimulus to expansion and a strength and tenacity to the tradition of German colonization which has been of lasting influence. For it was the descendants of the Hanseatic merchants who kept alive the colonial tradition in the fifteenth and sixteenth centuries; who revived German colonization in the nineteenth century; and who were responsible for the origins of the modern German colonial empire of our own day. Because of their far-reaching influence, therefore, they must command a brief discussion.

7

Medieval conditions—disorder, robbery, lack of good roads, unrestrained individualism, and the absence of a strong, central, protective power—gave birth to the Hanseatic League; and so long as those conditions prevailed it flourished, only coming to an end when the medieval age was succeeded by the modern. Indeed, the conjunction of two leagues, formed to cope with the economic restrictions and handicaps of the times, was responsible for the Hansa: the one, the Association of German merchants abroad; and the other, the League of North German cities at home.

The earliest appearance of a guild of German traders abroad was at Wisby on the island of Gotland in the Baltic, which, by the twelfth century, had become the center of trade. From the earliest times, the raw products of the Baltic lands, grain, wood, metals, fish, and wax had attracted the merchants of the North German and Wendish towns whose commercial activities we have already noted, were encouraged by Henry the Lion. Merchants from Lübeck, Soest, Münster, Dortmund, Bremen, later Cologne and Utrecht, belonged to the Association and, by 1287, their agreements, consummated in their assembly at Wisby, became binding upon the home cities. Because Wisby became somewhat inconvenient for the holding of a General Assembly, Lübeck, owing to its strategically geographical position, finally succeeded it as head of the Association.

At the same time, German merchants from Theil, Bremen, Liège and principally Cologne, established trading stations in Norway, Iceland,[5] Flanders and, most important of all, in England, where, shortly after the middle of the twelfth century, Cologne gained the right to have its own Guildhall and to be the head of the Association of Merchants, first called the Hansa. Lübeck, however, on account of its strength and position succeeded to Cologne's dominance in

London and, by 1281, the "German Hansa" there (still meaning only an Association of Merchants) received its privileges from the English king, Edward I.

While these Merchant Associations were being formed abroad, the other organization from which the Hansa sprang was taking shape at home. Since the beginning of the thirteenth century, alliances and leagues had been cemented between the north German cities for protection, for improvement of roads and for regularization of customs, laws and coinage. The most important of these was the League of the so-called Wendish cities, Lübeck, Rostock, Wismar, Stralsund, Greifswald. It was this League which finally gained supremacy over the others, incorporated within itself the separate Merchants' Associations abroad, inaugurated a successful war of the Wendish cities against Denmark, and finally emerged as the German Hansa. At its height, the Hansa came to include over seventy towns which were divided first into three, and then into four circles: the Wendish towns, with Lübeck the principal city; the Saxon towns, with Brunswick; the Westphalian towns, with Cologne; and the Prussian cities, with Danzig as their leader.[6]

As from the beginning, the principal scene of the Hansa's activity was the Baltic Sea, and one of the chief functions of the League was to gain concessions and trading rights from those princes whose lands, such as Russia, Sweden, Denmark, Norway, bordered the Baltic. Thus the German merchants gradually penetrated these countries by acquiring freedom from customs dues, from shipping fees, from native laws; and most important of all, by securing the right to establish that foundation of all trade colonies, the Factory or *Kontor*.

Factories generally embraced a number of buildings in

9

which lived the German merchants under the strictest regulations drawn up by the League, regulations almost cloister-like in the life which they dictated. An outstanding example of the Factories in the Baltic lands was the one at Bergen, Norway, which consisted of twenty-two buildings and housed from two to three thousand merchants, all of whom must remain unmarried. It was a community absolutely independent of Norway, governed entirely by German law and custom. Every contact with the natives of the country, aside from trading relations, was discouraged and indeed carefully guarded against by legislation in order that conflicts of any kind might be avoided.[7]

Naturally, such independent, self-sufficient communities like Bergen could exist only in the undeveloped lands of the Baltic and in England, states which were at this time both politically and economically weak. Of quite another character were the *Kontors* in Bruges and Venice. In Bruges, the German merchants lived among the townspeople and the Factory served principally as a warehouse; while in Venice, the Germans were without any independence whatever in the *Fondaco dei Tedeschi,* where they were obliged to dwell under the watchful eyes of the Venetians, hedged about with the strictest regulations as to their movements.

This brief description of the Factories has been elaborated to show that the Hanseatic League did not promote colonization, meaning settlement, in any sense whatsoever; even in the undeveloped Baltic lands it carried on a purely commercial colonization. The personnel within the *Kontors* was continually changing and there was no attempt to establish individual settlements outside the confines of the Factories. Nevertheless, the Hansa's influence upon German colonization was a very real one. In the Baltic lands especially, the Germans became the pioneers of commerce: they taught navigation, trading methods, commercial law; they carried goods from the Far East and Europe into northern lands and, although they did not mingle with the inhabitants, the life of their Factories, veritable oases of German religion, art, culture and economic life, could not help but leave an indelible impress upon those countries in the formative stage of their existence. The commercial expansion effected by the Hanseatic League carried German civilization far afield and might well have prepared the way for an extended political expansion had not the very force—a centralized dynastic nationalism—which Germany and the Hansa lacked, arisen in those same lands to destroy it and to expel everything German.

## *The Age of Exploration*

Although the material achievements of the Hanseatic League crumbled before the institutions of a new age, its spirit and tradition still survived. Its glorious and romantic past stimulated the descendants of the Hansa merchants to play their small part in the meagre opportunities open to Germany during the Golden Age of oversea expansion in the fifteenth and the sixteenth centuries. Recent research among the commercial records of Spain and Portugal and the papers of the prominent firms of the Rhenish cities, like those of the Welsers and Fuggers, has revealed a greater share of German participation in the trade of the Indies than has hitherto been appreciated, and more is doubtless yet to be discovered.[8]

At the beginning of the new commercial era, the north German towns took a lively interest in the Portuguese discoveries and the Hansa sent many of its vessels by the new waterways. The Rhine towns, also, being closer in touch with the eastern trade through Venice, at once realized the significance of the new routes. As early as 1503, the German firms of Nuremberg and Augsburg, such as the firms of Vöhlen, Fugger, Hochstetter, Hirschvogel, led by the Welser, formed a commercial establishment at Lisbon which developed into a large trading company and won rights from the king of Portugal to visit the East Indies. King Dom Emanuel gave the German company the right of precedence in the Indian trade, authorized it to use vessels built in Portugal and, in 1504, granted a charter permitting German merchants to establish their own law courts in Lisbon. The company dispatched three ships to the East, which returned laden with spices, pearls and cotton and brought in a return of one hundred and twenty per cent.[9] Its subsequent success, however, was prevented by opposition from the Portuguese and it was forced to go out of existence, having no national authority upon which to rely. But this first organized venture into the wealth of the Indies prepared the way for others, and showed that German merchants were alive to the new conditions and opportunities of world trade. Indeed the Welser had already been active elsewhere in the Portuguese possessions: they had established a settlement for sugar plantations in Madeira and also on the Canary Islands, which they later sold to Johann Bies, a Cologne merchant.

All contemporary efforts to penetrate the trade areas controlled by Spain, on the other hand, had proved unsuccessful, for the Spaniards excluded every foreigner. But in the year 1525, the Welser succeeded in entering the Spanish trade and founded a Factory in Seville. The following year, Charles V extended commercial privileges to the Germans, and the Fuggers likewise set up their Factory in Seville. The greatest opportunity arose, however, for the Germans in 1528, when Charles V, in return for a loan of a large sum of money, granted to the Welser the right to colonize and govern Venezuela.[10] For thirty years they held this land and it might have become a permanent German colony, had not the officials who represented them mismanaged affairs. Strife with the Indians and Spaniards followed, and handicapped by the lack of any national support the Welser lost the colony in Spain. In the meantime, some Augsburg merchants besides the Welser had established their Factories in other parts of South America—in La Plata and in Paraguay—but they found themselves unable to support and continue them.

With the exception of the Venezuela colony, all the other attempts of Germany during the period of colonization must be termed merely abortive efforts. For instance, in 1665, Johann Joachim Becher of Bavaria entered into negotiations with Holland in regard to the acquisition of the colony of New Amsterdam at the mouth of the Hudson River, but their negotiations were suddenly cut short by the English occupation;[11] also, the neighbor and brother-in-law of the Great Elector, Jacob of Kurland, possessed for a time Tobago, the smallest island of the Antilles, as well as lands in Gambia in West Africa; Martin Behaim of Nuremberg, a friend and companion of Columbus and Magellan, traveled under the patronage of the Portuguese and bequeathed to his native town a globe of the known world.

To be sure, Germany's record of colonial expansion seems paltry indeed in contrast to that of the other Powers during the great Age of Exploration; but, at least, it sufficed to keep alive the colonial tradition and to hand it down to the merchants of Hamburg and of Bremen who, in the early nineteenth century, were to lay so solidly the foundations of the modern colonial empire.

## Prussia's Colonial Policy

Finally, if the word "colonization" is to be interpreted in terms of a state-directed colonial policy pursued for both political and economic ends, then here too is Germany able to produce a record, intensive and ambitious, if brief and unsuccessful. For the Hohenzollerns, the rulers of Brandenburg-Prussia, upon whom had descended the political domination of the Hanseatic League, included a colonial policy within the sphere of their all-embracing rule, although they were never strong enough or free enough to prosecute it vigorously.

There is no doubt that the Great Elector was alive to the Hansa tradition as well as to the new age of colonization, and that it was his wish to foster both maritime and colonial development.[12] He had spent part of his youth in Holland where the advantages of world trade were exhibited to him, and he was made to realize, with all the rulers of the seventeenth century, that colonization was indispensable in maintaining the greatness of a nation among its peers. "Trade and commerce," he said, "are the most important foundations of a state."

Even before the close of the Thirty Years' War, the Great Elector attempted to put his ideas into practice. In 1647, seven years after his accession, he began the formation of an East India Company, but lack of money and the war with Sweden forced him to relinquish the project. Brought in touch with the sea upon the acquisition of Hither Pomerania by the Treaty of Westphalia (1648), he returned to his colonial policy, and sought to emulate the oversea endeavors of his maritime contemporaries. He purchased from the Danes, in 1650, Tranquebar and Fort Danesberg

14

on the southeast coast of India; built up a small navy with the assistance of the Dutch agents, Raule and Blonck, in his efforts to consolidate his new Baltic possessions; and sent out an expedition in 1676-1677 to reconnoiter the coast of Guinea, which resulted in gaining from the natives a protectorate on the Gold Coast between Axim and the Cape of Three Points.[13] The Great Elector then founded in 1682 an African Commercial Company to which he gave a monopoly of trade in this place for twenty years. In 1683, the agent of the company, Frederick von Der Groben, established a Factory and built the fortress *Gross Friedrichsburg*.[14] Two years later another agent built two more forts, and the natives of Taccorary placed themselves under Prussian protection, actions which greatly excited the envy of the Dutch. In 1686, negotiations for a naval base on Arguin Island were concluded and concessions for the Company were secured from France and Holland by the treaties of 1683-1685. The port of Emden, where the business was centralized, was enlarged and its operations were extended to Hamburg.

To the Orient, and to America also, the Great Elector directed his efforts in the hope of creating a colonial empire. He established an East India Company for trade with the East and negotiated commercial treaties with the Shah of Persia, arranging especially for the exporting of amber to Persia and the importing of raw silk to Prussia.[15] In 1685, he attempted a settlement in the Antilles and by a contract with the Danes gained a part of the island of St. Thomas, where he tried to maintain a slave station.

Like his father, Frederick the First of Prussia realized the importance of maintaining a colonial policy but he lacked his predecessor's energy and ability to struggle against

15

the ever-present adverse conditions. It is true that he bought half of Tobago in the West Indies from the Duke of Kurland in 1691, and attempted to resuscitate the African Company by numerous subsidies. Gradually, however, he became absorbed in European affairs as his ambitions to become king were encouraged by the emperor; he lost interest in colonies except for the pleasure afforded him in receiving the negro ambassadors from Guinea. His successor, Frederick William I, attempted to retrieve the financial situation of the African Company by transferring its rights to the East India Company, an expedient, however, which proved entirely unsuccessful.

One other Hohenzollern revived the colonial aims of the Great Elector and endeavored, for a time at least, to imitate him in that direction as well as in every other. For, before Frederick the Great became involved in the War of the Austrian Succession and its results, he appreciated the advantages of oversea expansion for Prussia and made some unsuccessful attempts to prosecute it: he endeavored to establish Asiatic trading companies, and to build up a commercial fleet.[16] In 1750, an Asiatic company was chartered at Emden which seems to have prospered for a few years, at any rate, paying twenty per cent interest in 1754 and having its prosperity sung in verse by the Brunswick poet Zacharia. Again in 1772, Frederick founded the Company of Maritime Commerce, and in 1780 he attempted to revive the Asiatic Company, but without success.

Prussia's efforts thus ended in 1775, so far as any material results could demonstrate, and her aims and ambitions far outstripped her achievements. Nevertheless, the early Hohenzollerns contributed the idea, if not the successful practice, of a state-directed commercial and colonial policy to Germany's historical tradition.

16

## Reasons for Germany's Failure

In the face of such a cumulative record embracing the various interpretations of "colonization," an explanation for Germany's backwardness becomes all the more imperative. Certainly it cannot be found in a lack of initiative and tradition, for we have seen in this brief review how colonial activity of some kind was present in every age, and persisted even under the most discouraging and adverse conditions. It would seem, therefore, that the reasons for Germany's conspicuous failure to retain any of her gains and to appear so strangely devoid of any colonial possessions, when she emerged as a great empire in 1871, must be sought rather in the individual and disunited character of her colonial achievement, and in the weakness and disorganization of her historical evolution. To this task, therefore, we must now address our attention.

## Private Initiative Carries on Alone

With the close of the Middle Ages, it is true that German colonization had well-nigh penetrated all of Central Europe through migration and conquest, while German trade had gained control of Northeastern Europe, of the Baltic and of the North Sea. In short the *Deutschtum* prevailed everywhere in those regions, but it did not endure because it was not a united *Deutschtum*. The emperors after Henry I and Otto I, who had promoted expansion during the tenth century, refused to have anything to do with it. Consequently, official fostering was short-lived, for their successors became so involved in Italian affairs and in imperial politics that they utterly abandoned a colonial policy. Instead, the princes, German and non-German, traders, missionaries, knights—separate units, in short—were

17

the pioneers, and their very success perpetuated their separateness and increased the political power of the individual or group in contrast to the united nation. The Holy Roman Empire, to be sure, stood as a shadow of power and might behind them, without which it may well be that their success would not have been so great, but its power was only a shadow and not a reality. It was too much of a shadow even to afford protection or to give the semblance of a union to these individual pioneers, whether princes, bishops, burgesses or merchants. Hence, disunion and individual effort became the guiding principles of German colonization as well as of German history, principles which were to obstruct its power and to postpone its triumph.

### German Separatism versus the Rise of Nationalism

Nowhere were those disintegrating forces better illustrated than in the decline of the Hanseatic League, the strongest factor making for German expansion which we have hitherto discovered. For it was not primarily the Commercial Revolution and the shifting of the trade axis from Central Europe to the Atlantic seaboard that caused the downfall of the Hansa; it was rather the stirrings of a dynastic nationalism—the very antithesis of German separatism—in Sweden, Denmark, Norway and in England, which commenced the League's destruction, to which the Commercial Revolution, the Protestant Revolt, and the Thirty Years' War were to give the finishing touches.[17]

The end of the fourteenth century and the beginning of the fifteenth marked the height of the Hansa; but, as the fifteenth and sixteenth centuries began to bring medieval conditions to an end and to introduce the dawning of the modern era, so did they likewise witness the waning of the Hanseatic League, that distinctly medieval structure. The decreptitude of this powerful institution, which had fitted the peculiar political exigencies of the Middle Ages, coincided with the transformation and the rejuvenescence of Europe. The Hansa no longer suited the changing conditions; therefore it too must perish.

It was but natural that the rising tide of a dynastic nationalism in the northern lands should make those countries chafe under the restrictions and monopolies imposed upon them by the Hansa. After driving out the Mongols, Russia, under the Czar Ivan III, began to assert itself, attacked the German power in Novgorod and, in 1494, led as captives to Moscow the fifty German merchants who remained there in the Factory. So perished the League in Russia. In like manner, Sweden, Denmark and Norway formed the Union of Calmar for their national protection in 1397; encouraged trading relations with the rising Dutch merchants whose geographical position made them freer than the Hansards, and who strove in every way to invade the Hansa's domain, even to capturing the North Sea fisheries. Finally, Lübeck was obliged to engage in disastrous wars with the Dutch, with the Danes and with the Swedes, ending with its practical downfall in 1536. The fall of the Factory at Bergen followed, which destroyed the League's power in the North. In the meantime, England had produced her own Merchant Adventurers; Willoughby and Chancellor had succeeded in opening a new route to Russia by the Arctic Ocean and the White Sea; and the London Muscovite Company took shape in 1555. British trade, promoted by the nationalistic Tudors, drove the Hansards off the seas.[18]

But the fifteenth and sixteenth centuries were times of growing ambition and self-assertion on the part of princes everywhere, and the League suffered not only externally but

19

internally therefrom. The German princes themselves began to resent the individual power of the burghers and merchants in those cities whose strength lay in the Hansa. They regarded with unfriendly eye the privileges, liberties and the inter-town alliances enjoyed by the League and, consequently, they began to curtail and to destroy the very framework of that Association. Indeed the supremacy of the trader and his individual independence had no place in an age when sovereignty was becoming self-conscious. Every prince, be his domain large or small, wished to bring each department of his realm, political, religious and economic, under his own control, and the economic had got entirely out of hand. Moreover, strife among the Hanseatic cities themselves was a natural concomitant of this growing idea of sovereignty. Danzig, for instance, resenting the selfish policy of Lübeck in her direction of the League, broke away and made a separate trade agreement with England; and the Dutch cities, such as Amsterdam for example, began their independent trade with Norway, Sweden and Denmark. Indeed, the Hansa was doomed even before the new western waterways destroyed the medieval trade routes and replaced the supremacy of the Baltic, Mediterranean and North Seas by the Atlantic Ocean.

Doubtless, without the rise of nationalism and the consequent disastrous competition resulting therefrom, the Hansa would not have been affected by the discovery of new trade routes for some time. For, in spite of colonial products, the demand for the ordinary necessities of life continued; and it was upon the trade in foodstuffs and clothing materials, the staples of life, that the Hansa depended. "The discovery of America did not cause an immediate commercial revolution: peasants and burghers did not at once change their diet of rye and fish and beer for spice and tea, nor did they discard their woolen and linen for cotton and silk. During the sixteenth and early seventeenth centuries, trade in colonial products—and Germany was supplied with these up the Rhine from the distributing centers in Italy and Holland—remained secondary to that of foodstuffs as is evidenced by the fact that, during one month in 1589, six hundred ships laden with grain from the Baltic entered Amsterdam. And this was at the time when the famous Spanish India fleet numbered forty ships." [19]

But the Hansa could not battle against the powerful dynastic nationalism animating its neighbors externally and its own princes internally, and so it easily fell a prey to the disintegrating forces of Protestantism and Particularism and, finally, to the destruction and devastation inflicted by the Thirty Years' War. In vain, the Hansa made an effort on the eve of the Thirty Years' War in 1606-1608 to strengthen itself internally by a union with the upper German towns whose object was to create a general league of German cities, but its effort ran counter to the Protestant Union and to the Catholic League and was therefore doomed to failure. Likewise, on account of Confessionalism and Particularism, the Hansa, in 1627, refused Kaiser Ferdinand's offer of an alliance which promised the League the monopoly of the Spanish-Indian trade in northern Germany in return for the maintenance by the League of a German supremacy in the Baltic.[20] The refusal of this alliance was followed by the death blow to the League inflicted by the Thirty Years' War. In 1669, the last General Assembly was called by Lübeck but, besides Lübeck, only eight towns were represented. The League was practically dissolved, and was destined thereafter to live only in its glorious history and traditions.

And with the downfall of the Hansa and the destruction of German commercial expansion came also the loss of much of the German colonization accomplished during the period. Dynastic nationalism on the borders of the empire, as well as within it, had become apparent in a violent reaction against the *Deutschtum:* the Hussite movement gripped Bohemia and Bavaria; the Jagiellon national dynasty in Poland drove back the German Orders from its borders; the new Russia, freed from the Tartar yoke, was not satisfied merely to drive out the German merchants but, under Czar Ivan IV, attacked Livland so that by 1661 the colony was lost to Germany and the Teutonic knights, and divided among its greedy neighbors, Russia, Sweden, and Poland; the Hungarian nobles regarded the German influence in Hungary with jealousy, and only their struggles against the Turks prevented them from entirely driving out the Germans.

Moreover, that shadowy power, the empire, was, itself, becoming more shadowy with the rising power of the German princes. German colonial expansion had always suffered from the weakness of its central authority; it was now to suffer more as that central authority grew weaker and the neighboring national states grew stronger. Russia, Poland, Sweden, Norway and Denmark were challenging the *Deutschtum* in the Baltic lands; England and Holland with the assistance of the Commercial Revolution were to destroy the last vestige of German commercial colonization; and Hungary, Poland, and Bohemia were reducing German influence and culture within their borders to a position of subordination. In a word, German colonial expansion was at a lower ebb at the dawn of the modern period than at the beginning of the so-called Middle Ages.

## Imperial Disorganization

And when the glorious epoch of oversea discoveries ushered in the modern era, the weakness of Germany's separate colonial efforts, as well as of her inherent national disorganization, continued to operate even more effectively to prevent her participation in the universal enterprise of exploration and expansion. The broadening of colonial activity to the world stage, with its all-compelling challenge to nationalism, found a backward and feudal Germany all too unable to cope with the enlarged opportunities so lavishly offered. Indeed, history presents no greater contrast than the one between Germany's capacity for colonial expansion and that of the other Western European states during the Golden Age of discovery. For, while Spain, Portugal, Holland, France and England enjoyed every advantage conducive to colonization, Germany suffered every disadvantage. The world movements such as the Commercial Revolution, the rise of nationalism, the Protestant Revolt, were just so many promoters of oversea activity in the Western European countries; but to Germany they were just so many deterrents.

Obviously, while all the Atlantic seaboard countries profited from their geographical position in the world revolution of trade, Germany, an interior state, suffered a loss. Even the Hanseatic cities, who alone possessed the necessary energy and wealth to engage in the new transatlantic enterprises, were handicapped by their unfavorable locations. At first there were only two routes to the new world for sailing vessels: the one from the north of Africa to the West Indies, by following the equatorial current and trade winds; and the other, from Iceland to Newfoundland by the opposite currents. Columbus sailed by the former, and Cabot by the latter, and not for one hundred years did the growing science of navigation make possible a direct passage. Indeed, it was not until the coming of the ocean steamship that Hamburg and Bremen became ports of world commerce.[21] The northern route was more accessible, but during the fifteenth and sixteenth centuries the Hansa towns had lost to Norway and to England their monopoly of the Iceland trade and, between 1486 and 1532, carried on commerce there only by force.

It has already been noted how the rise of dynastic nationalism was primarily responsible for the break-up of the Hanseatic League; but nationalism not only helped to destroy a large part of Germany's early expansion and all of her commercial colonization in the Middle Ages, it also prevented her from taking her place in the more extensive colonial movement of the new era. For the new national states, favored by their geographical position and strengthened by their centralized monarchies, were enabled to build up a new Spain, a new France, a new Holland and a new England oversea; while Germany, torn by feudal warfare between independent princes, which precluded any concentrated national activity necessary for the establishment of oversea dominion, was still floundering in the loose and disunited organization of the Middle Ages. Nationalism indeed was but another element of German disunion and consequent colonial incapacity.

Again, the Protestant Revolt and the Counter Reformation, so stimulating to colonial enterprise, especially in the new France and the new England, had exactly the opposite effect in Germany. There, Protestantism proved but another disruptive instead of constructive force and, together with nationalism, plunged Germany into the disastrous Thirty Years' War, the recovery from whose devastating results absorbed all her strength throughout the period which spelled the Golden Age of colonial expansion for Western Europe. For the Thirty Years' War left Germany at the Peace of Westphalia not only internally divided, economically ravished and impoverished, but also shorn by Sweden of Bremen, Bergen, Wismar and one-half of Pomerania, those colonial conquests of the Middle Ages along the Baltic Sea. As we have seen, the war was the death blow to the Hansa and all its works; Germany's prestige on the Baltic was lost as well as her ability to maintain any of the colonial settlements in the East.

Added to all these disasters, the Holy Roman Empire emerged from the war greatly weakened, for its authority had declined in the same ratio in which that of the nations of the western seaboard had increased. As has been demonstrated, the German merchant with the Hansa tradition back of him felt the same, if not a stronger, colonial urge as the merchants and traders in the other states of Western Europe; but unlike the other states of Western Europe, the unwieldy and disorganized Holy Roman Empire could afford him no national support, no mercantilist policy. All too true was the observation of the Württemberg publicist, Möser, who wrote a century later, "Not a Clive but a Hamburg Senator would command the Ganges today, had the efforts of the Hanseatic towns been supported by the old empire."

### Political and Economic Weakness of the Hohenzollerns

With the close of the Thirty Years' War, Germany became a geographical expression, and German history became that of her separate states, stressing once more the principle of individualism rather than of centralization. Thereafter, until the end of the nineteenth century, her colonial history was identified not with the German people as a whole, but only with that state which alone was strong enough to carry it forward, Brandenburg-Prussia.

But Brandenburg-Prussia was beset by too many difficulties to enable its rulers to promote a colonial policy with any success. Confronted by the task of resuscitating and establishing their kingdom politically and economically in Europe, they found themselves too weak, too financially embarrassed to maintain settlements and projects oversea and too beset on all sides by powerful colonial rivals. The Great Elector was obliged to relinquish his stations in India, the Orient, and America for lack of funds with which to maintain them, and they reverted to the Danes. The Dutch were all-powerful on the coast of Guinea and continually attacked the Prussian settlements there, aided by the French Corsairs, a new enemy which the War of the Spanish Succession had created. The fortunes of the African Company, consequently, went from bad to worse and became dependent upon the Prussian treasury. But in spite of subsidies its debt amounted to 900,000 thalers in 1691. Shortly afterward the French in Senegal and the Dutch in Guinea renewed their attacks and Frederick William I, having a greater desire for money wherewith to pay his soldiers than for oversea expansion, ceded to the Dutch all the Prussian African interests for the small indemnity of 7,200 ducats and twelve negroes. Thus Prussia disappeared from Africa in the year 1725.

In considering the failure of the Great Elector's efforts, it must also be remembered that had he not been so occupied with internal colonization in an effort to repair the terrible economic ravages of the Thirty Years' War, he would have had, perhaps, more success in external expansion. But he was obliged to repopulate and to develop his land so as to attract and to support those colonists like the Huguenots, the Dutch, and the Swiss, whom he called in and whose subsequent settlement and assimilation he bequeathed to his immediate successors.

In the same way Frederick the Great became so absorbed in making Prussia powerful in Europe that when urged to continue his colonial policy, he is said to have replied, "All distant provinces are a burden to the state. A village on the frontier is worth a principality two hundred and fifty miles away"; and when Joachim Nettelbeck,[22] a far-traveled burgher of Kolberg and a great agitator for Prussian colonization, presented a plan for a German colony in South America to be located in a region which he had discovered, Frederick the Great left his proposition entirely unnoticed. Indeed, in his *Memoirs of Brandenburg,* he never even mentioned the colonial exploits of his predecessors. The European wars and intrigues with which his reign was mainly occupied precluded any real colonial policy, and he himself was far too great a statesman not to recognize the overpowering strength of his rivals, in contrast to which the political ability of Prussia was too puny to permit of any expansion outside of Europe. As an illuminating illustration of the rivalry of the other Powers he had witnessed, just before he ascended the throne, the jealousy excited in England, France, and Holland by the efforts of the Emperor Charles VI to establish an East India Company in the Austrian Netherlands for the purposes of trade with the East and West Indies under the imperial flag, a project which had to be sacrificed to their adhesion to the Pragmatic Sanction.

It was not surprising, therefore, that Nettelbeck, continually agitating the subject, met a second rebuff from Frederick William II, Frederick the Great's successor, when he presented his plans for a plantation colony on the Corentyn River in South America, and for the revival of the Great Elector's colony on the Guinea Coast. It was his dream that the colony in South America would produce sugar, coffee, and other colonial wares for Prussia, and be worked by negroes secured at the slave station in Guinea.[23] But the intervention of the Revolutionary and Napoleonic Wars pushed any such notion of Prussia's expansion into the background, while the weakness of Frederick William II and Frederick William III rendered even more hopeless the prospect of any such activities.

Finally, it must be remembered that the Prussian colonies founded in the seventeenth and eighteenth centuries had only an ephemeral existence because they were imposed from above, and were at no time in favor with or supported by a state which was too weak to maintain them. Their collapse was the failure of a strong initiative on the part of the rulers to overcome the prejudices of a whole people, a people with very little political or economic foundation. Unlike the rulers of England, France, and Holland, the Great Elector and his successors had no middle-class to carry out their projects; they were obliged to depend on Dutch agents; and their country was too young to support the new colonization oversea, where it encountered too strong rivals. Indeed, all the adverse conditions which had beset German colonization from the beginning—the political weakness either in rulers or people inherent in the history of Germany, which forced her colonial history into subservience instead of prominence as in the other nations—was still active in the seventeenth and eighteenth centuries. The individual efforts of the Middle Ages had failed for the lack of a strong, central, national government; the state-directed efforts of the early Hohenzollerns had failed for lack of a strong, economic middle-class. Not until these two were coincident could Germany hope to achieve a real colonial policy.

# GERMANY'S LACK OF A COLONIAL EMPIRE

## NOTES

[1] *International Conciliation,* no. 144, *Treaty of Peace with Germany,* 1919, articles, 119, 128-158.

[2] Moon, P. T., *Imperialism and World Politics* (New York, 1926), p. 515.

[3] Thompson, J. W., "East German Colonization in the Middle Ages" in *Annual Report American Historical Association,* 1915, and *Economic and Social History Middle Ages* (N. Y., 1928), ch. xx.

[4] Schaefer, D., *Kolonialgeschichte* (Berlin, 1921, 2 vols.), 1, Pt. ii.

[5] Baasch, E., *Die Islandfahrt der Deutschen vom 15 bis 17 Jahrhundert* (Hamburg, 1889), p. 8-17.

[6] Lindner, T., *Die Deutsche Hansa* (Leipzig, 1911), ch. iv. For history of Hansa, see also, Barthold, F., *Die Geschichte der deutschen Hansa* (Leipzig, 1862).

[7] Simonsfeld, H., *Die Deutschen als Kolonisatoren in der Geschichte* (Hamburg, 1885), p. 24.

[8] Daenell, E., "Zu den deutschen Handelsunternehmungen in Amerika," in *Historische Vierteljahreschrift,* Bd. xii, 1910, p. 183.

[9] See Hümmerich, F., *Die erste Deutsche Handelsfahrt nach Indien,* 1505-1506 (Oldenburg, 1922).

[10] See Haebler, K., *Die überseeische Unternehmungen der Welser* (Leipzig, 1903).

[11] Simonsfeld, H., "Bayerische Kolonialpläne in 17 Jahrhundert," in *Augusburger Allgemeine Zeitung,* 1885, *Beilage,* nos. 172, 174, 176.

[12] Roscher, Jannarsch, *Kolonieen, Kolonialpolitik und Auswanderung* (Leipsig, 1856, 2nd ed.), p. 343.

[13] *Die Deutsche Kolonialzeitung,* 1884, p. 196.

[14] Beelitz, O., *Die deutsche Kolonisationen an der Westküste Afrikas* (Köln, 1885).

Koenig, E., *Benjamin Raule und die Flotte Friedrich Wilhelms des Grossen Kurfürstens* (Rathenow, 1887).

[15] Heyck, H., "Brandenbürgische-deutsche Kolonialpläne" in *Zeitschrift für die Geschichte des Oberrheins,* N.F., Bd. ii, p. 129.

[16] Ring, V., *Asiatische Handelskompagnien unter Friedrich dem Grossen* (1890).

[17] Simonsfeld, *Die Deutschen als Kolonisatoren,* p. 28ff.

[18] Lindner, *op. cit.,* ch. x.

[19] Hansen, M., *German Schemes of Colonization before 1860* (Smith College *Studies in History,* vol. ix, nos. 1, 2, 1924), p. 7.

[20] Simonsfeld, *op. cit.,* p. 40.

[21] Hansen, *op. cit.,* pp. 6, 7.

[22] See Köser, in *Marine Rundschau,* 1904.

[23] Joachim Nettelbeck, *Eine Lebensbeschreibung von ihm selbst aufgezeichnet* (Hamburg, 1863, 3 ed., 2 vols.).

## CHAPTER II

### PRIVATE ENTERPRISE PREPARES THE MIND AND THE WAY

NEVER before had so many auspicious coincidents smoothed the path for German expansion oversea as at the beginning of the nineteenth century.

In the first place, the change in economic theory and practice from mercantilism to *laissez-faire* had produced among the Great Powers a lull in the enthusiasm for colonies, if not, in some quarters, a positive aversion to them. The colonial monopoly of the sixteenth, the seventeenth, and the early eighteenth centuries had been broken. Both Spain and France were out of the race and England, in possession of the lion's share, had temporarily lost her appetite for more. At no time since the beginning of the modern era in 1500 had conditions been more favorable for Germany to enter the colonial field, so far as lack of opposition was concerned, than they were in 1815.

What is more, the Congress of Vienna, that liquidation of the map of Europe, presented a unique opportunity to secure some foothold for future expansion. Nettelbeck, now seventy-six years of age but still a colonial enthusiast, realized the golden chance for Germany to acquire colonies at the Peace Settlement. In 1815, he wrote to Gneisenau, one of the Prussian ambassadors to the Congress of Vienna, begging him to secure in the Peace, with England's permission, one of the French colonies for Prussia. He suggested Cayenne, or Grenada in the Antilles and other islands in the neighborhood of his proposed colony in South America.[1]

30

But Gneisenau, although as a young man he also had dreamed of founding colonies in the New World, replied that it was out of the question for Prussia without a navy to contemplate any such action; for colonial possessions would only bring her into dependence on the sea Powers.

Not only were conditions ripe externally for a vigorous colonial expansion, but internally a change had swept over the German people awakening them, broadening their horizon, and making them eager for adventure and discovery. Since the War of Liberation and the invigoration of a new national consciousness, they felt themselves to be more Germans than Prussians, than Bavarians or Saxons. The urge for national expansion experienced by the English, the French, and the Dutch during the sixteenth and the seventeenth centuries was now beginning to be felt tardily by the Germans in the nineteenth century. Besides, there was a widespread discontent with economic and political conditions during the years of reaction after 1815. Those idealists who had looked for better times as the result of the Peace were doomed to have their hopes dashed as they observed the old régime again in the saddle. Consequently, they transferred the realization of their idealism to other lands. Perhaps Goethe, in his *Wilhelm Meisters Wanderjahre,* best illustrates this longing and yearning of the German people for national self-expression at the beginning of the nineteenth century, when he says:

> Amerika, du hast es besser
> Als unser Kontinent, das alte,
> Hast keine verfallene Schlösser
> Und keine Basalte
> Dich stört nicht im Innern
> Zu lebendigem Zeit
> Unnützliches Erinnern
> Und vergeblicher Streit.[1a]

31

Idealism, moreover, was supplemented by practical experience: the difficulties and privations suffered by the Germans during the imposition of the Continental System and the high tariffs of the English after 1815 brought home to the populace as nothing else could the pressing economic need of colonies. To be able to enjoy coffee, sugar, and tobacco grown upon German territory oversea seemed highly preferable to paying exorbitant rates to the English or French, running the dangers of smuggling or to contenting oneself with acorns for coffee and coltsfoot for tobacco.

All these circumstances, accompanied by a constantly increasing population, proved most propitious for colonial expansion. But it was a repetition of her historic weakness that Germany possessed no government strong enough, nor economic basis stable enough to take advantage of the opportunity. The Germanic Confederation—that "geographical expression" created by the Congress of Vienna, was too weak politically and economically; too dominated by its powerful neighbors, Austria and Russia; too divided by customs barriers, and by an unarticulated economic system to embark upon any official colonial policy. Again, as in the Middle Ages, an impotent state relegated all colonial initiative to the individual. Hence, individual effort and achievement of every kind prepared the way for the ultimate, if tardy, acquisition of the colonial empire of our own day.

### German Publicists Create a Colonial Cult

That there were many people in Germany who realized the state of affairs just described is abundantly evident from the literature of the times. Indeed, as the nineteenth century advanced, publicists of all kinds, political economists, scientists, historians, and explorers, pointed out the necessity and the advantages of colonial expansion. As early as

1812, Heeren, the Göttingen historian, in his *History of the European State System,* recognized colonies as an integral part of the state; in 1817 Hans von Gagern urged in the German Diet that the states take some action in directing the ever-swelling volume of German emigration, and he was followed by Hornmayer in Bavaria and Perthes in Thuringia who advocated the same action on the part of their respective states.[2] Later, the nationalist historians, best represented by Treitschke and Droysen, echoed the same theme by urging the expansion and projection of German nationality. Treitschke especially had an enormous influence. He was appointed to a chair in the University of Freiburg-im-Breisgau in 1863, subsequently going to the universities of Kiel, Heidelberg and finally, in 1874, to Berlin.

By the forties, the political economists entered the field. Such men as Roscher and Wappäus preached colonization for the overflow of population as well as for the benefit of trade, and demonstrated the value of colonies as new production and consumption centers. They were led by List who broke with the prevailing *laissez-faire* and cosmopolitan school and urged colonialism as part of a national program. In his *National System of Political Economy* (1841), he advised a strong colonial policy in all its phases.

"A vigorous German consular and diplomatic service ought to be established . . . young explorers should be encouraged to travel through these countries and make impartial reports upon them. Young merchants should be encouraged to inspect them. . . . Enterprises should be founded and supported by stock companies and taken under governmental protection. Companies should be formed in the German seaports in order to buy lands in far countries and settle them with German colonists; also companies for commerce and navigation whose object would be to open new markets abroad for German manufacturers and to establish steamship lines. . . . Colonies are the best means of developing manufactures, export and import trade and finally a respectable navy." [3]

List's particular dream for the new Germany centered in the East in the Danube lands where fifty to sixty millions could be supported; a project in which he was upheld by Höffken, who saw Germany's colonial future in the Near East and, as editor of the *Augsburg Allgemeine Zeitung* gave his ideas great currency throughout the country. These men thus foreshadowed by half a century the great Berlin-Bagdad project, which was so to dominate Germany's colonial policy in our own day. [4]

Nor did scientists and explorers fail to play an important part both in urging the policy of expansion and in creating a knowledge of, and familiarity with, the advantages of oversea emigration. Alexander von Humboldt in his *Political Essay on the New Spain* (1811) has been called the founder of colonial knowledge in Germany. He pointed out, to be sure, the disadvantages rather than the advantages of plantation colonies, but nevertheless he awoke a great interest in them. [5] And von Humboldt was followed by a long series of men whose account of travels, researches in natural sciences, and whose geographical discoveries added material of inestimable value to a literature fast creating a colonial propaganda.

Since the end of the eighteenth century Germans had been interested in Africa: in 1829 Edward Rüppell's book on Nubia appeared, and in 1839 his work on Abysinnia; in 1830, Anton von Prokesch published his *Recollections of Egypt and the Near East* and in 1829, Christian Ehrenberg his *Natural History Journeys through North Africa and*

*West Asia.* Between 1840 and 1870, Gustaf Mann had studied flora in the region of the Niger; Dr. Bastian of Bremen had made a tour of the world, writing a book about Africa; Heinrich Barth of Hamburg had been the first European to explore the *Hinterland* of Kamerun; the geologist, Karl von Fretsch, had devoted himself to the mineralogy of Morocco; and Karl Mauch, upon returning from the Transvaal, had concluded one of his speeches with the words, "May this beautiful land some day become a German colony." [6] Finally, the expedition of Dr. Otto Kersten, Baron von Decken, and Richard Brenner in East Africa had called forth a request from the Sultan Zimba of Wituland for the official protection of Prussia, coupled with an offer to render all aid and hospitality to German travelers and settlers.

Nor had the New World lacked in publicity: the physician, Gottfried Duden, had published in 1829 his beautifully written and charmingly illustrated book, *Travels through the Western States of North America,* which created a veritable fever in Germany for emigration to Missouri; and Karl Postl, through his travel romances of 1824 and 1826 presented an alluring picture of natural conditions and of social life in the United States. [7]

A logical result of the activities of these scientists and explorers was the formation in 1868 of the *Central Society for Commercial Geography and German Interests Abroad.* [8] Founded by the traveler and explorer, Otto Kersten, it developed during the early seventies into one of the most important means for fostering German commercial interests oversea and at home, with its branches in all the leading cities it represented the only hitherto organized agency for promoting economic colonization. The monthly magazine, *Der Export,* its official organ, together with its many other publications, occupied a prominent place in colonial literature.

Considered as a whole, the voluminous productions of these publicists and doctrinaires during the first half of the nineteenth century may be said to have created a distinct colonial "cult" or theory. Its existence at the dawn of the empire is evident to the most superficial observer. Never can it be said of Germany, as it is so often observed of Great Britain, that she built up her colonial empire in a "fit of absence of mind." For while it may be an English characteristic to construct a policy *post facto,* it is equally a German habit to formulate *a priori* an abstract theory as a guide to practice.

In the meantime, while all this publicity and enthusiasm for colonization was being broadcast by the writers of the period, very practical individual achievements were in process, some of which actually paved the way for the founding of a colonial empire.

### Emigration

The most spectacular of these was the ever-growing emigration movement. After 1815 the number of emigrants steadily increased, to rise to a prodigious total between the years 1830 and 1870. Accurate official statistics are lacking but it has been conservatively estimated that 110,434 Germans left the Fatherland in the year 1847, 446,390 during the years 1855-1860, and 970,000 in the decade 1862-1870.[9] The first half of the nineteenth century also records innumerable expeditions for colonial settlement undertaken into the Americas, the Near East, into Africa, Australia, and Russia. Indeed, the governments of the separate German states became alarmed at this increasing exodus and consequently enacted stricter and stricter emigration legislation.

Space precludes a description of any but the chief of all these expeditions although an idea of their number and magnitude must be indicated.

The Americas, of course, claimed by far the greatest number of the emigrants. Immediately after 1817 an exodus of Rhinelanders, Württembergers, Westphalians, and other South Germans, seeking new homes oversea, began. Its number averaged about 6,000 annually until the year 1826, rising to 22,000 between the years 1830-1844, reaching 66,000 during 1856-1860, and as many as 128,000 persons in the year 1872.[10] The emancipation of Spain's and Portugal's colonies between the years 1817 and 1824 naturally attracted German colonial effort. For, although the Monroe Doctrine forbade the establishment of colonies by foreign powers, the United States, the empire of Brazil, and the South American republics did not prohibit but rather encouraged colonists. At the invitation of the Portuguese emperor of Brazil, a group of German colonists joined a company of Swiss emigrants who founded New Freiburg; and the naturalist, Freyreisz, was instrumental in establishing the colony of *San Leopoldo* in the Province of *Rio Grande du Sul* in South Brazil, whose population in 1853 had reached more than 11,000. *Tre Froquilhas* and *Torres* were founded on the coast in 1826 with the idea of serving the *Hinterland* but met with little success, because of the failure to complete improvements in transportation upon which their development was dependent.

In other provinces also, large German settlements were made: in *Sao Paulo,* whither Dom Pedro I invited a number of Catholic Rhinelanders in the year 1827, which later became the center of German Brazil and a parent from which other colonies sprang; as well as in the Province of *Santa Catharina* whose most significant colony at this time was *Sao Pedro de Alcantara*. Because of civil wars and the unsettled condition of these new republics, however, the German-emigrant settlements in South America did not prosper until the years 1840, 1850, and after, when they experienced a revival of interest largely caused by the failure of German efforts in North America and in the Near East, as well as by the vivifying influence of a commercial expansion.[10a]

It was due to this latter motive, the commercial, as well as to the political disturbances of the year 1848, that the Hamburg Colonial Society, founded in 1849, established the colony of *Dona Francisca* in the Province of *Santa Catharina,* in cooperation with Prince de Joinville, from whom the Society received its rights. The Hamburg merchants saw in it a great opportunity to increase their trade and so to injure their rival, Bremen. The Prince offered many inducements, such as the construction of a tariff-free port, freedom from direct taxes for ten years, exemption from military service, liberty of worship, and assistance in the acquisition of citizenship. The Society also offered the colonists many advantages such as land at a low figure, and it succeeded in importing 8,000 immigrants by the year 1868. *Dona Francisca* became the chief German settlement in South Brazil and even today the neighboring rivers bear German names.

The Province of *Rio Grande du Sul* also experienced a revival after 1850. Many new settlements were made, the mild, cool climate proving a great attraction. By 1872, for example, the number of Germans in the province had increased to about 60,000. They controlled trade and were prominent in commerce, industry, and agriculture. Hamburg, alone, sent fifty shiploads of goods there annually and, apparently, "a great future lay before this province as a support for German foreign trade and as an excellent acquisition for colonial expansion." [11]

"Assisted" emigration into Northern Brazil likewise prospered during the mid-century, for the Conventions controlling the slave trade were being enforced and the need of labor had become acute. Baron von Pereira established great coffee plantations in the Province of *Sao Paulo* which attracted a considerable number of emigrants. The practice, however, of maintaining the newcomers in what amounted to actual bondage until the debt consisting of their transportation, tools, land, and dwelling was paid by their crops created dissatisfaction and many complaints. As a result, warnings against emigration began to be issued by the home governments.

Other South American states, as well, offered inducements to German emigrants and settlements of all types sprang into life: in Chile, where the colony near Valdivia grew so fast that it ultimately alarmed the Chileans; in Argentina, where the future of the pampas was foreseen; and in Uruguay, wherein Liebig set up his enormous "Beef-Extract" factory. Plans were made and in some instances executed for emigration to Paraguay, Costa Rica, and Guatemala. The frequency of revolutions and consequent instability interfered with the success of all these establishments and Brazil continued to hold first place in German colonization in South America; although even her settlements ultimately met with a serious setback, due to the enactment of stricter and stricter legislation against emigration on the part of the German states as well as to the superior advantages offered by North America. The Prussian Rescript of 1859 [11a] forbade agents to solicit emigrants for Brazil which amounted to a virtual prohibition. It was followed by similar legislation on the part of the smaller German states and

39

adopted by the imperial government in 1872. This dealt, of course, a serious blow to German colonization in South America, although the colonies already established there continued to thrive and afford a striking illustration of what private initiative accomplished, not only without state support but actually in the face of opposition from the Fatherland.

To North America the flood of emigration had directed itself since 1820 in an ever-rising tide, and many had been the schemes projected to establish independent settlements. As early as 1835 a small colony was settled at Matamoras in Mexico on the *Rio Grande del Norte,* but on account of the climate, it did not survive. More elaborate and important, although meeting with the same disappointing results, were the plans of Bunsen, the Prussian Minister to England, who urged the seizing of lands in Mexico and in the two Californias. Bunsen did his best to persuade Frederick William IV to accept Mexico's offer to sell California to Prussia in 1842.[12] The plan included a canal to be cut through Panama and a gradual assimilation of Oregon and the Trans-Rocky Mountain regions, but needless to state none of it was ever realized.

Another more stable project which did materialize, although ultimately it too ended in failure, was the settlement in Texas projected by the *Company for Protection of Emigrants to Texas* founded in 1844 and sponsored by the *Mainzer Adelsverein,* whose leading spirits were Baron Castell, Prince von Swerigen, and Baron von Solms. Its real plan was annexation and with that hope it induced many immigrants to come, the number amounting to 7,000 in three years; but it failed to secure a direct grant of land and the disappointed settlers wandered to New York, to Cincinnati, New Orleans, or remained in Texas as nuclei about which subsequent waves of German emigrants gathered. The annexation of Texas by the United States in 1845, however, put an end to the hope of German colonization in Texas and brought to a close all dreams of German colonial settlement in or near the United States.[13]

Not alone were inexperience, mistakes of business management, and unfortunate choice of sites responsible for the failure of all these schemes of settlement in the New World; the rivalry of the leaders themselves, pulling the emigrants this way and that, must bear a large share of the responsibility. Emigration was not concentrated but scattered; diverse motives influenced leaders; and a multiplicity of leaders bid for followers. Illustrative of the complexity and variety of motive was the Texan scheme itself, for its real incentive was something more than a purely philanthropic desire on the part of the nobles concerned; it was rather their reaction to the founding in February, 1842, of a *Deutsche Kolonialgesellschaft* backed by the Syndic, Karl Sieveking of Hamburg, and having as its object the establishment around the world of a series of colonies bound together by a packet service. This company had already established a settlement at Chatham in New Zealand and its far-reaching plans for the control of emigration alarmed Bremen and the Rhenish towns who had so long profited from the American emigrant trade. Also, the nobility of Germany, fast losing their hold on the German peasantry as well as their wealth to the rising burgher class, hoped, perhaps, by the Texan scheme to establish a new feudal state oversea.[14]

Nor must the great German emigration to Russia during the first half of the nineteenth century be forgotten. For its numbers reached 250,000 between the years 1816-1826 and mounted, according to the *Almanach de Gotha,* in 1867

41

to 981,000 persons. Many of these were, of course, scattered throughout the Russian towns and cities as merchants, traders, and professional men of all types, but there existed as well actual German groups united and more or less segregated. These were: the evangelical colonies in Grusien with whose establishment the Baseler Mission had been active; the Protestant and Catholic colonies along the Volga which preserved a strictly German purity, the latter largely Mennonite; and the Protestant agrarian colonies in Bessarabia.[14a]

Many other plans of direct colonization also bid for German emigration urging it to the Near East where in Palestine in 1853 the *"Tempelgesellschaft"* was formed, resulting in the founding of seven settlements mainly composed of doctors, teachers, engineers, as well as peasants; to Greece where a colony was established at Herakli near Athens in 1833; to Hungary where German peasants were enticed by promises of fertile lands as they were also to upper Italy and Roumania; to Africa and to the Mosquito Coast of Central America. After 1840 also, emigration was very active to Australia, resulting in the organization of a colony of Prussian Old Lutherans at Hansdorf near Adelaide and in other settlements. The coincidence of political unrest in Germany of 1848 with the discovery of the Australian gold fields increased the number of Germans on that continent to about 8,000. But the long journey of one hundred and twenty-five days thither prevented the ultimate success of colonization there.[15]

A final proof of the extent of emigration during this period, is the existence of the national societies organized for its control and regulation. The tremendous increase in the numbers of emigrants, and in the variety of schemes for emigration during the decade of the forties made them neces-

42

sary, the figures rising from 28,000 emigrants in 1840 to 94,581 in 1846, to 109,531 in 1847, and to 251,931 in 1854.[16] The chief of these societies were the *Nationalverein für Deutsche Auswanderung und Ansiedlung,* founded at Frankfort am Main in 1848, and the *Berlin Verein zur Centralisation Deutscher Auswanderung und Kolonisation* organized in Berlin in 1849. The object of these organizations was to select the emigrants; to assist those requiring help; to foster nationalism among those leaving the Fatherland; and to help and direct them when they reached their destination.

## Missions

Closely allied to emigration in general were the achievements of the German missionaries during this period; and, like the emigration movement, missionary effort had crystallized into societies which became active centers of agitation for national expansion. Before 1870, at least eight strong societies for work abroad had been founded, of which the Barmen Rhine Mission, the Bremen Mission and the Baseler Mission were the most important. They encouraged trade and helped colonists and travelers wherever they carried on their work, and their publications and reports added just so much more to the colonial cult.

The Barmen Rhine Mission established its first settlement in Namaqualand in South West Africa. Knauer established a station there at Gibeon in 1863, and in 1864 Hahn was sent to organize a missionary colony on the coast of Otymbingue, "in order through the example of German efficiency and activity to influence the natives." As the missionary Büttner states in his book, entitled *Das Hinterland von Walfischbai und Angra Pequena,* this settlement is "the first piece of territory oversea acquired by Germans." Other stations were settled in Namaqualand: one at Windhoek, in 1867 and one at Grootfontein in 1873. Indeed, the missionaries became very much involved in trade throughout the region, gained a strong foothold and exerted a great influence upon German colonization. In 1868 Dr. Fabri, Inspector of the Rhine Mission, asked from the government protection of its work in the Herero land, but was refused. Nevertheless, by the year 1883, Fabri's society controlled ten stations or more, containing five thousand Christians, in South West Africa.

Contemporaneously, the Baseler Mission pursued its activities in a smaller way in Togoland. Originally founded in 1816 in Switzerland, it remained technically Swiss, but came to be composed almost entirely of Germans, who latterly supplied all of its leaders. In addition to its branches in India and elsewhere, the Baseler Mission began its work in Africa on the Gold Coast where it entered the English settlements as early as 1828. By dint of hard work, accompanied by a great loss of lives, it finally succeeded in establishing a station that numbered 23,848 members. In 1885, the Baseler Mission entered Kamerun where it very successfully combined its mission work with industrial enterprise in a way which presented a unique experiment of colonial administration.[17]

Among the South Sea Islands, German missionaries had also been active. Two missionaries had gone to New Guinea in 1855, several to North Borneo, to the Marshall Islands, and to the Samoan group.

## Colonial Merchants and Traders Found the Modern Empire

Among all the achievements, however, of spontaneous and individual effort during the first half of the nineteenth century, those of the commercial colonizers were the most effective. For it was upon their foundations that the German colonial empire of our own day was erected; indeed, without their preparation the colonial policy of modern Germany would have been impossible.[18]

With improved means of transportation and the destruction of the customs barriers, of which the *Zollverein* was the climax in 1834, German trade began to enter world trade by 1830. The markets of South America were thus opened to the weavers of the *Riesengebirge,* and the toys of *Sonneberge* and the stockings of *Apolda* were sought for by the outside world. The old commercial centers of the Rhine and the Hansa towns felt the tremors of renewed activity, an activity which demanded colonies, not for settlement but for economic development, the forerunner of the new colonization of our own day. Emigration had failed to establish German colonies in the strict sense of the word, because all the suitable areas for settlement had been occupied by the other Powers before Germany was strong enough to expand; commercial colonization was to succeed, on the other hand, because it demanded colonies in the tropics, which were as yet not entirely occupied.

The Hansa towns, in line with their old tradition, were the promoters of the new commercial expansion. Hamburg, Bremen, and Lübeck had never entered the *Zollverein.* They were free traders, controlled the bulk of Germany's foreign trade, and had always kept alive the Hanseatic tradition. They brought up their children with ships for toys when their little Prussian cousins were playing with soldiers, and they sent their youth oversea in large numbers. Africa had been the scene of their first activity: as early as 1833, Hamburg had established Factories on the west and southwest coast, the cornerstones as they were to prove of the German colonial empire; in 1844, the firm of Hertz and Son had sent

45

the first ship to East Africa, building up an export trade in cowry shells; [19] it was succeeded by the firms of Hansing and O'Swald, who began by establishing a trade with the west coast at Lagos, and then concentrated their efforts in East Africa at Zanzibar in 1860. So great was their success that in June, 1855, a trade treaty was arranged between the Hansa towns and the sultan of Zanzibar, which was subsequently extended to the North German Confederation in 1869 and later to the German Empire. The Zanzibar trading coast became the most important in East Africa and, by the year 1870, the Hamburg firm of O'Swald was controlling most of the trade, its only serious competitors being the Indian firms under English protection. In Witu, also, Richard Brenner, a traveling companion of Baron von Decken, established such friendly relations with the Sultan Achmed, a Suehli prince, who had won independence from the sultan of Zanzibar, that he offered, in 1867, to make a trade treaty with the Prussian government.

The successors of the pioneer work of Hansing and O'Swald in West Africa were the Hamburg business houses of Witt and Busch and Gaiser. But by far the most active firm in West Africa, dividing and subdividing itself and radiating out in all directions, was that of the Hamburg firm of Woermann. First entering Liberia in 1849, it penetrated and spread through the territories between Gabun and Kamerun. It founded a Factory in Gabun in 1862 and trading stations on the Kamerun River in 1864. Jantzen, a manager for Woermann, 1861-1871, and Thormählen, another agent, formed an independent firm, setting up a Factory in Kamerun in 1875. Their trade grew enormously, and by 1879 they owned Factories along the coast in Great-Batanga, on Bata Bay, and on the Ogowe River. Later, in 1879, two other managers for Woermann, Wölber and

Broehm, formed a partnership on this coast, thereby giving the House of Woermann a firm grasp on the entire district, and placing most of the commerce in its hands. Its packet boats carried on regular trade with all the West African coast, for Germany supplied the salt for most of this part of the world, and Hamburg manufactured the gin "so dear to the hearts of the blacks." [20]

Even the missionaries engaged largely in commerce in West Africa: in 1864, a stock company, with capital of 700,-000 M. was formed in Germany to support the commercial and religious work of the Rhine Barmen Mission at Otymbingue. This company bought the land and buildings of the Walfisch Bay Copper Company and carried on an extensive business. In the same way, the Baseler Mission, working on the Gold Coast in Togoland, established in connection with its trade a large Factory at Akra.

The following figures will illustrate the subsequent growth of German trade in West Africa arising from these foundations:

| Year | Exports to Africa | Imports to Hamburg |
|------|-------------------|--------------------|
| 1879 | 279,252 M. | 5,196,520 M. |
| 1880 | 335,080 | 6,735,090 |
| 1881 | 305,101 | 5,556,230 |
| 1882 | 417,513 | 8,475,100 |
| 1883 | 422,774 | 9,105,150 [21] |

Africa, however, did not represent the only stronghold of these practical colonizers. The Hansa towns were likewise pioneers of trade settlements in the South Seas. So great, indeed, was their influence there that, as early as 1858, a Prussian sea captain was asked whether Prussia was tributary to Hamburg.

The American captain, Wakeman, in his report [22] upon Samoa, writes in 1871 of calling upon T. Weber, agent of the Hamburg House of Godeffroy, and of finding him the controller of the Samoan copra trade. The House of Godeffroy became important on the island as early as 1857. It evidently realized that Samoa was, as Wakeman describes it, the Garden of the Pacific as well as a strategic commercial center. The firm began to buy land in 1857, and by 1859 monopolized all the trade. Its agent, Theodore Weber, entered the service as a lad, went to Samoa in 1861 and gradually assumed complete control. The North German Confederation assisted him by appointing him its official representative. It was due to his management that numerous trading depots in Oceania were created; that New Britain was added to the sphere of the firm's commerce in 1871; and that the traffic in oil of copra was organized on a vast scale. Besides copra, this House carried on trade in cocoa, coffee, and sugar. Each year, large ships left Europe for Apia, the headquarters of Godeffroy, said by Wakeman to be the best distributing center in the Samoan Islands. With its headquarters at Apia, the firm's activities ranged from Valparaiso to Cochin China. At the time of the Franco-Prussian War, its trade was tremendous: it controlled stations all over the South Seas, and the English referred to its head as the "South Sea King." [23] Rapidly the House of Godeffroy was outstripping the English, for whereas in 1868 there were thirty-four English ships in Samoan waters and twenty-four German, in 1871 there were twenty-six English and thirty-six German. Moreover, the activities of this firm were well known in Germany, or at least the House of Godeffroy endeavored to make them so. For in 1861, Johann Caesar Godeffroy founded the Godeffroy Museum in Hamburg to exhibit the geography, ethnology, and natural history of Samoa, for which purpose he sent out many expeditions. He also published the *Journal des Museums*

*Godeffroys* from the year 1871 until 1879, when the firm went out of existence.

In addition to Godeffroy in the South Seas, there was the firm of Hernsheim, which had established trade and acquired lands in New Britain in 1875, making its headquarters at White Bay on the Island of Matupi. These islands became valuable as a source of supply for workers on the German plantations in Samoa, whose organization and transportation this firm of Hernshein superintended. Hernsheim and Company also extended its business to the Caroline Islands, where it had interests in copra. These firms were forerunners of many powerful business houses trafficking in the South Seas.[24] Likewise in the Fiji Islands, Hamburg merchants had found sources of rich vegetable products, had bought plantations, and had invested considerable capital; one firm alone had made an outlay of two and one-half million marks.

Though, unfortunately, no definite trade statistics for the South Seas exist for these early years, the following figures compiled from English sources for the years from 1868 to 1870, and from the reports of German consuls from the years 1873 to 1878, will convey some idea of its growth and extent.

| Year | Total Number Ships Trading with Samoa and Tonga Islands | German Ships |
|------|-----|-----|
| 1868 | 65 | 24 |
| 1869 | 56 | 22 |
| 1870 | 70 | 28 |
| 1873 | 57 | 21 |
| 1874 | 75 | 36 |
| 1875 | 97 | 50 |

| Year | Imports | | Exports | | Ships | |
|------|---------|---------|---------|---------|-------|---------|
| | Total Marks | German Marks | Total Marks | German Marks | Total | German |
| 1876... | 1,606,000 | 1,290,000 | 2,566,000 | 2,386,000 | 149 | 89 |
| 1877... | 1,587,420 | 1,247,420 | 2,503,400 | 2,216,800 | 136 | 65 |
| 1878... | 1,595,000 | 1,395,600 | 2,576,400 | 2,427,200 | 120 | 72 [25] |

Such, then, was the status of economic ventures and settlements oversea about the middle of the nineteenth century. By 1870, German merchants and traders had made themselves prominent in Africa, in the South Seas and in South America, and their activities were the first symptoms of an unorganized and unarticulated colonial policy. Unconsciously this work went on and prospered. The majority of the German people did not know about the expeditions oversea nor the settlements of Hamburg and Bremen merchants in Africa and other parts of the world. But as Coppius remarks in his excellent monograph on this subject, "The quiet pioneer activities of our Hamburg merchants could not fail to exert a great influence upon the German people, even though they did not understand the significance of it." [20]

### The German States Ignore the Colonial Movement

Throughout this period of individual effort in colonization, official attitude on the part of the German states had been one of *laissez-faire*. Sporadic and scattered attempts had been made to induce both the single and the combined state governments to take some action but they had all come to nothing. In response to pressure for state aid, brought to bear by her emigrants, Prussia ordered her consuls in 1847 to make an investigation of the possibilities for concerted emigration; Württemberg and Hesse also considered the matter favorably and projected a plan to enlist the cooperation of the *Zollverein* in 1843. All of these schemes, however, were destroyed by the confusions of the year 1848.

At the German National Assembly in Frankfort in 1848 the matter was revived, and the unusual opportunity there offered for combined action was grasped. The statement that, henceforth, emigration was to be a matter for national concern was included in Article VI of the Constitution, and a law passed establishing an emigrant commission to regulate and to guide the national emigration. This law declared, however, that colonization as such was beyond the scope of the authority of the commission.[27] The gaining of a national commission was regarded as a great step forward, nevertheless, but the hope of the colonial enthusiasts was raised only to be dashed by the failure of the entire Frankfort scheme.

After the year 1848, the old régime returned to power; the old separatism of the states reasserted itself, and Prussia concentrated upon militarism and the maintenance of the established order. Emigration reached its mid-century climax carrying with it oversea many colonial enthusiasts and prophets of the new era. Consequently, the day of state-regulated emigration, to say nothing of state-directed colonization, receded still further into the future. Bavaria's futile attempt, in 1856, to divert her annual loss from emigration to Austria's gain by a joint supervision likewise failed, and the question did not enter the field of national politics until the era of Bismarck. "An attitude of resignation seemed to fall upon the German people as they groped abroad in one part of the world after another to find all of the desirable spots in British hands and as they contemplated a disunited Germany at home."[28]

During the fifties and sixties, however, this attitude of resignation diminished among the commercial colonists. As we have seen, German merchants and traders had made themselves prominent in Africa and in the South Seas and their well established Factories cried aloud for state protection; a protection as possible now for the state to extend over those unclaimed areas of the world, as it had been impossible for it to grant to its emigrants in the occupied countries like North and South America, the Near East, and

Greece. In contrast to the days of the Great Elector, the middle-class, the German merchants, had inaugurated this commercial colonial movement. It lacked state support just as the Great Elector's efforts had needed the support of a German merchant class and had consequently failed. Would it fail again, or had the time arrived when these two essential factors of a successful oversea policy—state aid and merchant activity—would cooperate? The answer rested with the creator of the new Germany—Bismarck.

## NOTES

[1] Nettelbeck, *Eine Lebensbeschreibung, op. cit.*, p. 456ff.

[1a] *Wilhelm Meisters Wanderjahre*, 1. *Buch*, 7. *Kapitel* and III *Buch*, 9 *Kapitel*.

[2] Hansen, *op. cit.*, p. 58.

[3] List, F., *National System of Political Economy* (1841). Translated by Lloyd, (London, 1916), p. 347.

[4] See *infra.*, ch. vii, p. 209.

[5] Sommerlad, T., *Der Deutsche Kolonialgedanke und sein Werden im* 19. *Jahrhundert* (Halle, 1918).

[6] Chéradame, A., *La colonisation et les colonies allemandes.* (Paris, 1905).

[7] Sommerlad, *op. cit.*, p. 24, footnote 3.

[8] Koschitzky, M., *Deutsche Kolonialgeschichte* (Leipzig, 1888, 2 vols.), 1, 123. Also see, *Schmollers Jahrbuch*, 1883, pp. 177-192.

[9] Koschitzky, *op. cit.*, i p. 71.

[10] *Ibid.*, p. 70 and note.

[10a] Sommerlad, *op. cit.*, p. 36.

[11] *Anlagen des deutschen Reichstages*, 1877, *Aktenstück*, no. 80.

[11a] Koschitzky, *op. cit.*, i p. 97ff.

[12] Wappäus, J., *Deutsche Auswanderung und Kolonisation* (Leipzig, 1846), p. 99.

[13] Hansen, *op. cit.*, p. 36, footnote 89.

[14] *Ibid.*, p. 28-29 and footnotes.

[14a] Koschitzky, *op. cit.*, i, ch. x.

[15] Hansen, *op. cit.*, ch. iii. Also Koschitzky, *op. cit.*, i, p. 72.

[16] *Ibid.*, p. 51.

[17] Koschitzky, *op. cit.*, ii, pp. 40ff., 103ff. Also see Mirbt, C., *Missionen in Kolonialpolitik in den d. Schutzgebieten* (Tübing., 1910). The Baseler Mission combined with the Baseler Trading Company (founded in 1859), which carried on a regular trading business with the natives like any com-

mercial company except that it did not sell alcohol and it handed over to the Baseler Mission its profits above 5%. These profits, the Mission proceeded to employ for the benefit of the natives. Cf. *supra.*, ch. xii, *note* 53.

[18] Von Hagen, M., *Bismarcks Kolonialpolitik* (Stuttgart, 1921), p. 18.

[19] *Manuscript Account of Adolph Hertz* by W. Hertz (Hamburg, 1867).

[20] Koschitzky, *op. cit.*, i, p. 244ff. See also, Coppius, M., *Hamburgs Bedeutung auf dem Gebiet der deutschen Kolonialpolitik* (Berlin, 1905), pp. 51ff.

[21] *Ibid.*, ii, p. 128.

[22] *Report of Captain Wakeman to H. Webb on Samoa, 1871* (New York, 1872).

[23] *Geographische Zeitschrift*, v, p. 494 (1899). See also, Coppius, *op. cit.*, p. 62.

[24] Koschitzky, *op. cit.*, ii, pp. 232-240.

[25] *Anlagen des Deutschen Reichstages, 1877, Aktenstück*, no. 80, p. 282.

[26] Coppius, *op. cit.*, p. 61.

[27] Hansen, *op. cit.*, pp. 61, 62 and notes nos. 181-185.

[28] *Ibid.*, p. 63.

# CHAPTER III

## BISMARCK INAUGURATES A COLONIAL EMPIRE

### Colonial Currents and Cross Currents

WITH the advent of the Bismarckian era, the age-old deterrents to a national colonial policy—political disunion and economic weakness—were summarily removed. After the successive triumphs from 1866 to 1871, a united Germany overflowing with superabundant energy had emerged; and the intense nationalism and patriotism engendered by the Wars of Unification found a natural outlet in an enthusiasm for expansion. Now that Germany had become a nation, she, like the other great states of Western Europe, must express her self-consciousness in the extension of her nationalism to a colonial empire; she too must pass through her phase of oversea expansion, and the impression of her individuality upon other lands.

And for Germany this newly aroused nationalism worked two ways, both centrifugally and centripetally, toward the encouragement of colonial foundations. For now, all those emigrant Germans who had left the Fatherland in the days of its weakness and insignificance—the days of the Germanic Confederation—clamored to be united to a glorified Germany. It meant something, after 1871, to say, *"Ich bin ein Deutscher Bürger"*; and petitions even from Latin America demanded the establishment of naval stations in Bolivia, in Ecuador, and Costa Rica.

More important in its influence upon expansion than the

54

removal of political disunion and the achievement of nationalism was, perhaps, the recovery of economic strength. Given a strong and united country after years of division and weakness, given the introduction of the Industrial Revolution with its consequent manufacturing and commercial boom, augmented by the billion-dollar war indemnity from France; and given the resulting overproduction of all kinds of commodities, what circumstances could be more favorable for colonial expansion? The era of security after 1870 developed industry and trade to a remarkable degree, as is too well established to need further exposition here; but the fact must be emphasized that "the commercial instinct is the origin of all colonial conquest," and hence there existed a veritable hothouse atmosphere for the culture of the colonial idea.

Furthermore, the extraordinary overdevelopment and overproduction led to speculation and inflated values, as is also too well known to need elaboration. The agrarian crisis coincided with industrial misery: ten thousand peasant proprietors were sold out each year by the Department of Justice; the new industry, thanks to free trade, was submerged under England's products; French merchandise triumphed; the sum available for industry from the war indemnity had been exhausted, and the terrible crisis and panic of 1873 resulted. The necessity of financial recuperation was widely felt, and when conditions proved too narrow at home both for capital and labor, the opportunity for expansion abroad was regarded favorably.

Voices from every phase of national life were not lacking to present all these circumstances to Bismarck in order to urge their demand for a national colonial policy. Lothar Bucher, a member of the Prussian Foreign Ministry, revived List's ideas on the eve of the empire by his articles in the

*Norddeutsche Allgemeine Zeitung* for February, 1867. He pointed out that everything which List had recommended for Prussia had been accomplished except the acquisition of colonies, and urged the speedy establishment of a colonial kingdom, naming Timor, the Philippines, and St. Thomas as objects. Likewise Friedel, in his book *Die Gründung Preuss-Deutschen Kolonien in der Indischen Ozean* (1867), emphasized opportunities for expansion in the Far East, especially recommending Formosa. Treitschke now supplemented his academic with his political influence, for he entered the *Reichstag* in 1870 where he remained for nearly twenty years. As every one knows, Treitschke stood for the imperialist doctrine in its fullest extent, and taught that Germany's most pressing need was the acquisition of colonies.

It is merely a crystallization of his earlier teachings when he writes in his *Politics:* "People from older states, who have been disciplined, go out and found new states. . . . Every virile people has established colonial power."[1] Reflecting Treitschke were the pamphleteers, Franz Mauer and J. Sturz, who recommended, respectively, the annexation of naval stations as footholds of national strength, and of the creation of a new Germany in Brazil.

Naturally the eve of the Treaty of Frankfort afforded a brilliant occasion for urging the cause of colonization as a means of strengthening the national economic and commercial welfare of the new empire. German merchants in Valparaiso, for instance, raised the question of taking possession of Patagonia; others advised seizing Madagascar, the Zulu Islands, the purchase of Danish St. Thomas. Many saw a golden opportunity to acquire colonies in the dictation of a victorious peace, and demanded that the Treaty of Frankfort should include some of France's colonial possessions. The traveler, von Weber, wrote in the *National Zeitung,*

September 20, 1870, advocating the acquisition of Cochin China, Tahiti, the Marquesan Islands, and Réunion.

Even after the peace settlement, enthusiastic colonists did not lose hope, but took refuge in propaganda, appealing still to the national sentiment. Some advocated annexing the Fiji Islands, the Hebrides, the Philippines, while from America came German voices clamoring for the acquisition of Cuba, Sumatra, New Guinea and Pondicherry. In 1871, Samoa was proposed as a naval station; *Das Kleine Journal* and *Die Welt Post* supported the cause, and pamphlets appeared advocating Germany's interests in the East.[2]

What is more, the imperial officials, Prince Albrecht of Prussia, chief of the navy, and Vice Admiral Livonius strongly advocated the acquisition of colonies. Germany had proved herself supreme on land; why, they asked, should she fail to strengthen herself upon the sea? In 1871 Wilhelmshafen became a naval base on the North Sea, and, in 1871, the Prussian Ministry of Marine became the Imperial Admiralty. Growing German trade demanded naval protection, and as navalism increased it paved the way for colonies. As Prince Albrecht, the "Builder of the German Fleet," expressed it: "For a growing people there is no prosperity without expansion, no expansion without an oversea policy, and no oversea policy without a navy."[3]

It would be an error to conclude, however, from the above discussion, that German public opinion generally was favorable to a colonial policy in 1871. Certain circumstances were most propitious for colonization. These included, as we have seen, an enhanced national consciousness expressed by Germans at home and abroad; a swollen purse requiring objects for expenditure, and then a depleted purse in need of large dividends regardless of risk; an abnormally inflated production demanding outlet markets; mushroom industries clamoring for raw materials; an overstocked labor market using emigration as a safety valve; and finally an evergrowing navy promising protection to oversea ventures and investments.

There were, on the other hand, many unpropitious features of the national life that were most inimical to the notion of expansion. With the exception of a few such personages as Bucher, Prince Albrecht and Admiral Livonius, the official circles and the ruling class absolutely opposed a colonial policy, because they recognized that a colonial policy involved expense and friction with other Powers; that it would interfere with the attainment of German security in Europe by means of concentration upon the strengthening of internal resources, and the maintenance of friendship with England. Politicians, ministers, and bureaucrats, the practical statesmen of the day, did not possess sufficient sympathy, understanding and imagination to appreciate the movement for the colonies which, as we have seen, was so far in a very embryonic and experimental stage. As a class they were too conservative to venture on untrodden paths.

Again the prevailing economic doctrine of the times, that of *laissez-faire,* would also prevent colonial expansion. This was the era of the ascendancy of the National Liberal Party, free traders, who considered colonies an anachronism. To be sure, a small group of economists composed of List, Wappäus, Wagner, and Roscher, had begun twenty-five years before to break away from the Manchester School, and to urge a colonial policy; but the predominant national school of political economy in Germany did not yet regard even German emigration from anything but the cosmopolitan viewpoint. Friedrich Kapp, a well-known representative political economist of the time, who became government commissioner for Germans in the United States in 1866, emphasized entirely the cosmopolitan idea of emigration. He was the author of several books on the subject, which showed no interest whatever in a narrow, nationalistic colonialism.

Despite, then, all the auspicious circumstances and all the work of individual colonists and enthusiasts reviewed in the foregoing chapter, it cannot be claimed with any accuracy that the country was awake either to the advantages or to the necessities of a colonial policy in 1871; on the other hand it was aware of many disadvantages.

But what of Bismarck? It has been necessary to examine the conditions and the national psychology with which he had to deal before we could understand his all-determining attitude.

### Bismarck's Attitude Toward a Colonial Policy

English interpreters of Bismarck generally pronounce him an anti-expansionist, or, at best, a late convert to colonization. Both his biographers and the historians of the period assert that he was emphatically opposed to a colonial policy in any form, until he was forced into it by the activities and importunities of the merchant class.[4]

It is true, say these English interpreters, that Germany embarked upon an era of colonization in the year 1884 when Bismarck was at the height of his power, but this was not due to his initiative. Indeed, the pioneers of colonization, they claim, achieved its adoption as a governmental policy in spite of his opposition and not with his assistance. Rather was it the result of the unaided efforts of the German merchants who had secured a foothold abroad and had consolidated at home into colonial societies all the political, economic, and religious factors making for colonialism. Bismarck is thus popularly represented as at first a vigorous opponent of expansion, and finally an unwilling convert; as a victim, in other words, of economic forces that were becoming too strong for him.

Such a rôle, it must be confessed, does not seem a suitable one for the Iron Chancellor, for he was much more accustomed to bending circumstances to his will than to fitting himself to circumstances. Hence it is not strange that a closer scrutiny of the origins of the modern German colonial empire would seem to recast him, not, it is true, as the founder of the German colonial movement, as the orthodox *Weltpolitiker* would have him; but as the man who was not, in principle, opposed to it, and who recognized and directed the *Weltberuf* of fifty million Germans.[5]

It cannot be denied, however, that there exists a great deal of evidence which apparently proves that Bismarck was in principle an opponent of colonization. There are, in the main, three arguments upon which this case rests. In the first place, nothing is easier than to cite from Bismarck's own speeches his reiterated and emphatic denial of any sympathy whatever with oversea expansion. His public utterances fairly bristle with such denials. Paradoxically enough, as the German Empire plunged deeper and deeper into her career of expansion, the more frequent and emphatic did his denials become. They range all the way from the brusque statement of the year 1871, "For Germany to acquire colonies would be like a poverty-stricken Polish nobleman providing himself with silks and sables when he needed shirts," [6] through the more dignified assertion in 1881, "As long as I am Chancellor we will carry on no colonial policies," [7] to the final decisive fiat of 1889, *"Von Haus auf bin ich kein Kolonialmensch."* [8]

In the second place there are the Chancellor's own acts

repudiating a colonial policy. Here, too, nothing is simpler than to point to innumerable measures directed not only against imperial expansion itself, but against the encouragement of such a policy by groups within the empire. To mention only a few at random: Bismarck in 1871 refused a French offer of colonies in Cochin China during the preliminaries of the Treaty of Frankfort;[9] in 1876 he rejected a proposal to establish a colony in South Africa put forward by a group of interested merchants;[10] in 1880 he ignored a plan for the colonization of New Guinea;[11] and in 1882 he announced in the official press that the political situation prevented the government from taking any part in the work of the *Kolonialverein*.[12]

The interpreters of Bismarck as an anti-expansionist, who rely upon these obvious manifestations of his faith and works to prove their case, must not forget, however, the principles of mid-nineteenth-century statecraft. Cavour, indeed, has revealed to us the rules of the game he played in company with his fellow statesmen when he says, "Now I know the art of deceiving diplomats: I tell the truth and they do not believe me." In terms of modern psychology the "defense attitude" was a favorite expedient of nineteenth-century diplomacy. Such Machiavellian practices worked both ways, and Bismarck was certainly never outdone by Cavour.

Finally, the third reason for the popular estimation of Bismarck as an anti-expansionist is a sound historical dogma; namely, that his one overruling aim, as demonstrated by all his policies, was to establish the security of Germany in Europe. Therefore, it is argued, he discounted the value of colonization and deliberately ignored it in order to concentrate entirely upon his chosen task. To believe Bismarck, in principle, a friend of colonies, however, would not necessarily contradict this well-founded dogma, but would seem to strengthen the evidence for it. For he sensed, as soon as any other statesman, the rising tide of economic imperialism, and he realized that without oversea expansion Germany could not hope to compete with the other nations, nor to attain her great ideal. Indeed, he came to perceive that Germany must foster colonization in order to secure and to maintain a position of supremacy in Europe.

When viewed from the angle of his colonial policy, Bismarck's chancellorship naturally falls into two periods: its inauguration from the year 1871 to 1884; and its stabilization and organization from 1884 to 1889, the latter to be discussed in the succeeding chapter. Again, the first period of inauguration divides into two distinct parts as Bismarck gradually developed his policy: the years 1871 to 1876 define a time of cautious preparation and watchful waiting; while the years 1876 to 1884 mark the initiation of official protection for all the commercial undertakings oversea, combined with an effective, if unadvertised, cooperation with all the colonialists, ending with the birthday of the German colonial empire, April 24, 1884.

### The Period of Watchful Waiting

Searching the first five years of the empire for evidences of colonial expansion, we discover that a decided unwillingness to encourage any colonial undertakings whatever characterized Bismarck's policy. Consistent with his refusal to accept the colonies proffered by France in 1871, already cited, he rejected innumerable petitions from government officials and German merchants at home and abroad to seize colonial opportunities, as well as requests from native rulers for the establishment of German protectorates. Importunities poured in from all sides and from every continent. The

German consuls in Samoa and Australia advocated, during 1871 and 1872, a speedy annexation of some point in Samoa or the Fiji Islands in order to protect German capital and industry so advantageously established there; [13] the customs commissioner in China urged the government to secure a foothold upon the Chinese coast; [14] a group of Bremen merchants earnestly petitioned that the Port of Saigon, a strategic naval base in China belonging to France, be demanded at the Peace of Frankfort; [15] and their petition was duplicated by the merchants of Hamburg, who demanded Cochin China, Miquelon, Martinique, and St. Pierre. [16] From the opposite side of the globe colonists in the Province of Rio Grande du Sul in Brazil demanded protection of their commercial interests so that, as they phrased it, "a modern colonial policy may be adopted"; [17] while from South Africa, Weber, who was developing a diamond mine, suggested the establishment of a German protectorate over the Transvaal. [18] As late as 1874, Bismarck refused the offer of the sultan of Zanzibar to place himself under German protection, [19] as he likewise treated the similar proposal from a land company in Borneo, enjoying the patronage of the sultan of Zulu, whose allegiance would thereby have been transferred to Germany. [20]

Again the Chancellor turned a deaf ear to the many vociferous colonial propagandists whom the glorious results of the Wars of Unification had inspired with an intense nationalism and patriotism. In fact, he quite dashed their hopes by officially announcing in the press that the new Germany contemplated no expansion, so fearful was he lest the voices of these colonialists should arouse the attention and suspicion of foreign Powers. [21]

In the face of these numerous and consistent refusals of cooperation with the colonists during the years 1871 to 1876

—which might be confirmed by many other examples—it would seem as though the case were adequately proved for those who call Bismarck an anti-expansionist. Further scrutiny, however, revealing his plans for the diplomatic guardianship of the colonists, his reasons for the refusal of their petitions, and the internal and external politics of the time, would seem to contradict so obvious a proof of opposition as the record appears at first glance to present.

Although Bismarck emphatically rejected and discouraged each petition for the establishment of a naval base for other territory, he did not neglect altogether the importunities for trade protection from these would-be colonists. To be sure, the official response to them was weak, but it was a response. It consisted in "diplomatic guardianship," which meant an extension of the consular service, and a dependence upon the offices of foreign consuls. To illustrate, the government rejected the proposed protectorates over Borneo, Zanzibar, and South Africa, and the acquisition of naval stations in China and Samoa, it is true; but it granted the petition of the Brazilian colonists for consular and postal service, and stationed consuls in Africa and in the South Seas in response to the demands of the merchants.

Moreover, whenever the Chancellor explained his action in refusing the plans and petitions for protection and colonization proposed between the years 1871 and 1876, he invariably assigned the same reasons: weakness and unpreparedness of the new empire, fear of exciting the antagonism of foreign Powers, and the lack of support for colonialism within Germany itself. For instance, he rejoined to the Hamburg merchants who urged his acceptance of France's colonies in 1871, that any colonial undertaking at that time was premature. He answered the demand for a naval station in China by saying that Germany possessed neither men nor money for such adventures, and could not afford to be "weakened from without." He explained to the sultan of Zanzibar that he was unable to accept his offer because he could not hope for support from the *Reichstag*. He admonished the consul in Samoa, declining his advice to colonize there, to "avoid any friction with the United States, to be most tactful, and to promote no independent policy." [22] All these explanations and admonitions, it would seem, implied a postponement of colonial expansion rather than a disapproval of it.

Furthermore, Bismarck's alleged reasons for delay assume all the appearance of genuineness if they are considered, as they must be, in direct connection, first with Germany's domestic affairs and, secondly, with her foreign orientation. Indeed, when one reviews the internal and external situation during those formative years of the young empire, from 1871 to 1876, it becomes clearly evident that an anti-expansionist policy was the only wise course to pursue. Engrossed first in his task of unifying and centralizing the empire, then absorbed in his bitter struggle with the Church, he had little opportunity to apply himself to colonization. It must also be remembered that the prevailing economic doctrine of the time, that of *laissez-faire,* would have the effect of restraining him, no matter how much he may have secretly believed in colonies, from projecting them at this time. For the Chancellor was temporarily, but strongly allied to the National Liberals, and so long as it served his ends to maintain such an alliance as a political expedient, he had to forego many policies dear to his inherently conservative convictions. He knew that as soon as the alliance with the National Liberals became no longer necessary, he would be free to become openly a Conservative once more. And it is significant, perhaps, that as soon as he did break with the National Liberals in 1878, he at once applied himself to protection and to its corollary—colonial expansion. Had he been quietly waiting until he no longer needed their support to do so?

In this connection it is interesting to observe that there is some evidence even before 1871, which shows that the idea of future colonies for Germany was not absent from Bismarck's mind. Article IV of the Constitution for the North German Confederation, which he prepared, reads: "the Law of the Kingdom shall be extended over the Colonies and the settlements in the lands oversea"; [23] a clause whose purport later appeared in the Constitution of the Empire in 1871. [24] Again, immediately prior to 1870 Bismarck, as the Chancellor of Prussia, rendered assistance to the mercantile house of Godeffroy in the South Seas: he encouraged the scheme of populating with German emigrants the land owned by the Godeffroy Company in Samoa; invested the Prussian consuls with extraordinary powers; granted arms from the royal arsenals and sent a warship to the island to protect German trade. Finally, a program of future colonization laid before him by Godeffroy elicited the promise of future aid; but the intervention of the Franco-Prussian War, and the consequent concentration upon empire-building at home, prevented its realization. [25]

And if internal affairs restrained Bismarck from embarking upon a colonial policy, so much more did external relationships. The guiding star of his foreign policy, the isolation of France, and the maintenance of friendship with England, inhibited any activity likely to cause friction with foreign Powers, especially when Germany was so young and her navy so weak. To have fostered anything at variance with the free trade principle oversea would at once have aroused the antagonism of England. No one grasped more clearly than this astute statesman the contrast between the positions of the two nations in regard to their colonial expansion: Great Britain, the "Sunday-child" of the European state system, with her natural, geographically protected base, could afford to be independent of other nations in building up her colonial empire; while Germany, the "Step-child," handicapped by her geographical insecurity in Central Europe, by her uncertain boundaries, her insufficient seaports, and by her ring of hostile neighbors, must of necessity subordinate her colonial expansion to her relationships with the other Powers, especially to the strongest colonial and naval Power, Great Britain.[26] Consequently, Bismarck realized that Germany's expansion oversea could only be carried on in cooperation with Great Britain, if at all;[27] and this realization goes a long way toward explaining the caution of those early years. Again and again, as we have already observed, the avoidance of "friction with other Powers" is given as a reason for refusing petitions from the colonists, and the express wish not to step on others' toes (meaning British toes) oversea is aired in the official press.

In view of all these considerations there exists no ground, as we see it, for pronouncing Bismarck an anti-expansionist, because of his stiff-necked refusal to launch the young empire immediately upon a career of colonization. His policy from 1871 to 1876, closely analyzed, would seem to imply a promise, a postponement, rather than a rejection of imperial expansion; a promise which was immediately fulfilled as soon as the avowed reason of political expediency; namely, the temporary alliance with the National Liberal Party, had disappeared.

## Bismarck Begins to Protect the Colonists

In the year 1876 a group of merchants led by Weber and Lüderitz presented again to the Chancellor the project of a German colony and protectorate in the Transvaal. On this occasion Bismarck did not curtly dismiss the petitioners, but received them with great courtesy, and expressed personal sympathy with their plans. He said that he had studied [28] the question for some years and had concluded that, "a great nation like Germany could not, in the end, dispense with colonies; but, as much as he was in principle in favor of the acquisition of colonies, he hesitated to embark upon colonization without adequate preparation and a definite impulse from the nation itself." He added that the political situation was unfavorable at that time—conditioned as it was by the jealousy of France, the sensitiveness of England, the *Kulturkampf;* but he held out the hope that something might be done in nine or ten years, "when there shall have been created a deep-seated national movement in favor of it." [29]

The above interview, which was not published until 1884, may be taken as a guide to the Chancellor's policy from 1876 to 1884, the period of protection for oversea interests.

For, if we consider these words spoken in confidence to colonialists, as the key to his subsequent actions, those actions become clear; otherwise they remain an enigma. On the one hand, they explain why he vigorously extended, after 1876, governmental protection to all commercial enterprise oversea, a course which always constitutes the first step of a colonial policy; while, on the other hand, they elucidate, as nothing else can, his apparent attitude of indifference, even of opposition, to colonization.

In other words, between the years 1876 and 1884, the

Chancellor appears to have played a double game. He secretly and indirectly pursued a policy of colonial expansion at the same time that he openly and officially repudiated it. He was feeling his way; he could afford neither to lose support at home, nor to antagonize the Powers abroad. His task, then, was to pursue a colonial policy and to create public opinion in favor of it without appearing to do so. He must of necessity encroach upon the preserves of the Great Powers, but must cause no resentment; in short, he must subordinate his colonial policy to his foreign policy. Only the methods of nineteenth-century statecraft, it will be admitted, could compass such a task. Why look, then, for his real purpose in his public utterances and in his open diplomacy?

Indicative of the changed attitude of the administration after 1875 is the long chapter of protective measures adopted by Bismarck for the benefit of the oversea traders; and as the years advance these measures grow bolder and more explicit. To begin with, he abandoned the policy of "diplomatic guardianship" and boldly protested to the other Powers whenever they overstepped the rights and opportunities of German traders and settlers oversea. Spain was summoned to account in 1875 for imposing customs duties upon German traders in Zuzuland,[30] and the attention of the British government was sharply called to the claims of the German settlers in Fiji, who had suffered eviction when England had annexed the island in 1874.[31] Moreover, to facilitate this new procedure, von Küsserow, a colonial enthusiast, was appointed Counsellor to the Foreign Office, and entrusted with the conduct of all the commercial affairs oversea.[32]

But it was the series of commercial treaties negotiated between the years 1876 and 1879, doubtless immediately instigated by England's aggressive action in Fiji, that marked the Chancellor's definite departure from mere "diplomatic guardianship" to active protection of the oversea traders. The Tongan Treaty, consummated in 1876, guaranteed reciprocal commercial freedom and the right to establish a naval station on the Vavao Islands, part of the Tongan group in the South Seas.[33] This was followed by the Samoan Treaty in 1879, which was the result of Germany's strong stand in those islands for the protection of her commercial interests, jeopardized, on the one hand, by the civil war waged between the native rival claimants to the throne and, on the other, by the claims of both England and the United States. The treaty, besides the usual trade advantage, ceded to Germany "rights which the Samoan government is forbidden to grant to any other nation," as well as the right to establish a coaling station on the island of Opolu.[34] Other treaties were signed at the same time granting Germany equal rights of trade with other nations, and three coaling stations in the Ellice and Gilbert Islands, Marshall, Ralick and Society Islands, in the Duke of York Islands, and on the northern coast of New Britain.[35]

It is true that in presenting all these treaties to the *Reichstag*, Bismarck officially and most particularly announced that the government contemplated no colonial policy, but only trade protection. The establishment of a naval base in Vavao should "not be considered as the establishment of a colony, an idea which the government distinctly repudiates," stated the preamble to the Tongan Treaty; while the *Deutscher Reichs-Anzeiger* published an explanation relative to the Samoan Treaty, that the government did not think of occupying the Samoan Islands, and contemplated no annexation of any kind. The government representatives adopted the same attitude in the *Reichstag* debates over these treaties when attacked and accused of a colonial policy by such radical opponents of it as Bamberger.[36] Von Bülow, for instance, replied, "The treaties represent, positively, no colonial nor monopolistic policy but merely the principle that where I have planted my foot there shall no one else be permitted to place his." [37]   Indeed, Bismarck and his representatives can be quoted *ad infinitum* in the documents and debates relative to the Tongan and Samoan Treaties as intending no colonial policy.[38]   The fact remains, however, that by these treaties, the Chancellor inaugurated a definite system of oversea trade protection and even endorsed the acquisition of naval stations, the inevitable introduction to annexation of territory.   Likewise, before the expiration of the year 1879, he established with England and the United States a joint municipal protectorate over Apia in Samoa.[39]

As already intimated, the all too threatening signs of a renewed interest in imperialism on the part of foreign Powers contributed effectively to Bismarck's change of policy: England had commenced her ambitious activities in Egypt, and in 1877 had annexed the Transvaal; France was on the eve of founding her second colonial empire; the United States was asserting her rights in Samoa.   Furthermore, Great Britain continued to ignore Germany's claims in regard to the indemnities of her Fiji Island settlers.   Bismarck had, significantly enough, revived the correspondence relative to this question on May 23, 1879.   His letter to the German ambassador in London had only elicited on June 17, 1879, the unsatisfactory reply from Lord Salisbury, that the matter had been brought to the attention of the Colonial Office.[40]   Furthermore, the Congress of Berlin in 1878 had served to bring both Bismarck and the German public into closer contact with international affairs, and it had revealed more closely the relative aims, ambitions, and strengths of the other Powers.

71

But, besides the pressure exerted from outside, internal changes influenced Bismarck in altering his hitherto cautious policy toward Germany's oversea interests: the year 1878 clearly marked the end of the "liberal era" in German politics for, by that time, Bismarck was ready to break with the National Liberals, and he signalized the break by his reversal of the fiscal system from free trade to protective tariff, a reversal fraught with significance for colonization. With the aid of the National Liberals, he had achieved his triumph of a centralized, united Fatherland in 1871, and he had allied himself with this alien group as a political expedient; now, he no longer needed their support and therefore found himself free and ready to return to more familiar principles and to more congenial friends. For the reversion to conservatism in 1878 gave him Conservatives and Clericals (won over respectively by a protective tariff and a diminution of the *Kulturkampf*) as his chief supporters in the *Reichstag* in place of the National Liberals; and to the Conservatives and Clericals, a colonial policy was not the anachronism it had been to his former political allies.

*The Chancellor Tests Public Opinion and Is Disappointed*

After 1879, therefore, refreshed by the clearer air of party politics at home and invigorated by the hostile atmosphere of a resurgent imperialism abroad, the Chancellor boldly projected a colonial policy in the *Reichstag*. He was too cautious, however, to label it as such. In 1880, he introduced the Samoan Subsidy Bill which proposed that the government should grant an annual subsidy to Godeffroy and Son to enable them to promote their trade in the South Seas.[41]

As will be remembered, the House of Godeffroy, a powerful Hamburg firm, had entered Samoa as early as 1857,

72

and by 1859 had monopolized all the trade. Trading in copra, coffee, cocoa, and sugar, it controlled many stations throughout the South Seas, and in 1871 had merited the name of "South Sea King" from the English. In 1878, however, the firm overreached itself in financial speculation, submitted to the pressure of borrowing money from Baring Brothers, of London, and in 1879 failed. Its failure not only spelled ruin for the extensive German interests of the South Seas, now in danger of falling into foreign hands, but seriously jeopardized Germany's political prestige in Samoa, where she had assumed a joint protectorate with England and the United States. Bismarck proposed to prevent such a calamity to Germany's oversea interests by officially underwriting a new company, *Die Deutsche-See-Handelsgessellschaft* which would rescue the Godeffroy interests from the grasp of Baring Brothers of London.[42] Of course, the presentation of such a bill to the *Reichstag* raised the issue of a colonial policy, and the Samoa Subsidy Bill became a test case of the whole colonial movement.

Throughout the course of the debates in the *Reichstag* over the Bill, as well as in the official documents and press, the government did not commit itself to a colonial policy, but it cautiously masked the question of colonial expansion, raised by the Bill, behind an impassioned appeal to national patriotism to protect German trade and prestige in the South Seas. The Samoan Subsidy, said von Küsserow, in urging the Bill, "is not a question of party, of free trade or protection of colonialism, but a question of the honor and glory of Germany."[43] He proceeded to exaggerate the imperialistic menace of England, to wave the red, black and white flag, and to expatiate at great length upon the threatened calamity, which Germany's failure to act would bring about in Samoa. Never once did the government meet squarely the issue of a colonial policy, although the Opposition, led by Bamberger, tore off the disguise of "national glory" and proclaimed the Bill an inauguration of state-directed colonialism.[44] The question of a colonial policy for Germany was thus openly discussed and attacked, and Bismarck was apprised thereby of the attitude of the country toward it. Significantly enough, he did not appear personally in the *Reichstag* during the debates. As the official *Norddeutsche Allgemeine Zeitung* announced, " . . . we hear that only a very acute neuralgic attack with which Bismarck has been afflicted for the last three weeks, prevented him from personally taking part in the debates." [45]

Finally, the failure of the Bill to pass the *Reichstag* [46] confirmed the Chancellor in his convictions that, in spite of the pressure from the oversea traders, it was unwise as yet to inaugurate an official colonial policy. Only in the first flush of his disappointment and anger over the loss of the Bill, did he discard all diplomacy and reveal his true position in the official press, as follows, ". . . It is probable that had the country been consulted, the verdict would have been very different. The Samoan Subsidy was a prelude to German colonial policy and the first practical expression of it. Neither the enemies of our greatness nor the doctrinaires of the Manchester School, will succeed in preventing Germany from embarking upon that course which other nations have followed to advantage." [47]

He was too astute a statesman, however, to make the mistake of openly pressing an already defeated issue in the face of a powerful opposition. He was also politician enough to realize that a policy which he had strongly advocated had been repudiated by a *Reichstag* already too independent; and he appreciated only too well the importance of not letting such a *Reichstag* get out of hand, especially at this crisis in political affairs. In the early eighties, the Chancellor's supporters were none too strong or numerous, for over against the union of the Conservatives, the Right Wing of the National Liberals and the Center, were ranged the Left Wing of the National Liberals,[48] the Progressives, the Poles, the Particularists, and the Socialists, and Bismarck was obliged to struggle against the opposition to his new fiscal policy and to his Social Insurance legislation. He felt that by the failure of the Samoan Bill his authority was compromised, his duty and policy injured by party strife, and that caution was necessary. Although by the Samoan Bill he had intended "to launch his *'Lieblingsplan'* "; namely, "a colonial policy," he fell back upon his maxim, " . . . it is impossible to launch a colonial policy without a national impulse."[48a]

Moreover, the failure of the Samoan Subsidy drove the Chancellor again into an equivocal position, after the Bill itself had forced him to show his hand in favor of colonies. Heartily in sympathy with expansion, as he had revealed himself to be in 1878, he became, during the years 1880 to 1885, firmly determined to establish a colonial policy for the empire, yet he considered it unsafe to do so. He dared not alienate the supporters of his policy in the *Reichstag* who, as we have already noted, were none too strong or numerous. Hence, it is during these years from 1880 to 1885 that Bismarck gives us the most interesting evidence of his double-dealing. For, on the one hand, there is abundant evidence to show his official and open repudiation of a colonial policy; while, on the other hand, everything goes to prove both his secret support and his furtherance of the colonial movement.

Six months, for example, after the failure of the Subsidy Bill, Bismarck was besieged by two capitalists interested in

oversea trade, von Hansemann and Mosle, for cooperation with their colonial plans. They belonged to the Right
Wing of the National Liberals, were very close to Bismarck
and probably cognizant of his attitude. But he rejected
Mosle's petition for a state subsidy to buy and develop land
in North Borneo, and refused von Hansemann's request for
a state-guaranteed steamship line between the Duke of
York Islands and other South Sea ports, as well as a plan
for the colonization of New Guinea. Indeed, he had von
Hansemann draw up a statement of trade conditions in the
South Seas which he published. It stated that, "After the
rejection of the Samoan Subsidy, it is impossible to take
any strong initiative in the South Seas." [49] Thus did he
allay any suspicion of governmental action in Oceania. At
the same time, however, he wrote to von Hansemann, " . . .
the country's inclination is not strong enough to warrant
support of this plan now." He also wrote to the Board of
Directors of the *Deutsche-See-Handelsgessellschaft,* who had
privately come to the rescue of the company upon the failure
of the Subsidy Bill and had assumed Godeffroy's debts, as
follows: "His Majesty and the German government appreciate the great service you have rendered the Fatherland by
supporting the German enterprises in the South Seas." [50]
Again in 1881, consistent with his official attitude, Bismarck
turned a deaf ear to the petition of the Barmen Mission in
Africa for protection and, in 1883, to the petition of the
brothers Denhardt for support of a proposed settlement
in Tana; but, at the beginning of the year 1883, he secretly
promised protection to Lüderitz, a Bremen merchant, long
active in African trade, and in April, 1883, he asked the
Hansa towns to submit suggestions for the protection of
their trade interests in Africa, with all of which he complied
by December of that same year. [51] He himself created in

1880 the Economic Council of Prussia to support his commercial policy, and the Council forthwith passed a resolution that the empire appropriate 100,000,000 M. to purchase territory for colonies. Indeed, he attempted to form such an Economic Council for the empire throughout the year 1881, but met with defeat.

On the other hand, whenever openly questioned in regard to an imperial colonial policy, the Chancellor emphatically repudiated it. His reply to a member of the *Reichstag,* in 1881, may be duplicated by his rejoinder, in 1883, to the Commerce Commissioner who recommended the annexation of Formosa: "Colonies only belong to a mother country in which national feeling is stronger than party spirit. The attitude of this *Reichstag* is such that it is difficult enough to maintain what we already have, even to support the army for home defense. So long as the empire is financially disabled, we dare not embark on such expensive undertakings . . . we cannot bear the burden of colonies, we can only support trading companies; but even for that it would be necessary to have a *Reichstag* which would have other and higher objects than constant discussions and the creation of difficulties for the administration." [52]

## *A National Colonial Impulse Arises*

As the years of the eighties progressed, however, forces both within and without the empire were removing those deterrents to an open colonial policy enumerated by Bismarck in 1876, and were preparing the way for him to pursue a bolder course. To be specific, a national feeling, an impulse for expansion, lacking in 1876, was becoming apparent and, secondly, the political situation both externally and internally had materially changed.

Since 1879, the friends of colonization, quick to sense

the significance for their cause in the Chancellor's shift to protective tariff, and alive to the rapidly increasing emigration statistics, were flooding Germany with a propaganda which based its arguments upon the vital political and economic necessity for colonies; upon a national interest calculated to arouse a strong patriotic emotion. Foremost among the many propagandists stood Hübbe-Schleiden and Fabri. The former, a lawyer and a statesman, was interested in a mercantile house in Hamburg, had been an explorer in equatorial Africa, and a merchant from 1875 to 1877 in Gabun; while the latter, for twenty-seven years Inspector of the Rhine Mission, had become convinced of Germany's need of colonies and had devoted himself to the cause by his books, by his articles in the press, by his speeches at innumerable gatherings, and by a many-sided correspondence with friends of a colonial policy, and with great industrialists.

Primarily, we may say, Hübbe-Schleiden represented the political, and Fabri the economic aspects of the question. It is Hübbe-Schleiden, however, who must be credited with having been the first to elevate the subject of acquiring colonies to the plane of a distinctively national policy. By far the most original and significant of any of the propagandists, he is the prophet of a new era for Germany, an era to be characterized by an intense, overgrown nationalism. He it was who cleverly linked up colonialism with the contemporary transformation in the *Weltanschauung* of the empire, from a liberal *laissez-faire* cosmopolitanism and internationalism to a conservative, individualized and narrow nationalism; and in so doing, he served further to accentuate and accelerate that change. He made the solution of the colonial question dependent upon the already visible change in the national mind of Germany; he identified himself with colonialism with the "younger generation," and the more advanced thinkers, and thereby gained for the movement that stimulating quality inherent in all movements which claim to have escaped from the reactionaries and to be apprehended only by "more enlightened minds."

A quotation from Schiller's *Wilhelm Tell* on the flyleaf of Hübbe-Schleiden's book, *Deutsch Kolonisation, "es lebt ein anders-denkendes Geschlecht"* gives us the keynote to his thesis, ". . . to the older generation, the term 'nationality' has only an ethnographical content, but for the younger it has a political." [53] Hence the outworn, international idea clung to by the past generation must not be allowed to block the ambitions of the present. That would seem suicide for Germany. Hübbe-Schleiden emphasized the fact that the development of a self-conscious national feeling as well as of a strong, oversea policy, which in trade and emigration acknowledge only a national flag, were questions of life and death for Germany's future. *"Los von Nord Amerika, Los von Gross-Britannien"* was his slogan. Likewise he exposed the "Free-trade Parody," as he termed it. He showed how the practice of free trade, instead of creating equal opportunity for all merchants, had enabled England to increase her control of world trade within two decades (1855-1875) from sixty-one per cent to seventy per cent.

A natural corollary to the foregoing argument was Germany's mission to spread her *Kultur* as a means of maintaining the *Deutschtum.* "In this manner a country exhibits before the world her strength or weakness as a nation." As Hübbe-Schleiden said, "How many inventions or discoveries are made by Germans decades before they are even thought of by Englishmen or Frenchmen, but are advertised to the world as of English or French origin. Hence prestige and *Kultur* become submerged." [54]

Supporting Hübbe-Schleiden in emphasizing the national political aspect of colonization were such men as von Weber, who recommended the annexation of the Transvaal, Moldenhauser, and Herman Wagner.

The economic side of the question of "life and death" for Germany was also exploited to the utmost by propagandists, and here it is Fabri who takes the lead. He wrote in 1879, when he thought the fiscal and commercial crisis would win for him a ready ear. In his book, *Bedarf Deutschland der Kolonieen?* he represented Germany as economically threatened, and emphasized the social results of noncolonization. He presented the question as one, not so much of political power and prestige, as of actual, national, material existence. "The colonial question is not primarily a *Machtfrage*. It is more a *Kulturfrage* since economic needs, in connection with general national crises, demand colonies." [55]

Fabri dealt in a practical manner with the ideas of the colonial theorists upon emigration, and focused attention upon what was rapidly becoming a dominant motive for expansion, the ever-swelling stream of emigrants from the Fatherland. He regarded emigration not as an isolated question, in the manner of the older colonialists, but as a subject closely connected with national and social questions; and many other writers, between the years 1879 and 1881, followed his lead in this respect. [56]

Naturally the flood of literature just reviewed, with its attempt to make the colonial question a national issue, did not go unchallenged by the opponents of a colonial policy. The warfare of pamphlets, books, and words that ensued, served at least indirectly the object of the colonial party to make the subject one of nationwide discussion.

These combatants of oversea expansion consisted, in the

main, of the older generation of cosmopolitans. They defined the issue squarely as one of nationalism versus internationalism, and opposed the effort of the propagandists to raise the debate to a national plane. Prominent among the opponents was Dr. Friedrich Kapp, the great mediator between Germany and the Germans in the United States, where he lived for twenty years. He represented the thought of a generation of Germans against whom Hübbe-Schleiden had directed his attacks. Indeed, Hübbe-Schleiden's book, *Deutsche Kolonisation* was a reply to Kapp's *Über Colonisation und Auswanderung,* in which Kapp argued that the "international protection of emigrants is the most pressing question of the day." He deplored the proposed adoption of a state-directed emigration as a definite attack upon individual liberty. Other supporters of the negative side of the controversy were Philippsohn, an associate of Dr. Kapp, Peltz, Loehnis, Fritz, and Zacharias.

### The Kolonialverein

More efficacious, however, than propaganda as a means of nationalizing the colonial policies was the work of the colonial party in founding the *Kolonialverein* in 1882.[57] Several societies had already appeared in Germany as forerunners of the *Kolonialverein.* The first of these, the *West Deutsch Verein für Kolonisation und Export,* founded by Fabri in 1880, was an offshoot from the *Central Verein für Handels-Geographie und Deutsche Interesse in Ausland,* which since 1868 had formed many branches, all emphasizing colonial interests. Next in importance as a forerunner was the Leipzig *Verein für Handels-Geographie,* which boasted objects similar to the *West Deutsch Verein.* In addition to these societies, there existed various others for exploration and travel; groups of Rhenish industrials like

Friedrichs, Hasenklever, and Heimdahl, who were very much in favor of economic expansion oversea; and the associations of Hanse merchants such as Woermann and Mosle, Godeffroy's successors.

Thus there were many movements, all unrelated, uncoordinated, and small in themselves, but there was no one concerted effort for colonization. A central organization which would unite all the various efforts was conspicuously lacking, although the preparation for it was complete.

The idea of a plan for one large, all-inclusive colonial society may be credited to three men, who gave it expression almost simultaneously: Freiherr von Maltzan, the naturalist; von der Brüggen, the traveler; and Prince Hohenlohe-Langenburg, the politician. The result of the cooperation of these three colonial enthusiasts was a summons to all those interested in colonization—the great industrials, representatives from societies, and the Boards of Trade of Frankfort and Offenbach—to meet in Frankfort to discuss the question of placing the colonial ambitions of Germans upon a broader base. The preparatory meeting was held on August 26th, 1882: it appointed a committee which issued on September 12th a circular embodying the objects of the proposed society and containing an appeal for members. The objects were stated as follows: "To extend to a larger circle the realization of the necessity of applying national energy to the field of colonization. To form a central organization for all the hitherto scattered efforts for expansion. To create some method for the practical solution of the question." The circular was then published in the papers, together with a manifesto addressed to the country which showed the need of increasing commercial outlets in order to establish and maintain close touch with Germans oversea, and called attention in quite an alarming way to

82

Germany's position which was growing more and more restricted abroad.

Many leading men responded to the call, particularly the industrial magnates of the west and south and members of those societies already organized. The *Kolonialverein* was accordingly founded, and its Constitution drawn up on December 6th, 1882, at Frankfort.[58]

The growth and success of the *Kolonialverein* in winning adherents to the cause were remarkable, for by December 31, 1883, after one year's work, it numbered three thousand, two hundred and sixty members and had footholds in four hundred and ninety-two places in Germany, and in forty-three abroad, including nineteen outside of Europe. Furthermore, it was strong enough to launch an official organ, the *Kolonialzeitung,* whose first issue appeared in January, 1884. The journal called upon all patriotic men to further the work of the colonial party. Its appeal was not political or partisan, but rather universal and national, and two years of active propaganda achieved wonders in shaping public opinion. Indeed, in one year from 1884 to 1885, the membership increased over three hundred per cent, rising to ten thousand, two hundred and seventy-five.

Another organization—*Die Gesellschaft für Deutsche Kolonisation*—was, in addition to the *Kolonialverein,* a molder of public opinion and influenced the growth of colonialism. It was founded by Karl Peters in Berlin on April 3rd, 1884, for the very practical object of raising capital to finance colonies in East Africa.[58a] When Dr. Peters attempted to win official interest for the new society, he encountered the lively opposition of the *Kolonialverein,* whose members thought that any scattering of effort would weaken the whole movement. An amalgamation of the two societies was proposed, but great difficulties lay in the way:

Peters advocated an active policy of immediate annexation; while the *Kolonialverein* was more cultural, more educational, more interested in supporting enterprises already started. Final amalgamation ultimately resulted, however, on November 19th, 1887, and the outcome was the foundation of a single great society, *Die Deutsche Kolonialgesellschaft,* which became a powerful and influential factor in the later history of the German colonial movement.

Coinciding with and stimulating this growth of a national desire for expansion within the country was the pressure of external circumstances demanding a definite policy on the part of Germany in regard to oversea territories. For, as a result of Stanley's and Livingstone's discovery of the Congo basin, the "international scramble" for Africa had set in; and between 1880 and 1885 the Great Powers of Western Europe all showed unmistakable signs of a thorough reconversion to the benefits of imperialism. The acquisitions of France in Tonkin and Tunis, of Italy in the Red Sea, and of England in India and in Egypt were so many witnesses of the altered point of view which had awakened free-trade England, and had inspired Jules Ferry to colonial acquisitions. All this activity on the part of the other Powers could not fail to strengthen Bismarck's decision, for, certainly, he was not blind to their too obvious ambitions.

Perhaps enough has been said to show how times had changed since 1876, when "a national impulse" for expansion was lacking. It remains to show how the international situation had also altered.

*A Favorable International Situation Presents Itself*

In 1876 Bismarck had enumerated as obstacles in the way of Germany's expansion, the *Kulturkampf,* the jealousy of France, the sensitiveness of England, and Germany's own unconfident position in international affairs. But by 1883 and 1884 the *Kulturkampf* was at an end; *"revanche"* under the administration of Jules Ferry had ceased to dominate France's foreign policy; and Germany was now in a position to defy the sensitiveness of England, for Bismarck had guaranteed her position in Europe by means of the Triple Alliance and the revival of a more formal Three Emperors' League (1881-1884). Moreover, Germany's subservient attitude to England, especially in the colonial field before 1875, had undergone a subtle change for several reasons: England had refused all Bismarck's offers of an alliance, the one in 1875 and one in 1879; [59] her aggressive action in Fiji had thrown into the limelight the conflicting Anglo-German colonial aims both in the South Seas and in Africa; and she exhibited no inclination to recognize Bismarck's support of her policy in Egypt which he, clinging to his old axiom of the isolation of France and the maintenance of friendship with England, continued to accord.

As an antidote to her increasing resentment toward Great Britain, on the other hand, Germany's relations with France had materially improved since 1875: the conciliatory Ferry had replaced the revengeful Gambetta and Freycinet as premier, and the well-disposed Saint-Vallier the intriguing Gontaut de Biron as French ambassador to Berlin; Germany had supported France at the Morocco conference in Madrid in 1880, had cooperated with her on the question of Greece's boundaries; and, finally, Bismarck had rendered valuable assistance to Ferry in acquiring Tunis and in helping France forget the "Gap in the Vosges," by the acquisition of a colonial empire.

But in addition to assuaging her injured feelings in regard to England, this improved relationship with France served to strengthen Germany's position in Europe. Indeed, the year 1883-1884 saw Germany's security in Europe attained. Hence, the creator of that security could afford to assume a firmer stand toward the other Powers than he had been able to do in 1875. Bismarck, to be sure, continued to subordinate his colonial policy to his foreign relations, but, having insured his foreign relations, he was no longer obliged to subordinate his colonial policy to the point of negation as had been the case before 1875; and, furthermore, he could not use his well-secured position in Europe to aid or to thwart the colonial ambitions of other nations.

## The Opportunist Grasps the Opportunity

The first evidence of Bismarck's new confidence in foreign relations, as applied to the protection of German traders, was his action concerning England and the Fiji Settlement. It may be remembered that England's ejection of Germans there in 1875 had exerted a telling influence in making him realize the necessity for German colonies.[00] Since 1875, the British government had ignored his claims in behalf of these dispossessed traders and was apparently proceeding unchallenged in its course of empire-building, irrespective of the rights of other nations: the governor of Queensland had occupied a section of New Guinea in 1883 and the Australian colonies had, in the same year, adopted a sort of Monroe Doctrine for the South Seas, opposing the annexation by a foreign power of any land below the equator. In May, 1882, Bismarck had deliberately revived the subject with Great Britain, but with no result. Consequently, in 1883, he assumed a bolder front, and peremptorily demanded the submission of the whole question of the Fiji settlers to a joint land commission to be composed of Englishmen and Germans. England seemed not at all disposed to consent to this proposal, and the diplomatic correspondence dragged

86

on with increasingly peremptory notes from Bismarck on
October 18 and December 27, 1883, and on April 8, 1884.
Not until June 19, 1884, did England agree to the estab-
lishment of a joint commission.[61]

The correspondence and the attitude of the Chancellor,
however, had their effect, for they served to create the impression in Germany that not only were England's commercial
and colonial methods a menace to the Fatherland, but that
any country might, in the same manner, infringe upon the
property rights of Germans anywhere oversea without
reparation. The affair stirred the people to a keen realization of the need of actual annexation in order to secure
adequate protection; even "the enemies of colonialism began
to debate the question favorably." [62]

But it was in Africa that the Chancellor pushed his confident nationalist policy to a climax; a climax which, in
conjunction with affairs in the South Seas, created an international crisis and precipitated an outburst of German
patriotism strong enough to launch a state-directed colonial
policy. During the early eighties, as we have seen, explorers
were directing the eyes of all nations toward Africa, that
continent which alone afforded great stretches of territory
as yet unclaimed, and the "Great African Hunt" had begun.
Here, also, Great Britain had been pursuing monopolistic
methods: in 1882, she had concluded with France a Colonial
Convention, negotiating a demarcation line for the extension of English and French territory northward from Sierra
Leone, and establishing high customs duties which were
keenly resented by German firms stationed in that region;
and, in line with the Anglo-French Convention, concluded
in 1884, the Anglo-Portuguese Treaty which established a
monopolistic control of the Congo river. This treaty met
with bitter and outspoken antagonism from German busi-

ness interests. The Boards of Trade of Hamburg, Solingen, Bremen, and Mannheim sent protests to the government, and the firms in Loanda dispatched representatives to Berlin to plead their cause.[63] Patriotic excitement spread throughout the Fatherland and an enraged public sentiment arose against England. The Chancellor noted the national resentment and turned it to his own account. He sent a protest against the Anglo-Portuguese Treaty to Portugal, April 18, 1884, and repudiated any intention of accepting its terms; at the same time, he instructed his ambassador in Paris to approach France with a proposal to unite the commercial interests of France and Germany in the Congo against England.[64] On April 24, 1884, he received a response wherein France promised her full support, and France's cooperation in maintaining the principle of equality of trade in the Congo finally led to the calling of the Congo Conference on November 15, 1884. Thus Bismarck attempted to isolate England, so far as her colonial aims in Africa were concerned, by drawing nearer to France, and he thereby encouraged and increased the growing anti-English sentiment already very prevalent in Germany.

Finally, England's well-known procrastination and pusillanimity in regard to her South West Africa claims [65] supplied the Chancellor with an opportunity to forcibly assert himself and crown his work with success. Shortly after Lüderitz, the Bremen merchant, had applied for imperial protection over his settlements in South West Africa in November, 1882, Bismarck had addressed a courteous note to England, (February 4, 1883) asking if England exercised any authority over the Angra Pequena region. "If not, Germany intends to afford her subjects in that region the protection which they need." The note conveyed the impression, however, that Germany "had not the least design of establishing a foothold in South West Africa," and would prefer to leave the responsibility of protection to England.

England replied to the note on February 23, 1883, that, "the Cape Colony government has certain establishments along the coast, but without more precise information as to the exact location of Lüderitz's Factory, it is impossible for the British government to say whether it could afford this protection in case it were required."

The reply was extremely evasive; and it appeared all the more so, since England had already declared that this part of the coast was outside her jurisdiction. Indeed, when Bismarck had asked the British government, on November 4, 1880, to extend its protection to German missionaries in this region on an occasion of a native war, England had replied (November 29, 1880), "The British government cannot accept responsibility for anything occurring outside of British territory, which includes only Whale Bay and its immediate region."

All this former correspondence, which had definitely delimited England's claims, had really made Bismarck's inquiries of 1883 superfluous, as he himself admitted; and it also indicated that the Chancellor had made such polite inquiries merely from the motive of wishing to maintain Germany scrupulously in the right, should a complication with England arise, and of desiring to quiet any suspicion of Germany's actual plans. The Chancellor also expected Great Britain to further German colonial policy in return for his invaluable support in Egypt.[86]

But Great Britain delayed her reply for nine months.[87] During this time she attempted to make the Cape government assert its claim to the territory beyond the Orange River; while Lüderitz, also, took advantage of the delay to seize the harbor of Angra Pequena and the surrounding districts. When England's answer finally reached Berlin in November, 1883, after two peremptory reminders from the Chancellor, Granville stated therein that, although English sovereignty had been proclaimed at Walfisch Bay and the islands off Angra Pequena, any claim to sovereignty or jurisdiction by a foreign power between Angola and Cape Colony would infringe England's legitimate rights.

To all patriotic Germans this dispatch placed England in the position of a dog-in-the-manger, and Bismarck's reply of December 31, 1883, demanded by what right or title England could claim sovereignty over a territory formerly considered independent; while his note revealed a tone hitherto lacking in his communications. He was sure of his ground and could afford to be defiant. And we need only to remember, in order to appreciate the full force of the Chancellor's diplomacy at this point, that its harsh tone synchronized with his ultimatum upon the Fijian claims, and with his promise of vigorous action in the South Seas. The cumulative effect of these clashes with England was not to be neglected.

From December, 1883, the thermometer of popular indignation and national chauvinism steadily and rapidly rose until April, 1884, when it finally indicated a state of feverish excitement. For England sent no reply to the note of December 31, 1883, and her procrastination aroused in Germany a keen resentment—a resentment augmented by articles in the official press, by the Chancellor's attitude toward Great Britain's aggressive interference with German trade in the South Seas, and by the Anglo-Portuguese Treaty of February, 1884. Bismarck realized that the crisis had arrived. He at once took advantage of the state of the popular mind, the "national impulse for expansion," and of Germany's security in Europe and dispatched the official proclamation to Lüderitz, declaring his settlements to be under imperial protection. With this stroke he inaugurated the German Colonial Empire on April 24, 1884, and the old Kaiser William I was able to announce, "Now I can look the Great Elector in the face when I cross the long bridge in Berlin."

## NOTES

[1] Treitschke, H., *Politics* (Berlin, 1898), trans. by Dugdale and DeBille (London, 1916).

[2] Zimmermann, A., *Geschichte der Deutsche Kolonialpolitik* (Berlin, 1914), p. 12.

[3] *Allgemeine Deutsche Biographie*, vol. xlv, p. 788.

[4] Dawson, W., *The German Empire, 1867-1914* (London, 1919), vol. ii, p. 17.

Ward, A., *Germany 1815-1890* (Cambridge, 1918), vol. iii, p. 158 *et seq.*

Lowe, C., *Prince Bismarck* (London, 1899), vol. ii, p. 207 *et seq.* Is a partial exception to this statement as notes a change in Bismarck's attitude after 1876.

Keller, A., *Colonization* (New York, 1908), pp. 539-543.

Keltie, J., *Partition of Africa* (London, 1893), p. 163 *et seq.* Speaks of Bismarck as open-minded after 1878.

Robertson, Grant, Bismarck (New York, 1919).

[5] Von Hagen, *op cit.*, p. 41.

[6] Poschinger, H., *Bismarck als Volkswirt* (Berlin, 1889, 2 vols.), vol. i, p. 63.

[7] *Ibid., Bismarck und die Parlementarier* (Breslau, 1894), 3 vols., vol. iii, p. 54.

[8] *Verhandlungen des deutschen Reichstages*, Jan. 26, 1889, p. 621.

[9] Canstatt, "Fürst Bismarcks Kolonialpolitische Initiativ," in *Zeitschrift für Kolonialpolitik*, June, 1908, p. 436.

[10] Hahn-Wippermann, *Fürst Bismarck, Sammlung der Reden, Depechen, Staatschriften und politischen Briefen* (Berlin, 1878, 5 vols.), vol. v, p. 4.

[11] Zimmermann, *op. cit.*, p. 21.

[12] *Ibid.*, p. 42.

[13] Hahn-Wippermann, *op. cit.*, vol. v, p. 185.

[14] Zimmermann, *op. cit.*, p. 11.

[15] *Anlagen des deutschen Reichstages*, 1870, Petition, no. 13, under no. 15.

[16] Poschinger, H., "Bismarck und die Anfänge der deutschen Kolonialpolitik," in *Kölnische Zeitung*, Aug. 19, 1907.

[17] *Anlagen des deutschen Reichstages*, 1872, Petition, no. 51.

[18] Weber, E., *Vier Jahre in Afrika* (Berlin, 1879), 2 vols., vol. ii, p. 543.

[19] Koschitzky, *op. cit.*, vol. i, p. 127.

[20] Herrfurth, K., *Bismarck und die Kolonialpolitik. Geschichte des Fürstens Bismarcks in Einzeldarstellungen,* vol. viii (Berlin, 1909), p. 6.

[21] Zimmermann, *op. cit.*, p. 22.

[22] Cf. *supra,* pp. 62, 63, footnotes, 15, 14, 19, 13.

[23] *Anlagen des Reichstages des Norddeutschen Bundes,* 1867, p. 11.

[24] Dodd, W., *Modern Constitutions* (Chicago, 1909), vol. i, p. 327, quoting *Section II, Art. 4* of the Constitution of the German Empire.

[25] Lowe, C., *Prince Bismarck,* vol. ii, p. 210.

[26] Rachfahl, F., *Bismarcks englische Bündnispolitik* (Freiburg, 1922), p. 7. *Deutschland und die Weltpolitik* (Tübingen, 1923), p. 84.

Rogge, H., "Bismarcks Kolonialpolitik" in *Historische Vierteljahreschrift,* 1922-1923, Heft, 3, 4.

[27] It is alleged by some writers that Bismarck even approached Great Britain in 1875 with offers of an alliance based upon cooperation in colonial affairs. Furthermore, it is claimed that he chose Lotha Bucher, that vigorous advocate of a German colonial policy, to go on this mission to England. Bucher was charged to offer Great Britain two things: either an alliance on the continent, which was (if true) Bismarck's first attempt to attach England to the Central Powers; or else, an alliance in the colonial field, to effect which he was "to draw up with England's help a far-reaching colonial program, to discuss in consultation with the British cabinet the colonial and economic development of Germany in the future and to try to discover a '*modus vivendi*' of cooperation in that direction." But England refused both offers. See Eckardstein, H., Freiherr, von., *Lebenserinnerungerungen und politische Denkwürdigkeiten,* 3 vols. (Leipzig, 1919), vol. i, pp. 296, 308, vol. ii, p. 102.

See also Stuhlmacher, W., *Bismarcks Kolonialpolitik* (Halle, 1927), pp. 120-124. He considers that there is not sufficient evidence for this mission of Bucher's. For a contrary view again, see Valentin, Veit, *Bismarcks Aussenpolitik, 1871-1890* (1922), pp. 18-22.

There is no reference to Bucher's mission, however, in *Die Grosse Politik der Europäischen Kabinette 1871-1914.* Edited by Lepsius, Mendelssohn-Bartholdy, Thimme (Berlin, 1922). See vol. iv, p. 4 note.

[28] As a student at the University of Göttingen, Bismarck had attended, more than any other lectures, those of von Heeren, Professor of World History, on political geography. Poschinger, H., *Bismarcks Portfeuille,* 5 vols. (Stuttgart, 1898-1900), vol. ii, p. 78.

[29] Hahn-Wippermann, *op. cit.,* vol. v, p. 22.

[30] *Anlagen des deutschen Reichstages,* 1877, *Aktenstück,* no. 205.

[31] *Weissbuch,* 1885 pt. ii, pp. 5-6. Also *Staatsarchiv,* vol. 44, pp. 13ff. Also, *Accounts and Papers,* vol. xlvi, pp. 339-457. See also, von Hagen, *op. cit.,* pp. 65ff. Von Hagen considers that England's action in Fiji convinced Bismarck of the pressing necessity for a German *Kolonialpolitik,* a view supported by Herbert Bismarck in *Die Grosse Politik,* vol. iv, p. 65.

[32] Poschinger, "Aus der Denkwürdigkeiten Heinrich von Küsserow," in *Deutsche Revue,* Feb., 1908, p. 189.

# BISMARCK INAUGURATES A COLONIAL EMPIRE

[33] *Anlagen des deutschen Reichstages,* 1877, *Aktenstück,* no. 80, pp. 279 *et seq.*

[34] *Ibid.,* 1879, *Aktenstück,* no. 239, p. 725.

[35] *Ibid., Aktenstück,* no. 239 and 1880, *Aktenstück,* no. 101.

[36] Ludwig Bamberger, a prolific writer on political economy and a very influential member of the *Reichstag.* He belonged to the Left Wing of the National Liberal Party, was a bitter enemy of Bismarck, and in 1880 was foremost among those who repudiated the National Liberal Party and formed the *Liberale Vereinigung.* (1833-1899).

[37] *Verhandlungen des deutschen Reichstages,* June 13, 1879, p. 1612.

[38] *Ibid.,* June 13, 16, 1879.

[39] *Anlagen des deutschen Reichstages,* 1880, *Aktenstück,* no. 101, p. 728.

[40] *Staatsarchiv,* vol. 44, pp. 13ff.

[41] *Anlagen des deutschen Reichstages,* 1880, *Aktenstück,* no. 101.

[42] There is abundant evidence to show that the Chancellor was hand in glove with the two great banking houses of Bleichröder and von Hansemann. Von Hansemann was the chief financial adviser of Bismarck, forming with Senator Gustaf Godeffroy, the head of the *Norddeutsche Bank,* the main links between national finance, the administration and colonial speculation. Moreover, von Hansemann was the father-in-law of von Küsserow.

[43] *Verhandlungen des deutschen Reichstages,* April 23, 1880, pp. 888 *et seq.*

[44] *Ibid.,* April 27, 1880, pp. 945 *et seq.*

[45] *Norddeutsche Allgemeine Zeitung,* April 25, 1880, no. 191.

[46] *Verhandlungen des deutschen Reichstages,* April 27, 1881, p. 960. The Bill was lost by 128 against 112 votes. The Opposition consisted of the Left Wing of the National Liberals, the Progressives, the Centrists and the Socialists. For details, see Townsend, M., *Origins of Modern German Colonialism* (New York, 1921), pp. 122ff.

[47] *Norddeut. Allg. Zt.,* April 28, 1880.

[48] Bismarck's adoption of protective tariff in 1878 had resulted in a split in the National Liberal Party. The Left Wing broke off entirely on August 30, 1880, under the leadership of Bamberger, Rickert, etc.; it formed the *Liberale Vereinigung,* endorsed all the traditional liberal ideas such as free trade, and joined the ranks of the Opposition.

[48a] Coppius, *op. cit.,* p. 67, also see *supra.,* ch. iii, p. 68.

[49] Hahn-Wippermann, *op. cit.,* vol. v, p. 72.

[50] Poschinger, *Aktenstücke zur Wirtschaftspolitik des Fürstens Bismarcks* (Berlin, 1889-1891, 2 vols.), vol. i, p. 372.

[51] *Weissbuch,* 1883, July 6, 7.

[52] Poschinger, H., *Bismarck als Volkswirt* (Berlin, 1889), vol. ii, p. 149.

[53] Hübbe-Schleiden, *Deutsche Kolonisation* (Hamburg, 1881).

[54] *Ibid.,* p. 48.

[55] Fabri, F., *Bedarf Deutschland der Kolonieen* (Gotha, 1879), p. 56.

[56] Von Scherzer, Dilthey, Liesenberg, Wölfing, Grünewald.

[57] See, *Die Deutsche Kolonialgesellschaft,* 1882-1907 (Berlin, 1908).

[58] *Ibid.*, pp. 9, 10.

[58a] See *infra.*, ch. v. p. 132.

[59] *Die Grosse Politik*, vol. iii, pp. 127-136, 458. See also Valentin, V., *op. cit.* See also Buckle, G., Life Beaconsfield, vol. iv, p. 486ff.

[60] See *supra.*, ch. iii, p. 69 and note 31.

[61] For Fiji Correspondence, see *Die Grosse Politik*, vol. iv, pp. 51, 52. *Staatsarchiv*, vol. 44, p. 73.

[62] Koschitzky, *op. cit.*, vol. ii, p. 145.

[63] *Die Kolonialgesellschaft, op. cit.*, p. 36ff.

[64] *Die Grosse Politik*, vol. iii, p. 437.

[65] *Ibid.*, vol. iv, pp. 1-108.

[66] See *infra*, ch. iv, pp. 101-102.

[67] Great Britain's delay in the affair is largely explained by the necessity felt by the British Colonial Office (Lord Derby) of consulting the Cape government and also by the failure of the British ministers, especially Lord Granville, to recognize Bismarck's colonial designs. They misunderstood his colonial policy as mere "election maneuvers." Granville's unawareness of Bismarck's colonial policy was due mainly to Lord Ampthill in Berlin, who failed to grasp the situation, and to Count Münster in London, who had no sympathy with his country's colonial ambitions.

Gooch, G. P., *History Modern Europe*, pp. 102ff., and Stuhlmacher, W., *Bismarcks Kolonialpolitik*, pp. 38ff.

Granville admitted Germany's right to be annoyed, see Correspondence of Granville and Herbert Bismarck, Aug. 20, 1884, *Die Grosse Politik*, vol. ii, nos. 751, 752.

# CHAPTER IV

## BISMARCK STABILIZES AND ORGANIZES THE COLONIAL POLICY UNDER THE SLOGAN "SAFETY FIRST"

WITH the inauguration of a state-directed colonial policy for the empire, Bismarck's work was not yet complete; its stabilization and organization remained to be accomplished. During the last five years of his chancellorship, therefore, we find him prosecuting his new policy of expansion at home and abroad, guiding it through the intricacies of foreign relations and finally organizing a definite program for its continuance.

### Friends and Enemies of the New Policy

As we follow the colonial history through these years, we must first take account of the political situation at home, and of the friends and enemies of colonization with whom the Chancellor had to reckon. Through the decade of the 1870's, the supporting parties of the government had been the Conservatives, the National Liberals, and even the Progressives who had rallied to Bismarck in the *Kulturkampf;* while the Social Democrats and the Center (because of the *Kulturkampf*) had sat in the Opposition. After 1880, however, the party line-ups had changed: the Conservatives, of course, remained staunch; but the National Liberals had split, mainly on the tariff issue; these secessionists, uniting in 1884 with the Progressives whose government alliance had ceased with the *Kulturkampf,* formed the *Deutsch-Freisinnige-Partei* and with the Socialists became the con-

95

stant opposer of the government; while the Center, some-what placated, but immensely strengthened after the *Kultur-kampf,* supported the government when it approved of its measures, such as the Social Insurance Laws and the Anti-Socialist Legislation, but cleverly held the balance of power in the *Reichstag.* To support his new colonial policy, there-fore, during the years 1884-1889, Bismarck could rely upon the Conversatives, most of the National Liberals, and on groups of merchants and industrials among the Progressives and *Deutsch-Freisinnige;* on the other hand he had to en-counter as a strong Opposition all the Radicals led by the *Deutsch-Freisinnige-Partei.*[1] They based their objections to colonization upon its patently capitalistic aspect, its danger of exciting friction with other Powers, and upon the general foolishness and futility of oversea possessions. In all these arguments the Socialists, who were, in any case, the natural enemies of the government, heartily concurred.

But a far more serious aspect of the Opposition was its partisan character. A party spirit apparently actuated the Radicals more than their liberal doctrines—a spirit of revenge and hatred of Bismarck and all his new policies, as well as of determination to contest his absolute control of foreign affairs. The same animosity likewise attracted to the Radical Opposition all dissident elements, who merely seized the colonial issue as something tangible upon which to fasten their antagonism to the government. Prominent among them was the Center party, led by Windthorst, Bis-marck's bitter enemy. Although the Catholic Center the-oretically and practically believed in a moderate colonial policy, it was still smarting from the *Kulturkampf* and, always posing as the party of economy, it resented the great expenditure required to support the colonies; it was becom-ing aroused by the proposed anti-Polish campaign and

finally, because of Windthorst's influence, it could not afford
to lose this unparalleled opportunity to combat the Chancellor. Hence the Catholic Party sacrificed conviction to
partisanship and joined forces with the Radicals. As the
Center held the balance in the *Reichstag* in 1884-1885, and
could determine any issue by combining with the Right or the
Left, its attitude created a serious problem for the government.

The chief method employed by this Clerical-Radical
Opposition to combat the colonial policy was to adopt
"obstruction tactics" carried to absurd extremes. It centered
its attack upon the Steamship Subsidy Bill [2] introduced by
Bismarck into the *Bundesrat,* in April of 1884, because it
regarded the proposed subsidy only as another measure to
further the colonial policy. Thus the Bill became the central
issue of the parliamentary struggle. It had had a long history, for the plan of a steamship line to the East, which it
proposed, had first come to Bismarck's attention in 1876.
He had not promoted it, however, until 1881, when he had
aired the project in the official press, and had requested the
imperial representative in Hamburg to sound opinion there
about it. Thwarted by the *Reichstag's* rejection of his me-
morial on the subject in May, 1881, he had temporarily abandoned the whole scheme, but he revived it in 1884, encouraged by the same stimulus of popular support which had
impelled him to send the telegram to Lüderitz. The Bill
provided for a government subsidy amounting to 4,000,-
000 M. annually for fifteen years, for steamship lines running to east Asia and to Australia. Primarily a commercial
measure its acceptance by the *Reichstag,* however, was, as
Bismarck himself declared when pressed, "decisive for the
colonial policy of the government," [3] since, "without steamship subventions, no colonial policy." [4] The struggle over

the Bill began on June 14, 1884, two weeks before the *Reichstag* expired. After its first reading the Opposition prevented its second reading by having it referred to the Budget Commission of which Windthorst was the chairman. To further embarrass the Chancellor, the Opposition blocked every bill proposed by him, and succeeded in creating an absolute parliamentary deadlock in the new *Reichstag* elected in the autumn of 1884.

Such then was the character of the pronounced domestic hostility to his new imperial policy, which Bismarck had to face immediately after its inauguration: the doctrinaire, Liberal-Radicals, plus all cautious citizens who traditionally opposed expense, risk, or any departure from the beaten path, and the far more dangerous parliamentary and partisan enemies represented by the Clerical-Radical majority in the *Reichstag,* supplemented by dissident nationalist groups, such as the Poles, Danes, and Alsace-Lorrainers, who were his traditional foes. But the very number and character of his enemies served, as always, to spur the Chancellor on to action, and we find him diligently and untiringly waging a campaign against this domestic opposition throughout the years remaining until his resignation in 1889; a campaign wherein two distinct strategems may be distinguished and which, considered together with the reaction of his enemies, comprises the colonial history of the period.

### Colonial Acquisitions Form Part of the Campaign Against the Opposition

In the first place, plans for colonial acquisition were executed with startling rapidity, for the best way to win support for a colonial empire was to have one. Consequently, Bismarck sent official orders to Dr. Nachtigal, an explorer whom he had appointed consul to West Africa

(April 17, 1884) at the behest of the Hamburg firms, to place certain districts there under imperial protection.[5] German commercial houses such as Woermann, Thormählen, Jantzen, and the merchant, Colin, largely active on the West Coast, had consummated treaties with the native chiefs, in spite of the competition and rivalry of the British who were very influential there. Nachtigal, realizing the urgency of the situation, lost no time in obeying orders, and arrived on the scene just one week ahead of Consul Hewett, sent on the same errand by the British. From the *S. S. Möwe* he visited and preëmpted with the German flag the Loos Islands and Dubreka in Senegal, the territory between the Niger Delta and Gabun, including the strip opposite the island Fernando Po in Biafra Bay, and Little Popo in Togoland. In consequence, Bismarck was able to announce on October 13, 1884, that all these districts (except the Loos Islands which reverted to Great Britain, and Dubreka which reverted to France) were under German protection.[6] Likewise, on October 1, 1884, he appointed Dr. Rholfs consul for East Africa, and extended imperial protection on February 7, 1885, to all lands acquired by the Society for German Colonization.[7] Thus, in Africa, empire building proceeded apace, and the protectorates of Kamerun, Togoland, and East Africa were added to that of South West Africa.

In the South Seas, moreover, activity was even more strenuous: the German New Guinea Company formed, on May 13, 1884, through the efforts of the bankers von Hansemann and Bleichröder, and the Chancellor himself, bought the shares of the *Samoa Handels-und-Plantagen Gesellschaft,*[8] until then in English possession, and established an oversea bank; like Dr. Nachtigal, an explorer, Dr. Finsch, was sent out ostensibly for scientific purposes but actually to unfurl the German flag in northern New Guinea; other explorers and merchants freely dispensed flags, nailed up signs entitled *"Kaiserliches Schutzgebiet"* on the palm trees, and made treaties with the non-resisting natives so that Bismarck, on December 23, 1884, notified the Powers that imperial protection had been extended to settlements on the north coast of the New Britain Archipelago.[9] All of these activities, of course, precipitated counter-activities on the part of Great Britain, urged on by the incessant demands of her Australian colonists.[10] But, finally, agreement with England was reached in 1885, by which the German imperial protectorates were allowed to embrace a quarter of New Guinea, rechristened Kaiser Wilhelmsland, a group of the Solomon Islands and other islands north of New Guinea later named the Bismarck Archipelago, and the Marshall Islands.[11] Thus the nucleus of a very respectable colonial empire was acquired in an astonishingly brief space of time, and it proved to be a very potent weapon in the Chancellor's hand in dealing with his refractory and obstructionist *Reichstag.*

### Diplomatic Skill Fosters the Colonial Cause

In the second place, Bismarck combated opposition to his imperialism, both at home and abroad, by his consummate skill in the conduct of foreign affairs. Always, as from the very first, he subordinated the colonial policy to the foreign policy; but in so far as it was possible he made international relations serve colonial ends. He exploited the difficulties and embarrassments of other Powers to further German expansion and yet not to jeopardize Germany's other interests. And at the same time he so manipulated the diplomatic chessboard as to sustain at home a national patriotic enthusiasm great enough to submerge objections to his colonial policy.

Two major orientations characterized this conduct of foreign relations during the decade of the eighties, orientations of which we must take particular note: first, a swing away from England toward France in contradiction to the traditional course; and then a return to the assiduous cultivation of British good-will. And Bismarck was able to assume this independent stand in his attitude toward Great Britain, because of the exceedingly propitious relations between Germany and the rest of Europe, which he had established by the year 1883-1884. Indeed, after 1883, for a short time at any rate, Bismarck could reap the rewards of his earlier toil in the enjoyment of that security which he had created. Protected, then, both by his Triple Alliance and Three Emperors' League, by the "splendid isolation" policy of Great Britain and, finally, by the temporary cessation of French *"revanche,"* he could afford to stack the cards in the game of foreign relations in order to further any project at home.

For the playing of such a game, Bismarck held a trump card; namely, Germany's attitude toward the activities of the other Powers in Egypt.[11a] With the crumbling of the Dual Control wielded by France and England over the Khedive, France had been growing ever weaker, and England ever stronger in that strategic neighborhood of the Suez Canal; and with England's increasing aggression, Bismarck had shown himself thoroughly in accord. After Great Britain's bombardment of Alexandria and victory at Tel-el-Kabir in the year 1882, Bismarck wrote to Granville that, "the friendship of the British Empire is much more important to us than the fate of Egypt," and added that he would

101

not even oppose annexation although he advised against it.[12] Indeed, there seems little doubt that Bismarck had deliberately advocated Great Britain's assertion of control in Egypt as early as 1877 as, of course, one more move in his isolation of France; for he spoke of it to Salisbury in that year and broached it again to Lord Russell in 1881.[13] Deeply appreciative of Germany's support, England did not hesitate to express her gratitude: " . . . we are extremely grateful to the prince," exclaimed Harcourt to Herbert Bismarck, then a member of the staff of the German Embassy in London (1883), "he could have upset the cart if he had wished. That we were left alone is due to Germany's good will." [14]

## The French Entente

But Bismarck expected something more from England in the way of gratitude than empty words. Indeed, he made it very clear in no unmistakable terms that the price of his support of England against France in Egypt was England's support of Germany's colonial ventures. He began to threaten to change his Egyptian policy—indeed to break with England altogether [15]—and to carry out his threat by forming, as we have already observed, a *rapprochement* with France on the Congo question. At the same time the wily Chancellor was only too well aware that England was the greatest colonial Power, and he seems to have become somewhat alarmed at his own temerity in reversing his policy and running counter to her aims, for her support rather than her animosity might, in the long run, prove more profitable for his own colonial ambitions. Consequently, he made an effort to bargain for her cooperation, securing himself at the same time, however, should his attempt fail, by a closer *rapprochement* with France. For on May 5,

1884, while the London Conference for the regulation of Egyptian finance was in preparation, he dispatched a *quid pro quo* note to England offering her the continuance of his assistance in her Egyptian schemes (of which she was greatly in need) in return for her help and cooperation in Germany's colonial ambitions, suggesting also the exchange of Angra Pequena in Africa for Heligoland as a symbol of good-will.[16]

It is apparent from the correspondence that Count Münster in London neglected to press the first part of the dispatch at the British Foreign Office.[17] For Count Münster, it must be remembered, was an Anglophile, had married an English wife, and evidently preferred not to consider as serious the colonial aims of his own country. His evasion of the real issue of this dispatch thus afforded Gladstone and Granville, when later reproached by Bismarck for not having replied to his important communication, the opportunity to claim that it had never been received.[17a]

Failing, therefore, to move England by repeated notifications [18] of the same type as the dispatch of May 5, owing largely to Münster's apathy, and the consequent misunderstanding by the British statesmen of the seriousness of Germany's aims, Bismarck plunged deeper and deeper into collaboration with her rivals, utilizing in a masterly manner their disputes with Great Britain to the advantage of Germany: he encouraged Russia, already closely bound to Germany by the Three Emperors' League, in her hostility to England in Afghanistan and he transformed his *"rapprochement"* with France into a virtual alliance. "If we find no justice from England, so we must seek closer alliance with the other sea Power, France," marks his decision to go over to the French side which he even proposed to strengthen by the creation of an "Armed Neutrality." For, on August

7, 1884, he wrote, " . . . the exclusive efforts of England to attain as far as possible the sole domination over near European seas will oblige the other commercial Powers to form an association among themselves as a counterpoise to the English colonial supremacy,"[19] and went so far as to direct Prince Hohenlohe, the ambassador at Paris, to broach the project to Ferry.

Meanwhile he pushed the plans for the calling of an international congress on colonial affairs. Many notes on the subject passed between Germany and France, indicating an harmonious understanding between them, for Bismarck saw here an opportunity to earn French support by this close cooperation in Ferry's ambitions.[20] Finally, on October 2, 1884, France notified Germany of her complete agreement with the latter's arrangements, and the German government issued on October 6, 1884, the invitations to the Congo Congress, over which Bismarck was to preside. The Congress commenced its sessions on November 15 in Berlin, thereby aligning Germany, by implication at any rate, with the great colonial Powers. Indeed, the fact that Bismarck, instead of a representative of Great Britain, the foremost colonial Power, presided at this, the first international colonial congress, and dictated with France the terms of the Congo Act, served to raise Germany's prestige at England's expense and to widen the breach between them. Entirely over England's head, the main provisions of the Congo Act were arranged, and the commercial and legal future of a large part of West Africa determined. Doubly protected by the recent renewal of the Three Emperors' League in March, 1884, which was strengthened by the harmonious meeting of the three Kaisers at Skiernewice, and by the French *rapprochement,* Bismarck could well afford to exploit—if only temporarily—the "splendid isolation" of England, and so insure, by means of the Congo Act, future security for German penetration into a large portion of the Dark Continent.

### The Quarrel with England Reaches a Climax

At the same time, Bismarck continued to foster German ire, for home consumption, against England, because of her attempts to block Germany in the colonial field; and, what is more, he no longer followed that path of impeccable scrupulousness which he had hitherto pursued, but stooped to sharp practices to gain his ends. He attempted both to exclude Great Britain from various colonial areas and, at the same time, to delude his own nation with the idea that Great Britain was monopolistically crowding Germany out of those very districts. For instance, in April, 1884, as we have seen, he sent forth Dr. Nachtigal with instructions to place under imperial protection certain territory in West Africa. At the same time he notified England that, "Nachtigal goes to Africa merely to verify information about the state of German commerce in that region," [21] although the *Kölnische Zeitung* made no secret of announcing his purpose of annexation, confirmed later by the German Protectorate, which was formally established in West Africa in July. How Bismarck must have enjoyed Gladstone's discomfiture may be imagined when he heard that England taking his statement on its face value, had ordered her agents to afford Nachtigal, who sustained the ruse by traveling as a merchant, all protection and courtesy. Recourse to the identical trick was had also later, in November, 1884, when to allay England's suspicions about Rohlf's appointment as consul to East Africa, Bismarck categorically stated that Germany had no intention of establishing a protectorate there; [22] a protectorate which he had evidently been plan-ning for some time, and which he subsequently declared three months later.[23] Again, as if to secure allies for Germany in South Africa, the Chancellor arranged a Convention between Germany and the Transvaal. He also received delegates from the Transvaal at Berlin on July 8, 1884, gave them a special audience with the Emperor, and fêted them so as to imbue them with a preference for German *Kultur* and a fear of Great Britain's monopolistic designs.

Likewise in the South Seas Bismarck, on the one hand, openly sought and gained the cooperation of England in securing a joint commission to settle the extension of either nation's claims in New Guinea, while, on the other, he secretly promised imperial protection to lands acquired by the New Guinea Company and even, on August 19, 1884, suggested the raising of the German flag over areas in New Britain and New Guinea. In reply, on September 19, Great Britain annexed New Guinea, with the exception of a part of the north coast, whereupon Bismarck protested that this act was contrary to the agreement. Lord Granville was therefore forced to limit the English annexation to the south coast "if all other claims are left to negotiation"; but Bismarck, interpreting this stipulation to read that "Germany could make acquisitions but England was debarred therefrom," proceeded to appropriate officially the north coast of New Guinea and the Islands in the New Britain Archipelago.[24]

Indeed, Bismarck seems to have lost all restraint in his quarrel with England, as the newspaper war between the two countries [25] indicated. Personally, he detested Gladstone and derived the keenest pleasure from his discomfiture. He initiated an entirely new and unwonted policy by publishing a series of *White Books,* all of which attempted to show the unjust treatment sustained by Germany at the hands of

England. The first three books dealt respectively with the Congo district and Biafra Bay, Angra Pequena and Samoa; they appeared during the height of the parliamentary struggle in December, 1884; while the two later books appeared in January and February, 1885, and presented the situation in Samoa and the South Seas.[26] Nor did the German press fail to mirror the official recklessness in adding fuel to the quarrel: the *Kölnische Zeitung,* for example, belligerently remarked, "if John Bull thinks he can block German colonial policy with all kinds of funny nonsense, he is wasting his efforts, for Germany is determined to hold on to what it has and it will pay him back in his own coin."[27]

To heighten the effect of the *White Books* in the quarrel with Great Britain, events both colonial and international played into the Chancellor's hands at the beginning of the year 1885, events which he did not hesitate to turn to his advantage. The news then reached Germany that the first German blood had been shed for German colonies, that disturbances had broken out between the natives and the Germans in Kamerun, and that King Old Bell Town and Hickory Town had been burned. The Chancellor immediately seized the opportunity to accuse the English of inciting the natives against Germany, as a means of dislodging her from Kamerun. He produced not a particle of real proof to support his accusations, although he presented as evidence a report, which he claimed to have received on November 24, 1884, from the Hamburg Syndicate, complaining of the actions of representatives of the English firm of J. Holt and Company, and of Buchanan, the British vice consul, in stirring up war. And to further support the illusion of England's aggression, he demanded Buchanan's dismissal.[28] He also raised a perfect storm about a Pole, Rogozinsky, quietly engaged in his own business in Kamerun, but whose name conveniently lent suspicion to his actions; denounced him in the *Reichstag* as a British agent, published a map of his evil designs, and demanded from Great Britain a formal repudiation of him and his works.[29]

Goaded to retaliation by all these recriminations, Lord Derby dispatched *H. M. S. Goshawk* to hoist the British flag at St. Lucia Bay where a German, Captain Schiel, in the service of the Transvaal Republic, was quietly securing land concessions; sent Sir H. H. Johnston into East Africa to circumvent German designs there, and ordered Sir Charles Warren to Bechuanaland to prevent the way to the north from being blocked. At the same time Great Britain resumed her liberty of action in New Guinea after Germany's annexations of December, 1884; yielded to Australia's pressure to assert British prestige in the Pacific before it proved too late; and seized what was left of that island. All these aggressions simply added more fuel to Bismarck's rage and he employed every means—the *Reichstag,* the press, and the diplomatic service—to pour the most vituperative reproaches and rebukes upon Great Britain and her ministers, the effect of which was not lost upon patriotic Germans.[30]

But colonial affairs did not alone favor the quarrel; the international situation as well enabled Bismarck to carry it to a triumphant conclusion. In the year 1885, Great Britain suddenly found herself unusually and peculiarly hard-pressed throughout her entire empire: in Egypt the fall of Khartoum and Gordon's death on February 26 weakened her prestige and strengthened the hostility of France; on February 13, Russia's army was at the gates of Herat, menacing the very borders of India; and the danger of a possible collusion between France and Turkey loomed large upon the horizon. It was only too patent that she could not afford to offend Germany any longer.[31] With his adversary in so weak a position in regard to her relations to the rest of Europe, Bismarck did not let slip the opportunity to exploit her difficulties from the vantage point of his own safe alliances; and he crowned his daring policy by publishing, on March 3, 1885, the imperial *Schutzbrief* over the lands in East Africa acquired by the East African Company, which he had again and again publicly refused to grant.[32] It is indeed interesting to note that the *Schutzbrief* was issued just one day after the closing session of the Congo Conference, and that the official press, the *Norddeutsche Allgemeine Zeitung* and the *Kreuzzeitung,* took no notice of it at all, while they featured articles about the Congo Act and the resulting friendship of Germany and France.[33]

### Bismarck Reaps the Results of the Quarrel

Such a thoroughgoing campaign against England and its subsequent triumph could not fail to arouse intense nationalism and patriotism within the country and, after January, 1885, these forces began to weaken the Opposition in the *Reichstag* as Bismarck had designed that they should. Hostility to the Chancellor waned before the wave of popular indignation and of patriotic pride that literally swept the nation. In March, 1885, the Steamship Subsidy Bill passed the *Reichstag* with a large majority, and Bismarck announced that at last he had found the "popular support" which he had demanded nine years before as indispensable to a colonial policy.[34]

His speech proved, however, somewhat premature because the Opposition was far from being permanently vanquished. It became more and more essential for the national government to supplement the work of the colonial companies as the colonial empire expanded and difficulties arose. The native uprisings and administrative expenses required financial support, which Bismarck's enemies in the *Reichstag* violently opposed. To secure the appropriations he was always obliged to win the support of the Center party, for the *Cartel* upon which he depended had only a narrow majority and the Center continued to hold the balance of power.

### Reconciliation with England Becomes Expedient

To add to the Chancellor's difficulties, he found himself suddenly confronted by an entirely altered foreign situation which prohibited his further exploitation of England's isolation: the year 1885 marked the fall of Ferry in France and a return to the *"revanche"* policy under Clemenceau, as witnessed by a no less definite movement than Boulangism; but the year 1885 also saw the downfall of his enemy, the Liberal Gladstone in England, and the accession of the more congenial Conservative, Salisbury. Bismarck, however, rapidly adjusted himself to the change: he recognized the destruction of the German-French *entente,* sensed at once the necessity of preventing any *rapprochement* between France and England, and lost no time in making friends with Salisbury and in gaining his support and cooperation for Germany's colonial projects.

As a matter of fact, Germany's reconciliation with England had already begun immediately after the crisis of February, 1885, and before the change in the British cabinet. For it was a cardinal principle of Bismarck's policy to keep on good terms with England, and the *rapprochement* with France was never, after all, destined to be anything but temporary. The fall of Ferry had revived hostility in Germany toward France, and Great Britain's concessions to Germany's interests had already commenced. Herbert Bismarck, sent once again to London in March of 1885 to explain the grievances of his countrymen, met with a cordial reception; even Gladstone, hearing his explanation, wished Germany "Godspeed" in her colonial career, welcoming her as "our ally in the execution of the great purposes of Providence," sentiments which were echoed by the Foreign Secretary in less pious phraseology and seconded by a large group in the administrative circles, to whom the Anglo-German quarrel had been extremely distasteful. The Prince of Wales, for instance, Chamberlain, and Sir Charles Dilke had strongly approved Germany's position on the colonies, and Harcourt, Secretary of the Interior, is said to have remarked that he "did not even know where Angra Pequena was." [35]

Moreover a definite settlement regarding the New Guinea boundaries had been reached in January, 1885, to be confirmed later in 1886, and the *"fait accompli"* in East Africa had been accepted. To prolong the quarrel would only have lent substance to the major criticism of the Opposition that, "a colonial policy inevitably produced dangerous friction abroad." What is more, the quarrel had served its purpose; the *Reichstag* Opposition had capitulated on the Subsidy Bill. Thus the dictates of both foreign and domestic policy demanded the cultivation of England's friendship for which Bismarck subtly paved the way by apologetically remarking in the *Reichstag,* "It is no wonder that when Great Britain's cousins the land rats take to the water, she is surprised, for she believes that 'Britannia rules the waves.' " [36]

On the other hand "cousin water rat's" friendship could not be cultivated too closely, because the revival of France's hostility strengthened the value of the German-Russian alliance, with which an English *entente* was incompatible so long

111

as Anglo-Russian rivalry in Afghanistan endured. But the handling of such a delicate situation presented no difficulties to Bismarck who was adept in maintaining such conflicting, coexisting relationships as those of Austria and Russia. As he told Busch on May 31, 1885, "Our policy must not necessarily be anti-English, but were it English, it might prove to be very much against our interests, as we must reckon with continental Powers." [37] Therefore, while he exchanged cordial letters with Salisbury,[38] he did not neglect to protest still against England's ingratitude; against British agents who blocked German colonial ventures, and even threatened again to support the Boers. A tone less sharp than that which characterized his protests to Gladstone, however, pervades these dispatches as his nonchalant references to the "pinpricks" of English traders and the "jingoism" of German colonists indicate.[39] Finally, however, the removal of Anglo-Russian friction in Afghanistan enabled him to abandon camouflage and by the close of the year 1886, Bismarck assured the British government that it could count upon his support of England in Egypt against France, as long as Germany's colonial claims received satisfactory treatment.[40] So ended the brief but bitter strife with England, which had served to initiate the German colonial empire; and in its stead ensued what Herbert Bismarck called the Anglo-German "colonial honeymoon."

### The Anglo-German "Colonial Honeymoon"

This second major orientation of Bismarck's foreign policy —the Anglo-German "honeymoon"—constitutes as natural a return to his traditional course established before 1875, as the brief and temporary *entente* with France was an unnatural departure from it. And it is not surprising that Bismarck strove to make the "honeymoon" endure throughout the remainder of his office, and even sought to transform it into a lasting bond by his negotiations for a British alliance in 1889, when one reviews the international situation of those years and remembers his slogan of "safety first."

In the first place, the Bulgarian crisis of 1886 drew the attention of all the Powers back to Europe, and raised in Germany the old ghost of a war on two frontiers. Also the expiration in 1887 of the treaty cementing the Three Emperors' League, the uncertainty of its renewal, and the effects of the Boulanger affair in France rendered the security of Germany not so assured as in the early eighties. In short, Bismarck was not so free any longer to oppose England; on the contrary, he felt the necessity, largely because of Russia's uncertainty, of creating an English *entente* against both his eastern and his western neighbors, which would also prevent any *rapprochement* between France and England. His old conviction that the only wise course for Germany lay in maintaining British friendship at all costs was more than ever confirmed, even when such a friendship involved the subordination and even neglect of his colonial policy.

At the same time he did not close the door to France, on account of his wish to further the oversea interests, and he saw again in Egypt, just as in 1883-1884, an opportunity to use a weapon against England in the colonial field.[41] Consequently, when France proposed a renewal of the Franco-German *entente* in 1886 against the English occupation of Egypt, the Chancellor first assumed a non-committal attitude, and then informed France that he would not oppose a Franco-German *entente* to get England out of Egypt.[42] Throughout the winter of 1886-1887, he remained passive in the Egyptian business, but in the spring of 1887, notified England that "our policy in Egypt must shortly change, if we cannot reach an accord in questions which are not so important as the eastern one." [43] As a result Salisbury gave in and withdrew from Zanzibar Holmwood, the anti-German British consul, who was blocking the development of German East Africa. As the eighties drew to a close, however, England grew so strong in Egypt that Germany's help ceased to be a determining factor. Hence Bismarck subordinated his colonial policy more and more to his foreign policy, dictated in turn by Germany's European position, which was none too secure. He strove for the English *entente,* the maintenance of the Russian Reinsurance Treaty, and the holding apart of the two flank Powers; eschewed all aggressive action in the colonial field, and returned almost to the caution of the early seventies.

## The Maintenance of the "Honeymoon" Demands Colonial Caution

Caution in colonial affairs was preëminently necessary during the years 1886 to 1889, when Great Britain was extending her empire in East Africa and laying the foundations of that great system whose goal was the Cape to Cairo plan. Keenly she resented the encroachments of the German East African Company, whose *fait accompli* in those regions she had been obliged unwillingly to accept. But, more serious than the official attitude was the bitter rivalry between the empire-builders themselves, the agents of the British East Africa Company, the British officials, and the German pioneers. Almost a state of war existed among them and, again and again, the irresponsible exploits of a Karl Peters, and the obstruction tactics of a fiercely anti-German British consul threatened to strain to the breaking point the bonds

114

of the Anglo-German "honeymoon" so solicitously fostered in the *Wilhelmstrasse* and in Downing Street. Bismarck avoided rendering assistance to the extension plans of the German East African Company, refused to endorse the Emin Pasha expedition, and officially repudiated the brilliant exploits of Karl Peters and others in planting the German flag in Uganda, Wituland and along the reaches of the Upper Nile.[44] For this same reason, also, he strove to maintain Salisbury's good will. As Herbert Bismarck wrote to Count Hatzfeldt in London, "Salisbury's friendship is worth more to us than the whole of East Africa; my father is of the same opinion." [45]

Finally, as the eighties drew to a close, and Russia grew more uncertain, Bismarck did not confine his caution locally to East African affairs, but applied it to his general colonial policy. He suddenly grew "tired of colonies," announced that Germany was satiated with colonial "quarrels and flag-raisings" and that, anyway, he himself had never been (*"von Haus auf"*) a *"Kolonialmensch."* He even talked about relinquishing some colonies, and went so far as to consider exchanging territory in Africa for Heligoland in the negotiations of an alliance with England in 1889—his last attempt to attach England to the Central Powers.[46] Doubtless the native wars in which the government had been obliged to intervene in Africa, the disappointing economic returns from those undeveloped regions—and the everlasting haggling with the *Reichstag* over appropriations, contributed to the Chancellor's "colonial weariness." But the exigencies of his foreign relationships, with their demand for "safety first," formed the dominating motive of his caution, as his continued quiet and steady support of the colonial empire and his constant, cleverly disguised struggle with the Opposition indicate.

115

### The Opposition Is Finally Vanquished

For, as it has already been observed, the Opposition was not vanquished even by the victory of the Subsidy Bill. It continued to annoy the government by disputing every colonial appropriation, and so to prevent the stabilization of the colonial policy. The Chancellor could not rest from his task. Obviously, however, he could no longer win the support of the hostile factions, led by the Center Party, with any such appeal to national patriotism against English aggression as he had been making since 1884; his *volte face* in foreign policy precluded the continuance of such a course. There remained other ways, nevertheless, of bidding for Catholic cooperation and, as usual, he was not slow to take advantage of them.

One of these opportunities was presented in 1886 by the dispute with Spain over the possession of the Caroline Islands. Harking back to her ancient rights conveyed by the Treaty of Tordiselas of 1493, Spain had always resented Germany's acquisitions in their region because they encroached upon what she regarded as her special sphere of influence. As early as 1875, Bismarck had protested against her interference with German commerce and, in 1877, in company with England, had negotiated a protocol with Spain which guaranteed freedom of trade. Since that time German interests had vastly expanded in the South Seas and, as a result, the government announced its intention, in August, 1885, of extending imperial protection to the German commercial stations on the Caroline Islands, which was confirmed by a flag-raising on the Island of York. As a reply, a storm of protest broke forth from Spain: patriotic Spaniards attacked the German embassy at Madrid, and war appeared imminent. Throughout the ensuing excitement the

Chancellor remained calm and peaceable, for with his ever-watchful eye, he discerned in the situation an opportunity to win both the support of the Center at home and of the Pope abroad (after the ill-will of the *Kulturkampf*). With a grand gesture, he referred the whole quarrel to the Vatican for settlement and agreed to abide by the verdict. As was to be expected, Pope Leo XIII awarded the Caroline and Pelew Islands to Spain, with freedom of trade, shipping and fishing to Germany, together with equal rights in the purchase of plantations and also a naval base.[47] The German comic press called it a "Solomon judgment" giving the honor of possession to Spain, and the practical use of the islands to Germany. But it was a masterly stroke of the Chancellor which helped to achieve peace with the Center party; a peace symbolized by the gorgeous Papal Decoration of brilliants which the Pope conferred upon him, the first Protestant prince to receive it.

But Bismarck's cleverest stratagem to win Center votes for colonial budgets was his open and vigorous championship of the Catholic anti-slave-trade campaign which was waged in 1888-1889. Authorized by the Pope, Cardinal Lavigerie was preaching a crusade against the cruelties of the Arab slave trade in East Africa throughout the summer of 1888; conventions in Cologne had demanded assistance from the German government, and Windthorst, the leader of the Center, had in November asked for official appropriations in the *Reichstag*. It was just at this time that the Arab uprising in East Africa obliged Bismarck to ask for 2,000,-000 M. to come to the rescue of the East African Company, as well as for authority to send an imperial commissioner into East Africa. The opportunity of connecting colonial policy with a popular, national, and above all Catholic issue was too good to be lost.

117

In defending the East African Bill in the *Reichstag*, Bismarck rested his whole case upon the necessity of suppressing the Arab slave trade in the interests of humanitarianism and Christian *Kultur,* and upon the duty of keeping faith with the other Powers in executing the provisions of the Congo Act against slavery; in other words, upon national honor. He insisted throughout his long speech that: "It is not a question of material support afforded to the East African Company; it is a question of civilization, of Christianity and of national obligation. . . . In company with England and France, the German government by signing the Congo Act has assumed the responsibility of christianizing and civilizing this great part of the earth's surface;" and he echoed Windthorst's sentiments that, "If we do not fulfill this obligation, we shall command respect neither in Africa nor in Europe." [48] So impassioned was his appeal to patriotism and humanitarianism that, in spite of the vigorous criticism and obstruction of the Opposition, the support of the Center party was won, and the Bill was passed. Thus for the last time did Bismarck screen his colonial activities behind a national issue which he had either created or encouraged.

### Bismarck's Colonial Program

Meanwhile, between the years 1884 and 1889, at the same time that he was stabilizing his new policy and winning a *Reichstag* majority for its support, Bismarck was organizing a program of colonial administration whose outstanding characteristics were moderation, non-aggression, and incompleteness. Indeed, he made his task of dealing with the opposition to his policy both at home and abroad much easier by announcing a limited and indirect colonial system, rather than by insisting upon the immediate annexation of territory by the empire. His original plan for colonies left all the responsibility to the merchants, and involved the empire in no expense "except for warships and consuls." With von Küsserow's help, the Chancellor outlined his program as follows: "The German empire cannot carry on a system of colonization like that of France. It cannot send out warships to conquer territory oversea, that is, it will not take the initiative; but it will protect the German merchant even in the land which he acquires. Germany will do what England has always done, establish Chartered Companies, so that the responsibility always rests with them." [49]

Bismarck's limitation and definition of Germany's new policy, laid down in close cooperation with the commercial colonists, those "princely merchants," as he called them, first found public expression when he expounded it in the Budget Commission on June 23, 1884. And on June 26, 1884, in the *Reichstag,* he skilfully met the objections of Richter that a colonial policy would involve expense and naval power and would precipitate wars, by falling back upon his apparently cautious and unambitious program which repudiated all conscious creation of colonies; "I would follow the example of England in granting to these merchants something like Royal Charters. . . . I do not wish to found provinces, but to protect commercial establishments in their own development. . . . We hope that the tree will flourish in proportion to the activity of the gardener, but if it does not, the whole responsibility rests with him and not with the empire, which will lose nothing." [50]

As we have seen, at this stage Bismarck was convinced of the unwisdom, from an international viewpoint, of embarking upon any vigorous policy. There are many indications, however, that as the struggle progressed, and as he grew more and more confident of ultimate success in winning the national support, he expanded his first unpretentious and unassuming plan. Early in 1885, we find him no longer talking merely about the empire's duty to protect commercial settlements, with all responsibility relegated to merchants, but about the value of colonies for their own sake. Indeed, he began to stress their economic aspect, and he prophesied the greatest national benefit therefrom. He thought that Germany should be economically independent. "Colonies would mean the winning of new markets for German industries, the expansion of trade, and a new field for German activity, civilization and capital," he said, and also, "Consider what it would mean if part of the cotton and coffee which we must import could be grown on German territory oversea. Would that not bring an increase of national wealth?" [51] It will be at once noted that these more purposeful utterances coincide with his triumph both over England abroad and over the Opposition at home.

To sum up, Bismarck never set forth a complete and exact colonial program, but administered it in homeopathic doses. As he himself remarked, "We have not evolved a fully developed colonial system which, like Minerva, sprang from the head of Jove and appeared fully grown at once, but we have allowed it to develop and shape itself." [52] He preferred rather to present a flexible program which, on the one hand, would be vague and elastic enough to escape the explicit criticism of the Opposition, and on the other, would be susceptible of change and addition as opportunity offered. As Fabri expressed it, "Bismarck limited his program of colonial policy to individual experiments without any initiative on the part of the government. This quieted suspicion and criticism and the responsibility appeared much less." [53]

## NOTES

[1] Rehm, H., *Deutschlands Politische Parteien* (Jena, 1912), p. 80ff.

[2] *Anlagen des deutschen Reichstages,* 1885, no. 111, p. 827.

[3] *Verhandlungen des deutschen Reichstages,* 1884, June 26, p. 1064.

[4] Poschinger, H., *Bismarck als Volkswirt,* vol. ii, p. 183, contains account of Bill in Budget Commission, June 23, 1884. See also, von Hagen, *op. cit.,* pp. 97-114.

[5] *Staatsarchiv,* vol. 43, pp. 246, 248.

[6] Hahn-Wippermann, *op. cit.,* vol. v, pp. 36-37.

[7] *Ibid.,* vol. v, pp. 163-165. See also, von Hagen, *op. cit.,* p. 510.

[8] *Staatsarchiv,* vol. 44, p. 91ff.

[9] Hahn-Wippermann, *op. cit.,* vol. v, p. 81.

[10] See *infra,* ch. iv, p. 106.

[11] *Staatsarchiv,* vii, 44, p. 260.

[11a] Eckardstein, *op. cit.,* vol. i, pp. 85, 281. Bismarck once said that the Egyptian situation provided Germany with a lever in her foreign diplomacy.

[12] *Die Grosse Politik,* vol. iv, pp. 31, 36-38.

[13] *Ibid.,* vol. ii, pp. 107-157.

[14] *Ibid.,* vol. ii, p. 48.

[15] *Ibid.,* vol. iv, pp. 51, 52.

[16] *Ibid.,* vol. iv, p. 50.

[17] *Ibid.,* vol. iv, p. 53. See also, Stuhlmann, *op. cit.,* pp. 40-42, 55, 56, 58.

[17a] *Hansard,* vol. ccxcv, March 12, 1885, p. 978.

[18] *Die Grosse Politik,* vol. iv, pp. 60, 77, 78, 93-94. On August 12, 1884, for instance, Bismarck wrote to Münster in London: "A continuation of the British policy will make us draw closer to France." But again Münster did not lay sufficient stress upon the proposed bargain, for he was not in sympathy with the German colonial movement and the idea of British support in return for German support of Great Britain in Egypt did not appeal to him. See Rogge, H., "Bismarcks Kolonialpolitik als aussenpolitisches Problem" in *Historische Vierteljahreschrift,* 1923, Heft, xxi.

[19] *Ibid.,* vol. ii, p. 414.

[20] Nowhere is Bismarck's cooperation with France at this juncture better seen than in his negotiations in West Africa which were carried on in opposition to Great Britain and in full accord with France. See *supra.,* ch. iv, p. 99. See also, *Die Grosse Politik,* vol. iv, p. 425.

[21] *Staatsarchiv,* vol. 44, p. 291.

[22] *Ibid.,* vol. 46, p. 119.

[23] In both the years 1880 and 1881, Bismarck had considered sending a consul to Zanzibar and also making a trade treaty with the Sultan, because of the many complaints from the German merchants regarding British interference with their affairs. It happened that Rohlfs was a friend of Bis-

marck's family, had traveled extensively in North Africa, and had gone at the Chancellor's behest in 1880 with a special message to the ruler of Abyssinia. In the fall of 1884, Bismarck had summoned Rohlfs quietly to Friederichsruh and had entrusted him with his plans. Subsequently, on October 27, 1884, he went again quietly to his post in East Africa. Three months later, the Chancellor declared a German protectorate in East Africa. See von Hagen, *op. cit.*, pp. 520ff.

[24] *Staatsarchiv*, vol. 44, pp. 207-213.

[25] Von Hagen, *op. cit.*, pp. 401-409.

[26] *Weissbuch*, 1885, pts. i, ii, iii.

[27] *Kölnische Zeitung*, Jan. 2, 1885.

[28] *Staatsarchiv*, vol. 44, pp. 322-324.

[29] Fitzmaurice, E., *Life Lord Granville* (Longmans, 1905), 2 vols., vol. ii, p. 368.

[30] *Verhandlungen des deutschen Reichstages*, March 2, 1885.
*Dis Norddeutsche Allgemeine Zeitung*, March 3, 4, 5, 1885.
Bismarck also personally attacked Malet, the English ambassador in Berlin. In the report of conversation, Malet tells how the Chancellor accused England of unparalleled egotism in claiming all the land in Africa which other Powers had not appropriated, and how he had administered a severe rebuke, saying that he felt that England was not treating Germany as an equal. He became so vehement in his charges that Malet begged him to state what he wanted. But Bismarck replied that it was impossible to come to any understanding with England since she had rejected his offer of cooperation of May 5, 1884, and that now his understanding with France stood in the way.
Hahn-Wippermann, *op. cit.*, vol. v, p. 89.
*Staatsarchiv*, vol. 44, p. 255.
Von Hagen, *op. cit.*, p. 489ff.

[31] Great Britain's anxiety to restore friendly relations with Germany may be well illustrated by Gladstone's letter to Granville, March 6, 1885. "I do hope that you are pressing forward the settlement of the north coast of New Guinea. It is really impossible to exaggerate the importance of getting out of the way the bar to the Egyptian settlement. . . . If we cannot wind up these small colonial controversies at once, we shall, before we are many months older, find it to our cost."
Fitzmaurice, *Life Lord Granville*, vol. i, p. 431.

[32] Von Hagen, *op. cit.*, p. 510.

[33] This incident would seem to confirm the view that Bismarck, while secretly in favor of the new colonial acquisitions, as his cooperation showed him to be, wished to postpone the official announcement until the Congo Congress had dispersed and to keep the matter as quiet as possible, so that the signatory Powers of the Congo Act would not become unduly excited over it.

[34] *Verhandlungen des deutschen Reichstages*, March 13, 1885, p. 1801.

[35] *Die Grosse Politik*, vol. iv, p. 174.

[36] *Verhandlungen des deutschen Reichstages*, Jan. 19, 1885, p. 532.

# BISMARCK STABILIZES THE COLONIAL POLICY

[37] Busch, M., Bismarck, *Some Secret Pages of His History* (London, 1898), 3 vols., vol. iii, p. 140.

[38] *Die Grosse Politik,* vol. iv, p. 132ff.

[39] *Ibid.,* vol. iv, pp. 145, 151, 168.

[40] *Ibid.,* vol. iv, p. 153.

[41] *Die Grosse Politik,* vol. v, p. 119.

[42] *Ibid.,* vol. iv, pp. 96, 156, 162.

[43] *Ibid.,* vol. iv, p. 168.

[44] See *Infra.,* ch. v, pp. 136, 137.

[45] Rogge, H., *op. cit.,* p. 433. In this connection, Bismarck had the *Nord. Allg. Zt.* say, "Our friendship with England is worth more than all the expeditions on the Upper Nile." von Hagen, *op. cit.,* p. 545.

[46] *Die Grosse Politik,* vol. iv, pp. 319-419.

See *infra.,* ch. vi, pp. 163, 164, for relation of this to the Anglo-German Treaty of 1890.

Bismarck even suggested to Crispi, at this same time, that Italy might like to buy some of Germany's colonies. Crispi, *Questioni Internazionali,* Milan, 1913, p. 219.

[47] *Staatsarchiv,* vol. 46, p. 176. See also, von Hagen, *op. cit.,* p. 562.

[48] *Verhandlungen des deutschen Reichstages,* Jan. 26, 1889, p. 619.

[49] Herrfurth, K., "Bismarck als Kolonialpolitiker" in *Zeitschrift für Kolonialpolitik,* Kolonialrecht, etc., 1909, p. 736.

[50] Hahn-Wippermann, *op. cit.,* vol. v, p. 42, p. 24. See also, Kohl, H., *Reden des Fürstens Bismarck,* vol. x, p. 196.

[51] *Verhandlungen des deutschen Reichstages,* March 16, 1885, p. 1864; Jan. 10, 1885, p. 524; June 26, 1884, p. 1073.

[52] *Ibid.,* March 13, 1885, pp. 1800 *et seq.*

[53] Fabri, F., *Fünf Jahre Deutscher Kolonialpolitik* (Gotha, 1889), p. 15.

# CHAPTER V

## THE COLONIAL COMPANIES FAIL TO FUNCTION

NOTHING could have been more logical than Bismarck's selection of the colonial company as the agent for his new policy. For he was interested in colonies primarily because they were a "business proposition" requiring national protection, and his interest had increased as the position of the German merchant in Africa and the South Seas became jeopardized by the imperialist encroachments of other Powers. With colonies as places to which Germans might emigrate—"official colonies," he called them—he had little sympathy. His colonial slogans, on the contrary, were, "The flag follows trade," and, "First the trader, then the soldier." [1] Again, nothing was further from his plan than to create imperial provinces, "hothouse colonies," [2] requiring like the French system officials, "boa constrictors," garrisons and troops. Indeed, it is doubtless colonies in this sense that he meant when he asserted, "I am no *Kolonialmensch.*"

### *The English Chartered Company the Model*

To execute his limited plan, then, Bismarck chose as his model the chartered company of the seventeenth and eighteenth centuries, because its two distinguishing features were the possession of sovereign rights and of complete monopoly, two privileges which were exactly suited to the age of weak national states in which it arose. Indeed, it was these two very features possessed by the chartered company of the old régime that attracted Bismarck in his search

124

for some system of colonial administration which would not involve the empire. For he wished to avoid as far as it was possible any governmental responsibility in the new possessions because of his system of alliances, which might be endangered by colonial frictions; because of the weakness of the German navy; and because of the expenses to which they would commit an unwilling *Reichstag*. Hence, he desired to leave to the companies the entire responsibility for administration and taxation, for the development of the land, for negotiations with the natives and for all local concerns. There was to be neither a colonial bureaucracy nor a colonial military; the empire was to interfere only for protection from other Powers—thus the title *Schutzgebiete*, protectorates. How independent Bismarck wished the companies to be and with what wide powers he desired to endow them may be gathered from his simple statement. "I intend to issue charters similar to the English Royal Charters . . . and I consider that one representative of imperial authority, whom we will call a consul, will be sufficient in the colonies." And, again, when the English Foreign Office inquired if Germany intended to proclaim its sovereignty over the territories acquired by Lüderitz in South West Africa, the Chancellor replied that "Germany intended to act in that region in the same manner in which England had acted in Borneo," [3] where the North Borneo Company had received in 1881 a charter giving it absolute sovereignty, the most liberal and independent charter possessed by any English colonial company in the nineteenth century. [4]

## Impracticability of the Chartered Company

But Bismarck's plan for the companies proved in its practical application a complete failure. As a matter of fact, only four such privileged companies as he envisaged were formed; namely, the East African Company, the New Guinea Company, the South West African Company, and the Jaluit Company; and, of these four, only the first two were chartered companies invested with sovereign rights; the trading companies in Togoland and Kamerun were too weak to exercise any governmental authority. From the outset the imperial government was obliged to administer these two districts; to appoint, first, imperial commissioners and then governors with all the paraphernalia of official machinery, which Bismarck had rejected as the "French system." Moreover, of the four privileged companies which really governed in their own right, only two, the New Guinea Company and the Jaluit Company survived after 1890. Even the New Guinea Company, owing to financial embarrassments, requested the imperial government, in 1889, to relieve it of all administrative powers; it received them back again in 1893, but only to collapse entirely in 1898. The Jaluit Company alone endured into the twentieth century, but it too relinquished its political authority in 1906.

The principal reasons assigned for the failure of Bismarck's original plan for colonial administration are that the German privileged companies lacked money, prestige, national support and were hence unable to develop the vast resources at their disposal, to control the native people, or to deal with foreign complications. Their capital melted away because of incompetent management, lack of experience, and unscrupulous and often scandalous behavior on the part of their governors. After 1885, the public had cooled off from the first colonial excitement; the business world, discouraged by the meager results of investments already made, became weary of the colonies. Administrative inefficiency and mistakes on the part of company officials precipitated native uprisings as well as misunderstandings with other colonial Powers, which necessitated imperial intervention and eventual withdrawal of the Societies from governmental control. A survey of the origins and fortunes of these companies will illustrate their incapacity for the responsibilities and powers with which Bismarck wished to endow them, as well as bring together those facts regarding the acquisition of the territories which they tried to control, hitherto scattered throughout these pages.

## The Company for South West Africa

The Company for South West Africa was founded in April, 1885, when Lüderitz handed over to it all rights to the lands which he had acquired in return for the sum of 500,000 M. It was a commercial stock company, a corporation, was capitalized at 800,000 M. and undertook the administration of all the territories, with the exception of those immediately adjoining Angra Pequena, which Lüderitz reserved for himself.

F. A. E. Lüderitz, the head of a large mercantile house in Bremen, had long been interested, as were all the Hansa merchants, in trading possibilities in Africa. It will be remembered that it was this man who, as spokesman for a merchant group, unfolded to Bismarck, in the year 1876, a complete scheme for founding a colony in South Africa and, although his plan was rejected, he won from the Chancellor a statement, at least, of the essential conditions for German colonization—a propitious international orientation, a navy, and a strong popular impulse.[5] Evidently, Lüderitz was not discouraged by his apparent rejection, for he took advantage of England's declaration in 1880,[6] limiting her territory to Whale Bay and its immediate vicinity, pursued his private ventures in that region, and finally, in 1882, took the first step to establish a German settlement where German missionaries had so long been active. Obtaining from Bismarck a secret promise that imperial protection would be forthcoming if he could acquire a harbor to which no other nation could legitimately assert a claim, he quietly sent his agent, Heinrich Vogelsang, in April, 1883, to take possession of the temperate port, Angra Pequena. To enlarge this settlement, Vogelsang was then dispatched into the interior to bargain for additional territory, with the result that Joseph Friedrichs, a Hottento chief, was persuaded to part with one hundred and fifty square miles of land in return for 200 rifles, 2,000 M., and an assortment of toys, mostly lead soldiers.[7] In August, Lüderitz himself went out and negotiated the purchase of the entire tract from the Orange River to latitude 26° S. How this territory was brought under imperial protection, and became Germany's first colony in the face of many complicating difficulties with England and the Cape government, who finally acknowledged its status in June, 1884, has been recounted at length.[8]

So soon as Lüderitz made sure of the security afforded by the telegram of April 24, 1884, which was reinforced by a visit from the imperial consul, Nachtigal, in the Möwe, during October of the same year, he set about developing the economic potentialities of the territory in a thoroughly German manner: he imported a botanist, a geographer, a mining engineer, and many other specialists. For a time, hopes ran high, but they were doomed to disappointment: the promised copper beds did not materialize, the farms seemed unable to produce. Lüderitz was all but ready to sell out his rights to an English company, had it not been for the efforts of the friends of colonization at home, such as Bleichröder and von Hansemann, the bankers, and, above all, the Chancellor himself, which resulted in the formation of the German South West African Company and saved the colony for the Fatherland.[9] Thereafter, Lüderitz disappeared both figuratively and literally from the scene, for he fell into the Orange River and was drowned.

It is evident that the size and potentialities of German South West Africa were such as to require power to administer and money to develop, two commodities which the Company for South West Africa, unfortunately, did not possess. It did manage, however, to add to its original holdings by negotiating treaties with the neighboring native chiefs, so as to extend the colony to the southern boundary of Portuguese Angola, making Germans masters of all the coast, but it was unable to extend eastward into the interior. It also organized three exploratory expeditions whose reports were somewhat discouraging. They pointed out that the coasts were rocky and inaccessible, that mineral riches were not abundant, that the best guano beds were all situated on the little costal islands which belonged to England, and that, finally, stock-raising could only prove profitable on the plateau where even there the pasturage was dry: a state of affairs demanding large sums of capital which were not forthcoming from skeptical investors at home. By the end of the first year the company had lost 45,159 M., and found itself financially unable to support a government of any kind, to explore the interior, or to control the natives. For this reason, it continually refused to accept the charter conveying sovereign rights, with which Bismarck offered again and again to invest it, according to his cherished plan. Indeed, instead of a charter, the Chancellor was obliged, against his will, to send in 1886 an imperial commissioner. Dr. Goering, to take charge of the interior, since the company was only pretending to function on the coast.

For two years this anomalous state of affairs lasted: on

the coast, the South West African Company nominally exercised sovereign rights without a charter over territories which it had acquired; while in the interior, the imperial commissioner governed for the empire. Obviously, such administrative confusion could not long endure: the company grew ever weaker as the competition from foreign companies became stronger and, in 1888, sank to the position of a privileged commercial company with monopoly rights over certain mining districts and lands. Dr. Goering then extended his imperial sway over the entire protectorate, and the company's political rule ceased, never to revive.[10]

Although German South West Africa was Germany's first colony, the only one entirely suited climatically to white settlement and, with its 835,100 square kilometers (one and one-half times the size of the German Empire), was second in size to German East Africa, it proved the most difficult and the most burdensome to pacify and to organize. The presence of extremely strong and independent tribes, like the Hereros, the Witboi, and the Bondelszwarts, kept the territory in a turmoil of native uprisings until 1906, while the nature of the country required tremendous sums of capital to develop: its inaccessible coasts demanded harbor construction; the high inland plateau so admirably suited to stock-raising necessitated irrigation; its mineral wealth needed expensive machinery to make it available; and the vast stretches of the country, unconnected by natural waterways, made the construction of roads and railways on a large scale inevitable.

### The East African Company

In East Africa, the same story of company rule was repeated, although there the East African Company assumed sovereign rights and enjoyed a longer life. As we have already recounted in a previous chapter,[11] Germany's commercial interest in East Africa dated as far back as 1844 and her trade had met with unusual success, reaching the considerable sum of three and one-half million marks annually, in 1875, an amount three times greater than that of the English. Since that time, the brothers Denhardt had penetrated far into Witu and had explored the Tana river. Appealing in the year 1882 to the government for support, they were referred to the ministry of the interior which had previously appropriated 5,000 M. for the Denhardt expedition because of its scientific value; but they were refused all imperial protection as had been the merchants and explorers in Zanzibar in 1874. Failing the latter, a private consortium was formed in Berlin which enabled Clemens Denhardt to purchase from Achmed, Sultan of Witu, a strip of territory between the Tana and Zuba rivers with full sovereign rights; a purchase designed to interfere with the activities of the Englishman, John Kirk, in that region and in 1888 included under the sovereignty of the East African Company.

In Zanzibar, events took quite a different course, as we have had occasion already to observe. There, Germans had apparently done little since 1875 to build upon the very substantial foundations already laid down by the merchants of the Hansa towns, although the expeditions of Sir Harry Johnston in the early eighties presented a serious challenge, and the English trade rivalry was keen. Suddenly Karl Peters appeared on the scene, reproaching the German government and the colonial party for their neglect of imperialism in general, and of the African continent in particular.

### Karl Peters Founds German East Africa

This impetuous and erratic son of a mild Saxony pastor had never settled down to a profession, apparently finding the strictures of such a life in his well-ordered Fatherland much too prosaic. While on a long visit to his uncle in England he had become thoroughly imbued with the national necessity for imperialism, but even more with the exciting and romantic adventures which it so glamorously offered to its pioneers. Returning home in 1883, he strove to find support for his many plans of colonial adventure, which ranged all the way from founding a colony in Brazil to helping the Boers against England, but which ultimately, due to the influence of Count Pfeil, an African explorer, resolved upon East Africa as a goal. Becoming thoroughly out of patience with what he termed the practical worthlessness, lethargy, and inaction of the existing colonial organizations, particularly that of the *Kolonialverein,* Peters and some kindred spirits exploited the opportunity for arousing patriotic sentiment, occasioned by the Kaiser's birthday, and founded a new Company for German Colonization on March 28, 1884.

Upon the strength of this company's financial support, Peters, Pfeil, Jühlke, and a merchant, Otto, set sail for East Africa in the autumn of 1884, with all the glamor of romantic adventure that secrecy, an alias, and the disguise provided by workmen's clothes could afford. When they arrived in Zanzibar, they found a telegram from Bismarck refusing imperial protection in advance to their adventures. Replying that they begged the government to keep its "protection" until it was asked for, they proceeded unmolested into the interior, as no one else, English or German, had the slightest suspicion of their real errand.[12] Their technique with the native chiefs was simple and direct: it consisted of a judicious distribution of childish presents plus an injudicious application of grog. In the happy and somewhat hazy mental state produced by the latter medium, the chiefs listened to the treaty articles, drawn up by Peters and read to them in the unknown, sonorous German tongue; then the German flag was ceremoniously raised and saluted with a salvo of gunshots; and the impressed and slightly befuddled chiefs obediently affixed their marks on the dotted line which signed away their rights.[13]

So effective did this method prove that Peters was back again within ten days on the coast, carrying a dozen treaties in his pocket, which covered the districts of Useguha, Ukami, Nguru, and Usagara, a region of about 60,000 square miles. Returning at once to Berlin, he besieged Bismarck for a *Schutzbrief* which, with his usual cautious hesitancy, the Chancellor refused at first. But, upon Peters' threatening to carry his treaties to Brussels to King Leopold, the Charter of Protection for the lands acquired by the Company for German Colonization (later transformed into the East African Colonial Company) was hastily issued, February 27, 1885, by the wily Bismarck with what *volte-face* policy we have already observed.[14] No doubt, both the international situation and his own plans for East Africa restrained the Chancellor from encouraging Peters until Peters' *fait accompli* could no longer be disregarded. Then, at the same time, the difficulties of England suddenly created an auspicious occasion for doing what, restrained by caution, he had distinctly told her he did not intend to do—namely, proclaim an East African protectorate.

The charter, or *Schutzbrief,* one of the only two which Bismarck succeeded in granting, is interesting as reflecting the plan which he was unable to carry out for all the colonies.[15] It is extremely brief and notable for two characteristics. First, it imposed only one condition upon the company in return for the many privileges received. As if to emphasize the Chancellor's wish that the companies be as independent as possible, the charter conveyed "all sovereign rights over the territories acquired by the company, jurisdiction over the natives and other inhabitants," on the one proviso that the company remain German. And, in the second place, it omitted to enumerate many obligations common to the charters granted by other nations during the same period, such as the prohibition of trade monopoly, which even the English charter for the North Borneo Company and all the English charters of the nineteenth century contained; the prohibition of slavery and sale of liquor; the duty of promoting the welfare of the natives, and the duty of building roads and harbors. These omissions may have been due to haste, to design, or to inexperience; but, whatever their cause, they render their author, the Chancellor, partially responsible for the flagrant misgovernment and many abuses of which the companies were guilty.

East Africa amply fulfilled Peters' desire for adventure and excitement, for added to the wild and unexplored nature of the hinterland, there was in the coastal districts the well-established authority of the sultan of Zanzibar as well as the keen rivalry of England with which to contend. The sultan, not without encouragement from Kirk, the English consul, sent a formal protest against the usurpation of the dubious rights which he claimed the East African Company had obtained by its flimsy treaties and began to mobilize. But Bismarck immediately replied by dispatching a small squadron of warships to the scene and a promise to respect the sultan's independence, which at once silenced the protest and established Germany in East Africa. Such a prompt display of decision and force scarcely harmonizes with Bismarck's caution and restraint toward Peters and confirms, we take it, his own preconceived plan, as indicated by the appointment of Rholfs, to plant the German flag in the eastern half of the Dark Continent.[16]

England, however,—or rather the English agents,—proved not quite so amenable as the sultan, and the adjustment of German and British claims and boundaries occupied several years. Immediately upon the receipt of its Charter of Protection, the East African Company had undertaken no less than eleven expeditions,[17] which added considerable areas to its original holdings, but brought the company directly into collision with both England and France, who, it was now revealed, had guaranteed the independence of Zanzibar by a secret treaty in 1862. Commissioners were appointed from the three nations to adjust the conflicting claims and we have the amusing but, alas, common spectacle of three great Powers dividing among themselves the territory of a little, weak nation on the basis of protecting that little nation's integrity. The decision reached in 1886 interpreted the sultan's "integrity" to consist of only his two islands, Zanzibar and Pemba, and a strip of the coast ten miles deep and about one thousand miles long, of which the German company was to have the southern six hundred miles, and the British company the northern four hundred, as spheres of influence. Back of the ten-mile limit, the southern half of the hinterland, from the mouth of the Rovuma River to the Umba River, and as far west as Lake Victoria Nyanza was apportioned to Germany—about 200,000 square miles; while the northern part, about 170,000 square miles, went to England.[18] Germany completed her area by leasing in 1888 the coastal strip bordering on her sphere with its harbors and customs from the sultan and, two years later, by purchasing the whole of his rights there for 4,000,000 M.[19] This addition secured her adequate seaports and the control of the coastal trade.

### The Company's Exploits Embarrass the Foreign Office

But the East African Company, in spite of its auspicious beginnings, failed utterly to fulfill Bismarck's hopes for his colonial program; on the other hand, it was unable to control the activities of irresponsible adventurers like Peters, who pursued their exploring and concession hunting regardless of international relations, and, on the other, it was unable to cope with the native insurrections which its inexperience as an administrator evoked. For the agreement of 1888 with England had left many other areas of rivalry unsettled; vast unexplored and unclaimed regions in the west, in the Upper Nile, in Uganda remained. And Peters, yearning for more excitement than the directorship of the East African Company with its prosaic problems of administration now offered, set out to conquer new lands.

Opportunity offered in the guise of a relief expedition to rescue Emin Pasha,[20] a German by birth, governor of the Equatorial Province in the British Egyptian service, who was reported besieged by fanatical Mahdi in the regions of the Upper Nile. That this expedition was but an excuse to checkmate the British and to acquire territories for Germany both in that section and in the coveted Uganda, the "pearl of East Africa," both Peters' own account [21] and the records of the Emin Pasha Relief Committee show. Results could not possibly have been better planned. For on Peters' arrival at the very gates of the Equatorial Province, he stopped to rest at the camp of two Englishmen, Jackson and Martin, who were temporarily away hunting in the bush. There he found waiting for them a letter from Stanley, containing the startling and somewhat disappointing (to Peters) information that he (Stanley) had found Emin Pasha. "What can have been the design of Providence in permitting me to advance so far only to find my labors were in vain," [22] exclaimed Peters, who shortly received an answer, however, by the simple method of reading further into the Englishmen's mail. Therein he found both an account of the distressing situation of the king of Uganda who, deposed by Mohammedans, was imploring the British to come to his assistance, as well as the proposition from Mackay, the director of the British East African Company, to Jackson, suggesting that this was the opportunity to conquer Uganda for the British. The "design of Providence" was clear: one object of rescue was substituted for another. It made no difference that Mwanga, unlike Emin, was not a German brother; Peters rushed to his relief, restored him to his throne, and concluded a treaty which placed Uganda under German protection. With the same careless disregard of consequences, Peters also invaded the French sphere of influence in Madagascar, as well as the Italian preserves in Somaliland—in the futile execution of his phantasmal dream to create a German "India" in Africa.

These irresponsible exploits of Peters were, moreover, duplicated by the erratic Emin Pasha who, having been rescued by Stanley, deserted the British colonial service for the German, to the amazement and disgust of the British. Disobeying the strict orders of Wissmann, the imperial commissioner, he invaded British rights in the region of Victoria Nyanza and soon afterward met a violent death from the Arabs, whom he had stirred up against himself.[23]

Meanwhile, the German Witu Company had encountered the keen rivalry and antagonism of the British East African Company in Witu. Always on friendly terms with the sultan of Witu, the Germans encouraged him to defy his superior, the sultan of Zanzibar, the friend of the English. Sworn enemies, the two commercial companies, backed by their respective sultans, created a delicate situation, both local and international, for Witu was considered to be under the aegis of the East African Company.[24]

Altogether, the agents and associates of the East African Company were seriously threatening the friendly relations of Downing Street and the *Wilhelmstrasse,* which the Chancellor had just succeeded in reestablishing, and wished most earnestly to maintain. How essential to Germany a good understanding with England was at this juncture, we have already had occasion to observe in regard to the new orientation of France.[25] Consequently, we find Bismarck seeking again and again to nullify the effect of these imperialistic adventurers in East Africa by publicly disavowing all official responsibility for them, and by continually assuring Lord Salisbury of Germany's good will, thereby erroneously giving the impression that he was opposed to colonies. He thoroughly disapproved of the Emin Pasha expedition, going so far as to state in the *Norddeutsche Allgemeine Zeitung*[26] that the administration "would regret any attempt to penetrate into England's spheres of interest . . . and that England's friendship was worth much more than any results which the expedition into the Upper Nile might secure." He absolutely ignored the treaties consummated by Peters in Uganda, Somaliland, and Madagascar, and refused to regard Witu, over which he declined to extend official protection, as anything but an asset with which to bargain with England, for as he declared, "The maintenance of Lord Salisbury in office is worth more to the German government than all of Witu."[27] The very fact that the Witu Company was getting out of hand and embarrassing the government was but another indication of the failure of his plan to administer the colonies by means of the colonial company, which seemed to become either too strong or not strong enough.

### The East African Company Fails to Hold Its Own

To add to Bismarck's disappointment in enforcing his program, the East African Company proved too weak to control the natives or to cope with English rivalry in its domain. In September, 1888, a serious revolt broke out—a native protest against the German administration of the customs. The Arabs, especially, saw their old and well-established slave trade endangered by the German officials, and formed the strongest element in the uprising. The entire coast was in insurrection, the company besought the assistance of the "powerful empire" and Bismarck found himself obliged, against his will, to intervene. How he cleverly secured the necessary supplies from the *Reichstag,* under cover of suppressing the slave trade and of upholding the honor of the Fatherland in executing the provisions of the Congo Act, we have already observed.[28]

In utter defiance of his colonial program, Captain Hermann Wissmann [29] was dispatched as imperial commissioner and German ships, German men, and German gold were poured into East Africa to quell the revolt. But Bismarck remained faithful to his colonial program by conserving to the company the exercise of its sovereign rights: he conferred on the commissioner only the power of proposing to the company all changes which he believed necessary for its welfare and security, together with those making for good relations with foreign nations.[30] In certain cases of major importance, Wissmann was empowered temporarily to proceed independently and, if necessary, against the company,

but when the revolt was suppressed the company again succeeded to its powers, although its jurisdiction was very limited and weak. All of its plantations were ruined and it had
to begin to reconstruct its economic work anew. Vohsen,
who had succeeded Peters as the company's director, successfully reopened negotiations with the sultan of Zanzibar,
and the company hoped to make up for lost time. But
maladministration and the conquistador behavior on the part
of adventurers like Peters brought the rule of the company
into bad repute and, finally, the Treaty of 1890 dealt it
its death blow as a chartered company. For the Anglo-
German Agreement of 1890 ceded to England, its hated
rival, the protectorate over the sultan, German claims in
Witu, Uganda, and Nyassaland—all districts where the
company and its agents had been most active.[31]

Although the Anglo-German Treaty of 1890 was consummated by Caprivi, Bismarck had begun negotiations for it in
1889, as the most effective means of repudiating those
dubious acquisitions, sponsored by the East African Company, and of establishing friendly relations with Great
Britain upon a basis which adventurers like Peters could no
longer disturb.[32] Its final settlement left to Germany the
full possession of the coast of the mainland, hitherto leased
from the sultan, and an extension of the boundary eastward
to the great lakes Tanganyika and Nyassa, which effectually
blocked the way for the realization of the British Cape-to-
Cairo dreams.

Altogether this area, which by subsequent minor boundary
adjustments reached with England, Belgium, and Portugal
in the years between 1904 and 1912, amounted to some
997,000 square kilometers, twice the size of the German
empire. It was Germany's largest colony and was poten-

tially extremely rich. Traversed by the long chain of mountains which extends from Abyssinia to Natal, in the eastern part of the Dark Continent, and which attains in the region of Kilimanjaro a height of more than 6,000 meters, it is able to defy the tropical, equatorial climate. For these highlands gradually descending to the coast, and representing varied climatic zones, provide healthful plantations for Europeans and a wide diversity of cultivation. Cotton, rubber, tobacco, coffee, sisal, cattle may all be raised in East Africa. Besides, the colony possessed a long coast line on the Indian Ocean, with excellent ports open to the eastern commerce, as well as similar access to the great land-locked lakes which form a gateway to the interior and to the western trade.

But the East African Company was too weak financially and politically to develop these magnificent opportunities so lavishly offered. With the increasing encroachment of imperial control, it relinquished its soverign rights and privileges in all those territories composing the East African Protectorate, which passed under the administration of the empire on January 1, 1891.[33]

In compensation for its many privileges the company, which resolved itself into a private commercial company, fared extremely well: it received an annual indemnity of 600,000 M. from the government to be raised through the customs, and numerous privileges such as the exploitation of the forests, the priority right of building railways, of establishing a bank and issuing money, a fifty per cent profit in all mining concessions awarded to other companies and, finally, a monopoly of land concessions over territory as yet unclaimed. As a private commercial company, it did much to develop East Africa, especially opening up the territory through roads, railroads, telegraph, and steamship lines.

## The Company Plan Fails in Kamerun and Togoland

But Bismarck was doomed to greater disappointment in the application of his colonial program than he had experienced in East Africa; for in both Togoland and Kamerun the colonial companies, in spite of their initial strength, never functioned as administrators. From the middle of the nineteenth century, German merchants had been exceedingly active on the West African coast.[34] As early as 1853 German missionaries and traders had established themselves in the English stations at Keta and Akra in Togoland and, in 1868, the Hamburg firm of Woermann had its own stations on the Kamerun River, later supplemented and extended by the firms of Thormähem and Jantzen. By 1880, the first German factories appeared in Togoland, founded by Broehm and Woelber of Hamburg, and the celebrated Vietor Sons of Bremen. In spite of the keen commercial rivalry of the British along the Gold Coast and on the Kamerun River, almost one-half of the West African trade came to be controlled by the Germans in 1883, and Woermann had established a steamship line to Hamburg.

But trade in these regions was extremely difficult because of the English competition and the opposition of the nations in Kamerun, who did all they could not prevent penetration into the hinterland, the value of whose treasures they appreciated. Here the British maintained a Court of Equity to which all traders submitted, and jealous British merchants incited the natives, in 1882, to demand a British Protectorate. Taking advantage of Great Britain's inertia in this respect, the Chambers of Commerce in both Hamburg and Bremen addressed a formal request [35] to the imperial government demanding a warship, a consul, a naval station at Fernando

142

Po and the establishment of a colony on Biafra Bay. As we have already observed, Bismarck lent a ready ear to their petitions, sent the armored cruiser *Sophie* and promised to appoint a consul. After a secret conference with Woermann, April 30, 1884, at which Nachtigal's instructions[36] to extend imperial protection over certain places in Kamerun, Togoland, and Angra Pequena were formulated, the latter was dispatched on the *Möwe*, with what sly scheme to outwit the British we have already heard.[37]

In the meantime, Lawson, a British agent, set himself up as king at Little Popo in Togoland and was bending every effort to interfere with the German merchants. But, owing to the presence of the *Sophie,* he was arrested and imprisoned on board. King Grigi and the princes of Little Popo, impressed by this "show of might," asked for German protection against the British, which was speedily granted on the arrival of Nachtigal in July, who signed a treaty with the king of Togoland and raised the German flag, for the first time in Africa, at Lowe and Bagida. Proceeding rapidly to the Kamerun River, Nachtigal hastily signed treaties with Kings Bell and Aqua, placing under the German flag Belltown, Aquatown, Didotown, and later Bimbia, Malimba, and Batanga. Scarcely had his orders been thus executed, and the coveted coast of Biafra Bay opposite Fernando Po been placed under German protection, than Consul Hewett appeared on the scene with his British treaty forms; but he was a week too late, and was obliged to take refuge in addressing protests to the German government and in inciting native revolts against the Germans.[38] Finally, in the general colonial settlement of the year 1885, brought about by Bismarck's diplomacy, an agreement with England was reached and the boundaries of Togoland and Kamerun were determined, to be later delimited by subsequent agreements with England in 1890, 1893, 1899, and with France in 1885, 1894, 1897, 1899, and in 1911.[39]

In Kamerun, Germany possessed an area of about 495,000 square kilometers, rising to extremely high mountains in the east, and having a well-watered plateau along the coast. The tropical climate, while favorable to the production of coffee, cocoa, rubber, and tobacco, is very unsuited to the white race, and limited Kamerun to a commercial and plantation colony. Doubtless for this reason, it was, next to New Guinea, the least known of the German colonies and its pacification and exploration were delayed and entrusted to the concession companies.

Since the original commercial companies, like Woermann and Jantzen, confined their activities to trade and refused to incur any responsibility whatever for administration or exploration, Kamerun was ruled from the outset as an imperial province. The government was obliged to maintain first the imperial commissioner and then the governor, his staff, and the military with no financial return from the commercial or concession companies,[40] who enjoyed all the benefits and assumed a minimum of responsibility; a system which was exactly the reverse of Bismarck's plan.

Togoland, however, presented the greatest failure of the Chancellor's colonial program because there no vestige of it was ever even tried. Not even a concession company with exceptional privileges, financial, administrative or economic, ever existed. Between the English colony of the Gold Coast and the French territory of Dahomey, this little area of only 87,200 square kilometers was slightly larger than Bavaria. A numerous and industrious native population of high grade cultivated the oil palm, ground nuts and maize, and extracted rubber from the interior; while foreign mer-

144

chants carried on a lively trade on the coast. No native uprisings have ever disturbed Togoland and, so peaceful and prosperous was its development that of all the colonies it alone was self-supporting. Like Kamerun, it was administered from the beginning as an imperial province by an imperial commissioner followed by a governor. Always has it been considered a colonial province and never a protectorate in the Bismarckian sense.

### The New Guinea Chartered Company Makes a Brave Effort

Turning now to the South Seas, we find the counterpart of the East African Company in the New Guinea Company, for it was the second of the two colonial companies to receive a *Kaiserlicher Schutzbrief* and to accept sovereign rights in full accordance with Bismarck's colonial program. The New Guinea Company was the successor to the *Deutsche-See-Handels-Gesellschaft,* for which Bismarck had attempted, unsuccessfully it will be remembered, to secure a state subsidy from the *Reichstag* in the year 1880.[1] It, in turn, was the successor of Godeffroy and Son, that firm of merchant princes and pioneers who had first opened up Samoa for Germany in the eighteen sixties, and had fallen into financial difficulties in 1879. In spite of its failure to secure a government subvention, the *Deutsche-See-Handels-Gesellschaft* had privately assumed Godeffroy's liabilities and, to Bismarck's great satisfaction, had continued to promote and to extend Germany's interest in the South Seas. So great was its success that by the year 1883, it was controlling eighteen trading stations in New Britain, the Hermit and Duke of York Islands, and was exporting copra to Germany at the rate of two to three thousand tons annually.[2]

Unlike the colonies in Africa, which were due almost entirely to private initiative, the South Seas' settlements were projected and fostered by the government from the beginning. For, on the one hand, the Pacific islands were more obviously valuable economically and commercially; and, on the other, which was of prime importance, they were strategically situated as coaling stations and naval bases, especially in view of the projected Panama Canal. German warships and official trade inspectors often appeared in the South Seas; but in the face of the rejection of the Samoan Subsidy in 1880, the government temporized with direct intervention for several years. After 1884, however, circumstances entirely changed, as we have already observed: the British were menacing the independent islands from their base in Samoa; Australia's aggressive imperialism was the subject of constant complaint on the part of the German consuls at Apia; and in the Marshall Islands, British ships continually interfered with the German labor transports.[43]

To meet the situation, Bismarck, as will be recalled, took a firm stand both in his correspondence with the British government and more directly by dispatching an imperial commissioner, von Oertzen, in August, 1884, accompanied by a small squadron of four ships, to take possession of the island archipelago to the north of New Guinea in the name of the German emperor.[44] While von Oertzen was decorating the principal parts of the numerous islands with the imperial colors, a syndicate of Berlin bankers, headed by von Hansemann, and secretly supported by the Chancellor, founded the New Guinea Colonial Company on May 26, 1884, with the avowed purpose of occupying the hitherto unclaimed northern part of New Guinea. In furtherance of this aim, Dr. Finsch, an explorer, was dispatched to the South Seas to play the same scientific-imperialistic rôle there, as his brother scientist, Dr. Nachtigal, was, at that moment, enacting so effectually in Africa. With two warships in the background, Dr. Finsch and his associates sailed about the coasts of New Guinea and New Britain, leaving a trail of German flags behind them until their supply was exhausted. The indignation aroused in Great Britain's South Sea colonies by this performance has been already chronicled, as has also been described the ensuing diplomatic tangle with England, and Bismarck's ultimate triumph, in the year 1885; namely, the recognition by England and later by France of Germany's new acquisitions.[45]

By this colonial "raid" Germany gained about one-fourth of New Guinea, the northeastern part, which was rechristened *Kaiser Wilhelmsland;* a group of the Solomon Islands, New Britain, the Duke of York Islands, and a huge collection of smaller islands to the north of New Guinea, all united under the title, the Bismarck Archipelago. To emphasize the permanency of these annexations, the names of the smaller islands as well as of the large groups underwent Teutonization. New Britain became *Neu Pommern;* New Ireland, *Neu Mecklenburg;* the Duke of York, *Neu Lauenburg,* and so forth.

Besides their importance as naval bases, coaling stations, commercial ports, these islands possessed a very real and potential economic value. Copra had from the earliest times constituted the most important product, but coffee, cocoa, tobacco, rubber, ground nuts, and hemp could be grown with great facility especially in the rich, fertile virgin soil of New Guinea, whose unexplored and undisturbed stretches offered boundless possibilities for plantations once they were opened up and made accessible. Tortoise shell, mother-of-pearl, ivory were all found in quantities and, later, rich phosphate beds were discovered on the smaller islands. Like the wild, undeveloped land, whose pristine beauty and luxuriant vegetation cast a spell over the explorers and settlers, the natives were most primitive and of low grade. Their indolence created a serious labor problem, necessitating the importation of coolies for the plantations and delaying the economic development of the islands.[46]

Meanwhile, the New Guinea Company had kept pace in its internal organization with its achievements in the South Seas: it absorbed the *Deutsche-Handels-Plantagen-Gesellschaft* and the firm of Robertson and Hernsheim and, on May 17, 1885, received its charter [47] from the government. More complete than that of the East African Company, this *Kaiserlicher Schutzbrief* invested the New Guinea Company with sovereign rights which were somewhat more specifically and precisely defined. For instance, where the charter of the East African Company gave it the right both to make and to execute the laws for the natives and other inhabitants, the charter of the New Guinea Company reserved the making of the laws to the empire; also, the New Guinea Company received a more widely defined monopoly, viz., "the exclusive right of taking possession of and of disposing of the unclaimed lands, and of concluding with the natives contracts relative to the soil and to the right of property." The charters of both societies, however, were qualified by a statute passed on April 16, 1886, which reserved to the emperor certain rights of sovereignty in the protectorates. They were: the right to promulgate laws defining the legal position of the protectorate, and laws applicable to the territory administered by the protectorate; the right to conduct all the foreign affairs; and, finally, the right to organize and to command all the military forces in the protectorates.

Also, like its predecessor, the East African Company, the New Guinea Company possessed all its prerogatives with no obligation to render any return therefor. These two great privileges, monopoly and freedom from service, which are not found in any other colonial charter of the nineteenth century, placed the German protectorates of East Africa and New Guinea in a peculiar and advantaged position, which made them resemble more nearly the colonial companies of the old régime than the modern English companies of our own time.

In spite of its unusual independence, however, the New Guinea Company, again like the East African Company, failed to succeed; [48] not because of unlicensed adventurers this time, but because of poor administration and of failure to develop its economic opportunities. It suffered from a too centralized control in Berlin; from corruption and ignorance on the part of its officials, who thought to solve the problems of administering the undeveloped country and the primitive inhabitants of the Pacific islands from their comfortable offices in *Unter den Linden.* This weakness at the center was reflected in the local administration where a veritably anarchy reigned. Since the company's officials failed to interest themselves in the country and its potentialities, there was always a constant turnover in personnel, as many as seventy-seven officials changing in one year. The fact that five years after the company's inauguration three-quarters of *Kaiser Wilhelmsland* remained uncharted on the map, represents some indication of the instability and lack of continuity in the administration.

It may be that the company was incapacitated for exercising economic and exploratory functions by the preponderance of bankers and speculators among its leaders and directors. At any rate, these "gentlemen of the green table" did not make efficient pioneers. Recognizing this handicap, the company sought to separate its economic from its political rôle in 1889 by creating a plantation company for the cultivation of coffee and cocoa. But all sorts of misfortunes beset its development program: the weather either burned or flooded the crops, the officials died of fever, the labor supply failed, the ships were wrecked. Discouraged by the poor results of its efforts, the company surrendered the administration to imperial officials for three years, beginning in 1889, but retained its other privileges. It recovered its full rights again in 1892, but fell rapidly into debt. At the end of its resources in 1895, it asked the government to relieve it altogether of its charter, a request at first refused, but finally granted in 1899. Like the East African Company, it received an indemnity of 4,000,000 M. from the empire, which it agreed to invest in plantations.[49] Unlike the East African Company, however, it failed, even as a private company, to benefit the protectorate: its finances went from bad to worse, it concealed its reports and records, and it won the ill-will of other companies in New Guinea by the exercise of its monopolistic privileges in detriment to their interests.

## The Jaluit Company

Much more successful than the New Guinea Company, and the longest lived of all the privileged companies was the smallest, the Jaluit Company endowed with special privileges in the Marshall Islands.[50] During the 1860's and the 1870's, the firm of Robertson and Hernsheim had been active there, and in 1878 had secured Jaluit as a coaling station for the government by a treaty with the native chiefs. Hernsheim, the merchant prince, was installed as consul. After the dispute with England, in 1885, about the South Seas, the imperial government extended its protection, April, 1886, to the Marshall Islands and the neighboring groups, the Brown and Providence Islands, situated to the northeast of the Bismarck Archipelago. At first, the firm of Robertson and Hernsheim refused a charter, declaring that it was not able to undertake the control of the islands; that it possessed neither money, ships nor soldiers and felt itself utterly unable to defend the islands against any warlike power. Since the merchants stood adamant in their refusal, the administration of the Marshall, Brown, and Providence Islands remained in the hands of a powerless royal commission. Finally, Robertson and Hernsheim united with the branch of the *Deutsche-See-Handels-Gesellschaft* represented in the islands to form, in 1887, the Jaluit Company. By a contract with the imperial government, this privileged company agreed to support the government officials in the islands in return for the following rights: the possession of all unclaimed land, the monopoly of the guano and pearl industries, and the right to be consulted about the laws.[51] Thus, the Jaluit Company never received a *Schutzbrief* or exercised sovereign powers.

This company met with unusual success: it never encountered any trouble with the natives, had the wisdom to leave the administration to the imperial officials whom it well supported; and, itself, concentrated upon the production of one commodity, the valuable copra. In 1901, the government extended its sway over the Caroline Islands, bought as a bargain from Spain after the Spanish-American War, but the company was able to assume the additional expense and even established its own steamship line, connecting its territory with these neighboring islands and with Hong Kong.

The competition from Australia, however, which had always miltated against the company, became very intense at this time, and, in 1906, the German government took over the rights of the company in order to display greater strength in the South Seas. After 1906, the Marshall Islands formed a province under the imperial government of New Guinea.

Doubtless the fundamental reason for the failure of the privileged companies was that they were out of date. The seventeenth-century system of great colonial societies enjoying sovereign, or nearly sovereign rights, was not in harmony with nineteenth-century conditions. The existence of strong national states precluded the companies from occupying a sufficiently important position. "Their independent political functions are less in an age of great states, and their commercial powers are not adequate to the strain and stress of contemporary life. Today, they are subordinate organizations for a political purpose, rather than independent organizations for purely commercial ends. They acted, however, as a screen for national expansion."

In spite of their failure and short duration, the rule of the privileged companies plays an important rôle in German colonial history. Without them, as we have seen, Bismarck would not have been able to carry his colonial policy so far, and to them, doubtless, is due the acquisition of so much oversea territory during the 1880's. Their results, however, were not, as we shall see, so beneficial, for the practice of concession and monopoly which they inaugurated left a baleful influence, postponing the adoption of a strong national colonial policy until, indeed, the year 1906. Although the privileged companies themselves disappeared, they resolved into commercial companies, perpetuating and multiplying the individual grants of land, of mining rights, and of concessions of all kinds which the government was obliged to win back. Until it was able to do that, Germany could not establish a thoroughgoing, scientific, and unified colonial empire.

## NOTES

[1] Kohl, H., *Die politische Reden des Fürstens Bismarck* (Stuttgart, 1892-1905), vol. xi, p. 281.

[2] *Ibid.,* vol. x, p. 197.

[3] Decharme, P., *Compagnies et sociétés coloniales allemandes* (Paris, 1903), pp. 80-84. See also von Hagen, *op. cit.,* pp. 84ff.

[4] Wiart, C., *Les grandes compagnies anglaises du XIX siècle* (Paris, 1899), ch. 1.

[5] See *supra.,* ch. iii, p. 68.

[6] See *supra*, ch. iii, p. 89.

[7] Koschitzky, *op. cit.,* vol. ii, p. 52ff.

[8] See *supra,* ch. iii, p. 89ff.

[9] Koschitzky, *op. cit.,* vol. ii, p. 98. See also, Zimmermann, *op. cit.,* p. 81.

[10] Sander, L., *Geschichte der deutschen Süd-West Afrika Kolonialgesellschaft* (Berlin, 1912).

[11] See *supra.,* ch. ii, p. 44.

[12] Peters, K., *Die Gründung von Deutsch-Ostafrika* (Berlin, 1906). *Lebenserinnerungen* (Hamburg, 1918).

Pfeil, Graf von, *Zur Erwerbung von Deutsch-Ostafrika* (Berlin, 1907).

[13] For the actual Treaties, see Koschitzky, *op. cit.,* vol. ii, p. 251ff.

[14] See *supra.,* ch. iv, p. 109.

[15] For the *Charter* itself, see Riebow-Zimmermann, *Die deutsche Kolonialgesetzgebung,* vol. i, p. 323.

[16] Von Hagen, *op. cit.,* p. 523ff.

[17] For an interesting first-hand account of these expeditions, see Rochus Schmidt, *Aus Koloniale Frühzeit* (Berlin, 1924), who was, himself, one of the leaders.

[18] Hertslet, E., *Map of Africa by Treaty* (London, 1909), 3rd edition, 3 vols. Vol. ii, p. 615.

[19] See *infra,* ch. vi, p. 162.

[20] Emin Pasha was really Edward Schnitzler, born in Germany in 1840. As a young man he had gone as a physician to Turkey and had lived for many years at the court of Ismail Halski, Pasha at Scutari. Upon the Pasha's death, he had married his widow, taken her to Germany and had then disappeared. Under an assumed name, he entered the service of the English in Egypt and finally became governor of Wadelai. See Schweitzer, G., *Emin Pasha* (Berlin, 1898).

[21] Peters, K., *New Light on Dark Africa* (Berlin, 1891).

[22] *Ibid.,* p. 360.

[23] Stuhlman, F., *Die Tagebücher von Emin Pasha* (Hamburg, 1916).

[24] Von Hagen, *op. cit.,* p. 543.

[25] See *supra.,* ch. iv, pp. 114-115.

[26] *Norddeutsche Allgemeine Zeitung,* August 14, 1889.

[27] Zimmermann, *op. cit.,* p. 160.

[28] See *supra*, ch. iv, pp. 117-118.

[29] Schmidt, Rochus, *Hermann Wissmann und Deutschlands Koloniales Wirken* (Berlin, 1925).

[30] To what extent Bismarck sought to efface the state in colonial management, even in the uprising in East Africa, may be illustrated by General Schmidt when he, himself, relates how he, as an officer under Wissmann, was obliged to secure his dismissal from the regular army in order to serve in the East African campaign.

[31] See *infra.*, ch. vi, p. 162 and *supra.*, ch. iv, p. 115.

[32] See in this connection, von Hagen, *op. cit.*, p. 547, note 1.

[33] For text of agreement, see Riebow-Zimmermann, *op. cit.*, vol. i, p. 382.

[34] See *supra.*, ch. ii, p. 46.

For a detailed account of German interests in West Africa before 1884, see Koschitzky, *op. cit.*, vol. i, p. 44ff., vol. ii, pp. 128ff., 190ff.

Also see, *Weissbuch vorgelegt dem Deutschen Reichstag*, 1885, p. 24.

[35] *Weissbuch*, July 9, 1883, p. 5, July 6, 1883, no. 3.

[36] See *supra.*, ch. iv, p. 99.

For Nachtigal's instructions, see *Staatsarchiv*, vol. 43, pp. 246, 248.

[37] See *supra.*, ch. iv, p. 105.

[38] Koschitzky, *op. cit.*, vol. ii, p. 190ff. Also see Buchner *Aurora Coloniales* (Berlin, 1884), p. 16ff.

[39] Hertslet, *May of Africa by Treaty*, vol. iii, pp. 903, 919ff., 619; vol. ii, pp. 653, 657ff., 662.

[40] See *infra.*, ch. vi, pp. 160, 170.

[41] See *supra.*, ch. iii, pp. 72-73.

[42] Koschitzky, *op. cit.*, vol. ii, p. 232ff. *Weissbuch*, 1885, pp. 131-135.

[43] Reports of consuls Stübel of Apia, Hahn-Wippermann, *op. cit.*, vol. v, pp. 75-76, and of Hernsheim of Jaluit, *Weissbuch*, 1885, pp. 131-150.

[44] *Staatsarchiv*, vol. 43, p. 349ff.

[45] See *supra.*, ch. iv, p. 100.

[46] Weyhmann, H., *Unsere Südsee* (Berlin, 1917).

[47] For text of *Charter*, see Riebow-Zimmermann, *op. cit.*, vol. i, p. 434.

[48] For account of New Guinea Company, see Decharme, *op. cit.*, ch. ii.

[49] *Das Kolonialblatt*, 1900, p. 227ff.

[50] Koschitzky, *op. cit.*, vol. ii, p. 302ff.

[51] For text, see Decharme, *op. cit.*, appendix x.

# CHAPTER VI

## IMPERIAL CONTROL

### *Bureaucrats and Colonels, Concessionaires and Culprits Rule the Colonies*

MANY circumstances beside their own failure conspired to replace the rule of the privileged companies over Germany's colonial territories by direct imperial government. Externally, national rivalry stimulated by imperialism, protective tariffs, and economic competition was emphasizing the importance of colonial possessions, and involving them in diplomatic relations with which the companies could not begin to cope. While internally, the insistent demands of the colonial party for a centralized national administration coincided with the accession of William II and his flamboyant ideas of *Weltpolitik*. Typical of these advocates for a reform of colonial administration was Fabri. In his book published in 1889, he demonstrated the ineffectiveness of the companies with their constant need of government support, and foreshadowed the complete transformation of the administrative régime with a replacement of company officials by an imperial bureaucracy.[1]

Again, the general public in Germany, which was after all the real supporter of colonial dominion, had become extremely hesitant about investing in oversea undertakings, because of the many failures and mistakes made by the companies. Many had lost heavily through the failure of the New Guinea Company and because of the wars of the East

155

African Company. Hence it was felt to be essential that colonial management be placed in the competent and responsible hands of the government, in order to create a popular confidence sufficient to attract the necessary capital.

### The Foundations of Imperial Rule Already Laid by Bismarck

What is more, the foundations of direct imperial control over the colonies had been already laid by Bismarck in practice if not in theory, so that the way was not unprepared. To be sure, he had ignored the importunities of the colonial party for the establishment of an imperial colonial office. But at that time in the late eighties, a wise caution, dictated, as we have seen, by the exigencies of his foreign diplomacy, demanded the rejection of any such strong measure at home promoting expansion, just as it required the repudiation of Peter's too vigorous acquisitions abroad.[2] Perhaps Bismarck's private acknowledgment of Fabri's book illustrates more accurately than his official public utterance his real attitude toward the subject.[3] He wrote to Fabri: "It is to be regretted that the colonial question has always from the very beginning been a party issue, and that appropriations for colonial purposes are only gained from the *Reichstag* after strong partisan opposition. The imperial government cannot depart from its original colonial program of merely extending support and protection to undertakings oversea; it cannot assume the erection of its own courts of justice in the colonies or the support of a bureaucracy and a military, so long as it is opposed by an antagonistic *Reichstag,* and so long as the national significance of colonies is not appreciated or supported by capital or business."[4]

The Chancellor was, of course, aware of the weakness of

his chartered companies but, as we have seen, he had invoked them as a screen to mask the action of the government and to blind the eyes of the Great Powers and, hence, he never openly acknowledged that his program had failed, or that he was in favor of a direct imperial administration. In the very last years of his chancellorship, we find him vociferously asserting that he had not altered his ideas on the subject, and that Germany must not depart from his original program. In the debates over colonial policy precipitated by the bill for appropriations and for the appointment of an imperial commissioner to be sent to East Africa in 1889, the Chancellor said: "I repeat that I am opposed to colonies, that is, to the kind of colonies where officials must be placed and garrisons established. . . . My present action is dictated only by pressing necessity. . . . I cannot burden myself with the reproaches of posterity that I failed to protect Germans and German territory. . . . If the locomotive of the empire has struck out on a new track for itself, I will not be the one to put stones in its way. . . . *Von Haus aus bin ich kein Kolonialmensch* and I entertain the gravest apprehension on the subject; but I submit to the pressure of public opinion, I yield to the majority." [5]

Nowhere do we find a more explicit example of his "defense attitude," for his actions scarcely confirm his professions, as they indeed never did where his colonial policy was concerned. For it has been already shown that, by 1889, the limits of Bismarck's original program, merely to protect the individual merchant, had been far exceeded. In Africa, the government had entirely abandoned the practice of chartered companies: it had administered Togoland and Kamerun from the outset as crown colonies; as early as May, 1889, it had installed an imperial commissioner in South West Africa; and in East Africa it had virtually super-

157

seded the East African Company when it dispatched von Wissmann to suppress the Arab revolt. Also, in the South Seas, the government had been obliged in 1889 to supplement the rule of the New Guinea Company at its own request. Thus Bismarck, consciously or unconsciously, had paved well the way for the direct imperial control of colonies, involving the sending of troops and the establishment of garrisons; while, at the same time, he had maintained the fiction of the chartered company.

### The Colonial Section of the Foreign Office Is Created

With all this preparation for a radical change in the colonial administration, it is not surprising that one of the first acts of Bismarck's successor, General von Caprivi, was to create, in April, 1890, an imperial colonial office, a section of the Foreign Office.[6] This constituted the first step toward an independent colonial administration. But it was still far from independent: until 1896, all the military affairs of the colonies were referred to the ministry of marine and all questions bearing on the general policy of the empire to the ministry of foreign affairs; only strictly domestic business involving the internal organization of the colonies was reserved to the colonial director and even then he was bound to the leadership of the Chancellor, under whose immediate protection this section of the Foreign Office remained.

Still, the colonial department possessed more independence than any other section of the Foreign Office; an independence greatly increased by the creation, in 1890, of the so-called Kolonialrat,[7] an advisory council composed at first of nineteen members representing not only those with economic interests in the colonies, like the representatives of the great commercial companies, but all classes of the population. As the *Norddeutsche Allgemeine Zeitung* remarked, "It was hoped that the colonial council would broaden and extend colonial interests instead of confining them to the theorists and those who were directly concerned." The Chancellor nominated the members from a list, which he invited the companies and all those who had important oversea enterprises to submit. Of the nineteen members originally named, twelve men, such as von Hansemann, Weber, and Woermann, represented the mercantile firms doing business in the colonies; two the *Kolonialverein*, two the missionary societies; and the remaining three were spokesmen for the interests of the general public. In 1895, the membership was raised to twenty-five, each member holding office for three years, and the circle of the council's contacts was thereby enlarged.

To be sure, the function of the *Kolonialrat* was purely consultative and advisory and, sometimes, as we shall have occasion to observe, its counsel was either unasked or ignored; even so, it lent a certain stability both to the external and internal colonial policy. With the colonial director, the colonial council constituted the special section of the Foreign Office that controlled all the oversea territories except Kiao-Chow (acquired in 1898) which had its own régime. Directly under the Chancellor, this form of central colonial administration endured until the year 1906, when the colonial director was promoted to a cabinet secretary and the colonial office was transformed into a separate department of state.

### Changes in Local Administration

Such a drastic change in the central administration of the colonies effected in 1890 was, of course, reflected in the local government. After 1891, governors, appointed by the

159

emperor and made directly responsible to him, replaced all the company officials, the imperial officers supported by the companies, and the imperial commissioners (as in Togoland and Kamerun). These governors combined the civil and military authority and wielded extensive powers. They had as assistants in each colony a certain number of high functionaries, such as a judge, a tax-collector, a postmaster who, in turn, possessed their own separate staffs. In the last analysis, however, the Kaiser retained sovereign power.[8]

### The First Colonial Director Encounters Many Difficulties

Dr. Paul Kayser, the first real director of the colonial department, was in some ways well prepared for his position. As a judge he had served his country in various capacities and, especially, had rendered expert service in the difficulties incident upon the German government's relations with the East African Company. First and foremost a bureaucrat, he had, nevertheless, some vision of the duty of the Fatherland to civilize and to develop her oversea possessions. "Military glory is not to be sought in the colonies," he once said, "the sole task of the armed force is to protect German traders. Government officials must place themselves at the service of commercial enterprises without losing sight of the interests of the natives."[9]

### Caprivi an Anti-Expansionist

But Dr. Kayser entered upon his administration under grave difficulties. In the first place, Bismarck's successor, Caprivi, was not a colonial enthusiast; by training, a soldier and politician, he was far more interested in imperial defense than in an extension of the empire, and he failed to envisage at all the economic advantage of colonies.[10] Besides, he had other preoccupations: he feared a Russian war, believed in continental expansion, and was intent upon improving the army. He would have preferred to relegate the colonies entirely to the control of companies, as England once did, but he realized that it was impossible, for, as he said, "We have no leaders to direct the companies. . . . Englishmen are accustomed to invest in the colonies, while Germans have so little confidence in the oversea policy that they prefer government securities which are considered safer." [11] At one time he declared in the *Reichstag* that he would regard it as a calamity were all of Africa presented to Germany as a gift.[12] Nevertheless, he felt that, so long as Germany had embarked upon a colonial empire, she could not withdraw without a loss of national honor and prestige. At least, Caprivi was alive to the political advantages of oversea territories, and saw in them a method of advancing Germany's position and defense; consequently, he used them as pawns in the game of international rivalry. He continued Bismarck's policy of subordinating colonial affairs to foreign diplomacy, but he did not have the same subtle reasons for so doing, nor did he employ the same consummate skill.

### The Anglo-German Treaty of 1890

Consistent with his outlook, and in harmony with William II's well-known disposition to maintain friendly relations with his grandmother, Queen Victoria, Caprivi lost no time in negotiating the Anglo-German Treaty of 1890 which, together with the non-renewal of the Russian Reinsurance Treaty in the same year, marked a critical departure in foreign policy, in fact the beginning of the so-called "new course" (*der neue Kurs*). By the terms of the Anglo-German Treaty, Germany accepted Chamberlain's offer of 1889 to hand over Heligoland for a colonial price: she recognized a British Protectorate over Witu and the Somali

coast in East Africa, transferred Uganda to the British
sphere of influence, agreed to a British Protectorate over
Zanzibar, excepting the coastal strip leased to the East African Company, and recognized the basin of the Upper Nile
to the borders of Egypt as within the British sphere; while,
in return, she received from Great Britain the promise to
urge the sultan of Zanzibar to sell the coastal strip to her,
the narrow corridor to the Zambesi on the western coast
(Caprivi's Finger), and the island of Heligoland,—greatly
increased in strategic significance since the cutting of the
Kiel Canal.[13]

The Kaiser put all the reasons for the exchange in a nut-
shell when he said: "I was firmly resolved to win back
Heligoland, that island lying close in front of the great
waterways leading to the principal Hanseatic commercial
ports. In the hands of the British it was a constant menace
to Hamburg and Bremen, and rendered impossible any
project for building up a navy. To exchange Zanzibar was
not a loss but a gain. For the importance of Zanzibar
would soon be a thing of the past, so soon as its value as a
port of trans-shipment was destroyed by the ports of Dar-es-
Salaam, Togoland, and Kamerun, rapidly becoming prosperous; but its importance lay in its being an asset for swapping
and thereby affording an opportunity to avoid friction with
England, to which Caprivi agreed."[14]

As was to be expected, the treaty, although popular with
the nation because of the acquisition of Heligoland, aroused
a storm of criticism from the colonial party, for it struck a
severe blow at their interests, not only locally in East Africa,
but also at their hopes and enthusiasm in Germany. "The
acquisition of Heligoland blinds every one to the losses sustained. With a pen's stroke, England has acquired a dominating position in East Africa. . . . Also we have lost the

coast."[15]  "Our colonial hopes in Africa are jeopardized and our colonial ideals have suffered a blow,"[16] complained the friends of colonies in vain. Even Stanley, the African explorer, exclaimed that "a new pair of trousers had been exchanged for an old trouser button," and Peters raged that "two kingdoms, Witu and Uganda, had been sacrificed for a bathtub in the North Sea."

Seeking to meet his hosts of critics, Caprivi did not improve matters, but rather strengthened a hundredfold the opposition of the colonial party. In an attempt to justify the treaty, he asserted that it was but a continuation of Bismarck's policy, which "set a high value on the relations with England," and had already opened negotiations for Heligoland.[17] This remark drew a sharp and scornful rebuke from the "dropped Pilot," now an embittered recluse in *Friedrichsruh,* who kept an ever-watchful, if hypercritical, eye upon his successor's colonial policies, and neglected no opportunity to vent his criticism with considerable venom in the press.[18] For while it was true that Bismarck had weighed the question of the cession of Heligoland, he had considered it as subordinate to a thoroughgoing understanding with England—for which he was always striving—and not as an end in itself. His reluctance on this point is very evident upon the two occasions when the matter was discussed. The first time, in May, 1884, Bismarck proposed that Great Britain cede the island to Germany in return for Germany's support in Egypt, and as a guarantee of friendliness, but not in return for a German colony.[19] Indeed, during the ensuing misunderstanding with England over the Angra Pequena affair, he expressed the fear that Heligoland might be offered by England in place of her recognition of Germany's claims in South West Africa, and he asked that the matter be dropped, because "Heligoland is only of secondary importance in comparison with England's attitude toward all of Germany's oversea interests." [20] "The question of Heligoland," he said, "must not interfere with the justice of our claims in Africa." [21] And again the second time in 1889, when Chamberlain, in conversation with Herbert Bismarck in London, proposed the cession of Heligoland to Germany in return for South West Africa, the Chancellor, in spite of the hearty approval of the Kaiser, postponed the question and instructed Herbert to "take no initiative in the matter." [22] "We must," he said, "wait until the English need us." [23]

In view of Bismarck's former attitude concerning the cession of Heligoland, therefore, his opposition to the Treaty of 1890 appears both natural and logical, for "the new course" had impulsively and recklessly consummated the exchange of territory without regard to any of the other factors of Anglo-German relationships. As he expresses it himself in his *Memoirs:* "Reference has been made to the fact that while I was in office I had set a high value upon relations with England. This is undoubtedly correct, but I had never believed in the possibility of a lasting guarantee of the same, and I should never have aimed at the sacrifice of a German possession in order to gain a good-will whose duration would have had no prospect of surviving an English ministry. The renunciation of equality in the commercial city of Zanzibar was a lasting sacrifice for which Heligoland guaranteed no equivalent." [24]

To have Bismarck, the beloved old Chancellor, thus come to the support of the colonial party against Caprivi,[25] went a long way toward changing their apparent defeat into victory, and did much to nullify the effect of the treaty. For, taking the treaty as a special grievance, the friends of colonial expansion founded on July 1, 1890, the Pan-German

League whose expressed purpose was "to arouse patriotic self-consciousness at home . . . and, above all, to carry forward the German colonial movement to tangible results." [26] Nor did this new expression of the colonial impulse forget its debt of gratitude to the old Chancellor; it at once elected him an honorary member of the League, and hailed him as the "Founder of the German Colonial Empire." [27] Although, indeed, Caprivi's words and attitude had "acted like streams of cold water, and his sarcasm had dampened all colonial enthusiasm," they ultimately instigated a counter colonial movement of no little strength.

## The "Colonial Weariness"

Besides the indifference of Chancellor Caprivi to colonial expansion, his lack of any program and his willingness to sacrifice colonies to political ends, Dr. Kayser had also to contend against the opposition of the *Reichstag*. Bismarck's colonial policy had been supported in the *Reichstag* by his *Cartel,* consisting of the National Liberals, the Center, and the Conservatives; the former party advocating expansion for economic, and the two latter parties for religious and patriotic reasons. But, even before Bismarck's resignation, the support of these groups had weakened: the National Liberal capitalists had become disappointed in the meager economic returns of the colonies; and the Conservatives and Center had disapproved of the wars, and of the cruelties practiced upon the natives by unscrupulous company officials and adventurers. As we have seen, Bismarck had all he could do to obtain sufficient appropriations to quell the uprisings in East Africa in the year 1889. After the new elections in 1890, the *Cartel* parties were placed in the minority in the *Reichstag* and hence the critics and opponents of the colonial policy; namely, the Socialists and the

*Freisinnige* had full play, and did not hesitate to use their opportunities. The Socialists, led by Bebel, asked embarrassing questions about the unsavory rumors of cruelties, graft, licentiousness, and lawlessness practiced by Peters, Schröder, and others in East Africa and Kamerun, questions which remained unanswered by the administration. So sharp, indeed, became the criticism of some of the colonial "heroes," so many and so dreadful were the scandals of colonial administrators uncovered in the *Reichstag,* that Dr. Kayser was forced into instituting an investigation, which resulted in Peters being brought to trial, convicted, and later dismissed from the imperial service.[28]

Also, the opposition of the *Reichstag* and its results had a distinct effect upon public opinion generally, tending to antagonize it toward all the colonial policy, thereby creating another obstacle for Dr. Kayser. For the investigations into the "colonial scandals" successfully aired all the seamy side of colonial administration throughout the country, and created an atmosphere of "colonial weariness." It certainly did not help the colonial cause to hear that the planter, Schröder, whom the governor had expelled from East Africa because of cruelty to his native laborers—among other things he had injured a native's child by idly throwing a bottle at him from his dinner table—had succeeded in returning to commit further iniquities through the influence of his brother, a member of the *Kolonialrat.* No more did it wring appropriations from an unwilling *Reichstag* to learn that Leist, the governor of Kamerun, had helped precipitate the Dahomeyan revolt by his inhuman cruelties inflicted upon women. Nor did it encourage investors in the colonial enterprises to learn that the celebrated Peters, whom an imperial judge in East Africa indicted for trial for his cruelties and illegal usurpation of authority, had been shielded by influential friends in Berlin and nominated for a semi-independent governorship over Tanganyika Province in the pay of the government. On the contrary, a strong reaction from the colonial sentiment of the early eighties set in: then, the people had seen the colonies as supplying a remedy for the annual national loss from emigration, as affording political prestige and economic opportunity; now, the popular mind of the early nineties regarded them as playfields for the bureaucrat, as battlegrounds for the militarists, and as so many excursion places for the unscrupulous adventurer—in short—possessions not worth the keeping.

Dr. Kayser's lack of support in the government, in the *Reichstag,* and among the people accentuated the third difficulty which confronted him; namely, economic depression: both the South West African Company and the East African Company were in a bad way financially; Togoland and Kamerun had found it difficult at first to get along; private capital was disinclined to invest in what appeared to be unprofitable enterprises oversea; and finally, the unsympathetic *Reichstag,* loath even to vote necessary appropriations for current expenses in the colonies, balked entirely at spending money to develop them. Indeed, the spirit for mercantile and industrial enterprise in Africa and in the South Seas seemed to have sunk to its very lowest point.

### Doctor Kayser Effects Some Progress

In spite of all these obstacles, however, Dr. Kayser seems to have attacked his task well: he did not hesitate openly to oppose Caprivi, he stood firmly for the colonial interests, and he gradually won national confidence and approval. Very tangible results stand to his credit both in his internal administration of the colonial office, and in the external development of the colonies themselves in spite of the wars waged with the natives: the *Kolonialrat* was established and enlarged and the system of the *Schutztruppe* (troops for protection) inaugurated and placed under the control of the colonial office instead of under the ministry of marine.[29] The number of white settlers in the colonies steadily increased: in Kamerun from 105 to 250, in Togoland from 35 to 96, in South West Africa from 750 to 2,025, and in East Africa to 1,250. The number of independent firms active in the colonies grew from 11 to 18 in Togoland, from 12 to 23 in South West Africa; and the independent plantations reached the number of 16 in East Africa with a capital of more than 8,000,000 M., of 7 in Kamerun, and of 8 in Togoland.[30] Likewise, welfare work among the natives had proceeded apace: instead of 6 missionary societies active in the year 1890, there were, at the close of Dr. Kayser's administration, 12 Protestant and 8 Catholic societies with a total of 145 stations; government schools had begun to arise; hospitals with laboratories were attacking tropical diseases; and, due largely to the efforts of the Colonial Society, at least a few experimental stations and botanical gardens were commencing to discover the agricultural potentialities of these strange lands. Closer and closer had grown the bond between the mother country and the colonies by the increase in transportation and communication facilities, notably through the East African Line and the Woermann Line to West Africa; as well as by the creation of a colonial literature. The colonial office published the *Kolonialblatt,* its official bulletin; a scientific journal made known all matters of interest to explorer and scientists; the Colonial Society chronicled every item of current interest in the colonies by means of its *Kolonialzeitung;* and the annual official reports traced their economic and material growth.

## Native Revolts

The progress of the colonies was very much hindered, however, by the constant revolts and punitive expeditions incident to the attempts of the new masters to extend and to assert their power; a state of affairs which characterizes the formative years of every nation's colonial history. In East Africa the power of the Arab slave traders in the Victoria Nyanza district was broken, the powerful chieftains of the Wahelis and the Mafites were subdued in the coastal sections, and German authority, after a difficult struggle, was extended to the Kilimandjaro region. Also in Kamerun, military affairs played the chief rôle in a successful attempt to penetrate the *Hinterland,* and to secure access to the great natural resources of palm-oil, ground nuts, ivory, and rubber. Between the years 1893 and 1895, the fierce Dahomeyans, the Bueas, and the Bakokos were all conquered. But South West Africa was the greatest sufferer from native unrest. There the constant fighting of the Hereros against the Hottentots, and their joint interference with the activities of the companies, necessitated drastic action on the part of the government which finally commissioned one of its most experienced officers, Major Leutwein,[81] to quell the revolt, which he succeeded in doing temporarily.

## The Concession Policy

But the first colonial director made some serious mistakes, which can be attributed very largely, however, to the system which he inherited and to the difficulties just reviewed, against which he was forced to contend. His first mistake concerned his unwise and unfortunate concession policy to all sorts of colonial companies; a policy which resulted in a virtual surrender to private initiative and to private ownership of most of the economic treasures of the colonies.[32]

Because of the lack of government support, Dr. Kayser had found it easier to induce private capitalists to subscribe for the economic development of the colonies than to raise money in the *Reichstag*. The wholesale granting of concessions, land, mining, trading, railroad building, and the like, was thus used as a means to attract the necessary but reluctant capital into the colonies, and the state was obliged to efface itself from these economic activities. The much needed capital responded to the lure but the "concessions" formed a very dark chapter in Germany's colonial history. Of course, Bismarck had begun this concession policy whch he first entrusted colonial administration to the merchants and then to the colonial companies; and the government had continued it, when it failed to grasp the opportunity to buy back the land and the mineral rights at the time of the dissolution of the privileged companies and had, instead, allowed new private societies to absorb these privileges. Now, the imperial administration crowned the evil by inaugurating a wholesale concession policy, under which the colonies were sadly and devastatingly exploited.

South West Africa, preeminently, was a victim to the concession policy. Its entire colonization was based upon grants of land, of mineral rights, and of railroad-building privileges and, by the year 1903, nine companies, many of them under foreign influence, controlled 32 per cent of its entire area.[33] For instance, the government gave a large tract of 227,000 square miles to the so-called "South African Company," really an English company under the influence of Cecil Rhodes, but formed in conjunction with Hamburg merchants. This company gained all the territory in which diamonds were found and wielded its influence over the smaller companies who mined diamonds, so that it possessed a monopoly. Also, it received the sole right from the government to construct a railway in South West Africa from the coast, by way of the Octavi mines, to the eastern boundary. Since it never built the railway and since its activities incited trouble with the natives, the government was forced to construct the Swakopmund-Windhuk line in order to provision the soldiers, whom it was obliged to provide to quell the uprising! [34]

In East Africa, likewise, the East African Company received in return for constructing a railway from Tanga to Korogwe not only the land to the width of three kilometers on each side of the track, but also a grant of 4,000 hectares in another place for each kilometer of finished road. [35] In fact, almost everywhere in the colonies, the custom was established of giving away to companies and individuals stretches of territory the size of the German states, land which in this way became permanently alienated from the ownership of the German nation.

### Officialdom Kills the Colonies

The second mistake which Dr. Kayser made was to over-emphasize the official, bureaucratic character of the colonial administration to the neglect of the economic. As we have seen, the colonial office allowed the national economic development of colonies to slip out of its hands through a too liberal concession policy and, hence, centered all its attention and effort upon the machinery of government, the only thing, indeed, which the nation had reserved for itself. This emphasis upon officialdom, or merely upon the political development of the colonies, seems most natural when one recalls Caprivi's attitude toward expansion and his interest in it, which was mainly limited to its value in his foreign policy.

Moreover, friends of colonies, aroused by Caprivi's indifference and by the Anglo-German Treaty of 1890, had worked up their indignation into a national and political grievance, that was not entirely unaided by the deposed national idol, Bismarck, in his retirement. The consequence was, that members of the militarist, imperialist, and monarchist parties, those who worshiped Bismarck, came to the rescue of the colonies, in spite of the "colonial weariness," to save them; they espoused the colonial cause and naturally impressed their character and their interests upon the colonial administration. Thus, the Conservatives and the National Liberals, especially the circles of officialdom, of the army, of rank and of big business ruled the oversea possessions. As a result the colonies abroad suffered from militarism [36] and bureaucracy, from financial mechanics, and from the lack of any sound economic development; while the colonial cause at home became a political and a partisan issue instead of a national affair. In other words, Germany had yet to learn that a successful colonial policy cannot be carried on alone by *Geheimrats,* generals, and capitalists, when the pioneers and settlers are lacking in plantation and forest; that it cannot be merely the sport of politicians in the *Reichstag.* The first colonial director, unfortunately, made the initial mistake of expending the resources of the country upon the creation of an elaborate system of control for the colonies before there was anything there to control. The administrative superstructure was too heavy, too expensive, and too oppressive for the economic structure and was, therefore, doomed to fall of its own weight.

What is more, these *Geheimrats,* generals, and adventurers who composed the colonial personnel were most unpractical: they possessed no experience, no education, no training for colonial service and, indeed, had not won their positions on that basis. Rank, title, gold lace, and uniforms apparently occupied the thoughts of many officials to the exclusion of all else. As a result, they took advantage of their positions to carry on unauthorized military raids against the natives, to indulge in all sorts of unlicensed excesses, and in illegitimate financial adventures which, as in the case of Peters and Schröder, brought the entire colonial policy into disrepute; a disrepute which, together with the "concessions," inflicted a handicap upon Germany's colonial record which demanded time and effort to overcome.

## NOTES

[1] Fabri, F., *Fünf Jahre deutscher Kolonialpolitik* (Gotha, 1889).
See also for the business man's point of view, Schroeder-Poggelow, *Unsere Afrikapolitik in den letzen drei Jahren* (Berlin, 1890). He states, "Bismarck's system is not forceful enough. The business man and the capitalist cannot carry on alone."
See also, *Die Deutsche Kolonialzeitung,* November 9, 1889, for the Petition sent to the *Reichstag* by the *Kolonialverein* asking for the establishment of a colonial office.

[2] See *supra.*, ch. v, p. 138.

[3] For an estimation of his real attitude, see Herrfurth, K., *Fürst Bismarck und die Kolonialpolitik* (Berlin, 1909). He states, "Bismarck einmal aussprach, es sei ihm unmöglich die innersten Falten seines Herzens dem Reichstag fortzusetzen und mit ihm über alle schwebenden Fragen *cartes sur table* zu spielen." p. 100.
Also see, Brodnitz, G., *Bismarcks Nationalökonomische Anschauungen* (Jena, 1902). He states, "Wir halten es nicht für unmöglich dass Bismarck den Geschichtspunkt in unseren Kolonieen neue Absatzgebiete zur erwerben nur deshalb so hervorhob um der Opposition die ganze überseeische Politik annehmen zu machen." p. 76.

[4] *Europäische Geschichtskalender,* 1890, p. 155. The comment of the *Kölnische Zeitung* on Fabri's book was: "It is no longer a question of whether we carry on a colonial policy or not. The greatest enemy of the colonial policy must acknowledge that the colonies are now parts of the empire."

[5] *Verhandlungen des deutschen Reichstages,* Jan. 26, 1889, p. 629 *et seq.*

[6] Zimmermann, *op. cit.,* p. 169ff.

[7] *Das Reichsgesetzblatt,* p. 179.

[8] For the legal and constitutional position of the colonies, which we do not attempt to discuss here, see Florack, F., *Die Schutzgebiete, ihre Organisation in Verfassung und Verwaltung* (Tübingen, 1905).

Hoffmann, H., v., *Einführung in das Kolonialrecht* (Leipzig, 1911).

[9] Speech at a dinner in Harburg, December 12, 1894. *Annual Register,* 1895, p. 269. Dr. Krauel, *Referent* in colonial office was actually the first director but only held office for three months.

[10] Friedjung, H., *Das Zeitalter des Imperialismus* (Berlin, 1919), vol. i, pp. 127-9.

Caprivi even once proposed selling South West Africa.

[11] Speech, May 12, 1890. *Europäische Geschichtskalender,* 1890, p. 70.

[12] See Hammann, O., *The World Policy of Germany* (New York, 1927, trans. by M. Huttman), p. 31ff.

[13] Hertslet, *Map of Africa by Treaty,* vol. ii, pp. 642ff. *Die Grosse Politik,* iv, ch. 29, viii, ch. 51.

[14] William II, *My Memoirs* (New York, 1922, trans. by T. Ybarra), pp. 55-56.

*Norddeutsche Allg. Zt.,* July 30, 1890, also stated in regard to treaty: "The government's endeavor was to preserve and to strengthen the relations between the two states."

[15] *Deutsche Kolonialzeitung,* June 28, 1890.

[16] Resolution adopted by the *Deutsche Kolonialgesellschaft. Die Deutsche Kolonialgesellschaft,* p. 62.

[17] *Verhandlungen des deutschen Reichstages,* 1890, February 5, p. 1351.

[18] *Die Hamburger Nachrichten.*

[19] *Die Grosse Politik,* vol. iv, p. 51 *et seq.,* p. 56 *et seq.,* p. 61 *et seq.*

[20] *Ibid.,* vol. iv, p. 408.

[21] *Ibid.,* vol. iv, p. 59.

[22] *Ibid.,* vol. iv, pp. 414-415.

[23] *Ibid.,* vol. iv, p. 417.

[24] Bismarck, *Gedanken und Erinnerungen,* vol. iii. (Stuttgart and Berlin, 1921), p. 147 *et seq.*

[25] For further confirmation of Bismarck's position in regard to the Anglo-German Treaty, see Penzler, J., *Fürst Bismarck nach seiner Entlassung* (Leipzig, 1897), p. 358. See also, Busch, M., *Some Secret Pages of His History* (New York and London, 1898), vol. ii, p. 547. Bismarck preferred to have Heligoland protected by English neutrality.

[26] Wertheimer, M., *The Pan-German League* (New York, 1924), pp. 25, 37.

[27] Kohl, H., *Bismarcks Jahrbuch,* vol. ii, p. 604.

[28] See *infra,* ch. viii, p. 230 and note.

[29] Zimmermann, *op. cit.,* p. 191.

[30] *Ibid.,* pp. 192-194.

[31] Leutwein, Major, *Elf Jahre Gouverneur* (Berlin, 1906).

[32] For the extent to which the companies gained possession of the col-

onies, see *Soziale Streitfragen,* Heft X, "Staat oder Gesellschaften in unseren Kolonieen."

[33] *Staats-Lexikon* (Freiburg, 1911), pp. 319, 328ff.

[34] Zimmermann, *op. cit.,* p. 213.

[35] *Ibid.,* p. 194.

[36] "There is great complaint against Caprivi for his policy which considers only the political government of the colonies and not their economic or cultural interests. He sends out military bureaucrats who have no understanding of the situation. To the Chancellor, the military activity seems to be the main thing. He seems to think that the officials in the colonies need do nothing but shoot men or lions." *Koloniales Jahrbuch,* 1895.

# CHAPTER VII

## COLONIAL POLICY AND *WELTPOLITIK*

### *The Kaiser Identifies the Colonial Movement with World Power*

AFTER the year 1896, the transition in Germany's position from chief Power in Continental Europe to a prominent world Power became apparent. Two factors were chiefly responsible for this transition: the rapid and astounding economic growth of the nation from poverty to riches, and the Kaiser's ambitious foreign policy known as the "new course."

### *The Industrial Revolution Demands a Commercial Revolution*

In no country did the Industrial Revolution bear such rich and prolific fruits so rapidly as in Germany. As if to compensate for its delay in coming, it began at once to shower a golden harvest which, within the span of a single generation, transformed an agricultural country into the second industrial nation of Europe. Between 1890 and 1910, for instance, Germany's steel industry grew seven times as fast as that of England in production; within forty years her foreign trade increased five times; her rural population sank from constituting sixty-three per cent of her population to thirty-three per cent; while the number of her cities of over one hundred thousand people rose from eight to forty-eight.

Bismarck's achievements of national unity, order, and peace had worked these wonders in Germany's industrial life, which increasingly and insistently demanded a larger scope for its fulfillment: social insurance legislation had protected labor and had rendered it prosperous and efficient before it could fall a victim to the evils of an unrestrained industrialism; early renunciation of *laissez-faire* had saved the country from its inevitable wastes; while the establishment of a strong imperial monarchy had inspired a Hohenzollern with the same enthusiasm for commercial and colonial expansion as had animated a Bourbon or a Tudor in the Golden Age of empire-building oversea. In other words, Germany's Industrial Revolution, instead of proceeding from the Commercial Revolution as had been the case with the Powers on the Atlantic seaboard, itself precipitated a Commercial Revolution by imperiously demanding world markets as an outlet for its giant industries, and by crying aloud for foodstuffs and raw materials wherewith to feed a rapidly growing population and its own insatiable machines. In short, the exact reversal of the economic process which had created modern industrial England and France took place in Germany; like the proverbial cart before the horse, her Commercial Revolution followed instead of preceded her Industrial Revolution.

### The Commercial Revolution in Turn Demands World Power

To facilitate this unusual procedure and to achieve for Germany an adequate position in the colonial field, almost entirely appropriated by the late nineties, was to run counter to the historical evolution of other nations and obviously to meet with many difficulties. In fact, an entrance into world trade and, consequently, into world power could only be

177

effected at this late date by a vigorous policy, to which Bismarck's cautious system of alliances and his safeguarded orientations to the other Powers would have to be sacrificed. But the Kaiser, confident of his own ability and of his young though giant-like nation, did not hesitate to embark upon this "new course," which, in a way, was forced upon him by the exigencies of Germany's economic life. He departed from Bismarck's safe system of the constant subordination of colonial expansion to foreign policy and, instead, he allowed his territorial ambitions to dominate those foreign relations. And, in so doing, he no longer confined himself to the economic motive for colonial acquisition which Bismarck and German tradition had so well established, but closely identified these acquisitions with political ends. And, because there remained at the end of the nineteenth century, so little unclaimed territory on the earth to be appropriated, the "new course" led the German colonial movement into that most modern expression of expansion, the securing of economic concessions and spheres of influence in already occupied territory—in a word, into economic imperialism.

### The Kaiser Applies the "New Course" to Colonial Policy

The "new course" in colonial policy was foreshadowed immediately upon the accession of William II, although it was not definitely adopted until after the retirement of Caprivi, who thoroughly believed in Bismarck's conviction that Germany was satiated, and who placed safety and defense before expansion. His Chancellor's attitude, therefore, and his own absorption with the navy restrained the Kaiser from any action in the colonial field for about five years. Always, however, he had shown himself sympathetic to the colonial movement even before coming to the throne, and he lost no time in specifically defining that sympathy when he took the reins of government into his own hands. As he himself tells us in his *Memoirs*, "Bismarck did not realize that his acquisition of colonies would oblige him to look beyond Europe and automatically force him to act politically, on a large scale, particularly in relation to England. The Foreign Office under Bismarck was too much concerned with the interplay of continental politics, had not sufficient interest in a navy, in England or in colonies, and possessed no experience in world politics. . . . England's psychology as shown in her constant although concealed pursuit of world hegemony was to the German Foreign Office a book sealed with seven seals." [1]

And that William II intended to break the "seven seals" one after another was only too evident. "The German empire has developed into a world empire," he declared to the Colonial Society upon the twenty-fifth anniversary of the Proclamation of a United Germany at Versailles in 1871, "and it is your duty, Gentlemen, to help me bind this great empire to the Fatherland." [2] "Colonial policy is only a branch of world policy which the German empire must follow for the protection of its continental position. The time of Germany's philistinism is over when she was oblivious to whatever went on in the world." Consequently, we find the Kaiser placing himself at the head of the colonial movement as a branch of his world policy, and making it the object of his assiduous care. [3] For he regarded the colonies as a means to an end and not as an end in themselves. Unlike Caprivi, who merely accepted the colonies because they were already there and employed them to promote his political aims in maintaining the hegemony of Germany in Europe, the Kaiser strove to acquire more colonial possessions in order to transform Germany's European hegemony into world power. In short, he saw in the further acquisition of oversea territories so many levers to be manipulated as a means of securing for the Fatherland the position in world affairs which his ambition desired her to occupy.[4]

### His Ministers Endorse the "New Course"

To realize such a purpose, the Kaiser took pains to surround himself with ministers who, unlike Bismarck and Caprivi, heartily endorsed his point of view. His new Chancellor, Prince Hohenlohe, appointed in 1894, was merely his agent, for the prince's advanced age and gentleness of character precluded any opposition whatsoever, and William II was virtually his own Chancellor until 1900. The aged prince was merely an echo of his royal master when he asserted in the *Reichstag* at the beginning of his régime: "The support of our colonial possessions is a command of national honor and a manifestation of our national prestige." [5]

But affording a stronger support to the new policy than mere acquiescence was Baron von Holstein. He had been head of the political department of the Foreign Office under Bismarck and had continued in his position at the Kaiser's request mainly because he had become a deadly enemy of his former master. As such, he was determined upon a reversal of the latter's policy, not only as a matter of conviction, but also as a means of personal revenge to prevent his or his son's, Herbert Bismarck, return to power. A man of strong intellectual attainments and of great political experience, von Holstein lacked, however, the cosmopolitan knowledge and the world outlook of the great Chancellor. He considered the acquisition of territory, as a means of increasing Germany's prestige, a matter of paramount importance and made it a cardinal aim of his policy which was, in the last analysis, *Machtpolitik.* This man, although not directly concerned with the management of the foreign policy, yet exercised a subtle and sinister effect upon it through the uncanny influence which he wielded over his associates in the Foreign Office; an effect which coincided with the ambitions of his royal master for at least ten years and persisted until his resignation in the year 1906.[6]

One of the votaries of von Holstein, and an apt learner of his expansion gospel, was Marschall von Bieberstein, chosen to succeed Herbert Bismarck as Foreign Secretary. This "State's Attorney" from Baden, as Bismarck had contemptuously dubbed him, was inexperienced politically, and utterly devoid at the outset of any familiarity with the world situation or of Germany's relation to it. An ardent admirer of von Holstein, he became an enthusiastic convert to the doctrine of world power, and a hater of England as an obstacle to Germany's colonial expansion. He admirably demonstrated this conviction in his speech to the *Reichstag,* February 13, 1896, in regard to the protection of German rights in South Africa, a speech which the *Kolonialgesellschaft* reprinted in a supplement to the *Kolonialzeitung* as evidence that the Foreign Secretary saw eye to eye with it upon the question of colonial policy.[7] Thoroughly imbued with the principles of the "new course," von Bieberstein accepted its doctrine of territorial expansion as a German imperative. Thus equipped, he entered upon the ambassadorship to the Sublime Porte in 1897, where his remarkable success in *Weltpolitik* demonstrated, as we later shall observe, the extraordinary effectiveness of his training.

Succeeding von Bieberstein as Foreign Secretary in 1897 was the famous von Bülow, who completes the group in the Foreign Office mainly responsible with the Kaiser for the identification of colonial policy with the struggle for world power. As Chancellor (in 1900), von Bülow's influence upon Germany's foreign affairs is too well known to bear repetition here. Merely a quotation from his speech introducing the first great navy bill of 1897, will suffice to indicate the acceleration which he lent to the "new course" as applied to the colonial movement. He declared: "The times are past when Germany left the earth to one of her neighbors, the sea to another and reserved heaven, where pure reason is enthroned, for herself. . . . We wish no one to be in the shadow but we also demand a Place in the Sun."[8]

## Popular Support Encourages the Kaiser

Besides the support of his own ambitions and of those advisers surrounding him, who agreed upon a forward movement in the colonial policy, the Kaiser had also the encouragement of big business, of the colonial party, of the Navy League and of the Pan-German League. It will be recalled that the latter had been organized as a protest against the Zanzibar Treaty of 1890, and that it had designated in its constitution "the promotion of an active colonial policy" as one of its aims. Consequently, it concentrated a large part of its energies upon the actual extension of the colonial empire, and never failed to arouse public opinion nor to incite the government to more vigorous action whenever any opportunity to acquire a territorial acquisition arose.[9]

With such cooperation from official and popular circles, it was to be expected that administrative promotion of colonial policy, both in its external and internal aspects, would characterize the years from 1895 to 1906: on the one hand, there ensued a feverish activity in the acquisition of colonies and spheres of influence abroad; and, on the other, there appeared a determined subordination of colonial government to the ends and aims of Germany's position in world affairs, a subject to be discussed in the following chapter.

### Germany Asserts Herself in Colonial Affairs

As a sort of prelude to actual annexations Germany began boldly to assert herself in regard to questions of oversea territories in an attempt to be treated as an equal. As if to gain self-confidence for active participation in world politics, the Foreign Office commenced to act with a bluntness, especially toward England, which marked a decided break with the Bismarckian tradition of cautious diplomacy and which was, after all, but a reflection of that childish bluster and bad manners which characterized the Kaiser's entire foreign policy between the years 1895 and 1905.

Nowhere was this new attitude more evident than in Africa, although clashes in Samoa and in the South Seas were not lacking. For the adoption of world policy, naturally, brought Germany's and England's aims into conflict, as the Kaiser meant that it should. The Anglo-German "honeymoon," so felicitously arranged by Bismarck, was at an end and the treaty of 1893, which gave Germany the right of way to Lake Chad and to the Chari in Kamerun, marked the conclusion of amicable Anglo-German relations for some years. Points of antagonism inevitably and continually arising were not smoothed over as formerly but were magnified: Great Britain indirectly favored the native revolt in South West Africa, and objected to Germany unloading arms in Walfisch Bay; Germany refused to see England's difficulties in Egypt and formally protested, with ultimate success, against the Anglo-Belgian Treaty of 1894, whereby England exchanged a piece of the Soudan, in defiance of the Congo Act, for a strip of the Congo between

Lake Tanganyika and Lake Albert Nyanza, which would have restored the connection between South Africa and Uganda.[10] In 1893, Hatzfeldt in London was instructed to tell Lord Rosebery that "Germany would feel obliged to exercise greater reserve in her general attitude toward England unless she adopted a different attitude toward Germany's colonial interests," [11] and in 1894, he intimated that "advocacy of England's interests must not be expected of us any longer."

### The Kaiser Attempts a Boer Protectorate

The outstanding example of this changed and defiant attitude of Germany is her well-known and open support of the Boers against England, throughout the years 1895-1896, which consisted in sending warships to Delagoa Bay, protests against Jameson's activities, and finally culminated in the famous Kruger telegram, congratulating President Kruger on "preserving the independence of his country." [12] Indeed, if the interpretation of the Kruger telegram sustained by recent revelations be accepted, we now know that something more even than support of the Boers lay behind that dispatch; that the telegram was, in effect, an indication of the Kaiser's real wish to land troops and to bring about an annexation of territory. For the following entry was made by Foreign Secretary Marschall von Bieberstein in his diary on the day on which the Kruger telegram was sent: "January 3rd, 1896. At 10 o'clock conference with H.M. H.M. unfolded somewhat astonishing projects. A protectorate over the Transvaal, but I talked him out of that at once. Mobilization of the Marine Infantry. The dispatch of troops to the Transvaal. And upon the Chancellor's objection: 'That would mean war with England,' H.M. replied, 'Yes, but only on land.' Then it was resolved to send Scheele (governor of German East Africa) to the Transvaal to reconnoiter. Also an unfortunate idea. Finally, H.M., at my suggestion,[13] sent a congratulatory dispatch to President Kruger." This significant entry would seem to show that the Kruger telegram, always considered to be the climax of the Kaiser's hostility toward England in South Africa at this particular time, was, after all, the least of other evils. What the Kaiser really desired was something far in excess of a mere congratulation. "The telegram was the way out of a dilemma, an emergency exit." [14]

As further confirmation of the Kaiser's ambitions in South Africa is his attempt, three days after the sending of the Kruger telegram, again to carry out his plan of establishing a German protectorate over the Transvaal by landing troops in Delagoa Bay, and by taking possession of the Portuguese port of Lorenço Marques. On January 16, 1897, he wired this proposal to the Chancellor, who endeavored, successfully, to prevent his action by pointing out "with no unrestrained language," in a return telegram, that "isolated Germany cannot go to war with Great Britain." At the top of his document, the Kaiser wrote, "I differ but acquiesce," and at the end, "The forfeiture or non-acquisition of Delagoa Bay will have to be heavily paid for in the future, and we shall some day deeply regret it." [15]

Marschall's restraining influence upon the Kaiser, which he further confirmed by advising Kruger to adopt similar moderation, was doubtless due to the failure of the German Foreign Office, first, to induce England to join the Triple Alliance by treaty, and thus undertake definite obligations in regard to the furthering of Germany's colonial interests;[16] and second, to its failure to form a bloc of continental Powers against England. For, both in October and December, 1895, the Kaiser asked England to join the

185

Triple Alliance under threat of opposition by the other Powers, a proposal which England ignored. As a result, the Kaiser directed notes to the embassies of Italy, France, and Russia December 20, 1895, proposing the organization of a continental bloc against England.[17] But again he met with failure: Italy felt itself master of the situation; France dropped the suggestion but communicated it to England; and Russia replied that Germany was attending to European interests in the Transvaal. Although Germany's efforts bore no result, they are significant of her willingness to subordinate her European alliances to her colonial policy, which was the direct opposite of Bismarck's procedure and highly indicative of the "new course," *Weltpolitik*.

### Germany Achieves a Naval Base in the Far East

But there were other areas of the world where the Kaiser could pursue what is sometimes referred to as his "hysterical expansionism," unhampered by England's actual occupation, and hence by the restraining hand of his more diplomatic ministers. Indeed, after 1897, we see the beginning of the "storm and stress" period of German colonial policy. The Kaiser's mania for acquiring new colonies, no matter whether they had any value or what international complications they might entail, grew from day to day. Germany had made no additions to her oversea territories for more than a decade, so she grasped every opportunity presented by the kaleidoscope of world affairs to seize even the smallest island or the slightest economic concession.

In one instance, at least, strategic points of seizure were studied out beforehand by experts with true German thoroughness. For a long time the project of securing a naval base in the Far East to protect German commercial interests had been discussed in both naval and colonial circles. As early as the first years of the empire, Dettering, the customs commissioner in China, had proposed that a foothold be acquired there,[18] and Bremen merchants had urged that Saigon, belonging to France, be acquired by the Treaty of Frankfort;[19] but Bismarck had flatly refused. Now, in 1897, when Germany was rapidly building a navy, and extending her economic and political interests in the East, the question was revived. But the circumstance which made it particularly urgent was the fact that Germany, a participator in the East Asiatic Triple Alliance, had emerged therefrom, unlike her partners, empty-handed except for two meager commercial concessions, one at Tien-Tsin and the other at Hankow.

Consequently, Richtenhofer, the geographer, and von Tirpitz, the admiral, were commissioned to seek for an ice-free port; one which would at the same time give access to a useful hinterland and would avoid any conflict with Russia.[20] Many letters passed between the Foreign Office and the ministry of marine until, finally, the choice fell upon Kiao-Chow on the Shantung Peninsula.[21] Fortunately for the Kaiser's plans, two Catholic missionaries were opportunely murdered by the Chinese in this very Shantung province. The incident provided the Kaiser with an excuse for his longed-for seizure—how keenly desired, only his telegram to the Foreign Office can adequately illustrate. "We must take advantage of this excellent opportunity before another great Power either dismembers China or comes to her help! Now or never!"[22] And he immediately dispatched Prince Henry of Prussia with a squadron, "to make clear to the Europeans in China, to the German merchants and, above all, to China herself that the German Michael has planted his shield firmly in the soil."[23]

As was fitting to the new international relationship established by the Triple Alliance in China, Russia's consent had first been asked for this important move. It was obtained mainly through the informal and casual conversations and correspondence of the Kaiser with the Tsar, for the Russian Foreign Secretary was inclined to place difficulties in Germany's way, since Russia had her eye on Tsingtao, a port on the south coast of the Shantung Peninsula and could, moreover, claim the right of prior anchorage in the harbor of Kiao-Chow, the Russian squadron having wintered there. The Tsar was quite willing to waive this rather insecure claim, however, on the understanding that Russia have Port Arthur instead. How fully in accord were Russia and Germany on this spoliation of China may be judged from the following telegram sent by "Willy" to "Nicky" on December 19, 1897:

> Best thanks for kind wishes for Henry. Please accept my congratulations at the arrival of your squadron at Port Arthur. [It had gone there for the winter.] Russia and Germany at the entrance to the Yellow Sea may be taken as represented by St. George and St. Michael shielding the Holy Cross in the Far East and guarding the gates of the Continent of Asia.—Willy.[24]

To shield the Holy Cross and guard the gates of the Asiatic continent more effectually, the Kaiser proceeded to negotiate a treaty with China, consummated in March, 1898, whereby Germany leased the shores of the Kiao-Chow Bay—about 200 square miles—for 99 years with the right to fortify and to administer the leased territory as if it were hers, to build two railways into the interior to join the projected Chinese system, to exploit the mines found near the railways, and to enjoy special preference for German capital and materials on public works in Shantung. Germany had acquired much more than a naval base; she had gained an economic sphere of influence,[25] although it was primarily chosen for its political and strategic value.[26] "Without a foothold in eastern Asia," explained Marschall, "we should be in the air alike on the economic, maritime, and political plane"; but it seemed to have escaped both him and his royal master that the "foothold" had been secured at the cost of Great Britain's increased hostility, of France's suspicion, and of the indignation of the rising Far Eastern Power, Japan.

### An Anglo-German Treaty Gambles on the Portuguese Colonies

Earlier in the same year, 1898, an unexpected change in British diplomacy afforded the Kaiser one more opportunity to identify colonial acquisitions with his world policy in still another area, and definitely to acquire further holdings —or rather the prospect of them. For, in 1898, Great Britain found herself hard-pressed by the serious and unremitting opposition to her imperial ambitions exerted by France in Africa, by Russia in Asia and, now apparently, by Germany also in the Far East. As a result, she finally turned to Germany as a last resort since Germany was, after all, the strongest military Power in Europe. Besides, it will be recalled, Germany had been angling some time for an English alliance. Even after Great Britain's disregard of her offers to tie up to the Triple Alliance in 1895-1896, Germany had kept the way open by casual and discreet suggestions of cooperation, especially in colonial affairs,[27] which von Bülow, the successor to Marschall as Foreign Secretary in 1897, continued as he considered an English alliance "an aim which we must never lose sight of."

To Chamberlain's direct proposal, therefore, that if Germany stood by England, England was ready to support her if she were attacked, von Bülow responded with a caution induced by the fear of injuring Russo-German relations; a caution that was transformed into a suspicion when he heard of the correspondence of the Tsar and the Kaiser, which revealed that England had already similarly approached Russia.[28] The Kaiser also was skeptical and for the same reason. "The Franco-Russian Alliance would become much closer if we identify ourselves with England."[29] But, at the same time he approved of not letting England's offer of an alliance go altogether, because "a friendly England gives us a spare card against Russia, and, besides there is a prospect of our acquiring colonial and commercial treaties with England."

And so events proved. A request from Portugal for a loan provided for a *rapprochement* between England and Germany over the disposal of the Portuguese colonies, for Portugal was in a bad way financially, and was obliged to mortgage her colonies in order to secure financial assistance. This *rapprochement,* moreover, suited the more experienced Salisbury much more than the alliance which he had always opposed, for he saw in it an opportunity to purchase immunity from German interference in the Boer region, without the inconveniences of a binding political agreement. Consequently on August 30, 1898, an Anglo-German Treaty was consummated which provided for the division of the Portuguese colonies of Angola and Mozambique into spheres of influence between Germany and England, should Portugal become insolvent and offer her colonies as collateral for a loan, which she seemed to be on the point of doing. In the event of the treaty taking effect, England's share of Angola reserved to her the much disputed Delagoa Bay with the harbor of Lorenço Marques, which would put an end forever to the Kaiser's ambition, as revealed in the Kruger telegram, to effect a Boer protectorate. Germany's share, on the other hand, secured to her southern Angola, northern Mozambique, and Portuguese Timor in the South Seas.[30]

How far short Germany's promised share of the bargain fell of her desires may be gauged by the list of coveted territories submitted to England, during the negotiations in July and August of 1898. It included: in West Africa, Walfisch Bay, the island of Fernando Po, Angola, a naval base on the Canary or the Cape Verde Islands, and the extension of Togoland to the Volta River as the boundary line between it and the Gold Coast; in East Africa, Zanzibar with the island of Pemba, and the extension of East Africa southwest to the Zambesi and the Schire rivers as boundary lines; in Asia, the Portuguese island of Timor, the Sulu Archipelago and at least one of the Philippines (Mundanaro); in the South Seas, the Caroline and Samoa Islands.[31] This list also indicates how fast Germany's appetite for colonies was increasing since her transition to world power, as did likewise the Kaiser's temperamental outburst, during a hitch in the proceedings, when he declared that Germany required a colonial empire, and that she meant to develop one with or without Great Britain.

But, in any case, England got the best of the bargain, for unknown to Germany she practically nullified the Treaty of 1898 by the so-called Treaty of Windsor with Portugal negotiated the following year.[32] This treaty confirmed earlier treaties by which England and Portugal, always friendly, had bound themselves mutually to protect each other's possessions, and, without contradicting the Anglo-German agreement in letter, it destroyed it in spirit, for it encouraged the Portuguese to avoid so encumbering their colonies with loans that they would be forced to sell; and, of course it was only their willingness to sell or failure to meet the loan obligations that would bring the Anglo-German agreement into operation.

About the only gain accruing to Germany, as a result of the Anglo-German understanding, was that Great Britain could not independently acquire economic or political privileges and rights in the Portuguese colonies bordering upon Germany's possessions. Even the apparent cooperation which the treaty implied was only a hollow semblance after all, vitiated as it was by the so-called Treaty of Windsor, a semblance which became more and more apparent as the Kaiser sought to satisfy his colonial aspirations in other areas. Indeed, the very fact that England sought to nullify the Anglo-German understanding is indicative of the mistrust which the Kaiser was sowing in his drive for world power.

## High Hopes in the South Pacific

For the acquisition of one naval base in the Pacific, Kiao-Chow had only whetted Germany's appetite for more, and she naturally turned to the South Pacific, where she had already laid substantial foundations for occupancy. Since the eighteen seventies, the German government had recognized the strategic importance of this area, especially in relation to the Panama Canal and, as we have seen, had neglected few opportunities to subsidize and strengthen the position there of German merchants and traders. Now, in 1898, the outbreak of the Spanish-American War suddenly projected the whole region into the limelight, and also afforded the Kaiser the necessary troubled waters in which to fish for colonies.

Indeed, on May 11, 1898, a veritable fishing rod was placed in the Kaiser's hand by Prince Henry of Prussia, then in command of the Asiatic squadron. He cabled from

Hong Kong that the Filipinos had decided upon a rebellion, and that they "would gladly place themselves under the protection of a European Power, especially Germany."[33] This the prince had from a reliable German merchant from Manila. The ensuing correspondence between the German ambassadors in China and the Philippines and the Foreign Office, between von Bülow and the Kaiser shows that, at first, the idea of establishing a German protectorate over the Philippines was seriously considered, but ultimately rejected because of Germany's naval weakness, of the menace of the other Powers, and because of the danger of supporting revolution against the "principle of legitimacy." Rather, the Kaiser and von Bülow agreed, it would be better for German colonial interests in the long run to neutralize the islands for the present until the aspirations of the United States therein as well as the attitude of Great Britain—thereto—could be more definitely ascertained; failing neutralization, however, they were both determined to demand adequate compensations for Germany, should the islands fall into the hands of another Power.[34] Consequently, Admiral von Diederichs was dispatched to Philippine waters with a large squadron ostensibly to protect German lives and property—that time-worn subterfuge—but actually to be on the spot to watch developments, to take advantage of any unexpected turn of affairs or, at least, to grab a naval station if the estates of Spain were suddenly liquidated; and, at the same time, Ambassador Hatzfeldt in London was instructed to sound the British government on its attitude toward neutralization.

The outburst of anti-German feeling in the American press, occasioned by the well-known friction which ensued between Admiral von Diederichs[35] and Admiral Dewey in Manila Bay, not unencouraged by the British,[36] served to demonstrate that the United States was determined to annex the Philippines and that Great Britain would support her. These facts, added to the failure of the neutralization plans, apparently convinced the German Foreign Office that its only course was to demand a division of the colonial spoils in cooperation with, rather than in antagonism to the powerful American Republic. As a result, Germany proposed to the United States a colonial deal: Germany to secure Samoa, the Caroline Islands, and naval stations in the Philippines in return for German support of American occupation. In fine, the German ambassador in Washington, von Holleben, was ordered to drop the suggestion that, if properly compensated with "coaling stations, maritime *fulcra,* and the like, Germany was in a position to be of much greater assistance to the United States than was England." And his orders began with the significant words, "His Majesty, the Emperor, deems it a principal object of German policy to leave unused no opportunity which may arise from the Spanish-American War to obtain maritime *fulcra* in East Asia. . . . It would, therefore, be of practical use for America, in case she considers territorial expansion, to assure herself of the friendly attitude of Germany by the practical application of 'live and let live'." Hatzfeldt was instructed to make the same suggestion to the American ambassador in London and, on July 9, Ambassador Andrew D. White in Berlin was approached.[37] The argument was strongly urged that Germany should receive some reward for her neutrality in the Spanish-American War, and her rejection of all opportunities to become the leader of a European intervention against the United States in order to preserve the monarchial principle. Although, at first, extremely hospitable if not encouraging to the German proposals,[38] White, upon receiving advices from home, postponed the whole discussion of colonial settlements until peace had been effected between the United States and Spain.

Germany, however, even though thoroughly convinced of the wisdom of not further arousing the ill-will of the United States for the ultimate success of her annexation plans, had too strong an appetite for colonies to allow the matter to drop and so turned to Spain. The ambassador at Madrid was instructed to inquire Spain's plans for the Philippines, the Sulus, the Carolines, and other South Sea islands, as well as for the Canaries and Fernando Po; and to concentrate on the acquisition of the Ladrones and Carolines, after the fate of the Philippines was learned from the Spanish-American Peace Protocol of August 13, 1898. Due to German persistence, therefore, and despite Spain's reluctance to settle anything before the conclusion of final peace with America, a lien upon the islands of Kusaie, Ponape, and Yap of the Caroline group was secured by a secret provisional agreement of September 10, 1898, according to which Spain promised to sell them to Germany, subject to the decisions of the Spanish-American Treaty and, in addition, "to grant Germany favorable consideration in any future disposal of Spanish insular possessions." [39]

Nor did the German Foreign Office cease for one instant to persist in the realization of its lien upon these islands; for it bent all its diplomatic efforts both to retain them and yet not to antagonize the United States. Thus it entered a formal protest when the United States, in her negotiations with Spain expressed a desire for the island of Kusaie (Strong Island) in the Caroline group as a cable station, claiming that American occupation there would prove strategically dangerous to Germany.[40] Yet, at the same time, in order to avoid any appearance of aggressiveness, the

Foreign Office informed Reid, who was negotiating the Spanish-American Treaty at Paris, that Germany would waive her claim to the Sulu Islands, although next to Spain she had the strongest claim to them, if the United States in turn would award her a naval station on one of them, and put no obstacle in the way of her acquiring all the Caroline group, the Pelew, and Marianne Islands, except Guam.[41] While these negotiations were being discussed backward and forward, Germany, as a measure of precaution, signed a second provisional treaty with Spain on December 10, 1898, by which Spain agreed to sell not only all the Carolines, but also all the Pelews and Mariannes (except Guam).[42] With another conciliatory gesture to the United States, Germany revealed the bargain and asked for official assurance of non-interference. This she received, but not without a reproach from Secretary Hay for her protest in regard to Kusaie and her secret arrangements with Spain.[43] Although plainly offended, she nevertheless restrained herself and allowed the United States to occupy Wake Island, in spite of her contention that it was one of the Marshall group.

Finally, the completion of the Spanish-American Treaty terminated this anxious diplomacy and the German-Spanish Treaty, based upon the two previous provisional agreements, gave Germany in return for $4,200,000 sole possession of the Caroline, Pelew, and Marianne Islands (except Guam), together with the right of first option in case Spain decided to dispose of Fernando Po.[44] The United States had not acquired a cable station in the Carolines, nor had Germany gained a coaling station in the Sulus, which went entirely to the United States, who also retained Wake Island. With her new possessions, Germany added a host of small coral islets and lagoon islands to her colonial empire. Thus the Kaiser's desire for naval stations and cable landings—

strategic footholds in the game of *Weltpolitik*—had been secured, but nothing of economic value.

Indeed, the entire negotiations incident to the Spanish-American War confirmed the general trend of Germany's colonial policy toward world power: first, the unswerving persistency in her effort to secure the "maritime *fulcra*," whose success was described by von Bülow when he presented the Spanish treaty to the *Reichstag* by the words: "Now Germany's possessions in the South Seas are complete and this treaty together with the one with China regarding Kiao-Chow are milestones along the same road, the road of *Weltpolitik*";[45] and second, the disregard of her relations to her European neighbors, especially England. Certainly, Germany's diplomacy during the Spanish-American War affords another striking example of her oftentimes reckless course of subordinating her European policy to her colonial expansion. For when it became apparent that Germany's attitude was alienating American good-will,[46] thus throwing that powerful state on the side of Great Britain against her and decreasing her chances of colonial gains, the German Foreign Office adopted (after July, 1898) a policy of studied concession toward the United States in order to detach her from England. In fact, it definitely offered Germany's support in place of England's; and from July, 1898 until the conclusion of the Spanish-American Treaty endeavored earnestly, as we have seen, to harmonize Germany's appetite for territorial acquisition with America's annexationist plans and aims. As the Kaiser expressed it, when he restrained von Bülow from sending a German warship to the Caroline Islands when their disposition was uncertain, "It is the task of diplomacy to avoid difficulties and misunderstandings with the United States so long as that is compatible with the dignity of the empire." [47]

But while this policy met with success, as we have seen, in achieving Germany's colonial objects, it wrought havoc in her relationship to England: it interfered with Great Britain's plans of an Anglo-American alliance; [48] it accentuated their colonial rivalries and definitely incited Great Britain to attempt to block Germany in the Pacific. There would seem to exist little doubt that the whole affair contributed generously to the fast-growing feeling of competition and cross purpose in the colonial field in general, and to the immediately ensuing difficulties of adjusting Anglo-German claims in Samoa in particular.

## The Samoan Islands are Apportioned with Diplomatic Difficulty

Less disappointing to Germany, than the Anglo-German Treaty of 1898 proved to be were the results of the new Anglo-German accord of 1899 in Samoa, whose consummation was but another indication of Great Britain's desire to accommodate the strongest military power in Europe. The tripartite condominium [49] arranged by Bismarck in 1879, under which Samoa had been living in anything but a peaceful manner, had come to grief upon the death of King Malitoa, with whom the treaty had been made. Rival claimants disputed the throne: Malitoa's son, Tana, secured the support of England and the United States, thrown more closely together because of Germany's attitude in the Spanish-American War; while Mataafa, returning from exile on a German warship, gained the assistance of Germany. Realizing that such a divided rule, which was nothing but anarchy, was leading to native civil war and to serious disagreement among themselves, the three Powers were forced to seek another solution.

The negotiations concerning it dragged on for over a year,

198

so complicated were they by all kinds of conflicting influences: the British and American community of interest on the one hand, and England's need of Germany's good-will on the other; Germany's sentimental attachment to Samoa as the scene of her first colonial ventures, and Australia's antagonism to any increase of Germany's power in the South Pacific; America's desire to maintain Samoan independence, and Germany's and England's desire to subordinate Samoa to their commercial interests; and, finally, the Kaiser's deep dislike of Salisbury, which was shared by von Holstein, and his childish grievance at not having been invited to his grandmother's birthday party! [50]   Out of this tangled situation two solutions emerged: Germany to cede her interests in the islands to England in return for compensations elsewhere; or England to cede the chief island, Opolu, to Germany, receiving in turn compensation from Germany's other islands in the neighborhood.

Compensations for Germany were favored by the majority of the *Kolonialrat* (colonial council) and a tentative settlement on that basis was reached.   Germany was to transfer her rights in Samoa to England in return for the Solomon Islands and a portion of the Gold Coast.   But von Bülow and the Kaiser were influenced by the opposition of von Tirpitz, who foresaw the growing strategic importance of Samoa.[51]   The admiral succeeded in arousing a strong public opinion in Germany against the settlement.   He argued that Samoa was German and must remain so, although, as a matter of fact, most people in Germany did not know whether Samoa was "fish, fowl or foreign queen." Consequently, the decision was rejected.   Fortunately for Germany, however, the sudden outbreak of the Boer War enabled her to assume a stronger tone toward Britain so that she reversed the arrangement.   By the final treaty of

November 1899, Germany received the islands of Opolu and Sawai; the United States the islands of Tutuila; while England secured as compensation the Tonga Islands, the larger part of the Solomon group, a rectification of the boundary of the *Hinterland* of Togoland and Germany's renunciation of extra-territoriality in Zanzibar.[52]

The negotiations over the treaty had been extremely difficult, and they left scars of ill-feeling in Anglo-German relations which were slow to heal. At one stage Germany threatened to break off diplomatic relations and only Salisbury's shrewd diplomacy, which knew how to avoid a quarrel by the tactics of delay, prevented a break.[53] Doubtless, also, the friendly relations established meanwhile between the Kaiser and Cecil Rhodes had much to do with the peaceful termination of the Samoan difficulty, as it proved, to Germany's advantage. For, at the suggestion of von Liebert, the governor of East Africa, Rhodes had visited Berlin in March 1899, for the purpose of exchanging ideas with the German government regarding his plans for the promotion of the Cape to Cairo railroad. The Kaiser and von Bülow, evidently considering that it would be better for German interests to cooperate with the scheme than to oppose it, received him cordially and pledged their country's support in return for his promise to use German materials on the railroad where it crossed German territory, to employ only German signalmen, and to build a line within the German boundaries to Tabara. Rhodes then asked permission to construct a cable through German territory, a project strongly supported by Dr. Scharlach of Hamburg, who had attempted to do so in 1893. The Kaiser and his Foreign Secretary granted the privilege with the proviso that the stations on German soil be under German control. They then took advantage of the occasion, made so propitious by such harmonious negotiations, to invoke Rhodes' influence on **Germany's** behalf in Samoa, which, in return for his friendly reception in Berlin, the latter proceeded to use. "Your emperor was very good to me," Rhodes wrote to a German friend, "I shall not alter my determination to work with the German colonies in Africa." [54] Thus did economic cooperation facilitate political agreement.

The determining factor, however, in England's capitulation in Samoa was her isolation. She could not afford to alienate Germany, who was becoming ever more menacing on the sea, and for that reason was obliged to submit to the Kaiser's rudeness, peevishness, and childish blustering. When he recklessly threatened that cooperation with England in international politics was only possible if Samoa was secured, and that he would not go to England as long as Lord Salisbury was in power, England gave way and even apologized for not inviting him to the queen's eightieth birthday celebration.[54a] So far had the desire for colonial gains advanced Germany on the road of world power, an advance, however, not unattended by British ill-will.

### *Restrained Ambitions in the New World*

Nor did the New World along with Asia, Africa, and the Pacific escape the effects of the Kaiser's strenuous prosecution of a colonial policy for the sake of world power, although here it would appear that Germany's activities were by no means so great, as it has hitherto been the custom to represent them.

A former chapter has described the success and failure—mostly the failure—of German colonial schemes in North and South America prior to 1860. Also, the flood of emigration to the New World, which characterized the middle of the nineteenth century and the first two decades of the empire, has been mentioned. For, despite the Prussian rescript of 1859, German emigration principally to Brazil and Argentina continued to increase and, as we have noted, influenced considerably the colonial movement of the eighties. By the year 1896, there were some 400,000 Germans settled in Latin America scattered throughout Mexico, Guatemala, Venezuela, Brazil, and Chile; German investments had reached about half a billion dollars; while German ships were carrying a goodly amount of South American commerce and German trade amounted to some $146,000,-000.[55] All of this activity was initiated by individual effort although the government, consonant with its policy followed since 1871, assisted by negotiating commercial treaties and by protecting and supporting mercantile and financial interests. Prior to 1896, however, there seems to have been no conscious administrative colonial policy of aggression in Latin America; indeed, the Prussian rescript upon emigration remained in force until that year.

The Spanish-American War, of course, attracted both popular and official attention to the colonial potentialities of the New World, as was only natural in this era of *Weltpolitik*. In fact, so great was Germany's interest in Latin America, and so aggressive her designs upon it purported to be, that her attitude assumed in the eyes of even responsible Americans the proportions of a "conspiracy," best described by Thayer in his *Life of John Hay* under the chapter caption, "The German Menace Looms Up."[56] In 1901, even the American Secretary of State made a statement about the "menace" of Germany in South America, emphasized by a speech by Senator Lodge declaring the Monroe Doctrine to be threatened, both of which occasioned wild excitement.[57] All sorts of rumors about Germany's designs were afloat: in 1901-1902 it was declared that the Kaiser was negotiating with Mexico to acquire a strip of territory along the coast of the Lower California peninsula including two good harbors;[58] in the same year there was a persistent story that Germany was looking for a coaling station on the Caribbean Sea, the island of Margarita off Venezuela;[59] suspicions of the Kaiser's influence in the Caribbean were very lively in 1905, and the report that the Hamburg-American Company was about to establish a coaling station on the island of St. Thomas threw Senator Lodge into a panic.[60] Moreover, the South American states shared the general alarm concretely expressed by Senator Barbosa in the Rio Congress in 1903 and by the Rio press.[61]

Sifting this alleged "plot" of Germany to acquire colonial territory in Latin America, we are forced, through lack of confirmatory evidence, to the conclusion that the rumors regarding it were due rather to the extravagant expressions and noisy activities of the colonialists, Pan-Germans, and naval circles in Germany rather than to any official action or policy on the part of the government. For, at the time of the Spanish-American War, and immediately afterward, many articles appeared from the pens of the colonial enthusiasts, urging territorial acquisition in South America and defiance of the Monroe Doctrine; while, as we have observed, the tenor of the German press was violently anti-American.[62] Books and articles, such as those of Professor Unold of Munich, Wintzer, Sievers, Wangemann, Leyser, and Professor Arnold of Jena, admonished the German people that, "they were marked to be the teachers and the economic and political leaders of Spanish and Portuguese Americans";[63] that, "here in southern Brazil, a glorious future awaits us";[64] and that, "German emigration should not be directed to South America unless the question whether Germany means simply to obey the American order of hands off in South America is first answered in the negative." [65] So widespread were these ideas in Germany, that Mr. Jackson of the American embassy in Berlin wrote to the home government in 1897 that in his opinion, "Germany is opposed to any international recognition of the Monroe Doctrine," because she "expects to benefit from the anticipated breaking up of the United States of Brazil." [66]

At the same time, German individual enterprise was conspicuously active in the New World between the years 1900-1903: three extensive exploratory expeditions were carried on in Brazil; German merchants were pushing the Rio Grande-Northwestern Railway; the Hansa merchants purchased all the ships of the Brazilian Lloyd; and by the year 1903, German trade had reached third place in Brazil, Argentina, and Uruguay. [67]

On the other hand, there is no evidence as yet to prove that the German government ever instigated these activities, or had any designs of territorial conquest; while there is considerable evidence to show that it limited its *Weltpolitik* in the New World to the protection of its nationals and their financial interests. As we have seen, it was during the Spanish-American War that the Foreign Office decided it to be for the best interests of German colonial policy to cooperate with, rather than to oppose the United States. And even prior to that time it had cleared itself of the rumor, very disturbing to the United States, that it was negotiating for one or more of the Danish West Indies and had, in 1892, rejected outright Baron von Reuter's offer of a 1,600,000-acre tract acquired by him in Colombia as a German colony to which emigration might be directed. Consistent with this policy of non-acquisition, the Kaiser refused the gift of a naval base in the Dominican Republic proffered by its president in 1898, replying that he "would not fall into such a trap," nor did he wish to "set himself at variance with the United States"; [68] and what was more attractive to the Kaiser at this time than naval bases?

Furthermore, the Kaiser and the Foreign Office took pains in 1901 specifically to declare that "the German Government had no purpose or intention to acquire the smallest foothold in South America or the Caribbean Sea"; [69] while the German embassy at Washington declared that, "all reports circulated concerning German plans of conquest in South and Central America are lies and slanders of our enemies." [70] Again, in 1903, the German ambassador in Washington assured Roosevelt that Germany had no thought of acquiring territory in Central and South America. [71] On March 19, 1903, von Bülow made a similar statement in the *Reichstag*, [72] and soon afterward set forth Germany's Latin American policy in an interview with the press. [73] Likewise, Prince Henry of Prussia on his visit to the United States was instructed in 1902 as follows: "Should the Americans manifest concern about German ideas of acquisition or of influence as regards Central and South America, that should be disclaimed as an absurd phantasy by pointing to the pacific character of His Majesty's policy and to the many problems we have to solve elsewhere in the world, without, however, imparting the character of a solemn declaration to such a rather ironical denial." [74] Again, at the outbreak of the Great War, the German ambassador in Washington took particular pains to deny the rumor that Germany intended, if victorious, to "seek expansion in South America"; while ex-Colonial Secretary Dernburg publicly stated that if the United States desired more assurances on this matter, such assurances would be forthcoming, but that: "We have already laid before the government of the United States an official note stating that Germany would not seek any expansion in South America." [74a]

In the face of these avowals, which, whatever their historical value, at least cannot be contradicted by any evidence of official plans for territorial acquisition during this period, it would seem that the only truth to be found in the "German plot" consisted of schemes and efforts, concocted by German naval and colonial circles. It is doubtless true that these did exist, but it cannot be ascertained that they were in any case supported by the government.

While official Germany thus repudiated by word and deed any concrete opposition to the Monroe Doctrine by attempts to annex territory, and deemed it the better part of wisdom not to antagonize the United States, she found no small outlet for her *Weltpolitik* in her strenuous defense of her nationals and their interests upon every and all occasions. Thus in 1897, when Lueders, a German subject, was unjustly and harshly punished by the Haitian government, his Fatherland sent men-of-war and under threat of bombardment secured damages and an apology. "We are not merely satisfied with the freeing of Lueders but have a right to demand some compensation from the Haitian government," blustered von Bülow in the *Reichstag.*[75] Very drastic action was again taken against Haiti during her civil war in 1902; German warships were continually paraded in Caribbean waters to impress the Latin American states with the fact that the German empire had become a world Power; and the coercion of Guatemala was discussed in 1902.

The culmination of this policy during the era of *Weltpolitik* may be seen in Germany's action in the Venezuelan imbroglio of 1902-1903. Here Germany in cooperation with

Great Britain "coerced" Venezuela for the purpose of enforcing their joint claims to the point of sinking her ships and bombarding her forts, but desisted, and agreed to the submission of these claims to arbitration, so soon as the pressure of public opinion both in the United States and Great Britain was seen to be injuring her best interests—namely friendship with the United States. A careful scrutiny of the controversy reveals no ulterior German motives to acquire territory.[76] On the other hand, the Foreign Office assured the United States at the outset that, "under no circumstances do we consider in our proceedings the acquisition or permanent occupation of Venezuelan territory;[77] that it had "no intention whatever to proceed beyond a warlike blockade";[78] while the German ambassador in London told Lord Lansdowne that, "the United States knows full well that we do not wish to establish ourselves in Venezuela."[79] What is more, the Kaiser thought to take shelter behind the warlike activities of the British when he said, "Let the British be active, then we can take a back seat . . . then the English can take the criticisms of America."[80]

Were any further proof required to establish the fact that the German government had no secret motive to acquire territory, either in the Venezuelan affair or upon other occasions that offered, but solely wished to protect its subjects and their interests, as well as to assert its prestige in Latin America, the fact that it turned a deaf ear to the demands of the annexationists at home would supply it. For in 1903, after the Venezuelan matter was submitted to arbitration, widespread dissatisfaction with the settlement was voiced, and many joined the Pan-Germans and colonialists in again reviving the propaganda for acquisitions in the New World. The Monroe Doctrine was denounced and it was asserted even by the moderate *Grenzboten* that, "We cannot and will not allow ourselves to be shut out from the only portion of the globe still open to us." [81]

That the German government would have liked nothing better than to follow the lead of these annexationists and to acquire colonies in South America, as it was doing in Asia and the Pacific, goes of course without saying, because this was the whole trend of its colonial policy. [82] But while the Kaiser evidently considered it safe to be reckless in regard to his foreign relations where the European Powers were concerned, for the sake of his world position he adopted, as we have noted, a very different and cautious attitude toward the United States. May it not be, however, that one motive behind his all-too-obvious bidding for the support of the powerful western republic against England was for the furthering of his designs, against that very nation, his most formidable rival in the colonial field; and is it not likely that his earnest effort to take the United States away from Great Britain, even when that course necessitated restraint in colonial advance in Latin America, was part and parcel of his larger game of *Weltpolitik?* [83] Finally, when one reflects upon the British suspicion and ill-will, which this studied policy of friendship for the United States occasioned, especially during the Spanish-American War, [84] the question arises whether it was not as equally detrimental to Germany's position in Europe as were the other methods which, we have noted, the impulsive Kaiser employed in his subordination of his foreign relations to the prosecution of his colonial policy.

## The Kaiser Turns to Turkey

But the Kaiser's promotion of imperialism for the sake of world power did not exhaust itself in Africa, the Far

East, nor in the South Seas, but focused nearer home upon the Near East. Nothing illustrates more clearly William II's break with the Bismarckian colonial tradition, induced by the adoption of world power, than does his Near Eastern policy; and doubtless because it necessitated such a drastic change in Germany's diplomatic trend, it was the last section of the globe to feel the effect of the "new course."

Early in the nineteenth century, as has already been recounted, colonial propagandists and sympathizers realized the possibilities which the Near East held for the economic expansion of the Fatherland, whose need they so shrewdly foresaw. List, Höffken, the editor of the *Augsburg Allgemeine Zeitung,* drew attention to the importance of the Near East as a field for colonization, while von Moltke and Rodbertus indicated Asia Minor as the future spoil of Germany.[85] Although their advice had no effect upon the Prussian government, individual enterprise, as was always the case in Germany's colonial history, translated their ideas into practice: many small agricultural colonies were founded such as *Gutland,* a project of the *Deutsche Weinbau Gesellschaft* in the sixties; schools, hospitals and other German agencies were planted throughout the lands nearest Europe, and, in 1853 the most ambitious undertaking, the *Tempelgesellschaft,* was organized in the Holy Land, to which doctors, teachers, engineers, as well as peasants attached themselves, resulting in about seven settlements.

According to the usual story, these private enterprises faltered for lack of financial and state support, but they prepared the way for a more stable element, namely, the investors. For as soon as national unification had rendered German economic interests strong enough, the latter began to penetrate the Near East in earnest and to compete with the English and French firms already entrenched there, a competition rendered continually weaker by the waning of British and French influence in that region during the two decades succeeding the Congress of Berlin. As early as 1872, von Pressell, an eminent German railway engineer, was retained by the sultan to develop plans for railways in Turkey, and the bankers Bleichröder, von Siemens of the *Deutsche Bank,* and von Kaulla of the *Würtembergische Vereinsbank* of Stuttgart became interested in his projects. In the year 1888, a German syndicate under the leadership of von Siemens was formed, gained a concession from the Ottoman government to continue the Haidar-Pascha line, of which it had obtained control, to Angora with a conditional right of further extensions.[86]

Naturally, the trader followed the investor and during the twelve years from 1888 to 1900, Germany's economic expansion into the Near East was one of the wonders wrought by her Industrial Revolution. Whereas in 1898, "the trade and finance of Turkey was practically monopolized by Great Britain and France, the Germans (in 1900) were by far the most active group in Constantinople and in Asia Minor. Hundreds of German salesmen were traveling in Turkey. . . . The Krupp-owned Germania Shipping Company was furnishing torpedoes to the Turkish navy; Ludwig Löwe and Company, of Berlin, was equipping the sultan's military machine with small arms; Krupp of Essen was sharing with Armstrong the orders for artillery. German bicycles were replacing American-made machines. . . . In 1899, a group of German financiers founded the *Deutsche Palästina Bank,* which proceeded to establish branches at Beirut, Damascus, Gaza, Haifa, Jaffa, Jerusalem, Nablus, Nazareth, and Tripoli-in-Syria."[87] During this period (1888-1900), Germany's exports into Turkey rose from 2,300,000 M. to

30,400,000 M., and her imports from 11,700,000 M. to 34,400,000 M.

Until this time, the year 1898, the imperial government had played no part in this active economic penetration of the Ottoman empire. Indeed Bismarck had taken particular pains to subordinate it to Germany's political relations to the Near East and to the other powers, in harmony with his consistently pursued method of "limited liability." Here, as always, he allowed the economic motive of expansion to dominate, and avoided the political for fear of jeopardizing his system of alliances. When giving his consent to Dr. von Siemens, Director of the *Deutsche Bank,* for the railway concession of 1888, he expressly stipulated that Germany's Turkish policy must be made subordinate to her Russian policy, for he never forgot that the price of Russian friendship, more desirable than ever in the year 1888, was a free hand in the Near East. The very phrase that he used in his letter to Dr. von Siemens, "The danger involved therein (the railway concession) for German *entrepreneurs* must be assumed exclusively by the *entrepreneurs*," [88] is but an echo of the slogan of his original colonial program, "The entire responsibility rests with the merchant, and not with the empire." [89]

Again, Bismarck had always resisted the young Kaiser's ever-growing interest in Turkey. He thoroughly disapproved of the latter's ostentatious visit to the Sublime Porte in 1889, whose implication he had been obliged to explain away to the Tsar, by assigning it to the Kaiser's sight-seeing desire to visit Constantinople rather than to any political purpose. And he had only consented to the appointment of a German military mission to Turkey, under the command of General von der Goltz, upon the urgent insistence of Count Hatzfeld, the German ambassador at

Constantinople, because he felt it was an insurance against the danger of Pan-Slav and anti-German elements in Russia gaining ascendency at the court of the Tsar.[90]

But all this cautious and skillful diplomacy, William II was to cast to the winds in his reckless pursuit of German expansion for world power. Always he seems to have realized the possibilities of the Turkish empire as compensation for Germany's limited colonial opportunities outside of Europe, although he appears to have formulated no definite plan for the political penetration of Turkey until 1898. There were many signs, however, of his sympathy with the German-Ottoman economic *entente,* which so admirably paved the way for his ultimate political alliance: his visit to Sultan Abdul Hamid the year of his accession, although so plausibly interpreted by Bismarck, had a distinct political complexion, as the resulting favorable commercial treaty ratified by the German and Turkish governments in 1890 confirmed; he was utterly indifferent to the sufferings inflicted upon the Christians at the hands of the Turks, although generally a sympathizer with Christian martyrdom when it served his imperialist interests; he presented his portrait to Yildiz Kiosk; and, finally, he appointed Marschall von Bieberstein [91] to the ambassador's post in Constantinople, as we have seen, the very best member of the diplomatic corps he could possibly have selected to build upon the already strong foundations of German-Turco understanding laid down by his predecessors, Haztfeld and von Wangenheim.

Taking advantage of the favorable political situation for Germany, which prevailed both in the Near East and in Europe in the late nineties, the Kaiser hastened to bring his Turkish policy to a climax, and to merge the German-Ottoman economic *entente* into a political alliance. The outward and visible sign thereof was his famous and spectacular visit to the sultan in 1898, on which occasion he shrouded his imperialistic designs with the same religious camouflage as he had employed in China: the dedication of a Lutheran Church in Jerusalem with Oriental pomp and ceremony; the hoisting of the imperial standard on Mount Zion, and the gift of hallowed land to the Roman Catholic Church; all exercises of such piety that they drew from Abdul Hamid an expression of admiration for the Kaiser's truly religious spirit, and his deep understanding of the meaning of religion.[92] In addition, the Kaiser capped his religious exercises by pledging his eternal friendship and that of the German people to all Mohammedans, possessed with the idea that in case of war they would start rebellions in the colonial territories of Germany's opponents, Russia and England. It was a fantastic and dangerous plan, and but another indication of William II's pursuit of German expansion and world power, with not the slightest regard to international consequences.

## The Bagdad Railway

Nevertheless, just as the "planting of St. Michael's shield" among the heathen Chinese had secured no inconsiderable results for world policy in the Far East, so did Protestant-Lutheran patronage of the followers of the Great Prophet bear similar fruits for *Realpolitik*.[93] Chief of these was the promise of the concession from Turkey to continue the Anatolian Railway from Konia to Bagdad and the Persian Gulf. Until 1898, this railway had been, like the railways of France and England in the Near East, short lines within their respective spheres of influence. Now, the German plan was to establish a unified system of railways: to connect Turkey with Anatolia, the old homeland, with Syria and Mesopotamia as far as Persia, Arabia, and Egypt; to revive the once fabulously fruitful Anatolian upland and to grow cotton in Mesopotamia; to gather the Anatolian mineral wealth of antimony, chrome, copper, iron, coal and to exploit the oil wells of Mesopotamia and Syria; to develop and control, in short, this valuable stretch of territory for Germany's economic and political benefit.

Such a plan was obviously replete with materials for international rivalry and conflicts: conflicts practical and immediate between French and British railway and shipping interests as well as commercial competitors; and clashes less tangible in the realm of world politics, due to Russian and Austrian contradicting ambitions, England's fear for the route to India, and France's ancient position of social and financial influence in the Near East. Thus it was evident from the start that the prosecution of this imposing plan, the financing of this railway to be built in sections, depended to a large extent upon world politics, upon the alignment of the European Powers and, as such, contained a peculiar fascination for the Kaiser, embarked as he already was upon the game of world power, played so largely with the cards of imperialist expansion. "As the political barometer rose and fell, so rose or fell the prospects of the enterprise," and as the prospects of the enterprise prospered, so mounted the German barometer of world power.

As was to be expected, then, Germany's attempt to realize her promised concession of 1899 was met at once by opposition, especially from Russia, and the route of the railroad had to be altered to avoid its running too near the Russian frontier. But the Russian hostility to the Railway remained, for it was bound to be a thorn in the side of those Powers who aimed at preserving the "Sick Man," and disliked seeing a tonic administered to him, especially by such a strong hand as Germany's.

Mainly for the same reason the British government opposed the project, although the German attempt to include British stockholders and directors in the syndicate of the Bagdad Railway Company very nearly succeeded. As long as England had been interested in preserving the integrity of Turkey, there had been no fear of her opposition; but, since 1895, when Lord Salisbury had announced that Turkey was "rotten," there was little hope of her support for reasons of imperial strategy, supplemented, after 1899, by her natural resentment of Germany's refusal of her proffered alliance; by Germany's menacing position in the Far East and in the Pacific, accentuated by the Navy Bill of 1898, and by Germany's refusal to agree with England's interpretation of the Yangtse Agreement of 1900; [94] by all the irritation and ill-feeling incident to the settlement of the Samoan affair; and finally, by the death of Queen Victoria and the snapping of that personal tie, which had so often held in spite of stress and strain between the Foreign Offices.

And England's hostility was very concrete: in 1903 Balfour, at first favorable to the project, ultimately yielded to the pressure of British public opinion and rejected the plan of British cooperation; [95] while Lord Lansdowne, Secretary of State for Foreign Affairs, raised difficulties about the proposed terminus of the railway at Koweit, the only good harbor on the north shore of the Persian Gulf, by publicly announcing that his government would regard the establishment of a naval base or fortified port in that region as a very grave menace to British interests which, "we would certainly resist with all the means at our disposal." Indeed, the German terminus at Koweit had already been effectually blocked by a secret agreement with the sheik to enter into no international agreements without the consent of the British resident adviser. [96]

215

Like the English, the French bankers approved of the Bagdad Railway Syndicate and actually subscribed thirty per cent of the capital; even Delcassé was interested in it as a means of diverting Germany's imperialistic designs away from Morocco. But in 1903, on the eve of the conclusion of the *Entente Cordiale,* Delcassé now more secure in Morocco, submitted to the influence of French traditional Eastern policy and also to the pressure exerted by Russia, echoed Balfour's reasons for opposition in the French Chamber, and prohibited trading in Bagdad Railway shares on the Paris Bourse.

In the meantime, in spite of the widespread hostility from the Powers, Germany had realized her tentative plan of 1899 by obtaining in March, 1903, a definite contract or concession from the Turkish government to carry through the Bagdad Railway via Konia—Adana, Nisibin, Mosul—Bagdad-Basra to Koweit on the Persian Gulf, with branches to Aleppo, Urfa, Khanikin and other cities north and south of the trunk line. In October, 1904, the line was opened as far as Konia, and one more triumph was added to the Kaiser's already successful record of world policy. But, once again, he had subordinated his foreign relations to imperialistic expansion, with what portentous sacrifice of Germany's friendly orientation to the other Powers, the foregoing account of Russian, British, and French hostility has made apparent.

### The Railway a Symbol of Imperialism

Finally, the contrast between the Kaiser's plan to use the Bagdad Railway for political ends, as a colossal mortgage for empire, and the absence at first of any imperialistic designs on the part of its promoters and supporters, will serve to confirm his definite identification of the colonial movement with *Weltpolitik,* which has been the thesis of this chapter. For, while the German people predominantly applauded and acclaimed the Bagdad Railway as a great patriotic adventure, many, at first, either failed to grasp its political import or else repudiated it altogether.

From the very beginning, when List had advocated a *"Drang nach Osten"* in the thirties and forties, there had been no thought of a political purpose or any threat to British supremacy in India. In fact, the German movement eastward was to be "accompanied by a Prussian-British alliance and through the German manufacturing cities of the Rhine, the German farm lands of the Danube, and the German plantations of Asia Minor were to run the lines of the London-Calcutta Railway! [97]

To the great mass of the German people, then, in 1900, the Railway was a vast business and economic undertaking and little else. Its promoters, von Siemens and von Gwinner, strove arduously to include British and French capital in its organization and control. In fact, they almost reached an agreement whereby the board of directors was to consist of eight Germans, eight Frenchmen, eight Englishmen, and six others appointed by the Turkish government and the Anatolian Railway Company. Indeed, von Gwinner's one concern was to guarantee the financial success of the project, and he often found the interference of the German government in his plans extremely embarrassing. [98] Even Paul Rohrbach himself, who later showed how the Railway might be employed as a strategic menace to England, expressed his belief, in 1903, that its promoters contemplated no political or diplomatic ends.

What is more, the project was not conspicuously pushed by the colonial circles in the same way in which territorial acquisitions were urged. The Pan-German League, for instance, in 1904, did not consider the Near East a potential

217

field for colonization or exploitation. It claimed that, were Germany to consider that section as a possible sphere of influence, she would need a Mediterranean fleet and would antagonize both England and Russia.[99]

Contrast with these non-aggressive and non-imperialist aims of the German people, even of the colonialists and the promoters of the project itself, the many evidences of the purpose of the Kaiser's government to effect a political alliance with Turkey of which the Railway was the tangible symbol. These have been, for the most part, already reviewed, but let us add a few high lights to the picture. In 1897, Germany withdrew her ships while those of the other Powers were making an end of Turkey in Crete, and remarking upon this in the *Reichstag,* von Bülow observed, "It is not necessary that everyone in the European concert play the same instrument: in crises, one plays the drum, another the trumpet and a third the kettledrum; but Germany has chosen to play the flute of diplomacy and persuasion at Constantinople. If conflict arises, therefore, we will stand to one side; if the situation becomes serious we will lay the flute on the table and leave the concert hall."[100] In 1898, the Kaiser declared in his speech from the throne, "I trust that my visit to the Turkish Empire promises the ultimate drawing together of these two nations."[101] Subsequently, he always referred to the Bagdad project as "My Railway."

But the strongest contrast between the government's aims and those of the Railway's projectors is demonstrated by the activities of Marschall von Bieberstein,[102] that *Realpolitiker,* ambassador to the Sublime Porte from 1897 to 1912, and the most zealous champion of the idea that Germany's colonial future lay in Asia. One of his very first *Reports* developed the theme that Germany needed room for economic expansion, and that this could only be achieved by the state in Turkey through the Railroad.[103] The same thought permeated all his subsequent memoranda, and demonstrated to von Bülow that Germany's policy in the East must be placed on a new basis consonant with that ideal. In this connection he maintained that Bismarck's remarks about the "bones of a Pomeranian Grenadier" had lost all their relevancy. As every one knows, Marschall became the trusted adviser of Abdul Hamid and worked with exceeding great craft for his master's ends. Whenever he presented a *Report* upon the Bagdad Railway, he referred to it as "Your Most Gracious Majesty's glorious undertaking." He heartily disapproved of British cooperation in the project, and was largely responsible for von Gwinner's sudden withdrawal from London in 1903, whither he had gone to negotiate Great Britain's share and cooperation in the scheme.[104] In short, Marschall von Bieberstein, the Giant of the Golden Horn, was the chief protagonist as well as the most potent instrument of the dominating point of view in German administrative circles which under secretary Mühlberg thus succinctly expressed: "With a bow to the British Lion and a courtesy to the Russian Bear, we will worm our way little by little down to the Persian Gulf." [105]

## NOTES

[1] William II, *My Memoirs* (Trans. by T. Ybarra, Harpers, 1922), pp. 8-9.

[2] *Die Deutsche Kolonialgesellschaft, op. cit.,* p. 104.

[3] At the Provincial *Landtag* of Brandenburg, the Kaiser enthusiastically declared himself to be a friend of *Kolonialpolitik,* "following in the steps of the Great Elector." *Deutsche Kolonialzeitung,* March 15, 1890.

[4] He also said: "My grandfather founded the empire, my father was a victor in the great battles, it is my duty to the nation to create for it a place in the world." Friedjung, H., *Das Zeitalter des Imperialismus* (Berlin, 1922, 3 vols.), vol. i, p. 148.

[5] Friedjung, *op. cit.*, vol. i, p. 236, quoting Hohenlohe's speech in *Reichstag*, December 7, 1897, upon occasion of the first great Naval Bill.

[6] See for Holstein, Rachfahl, F., "Die deutsche Aussenpolitik in der Wilhelmischen Aera" in *Einzelschriften zum Politik und Geschichte*, no. 6, 1924.

[7] *Die Deutsche Kolonialzeitung*, 1896, p. 929.

[8] *Verhandlungen des deutschen Reichstages*, 1897-1898, vol. 1, p. 60.

[9] Wertheimer, M., *The Pan-German League* (New York, 1924), p. 160ff.

[10] *Die Grosse Politik*, vol. viii, p. 459.

[11] *Ibid.*, vol. viii, p. 402.

[12] *Ibid.*, vol. xi, no. 2610. Indicative of Great Britain's resentment is the comment upon the telegram made by the *Morning Post*: "The right answer to this telegram would be the assembling of the British fleet in the Channel: the English nation will never forget the dispatch, but will always think of it in connection with her foreign policy." See Friedjung, *op. cit.*, vol. i, p. 202. Also, the *Saturday Review* stated on September 11, 1897, "In the Transvaal, on the Cape, in Middle Africa, in the South Seas, Germans compete with English. Should Germany be destroyed, there is not an Englishman in the world who would not be the richer. *Germania esse delendam.*"

[13] This suggestion Marschall owed to the colonial director, Doctor Kayser. Ludwig, E., *Wilhelm der Zweiter* (Berlin, 1926), p. 193.

[14] *Die Grosse Politik*, vol. xi, p. 32, footnote. See also, F. Thimme, "Die Krueger Despesche" in *Europäische Gespräche*, May-June, 1924, pp. 201-244. Hammann, O., *World Power of Germany*, p. 68ff., and Brandenburg, E., *From Bismarck to the World War* (Trans. by A. Adams, London, 1927), pp. 84-85.

[15] *Die Grosse Politik*, vol. xi, p. 36.

[16] *Ibid.*, pp. 8, 251.

[17] *Ibid.*, ch. 64.

[18] See *supra.*, ch. iii, p. 63.

[19] See *supra.*, ch. iii, p. 63.

[20] Von Tirpitz, A., *My Memoirs* (New York, 1919, 2 vols.), vol. 1, ch. 8. *The Kaiser's Memoirs, op. cit.*, pp. 64-67. *Die Grosse Politik*, vol. xv, pp. 1, 5, 7.

[21] *Die Grosse Politik*, vol. xiv, nos. 3645-3685. See also, *British Documents, Origins of War*, 1898-1914, Gooch and Temperley, Eds. (London, 1927), vol. i, p. 4ff.

[22] *Ibid.*, vol. xiv, nos. 3686, 3689.

[23] *Kaiser's Memoirs, op. cit.*, p. 65.

[24] *Die Grosse Politik*, vol. xiv, nos. 3679, 3743.

[25] MacMurray, J., *Treaties and Agreements with and Concerning China*, 1884-1919 (New York, 1921), pp. 112, 240, 248, 252.

[26] *Die Grosse Politik*, vol. xiv, no. 3778. von Bülow sums up Germany's position in China.

[27] *Die Grosse Politik*, vol. xi, p. 385, vol. xiii, p. 7. The Kaiser remarked to the British ambassador that, since Germany could not develop

all of her colonies at the same time, it might be best to retain one and exchange the others with England for coaling stations.

[28] *Ibid.,* vol. xiv, p. 250.

[29] *Ibid.,* vol. xiv, p. 217.

[30] *Ibid.,* vol. xiv, p. 347ff. See also Moon, *op. cit.,* p. 119.

[31] *Ibid.,* vol. xiv, no. 3806. See also, *British Documents, op. cit.,* vol. i, ch. ii.

[32] *International Conciliation,* no. 127, pp. 281, 289.

[33] *Die Grosse Politik,* vol. xv, pp. 33-34.

[34] *Ibid.,* vol. xv, pp. 33, 38, 39.

[35] Keim, J., *Forty Years of German-American Relations* (Phila., 1919), pp. 221ff.

Shippee, L., "Germany and the Spanish-American War" in *Am. Hist. Review,* July, 1925.

*Autobiography A. D. White* (New York, 1905, 2 vols.), vol. ii, p. 160.

Rippy, J. F., *Latin America in World Politics* (New York, 1928), pp. 166-167.

*Die Grosse Politik,* vol. xvi, nos. 4150-4160.

[36] *Ibid.,* vol. xv, p. 62 note.

[37] Letter of Bülow to Holleben in Washington, *Die Grosse Politik,* vol. xv, pp. 44-45. This same thought was more completely elaborated to Hatzfeldt in London, who was instructed to make the same suggestion to the American ambassador there. *Die Grosse Politik,* vol. xv, pp. 47-52.

[38] Mr. White seemed favorable to the idea when interviewed. *Die Grosse Politik,* vol. xv, pp. 54-59. Also see *Autobiography Andrew D. White* (New York, 1905, 2 vols.), vol. ii, p. 169ff.

[39] *Die Grosse Politik,* vol. xv, pp. 75-77.

[40] *Ibid.,* vol. xv, pp. 82-84.

[41] *Ibid.,* vol. xv, pp. 82-83.

[42] *Ibid.,* vol. xv, pp. 90-94.

[43] *Ibid.,* vol. xv, pp. 94-98.

[44] *Ibid.,* vol. xiv, nos. 3801, 3806, and vol. xv, no. 4167.

[45] *Verhandlungen des deutschen Reichstages,* 1898-1900, vol. iii, p. 2895ff.

*Die Grosse Politik,* vol. xiv, no. 3778.

[46] The German press made a violent attack against the American "intriguers." Eckardstein, *op. cit.,* vol. i, p. 99ff. He speaks of the "dangerous hash" which the naval and colonial factions cooked up in the Pacific."

[47] *Die Grosse Politik,* vol. xv, pp. 91-101, note.

[48] Rippy, *op. cit.,* p. 180 and note. See also Report conversations of Hatzfeld and Salisbury, *Die Grosse Politik,* vol. xv, p. 39 and note.

[49] See *supra.,* ch. iii, p. 71.

[50] *Die Grosse Politik,* vol. xiv, pp. 575, 585, 606, 615, 620, 623.

[51] Von Tirpitz's memorandum, *Die Grosse Politik,* vol. xiv, p. 660.

[52] *Die Grosse Politik,* xiv, p. 666ff.

von Bülow called Germany's gain only an "appetizer (Vorspeise)," but the Kaiser displayed his gratitude by promoting Bülow to the rank of Count.

[53] Eckardstein declared that Salisbury was well-disposed until annoyed by the tone of the Kaiser's dispatches, which assumed the character of daily tirades. "I will not be dictated to by Berlin with a stop-watch in its hand," said Salisbury.

See also, *British Documents,* vol. i, nos. 136, 137, 141.

[54] *Die Grosse Politik,* vol. iv, p. 51, vol. xiv, no. 4068.

*Kaiser's Memoirs,* p. 89.

[54a] *Die Grosse Politik,* vol. xiv, pp. 606, 615, 620-623.

[55] Sievers, W., *Südamerika und die deutschen Interesse* (Stuttgart, 1903).

[56] Thayer, W. R., *Life and Letters of John Hay* (1915).

[57] Bonsall, L., "Greater Germany in South America," in *North American Review,* vol. 176, 1903, p. 58.

[58] *Hay Papers,* undated, Choate to Hay, 1902.

Keim, J., *op. cit.,* p. 279.

[59] *U. S. Dept. State, to Germany,* vol. 21, no. 1186, April 10, 1901, Hay to Jackson.

[60] *Roosevelt-Lodge Correspondence,* vol. ii, pp. 135-138.

[61] Bonsall, *op. cit.*

[62] Although immediately after the war the press generally changed its attitude to support the government.

[63] Unold, J., *Das Deutschtum in Chile* (1899), p. 62ff.

[64] Leyser, H., quoted by Bonsall, *op. cit.,* from his book on Santa Catharina.

[65] Wintzer, W., *Die Deutschen in Tropischen Amerika* (1900), p. 78ff.

[66] *U. S. Dept. of State, from Germany,* vol. 64, no. 161, October 29, 1897, Jackson to Sherman.

[67] Sievers, W., *op. cit.*

[68] *Die Grosse Politik,* vol. xv, pp. 109-111.

[69] *U. S. Dept. of State, from Germany, numerical file* vol. 547, *memo.* November 16, 1901.

[70] *Ibid.,* vol. 30, October 11, 1901.

[71] *Die Grosse Politik,* vol. xvii, pp. 291-292.

[72] *Verhandlungen des deutschen Reichstages,* March 19, 1903.

[73] Rippy, *op. cit.,* p. 152, note.

[74] *Die Grosse Politik,* vol. xvii, no. 5106.

[74a] *Ibid.,* p. 152 and *note.* Obviously, with the entrance of the United States into the World War, the attitude of the German government changed to that adopted by an enemy nation. All sorts of rumors arose of German designs in South America, in Central America and in Mexico. There is no doubt that such designs and actual intervention existed, especially in Cuba, Haiti, Brazil and Mexico, to a considerable extent. Whatever may prove to have been its exact extent in the light of future investigation, such intervention would appear to belong to the military strategy of warfare rather than to the processes of colonial expansion. At any rate, no official plans

or aims for permanent colonial acquisitions in Latin America can be found in the statements of war objectives as can be found for German expansion in Africa and Asia. See *supra.*, ch. xii, pp. 370 *et seq.*

[75] *Verhandlungen des deutschen Reichstages,* 1897-1898, vol. ii, December 6, 1897.

[76] Rippy, *op. cit.*, pp. 196-199, contains a thorough examination of the evidence. Likewise, there seems to exist no evidence for Germany's alleged designs in Nicaragua later.

[77] Dennis, A., *Adventures in American Diplomacy* (New York, 1928), p. 285.

[78] Quoted by Rippy, *op. cit.*, p. 196, note 44.

[79] *Die Grosse Politik,* vol. xvii, p. 263.

[80] *Die Grosse Politik,* vol. xvii, no. 5102.

[81] Quoted by Rippy, *op. cit.*, p. 147.

[82] See Kaiser's marginal comments upon *Report* of von Stern's conversation with Roosevelt about Venezuela affair, which reveals his great interest in South America, *Die Grosse Politik,* vol. xvii, pp. 291-292.

[83] This is very evident in correspondence with U. S. regarding Samoa, *U. S. Dept. of State, to German Embassy,* vol. 12, p. 368, *memo,* April 13, 1899.

*Dept. of State, numerical file* 547 (undated following *memo.* August 31, 1899).

[84] Rippy, *op cit.*, p. 168.

[85] See *supra.*, ch. ii, pp. 34-35.

[86] Earle, E. M., *Turkey, The Great Powers and the Bagdad Railway* (New York, 1923), ch. iii.

[87] *Ibid.*, p. 37.

[88] *Ibid.*, p. 41.

[89] See *supra.*, ch. iv, p. 119.

[90] Earle, *op. cit.*, p. 38, note 18.

[91] See *supra.*, ch. vii, p. 181.

[92] *Die Grosse Politik,* vol. xii, pt. 2, no. 3338.

[93] These are described in detail by von Bülow, see *Moon, op. cit.*, p. 240.

*Die Grosse Politik,* vol. xii, no. 3347 note.

[94] *Die Grosse Politik,* vol. xvii, p. 39.

For England's disappointment over Germany's withdrawal from Russian opposition, which she had hoped to secure from the *Yangtse Agreement* of 1900, and its consequent effect upon her own opposition to the Bagdad Railway, see Helfferich, K., *Die deutsche Türkenpolitik* (Berlin, 1921).

[95] Earle, *op. cit.*, p. 180ff.

[96] *Ibid.*, p. 197ff.

[97] Hansen, *op. cit.*, p. 19.

[98] Moon, *op. cit.*, pp. 245-246. Also, Earle, *op. cit.*, ch. vi.

[99] Wertheimer, *op. cit.*, pp. 170-171.

[100] *Verhandlungen des deutschen Reichstages,* 1897-1898, vol. 2-3, pp. 907-8, February 8, 1898.

[101] *Ibid.,* vol. 1, p. 3.
[102] For best account of Marschall von Bieberstein, see Bettelheim, *Biographisches Jahrbuch,* vol. xvii.
[103] *Die Grosse Politik,* vol. xvii, no. 5247, vol. xii, pp. 560, 561, 565. The Kaiser wrote *"Gut"* on this Report.
[104] Eckardstein, *op. cit.,* vol. ii, p. 178.
[105] *Ibid.,* p. 177.

# CHAPTER VIII

## THE NEW COLONIAL POLICY BECOMES A NATIONAL ISSUE

### The Crisis of 1906-1907

THE identification of colonial policy with the ideals and methods of *Weltpolitik* was not confined to its external aspect, but was applied to its internal administration as well. Official promotion and direction of the colonies themselves kept pace with imperial zeal in acquiring new territories abroad; but in so doing it sacrificed their economic development and internal welfare to the one all-absorbing aim of political prestige and world power. In other words, the character of the colonial administration, during the decade 1896 to 1906, illustrates the same break with the Bismarckian tradition and the economic origins and aims of German colonization, which we have seen the Kaiser's feverish activities oversea had already initiated. While the government was extending its possessions and transforming colonial expansion into imperialism, it was seeking to impose its ideas of the acquisition, use, and administration of colonies upon the German people and, encountering their opposition, made a determined and high-handed effort to win or to coerce popular and party consent.

### Political Bureaucracy Dominates the Colonies

From the beginning, the Kaiser and von Bülow had relied politically, for the support of their aggressive external colonial policy, upon the Conservatives and National Liberals, over whom Germany's astounding economic prosperity and rapid rise to the position of a world Power had cast a spell of enchantment. Hence, their ideals, militarism, bureaucracy, economic imperialism or exploitation, having been justified by success, prevailed in guiding the internal colonial administration, and accentuated those unfortunate tendencies which we have seen already established during the period of the colonial companies and the first chapter of imperial control.[1]

It is true that Dr. Kayser's withdrawal from the colonial office in 1896 had given place to Richthofen, a former councillor, who possessed a broader outlook and a greater appreciation of the economic value of oversea possessions for the entire nation. His experience as a foreign consul and as an official in the Foreign Office had given him a thorough understanding of England's colonial empire and of the world situation; while his service on the debt commission in Cairo had introduced him to international finance. Contrary to the prevailing mind of the colonial department, he regarded Germany's colonial policy from the standpoint of a national and not an individual business man, realized that the rule of the militarist, the adventurer, the politician, and the exploiter would have to cease, and desired to establish a stable, wise, and intelligent colonial administration from which the nation as a whole might profit. But he had inherited an unfortunate legacy from Dr. Kayser, and circumstances everywhere seemed to be against him: the recent nomination of Major Liebert to the governorship of East Africa, as successor to the wise and excellent Major Wissmann, prevented him from avoiding a stern militaristic rule there; difficulties regarding English, French, and German boundaries in West Africa monopolized his attention in that region; a scourge of rinderpest devastated South West Africa; and finally, huge appropriations amounting to 5,000,000 M., which might have been expended upon the economic development of the colonies, were directed toward acquiring a foothold in China.

Upon the accession of von Bülow to the Foreign Office in 1897 and to the chancellorship in 1900, and the consequent closer identification of colonial acquisitions with world policy, it was but natural to find the internal administration of the colonies subordinated to the same end. For by 1900, Germany's success as a world power had emphasized the advantages of her oversea territories in creating political prestige, and had blinded her more and more to the imperious need of their national assimilation and of their economic development for the country's welfare. The official, military, and bureaucratic class, more deeply entrenched in the government than ever before, continued to dominate the colonial office, ably assisted by the National Liberals; and those representatives of big business, the economic imperialists, were enjoying to the full the exploitation of the colonies for their individual interests under the eager protection of the military.

Von Bülow's appointees, who succeeded Richthofen as directors of the colonial department, well represented the bureaucratic character of this overweening political domination: first Dr. von Buchka, a Conservative jurist who knew no more about the colonies than what he had learned as a member of the Colonial Society, although the *Deutsche Allgemeine Zeitung* commended his appointment because of his familiarity with commerce and shipping gained from his long residence in Rostock; [2] second, in 1900, Dr Stübel, the consul in Chile, whose chief recommendation for the position seemed to be that he had spent so many years away from home in the consular service in the United States, China, Denmark, and Samoa, that he was entirely out of touch with colonial affairs and could be counted upon not to interfere with the intrigues in parliamentary and official circles; and finally, in 1905, Prince Hohenlohe-Langenberg, the son of one of the founders of the *Kolonialverein,* who had been secretary at the legation in London, and regent for the young Duke of Coburg-Gotha, and who failed utterly to master the difficulties in the colonial department. Even if Dr. Buchka, Dr. Stübel or Prince Hohenlohe had had any inclination to reform the colonial department and to free it from the militarist, the capitalist, the adventurer, and the politician, their utter lack of knowledge and preparation for their position obliged them to submit to the group already in control.

These imperialists, led by von Bülow, conducted the internal colonial policy with a high hand and with only a very slight regard for the welfare, present or future, of the colonies, so long as their own private interests were served and the greed for world power on the part of their ruler gratified. Illustrative of the essentially un-economic and un-national policy of their administration were the two great concessions granted in 1898 and 1899 in Kamerun, which conveyed the same unlimited freedom to plunder forests and lands as the companies in the new French Congo possessed. The German-Belgian Company for Southern Kamerun, founded in Hamburg, received from the government an immense tract of 9,000,000 hectares *in perpetua* to exploit the territory for rubber. Since no obligation whatsoever rested upon the Company, in return for the absolute rights over land and people which it received, the grant was a virtual donation. Because of its financial success, the Company for Northern Kamerun quickly followed it, in

1899, and gained a concession of unrestricted rights over one-fifth of the entire territory.[3]

Because of the popular outcry in Germany, the latter grant was qualified to some degree by services, which the Company for Northern Kamerun was pledged to render to the state. It agreed, for instance, to guarantee freedom of trade, to subscribe 100,000 M. to the exploration of the Lake Chad region, to build roads, canals, railroads and to maintain steamships, to complete the exploration of the territory and to establish plantations and factories. Besides, the company was placed under the supervision of the Chancellor, who appointed a representative to attend the directors' meetings and to examine the books. But, in spite of this, the companies had things pretty much their own way, exploiting the territory at the expense of the natives and of the nation; the latter in two ways, since foreign capital was encouraged to invest heavily. In fact, the Company of Southern Kamerun was principally Belgian, just as that of South West Africa came to be more English than German. Herr Sharlach of Hamburg, the director of both of these companies at the same time, was principally responsible for this extensive alienation of German property. Indeed, so profitable did he find such enterprises that, altogether, he belonged to the administrative boards of eleven different colonial companies.

Another land grant of 12,000 square miles and all that was contained therein was made to an East African pioneer, Deuss, for a period of ten years, accompanied by no obligations whatsoever, while the New Guinea Company received outright a tract of 5,000 hectares at the time of its dissolution, a proceeding that was consummated by the Chancellor alone with no reference to the *Kolonialrat*. The *Kolonialrat* asserted itself, however, in the case of Deuss and succeeded in altering the terms of his concession.

## Maladministration Arouses Criticism

These flagrant and high-handed usurpations of the nation's property began to arouse criticism from all sides in the press, as did also a revival of the colonial "scandals." [4] As we have already heard, Peters had been brought to trial in 1896, specifically for unjustly condemning to death a native servant, whom he claimed was plotting with hostile chiefs against him; was found guilty and dismissed from the colonial service in the following year.[5] Leist, governor of Kamerun, 1893-1894, was accused of atrocious cruelty, including the beating of women, in suppressing the Dahomeyan uprising, so that he, too, was forced before the disciplinary court and out of the service. Wehlan, an imperial judge in Kamerun, met the same fate for cruelty in 1896, as did also von Horn, the governor of Togoland, who had tortured to death a native chief by flogging him and chaining him to a flagstaff for thirty-six hours. In the case of the latter and that of von Puttkamer, governor of Kamerun in 1905, a perfect wild-fire of scandal arose. The native chiefs had kept a record of von Puttkamer's arbitrary and outrageous acts committed against their people and had communicated directly with Berlin. So damaging were these reports that attempts were made by the colonial department itself, it was charged, to prevent investigation; state documents were claimed to have been abstracted from the official files and the whole administration was accused of complicity. Von Puttkamer, however, was later brought to trial and dismissed. At least it can be said that the colonial administration failed to uphold its undesirable appointees, once their notorious behavior brought discredit upon it and the whole colonial policy.

Loud also in censure of the colonial department was the

Pan-German League and all earnest colonialists.⁶ They condemned the government's land concessions and its mistakes of local management; they urged greater zeal in economic development, in building of railways, in stricter selection of colonial officials and in the financial reorganization of the colonies.⁷

### The Government Encounters Parliamentary Opposition

More serious for the government, however, than the criticisms of the press and of interested groups, were the attacks in the *Reichstag* from the Center, the *Freisinnige* and the Socialist parties who, after 1900, began to form a solid bloc of opposition against the colonial policy, whose selfish character and stupid mistakes they spared neither time nor rhetoric to describe. To be sure, the Catholic party had been finally won over to the colonial policy by Bismarck, but its support was never whole-hearted nor free from criticism. It resented the expense, deplored the warfare, cruelties and maladministration, and finally became thoroughly disgruntled when Prince Hohenlohe, one of the leaders of the Evangelical League, became colonial director. Among other things, the party claimed that Catholics were discriminated against in colonial offices and that all the appointments went to Protestant National Liberals or Conservatives.

Of course, the Kaiser and von Bülow could withstand the opposition of the Socialists and the *Freisinnige,* which they always expected on all of their measures. But they could not afford to lose the support of the Center, especially for their navy and army bills, so essentially a part of their world policy, which the Center had, in the main, aided and abetted through the nineties. When the Catholics joined the Opposition, therefore, and began to block every colonial

231

appropriation and project, it created a serious problem for the government; in fact the identical problem, it will be recalled, which the same party had created for Bismarck in his struggle over the Subsidy Bill in 1885.[8]

## The Socialists Combat Colonialism

Joining the Center in its opposition to the colonial party were the parties of the Left, the *Freisinnige,* and the Socialists; but the Socialists constituted its strongest ally. Since 1886, this party had increased in direct ratio to the rising bourgeoisie, made rich and strong through the results of the Industrial Revolution, and, in 1906, held 79 seats in the *Reichstag.* Since the days of Bebel's voluminously worded arguments against Bismarck's colonial policy, it had formulated a concise anti-expansionist and anti-imperialist creed, and had incorporated it into the articles of its belief. Every annual Socialist convention during the years 1903-1906 went on record as fighting the colonial policy.[9] At Bremen, for instance in 1904, where a heated discussion of the colonial policy took place, they vowed, "The Social Democrats are all united against the colonial policy, carried on in behalf of the capitalist world. . . . Under no circumstances do we recognize the capitalist colonial policy." [10] For they had come to the conclusion that modern colonial expansion was based entirely upon a capitalist motive and hence, to the Socialist mind, every evil might be expected to result therefrom. The trenchant statement of Franz Mehring writing in *Die Neue Zeit* expresses this attitude admirably: "Colonies are merely trading stations. The capitalist system plays the rôle of capital accumulation. It enriches the shipping trade and assures a world market. . . . Colonial policy in Germany was called into being when capital at last stood on its own feet and was ready to take the next step." [11]

Again, the *Socialist Handbuch* instructed the members of the party, "to fight the colonial policy because it affords opportunity for senseless economic ventures on the part of a few capitalists and enriches them, while increasing the taxes which bear so heavily upon the working class." [12]   And, in confirmation of their theory, the Socialists pointed to the Colonial Congress, held in 1905, which adopted a resolution to bring in a new navy bill as a result of the sentiment of the Assembly, "that colonial markets must be kept open, hence a fleet of ironclads is necessary as they (the colonies) cannot exist without a background of guns." [13]

## The Center and the Socialists Condemn the Colonial Policy

Led by these two parties the parliamentary struggle raged between the years 1903 and 1906, fanned into a flame by a series of severe native revolts.   These serious uprisings [14] in East Africa, in Kamerun, and two in South West Africa—served concretely to discredit the entire colonial administration and their suppression demanded an outpouring of men, money, and supplies in such quantities as seriously to embarrass and handicap the government if they were not forthcoming.   Finally, the continued opposition to the colonial estimates constituted a deadlock in the *Reichstag,* which precipitated the second parliamentary crisis in Germany's colonial policy, a policy this time on trial not only for its continuance but for its future character, should any future, at all, be accorded it.

The leaders of the campaign against the government proceeded first to tear to shreds the veil of patriotic idealism,

233

with which the imperialists sought to disguise their selfish and, in many instances, distinctly unpatriotic colonial rule. With bitter sarcasm, Erzberger and Roeren reduced to absurdity the claim that the "German flag, carrying the cross and *Kultur* was winning the African continent for civilization and Christianity." [15] They exposed in no unrestrained language the oppression, even enslavement of the natives; their swindling and exploitation by the traders who bring in the *"Schnapps* and the *Pulzwaren";* the robbing of their lands and cattle by the big companies; and the cruelty of the forced labor on the plantations, in the mines, and on the public works.[16] They held up to ridicule, as shining examples of German and Christian *"Kulturträger,"* such men as Peters, Wehlan, Puttkamer, Arenberg, Leist, and Wegner, who had used their official positions to further their own ambitions, to give play to their own licentious passions. and with whose "scandals" the press and the country had rung for years past.[17]

Unfortunately for the administration, there coincided with this outburst of criticism and this partisan attack in the *Reichstag,* a most severe native revolt of the Hereros in South West Africa, which was crushed by the government in such a manner as to lend concrete vindication to the charges of cruelty and ill-treatment. In fact, it was, as the Socialists pointed out, the grasping policy of the land companies in South West Africa in seizing more than 32 per cent of the natives' land which had precipitated the Herero rebellion. To make matters worse, the government had sent out General Trotha who had proclaimed that the "Herero people must leave the land. If it refuses I shall compel it with the gun. I shall assume charge of no more women and children, but shall drive them back to their people or let them be shot at." And, as a result, they were driven into the desert where nearly 14,000 starved; while at the same time the government appropriated their land.[18]

Turning from the ill-treatment of the natives, the critics of the colonial policy next exposed the tremendous profits and advantages of economic exploitation enjoyed by the capitalists in the colonies; an exploitation that was assisted and protected by the state and for which, they claimed, the German people had to pay. Here the Socialists distinguished themselves in the debates, for they attacked the sins of bourgeois capitalism with the same religious fervor as the Catholics had condemned those trespasses against the decalogue—murder, robbery, and lust. They demonstrated with statistics that all the mining rights of South West Africa were in the hands of individuals, syndicates, and companies, many of them foreign, who had acquired them *gratis* from the government, and were now profiting from their increased value created by improvements such as railroads, harbors, roads built by the government at the expense of the German "Michael," the taxpayer.[19] For instance, the German Colonial Company of South West Africa was said to have made a pure gain of 7,000,000 M. on land sold in the vicinity of the harbor of Swakopmund, where the government expenditure of 7,000,000 M. on docks and other improvements had tremendously increased property value.[20] They showed that government subsidies were granted to commercial companies, such as the Jaluit Company, who received annually 120,000 M., and yet enjoyed the profits of a monopoly by forcing the administration to demand an export duty of 30 M. per ton on copra;[21] and that imperial guarantees were given railway companies ranging from 3½ per cent to 4 per cent interest, sometimes even 6 per cent, on the capital invested, in addition to all kinds of concessions such as land, use of stone quarries, water power, and forests.[22]

The Socialists spared no effort to demonstrate that railway building in the colonies was a sort of "mutual benefit society," composed of state officials who granted subsidies and concessions to the companies, of which they were generally directors, like under secretary Fischer who, "has had his hand in every pot which has been on the colonial fire"; [23] of bankers who charged high rates of interest for loans; of the industrialists and contractors who supplied the iron and steel; and even of authors, one of whom received 5,000 M. for writing a book describing the glories of the locality and strongly recommending the building of and investment in the railway.[24]

Nor did the Socialists hesitate to come even nearer home and reveal the political graft existing in the monopolies secured by the supply and transportation companies which served the state in all the colonial departments. They pointed out that the firm of Tippelskirche, military outfitters, who had secured since 1896 long-term contracts, were making profits ranging from thirty to forty, sometimes to one hundred per cent. Their method, it was shown, consisted in selling harness to the government for 2,000 M., which had cost them but 900; infantry boots for 23.30 M. per pair, for which they had paid but 18.20 M. but had lacquered at a cost of 25 pfennigs, so that "boot blacking proved a very profitable business." [25] This firm had been bleeding the government for nearly ten years, greatly facilitated by the fact that one of its directors, Herr Podbielski, was at the same time Prussian Minister of the Interior, whose influence effected the huge contracts. Likewise, the Socialists did not spare the famous shipping firm of Woermann of Hamburg, who had secured exclusive transportation rights to certain African ports and, they claimed, was charging the government 31.50 M. per ton for freight from Capetown to

Lüderitz Bay, a journey of two days, while the regular price from Hamburg to Vladivostok, a voyage of fifty-six or sixty days, was only 23.50 M. per ton.[26] Nor did minor firms escape the Socialist probe, such as Kade, apothecaries of Berlin, who controlled a monopoly of all drug supplies and, it was discovered, served also as middlemen and sold to the government horseshoes, blankets, photographic apparatus at apothecary prices; and Lenz, railway contractors, who were often referred to in official documents as the "German Colonial Railway Building and Construction Company."[27]

## The Colonies Shown to be a Liability Instead of an Asset

Forced to admit the truth of many of these charges made by Erzberger and Bebel which were thoroughly supported by statistics, state papers, and letters of missionaries and travelers, von Bülow and his parties of the Right were obliged to retreat to their last bulwark of defense; namely, the economic value of the colonies. This point they strove to prove but, considering how little attention they had paid to developing the oversea territories for the benefit of the nation, it is not surprising that such a justification for their colonial policy availed them little.

Here, again, the Socialists took the lead in the debates, for they were well prepared to attack the stock argument of the capitalist-imperialist—the necessity of creating a "self-sufficient state." They showed that so far as supplying food to Germany, the colonies mainly produced raw materials for industry, such as rubber, copra, cotton, ivory, and that the foodstuffs, like coffee, cocoa, palm-oil which they did produce, were so small in comparison with the amount Germany imported from other countries as to be not worth the expense of colonies.[28] In other words, Bebel claimed, the state took

237

the bread and meat out of the mouths of its workmen by taxes to support the colonies in order to give him cocoa beans from Kamerun "worth their weight in gold." "A glass of milk produced on an African farm is dearer than a glass of champagne for the German workman," [29] he asserted. Besides, all the colonial imports came in under a heavy duty which caused the Socialists to ask "Why," if the import of food is so essential. "The answer simply sets up a vicious circle, for tariff, the capitalists reply, is necessary to support a navy, to protect colonies which provide cocoa and coffee which one could buy cheaper were there no tariff."

Bebel clinched his argument by citing the trade statistics which, even to an impartial eye, showed how insignificant the colonial trade with the empire had proved, especially when one compared it to the total German foreign trade. In 1904, the colonial trade amounting to 64,459,000 M. was only one-half per cent of the total foreign trade which reached 13,278,100,100 M.; [30] and in view of how much the empire had sacrificed for it, it became even more insignificant. As Bebel put it, "Germany's trade with the British empire amounted to 2,700,000,000 M. in 1905 and did not cost Germany one cent; and if Germany should lose all her trade with Denmark (300,000,000 M. in 1905) it would mean much more than if all her colonial trade (64,000,000 M. in 1904) 'went to the devil'." [31] Even the commercial hopes of Kiao-Chow had not been realized. The official report [32] itself had stated that "The people of Shantung desire the cheapest wares and carry on a great trade with Japan." Indeed, the commercial reward reaped by Germany for securing this "place in the sun" was, according to the figures for the year 1904, 7,705,000 M. worth of exports, consisting mainly of military and construction supplies, and 38,000 M. worth of imports, which remained to be balanced against an imperial grant of 14,660,000 M. [32a]

In the same thoroughly scientific manner, with the aid of statistics, the Socialists disposed of the "patriotic-capitalistic" argument that colonies were necessary for the rapidly expanding German population. They called attention to the fact that most of the colonies were unsuitable for European settlement; that even to South West Africa, the best colony for Europeans, only 2,500 Germans had gone in the past ten years; and that in the year 1903, there were only 5,125 Germans,[33] all told, in all the colonies including 1,567 officials and military. Finally, they claimed that the accompanying figures showed very little inclination on the part of the German people to settle in their undeveloped colonial possessions, to which they much preferred the highly industrialized United States of America.

| Year | Africa (except South West Africa where no figures obtainable due to uprisings) | Asia [34] |
|---|---|---|
| 1904 | 1,919 | 525 |
| 1905 | 2,278 | 577 |
| 1906 | 2,704 | 693 |

Did anything remain of the capitalists' "economic-necessity" argument after these devastating revelations; the Socialists dealt it its final blow by presenting to the *Reichstag* a survey of the expense accounts of the colonies. They demonstrated that by the year 1906, no colony except Togoland was self-supporting and that all the others required annual imperial grants of unprecedented amounts. In 1903, the imperial grant for East Africa was 5,365,000 M., more than twice as much the total amount of the German imports for that year;[35] in 1904, the bare support of South West Africa cost 32,000,000 M., and added to the cost of administration and the imperial subventions, there were unusual and extraordinary expenses for buildings, public works and, above all, for the suppression of uprisings; whereas, the total trade with all the colonies in the year 1902 had only reached the same amount.[36] Again, in 1903, Kiao-Chow alone had cost the empire 12,420,000 M., which had been expended in railroads, harbors, and supplies, with nothing accruing to the Fatherland therefrom.[37] And the insurrections, during 1904-1906, in South West Africa, East Africa, and in Kamerun had enormously increased the demands on the German people: South West Africa cost 110,575,000 M. in 1904, 154,591,000 M. in 1905, and in 1906 the war alone amounted to 102,067,400 M., while the entire Herero uprising sent in a bill to the government for 323,260,000 M.[38]

Finally, how great a liability rather than an asset the colonies were to Germany was set forth by the Socialists in the following table giving the total colonial costs, revenue, and imperial grants for the years 1903-1906.

| Year | Colonial Costs | Colonial Revenue | Imperial Grants [39] |
|------|----------------|------------------|----------------------|
| 1903 | 42,104,000     | 9,351,000        | 27,371,000           |
| 1904 | 147,288,000    | 11,586,000       | 26,896,000           |
| 1905 | 204,291,000    | 15,636,000       | 75,928,000           |
| 1906 | 168,988,000    | 17,080,000       | 113,944,000          |

No matter what benefit, economic or commercial, the colonies had been to the empire, according to the claims of their supporters in the *Reichstag,* a glance at the foregoing and following tables would demonstrate, so the Socialists asserted, the tremendous drain they had been upon the Fatherland.

IMPERIAL APPROPRIATIONS FOR COLONIES 1884-1906 [40]

| | |
|---|---|
| East Africa | 93,116,000 M |
| South West Africa | 94,145,000 |
| | 323,260,000 |
| Kamerun | 25,510,000 |
| Togoland | 3,759,000 |
| New Guinea and Marshall Islands | 7,070,000 |
| Caroline, Pelew, Marianne Islands | 2,641,000 |
| Samoa | 1,374,000 |
| Kiao-Chow | 102,167,000 |

## The Parliamentary Struggle Reaches a Crisis

By 1906, this parliamentary struggle had reached a climax: in March the *Reichstag* reduced by 15,000,000 M. the estimates for maintaining the expeditionary force in South West Africa, and indicated that it wished the troops to return; and it rejected the subvention for the South West African railway and cut down the amount appropriated for the indemnification of the colonists whose property had been injured in the Herero uprising. When von Bülow proposed in the *Reichstag* that the colonial department be transformed into a separate colonial ministry, Bebel countered by declaring that an independent colonial office would only enable the government to pursue a more ambitious policy in the spirit of the Kaiser's assertion that, "Wherever in the world he could find a nail to hang his shield, there he would hang it." Finally, aroused to indignation over the astounding amount of the budget, 265,752,000 M., demanded for the year, the Opposition caused the rejection of the supplementary estimates of 29,200,000 M. for South West Africa. As a reply, von Bülow arose, drew from his portfolio and read the decree of dissolution which the Chancellor had signed that morning.

## Colonial Policy Becomes a National Issue

The electoral campaign that ensued was characterized by two things. In the first place, there was the unprecedented interference of the imperial administration, who at once squarely defined the issue as one of world policy. "Germany's position in the world is menaced. The forthcoming election will decide whether Germany is capable of developing into a world Power from a European Power," challenged the *Norddeutsche Allgemeine Zeitung.*[41] And

241

to guide the decision, Dr. Dernburg, the new colonial director, with the Chancellor behind him, directed the electioneering for the government. A "captain of industry" and formerly president of the Darmstäder Bank, he had been selected on account of his business ability by von Bülow, at the height of the parliamentary quarrel in September, 1906, to succeed the inefficient Prince Hohenlohe. His speeches, which had been delivered in the *Reichstag,* to explain the glowing promises of the new business and economic program for the colonies, were distributed as election pamphlets.

In the second place, the campaign was notable because of the attitude of the *Freisinnige Partei,* a party of the Left who had always opposed the colonial policy but who, now, for the first time adhered to its erstwhile enemies, the Conservatives and National Liberals, the parties of the Right. Its surprising shift in position during the struggle and at the time of the election, was due to a combination of causes: its liberal dislike of the Catholic Center, the loss of its leader, Richter, pleasure at the compliment the Chancellor paid it in his election manifesto, asking for its support on patriotic grounds, and finally, its declining opposition to world power. The addition of this party to the government's side added greatly to the latter's strength, for it left the Catholic Center and the Socialists to fight, two to three, against the Conservatives, National Liberals, and itself.

The nationalistic societies also rallied to the support of the government and proved of invaluable assistance: the Navy League, the Colonial Society, the Pan-German League, and the Association for the Suppression of Socialism. Through their nation-wide organizations, admirably equipped with machinery for the purpose, they disseminated the appeal to "patriotism" and "the honor of the Fatherland," whose ringing challenge lost nothing at their hands.

## The Triumph for World Policy

With all this highly efficient and patriotic support, it was not surprising that the government polled a tremendous victory on January 25, 1907. The Socialists' seats were reduced from 79 to 43, the Center's from 205 to 180, and these two parties henceforth sat in the minority over against the formidable strength of von Bülow's hybrid Conservative-National-Liberal and *Freisinnige* bloc. On the election night, thousands of people crowded to the palace to give the Kaiser an ovation. His representative, von Bülow, appeared at a window to acknowledge the cheers, and could not have better expressed the significance of the victory than by quoting, as he did, from his predecessor, the great and beloved Chancellor, "You have placed Germany in the saddle and now she can ride." [2] The election had overwhelmingly endorsed the Kaiser's *Weltpolitik*.

## NOTES

[1] *Supra.*, chs. v, vi. For summary of party support, see *Kolonialzeitschrift*, December, 1902. "Die d. Kolonialpolitik, die Parteien und das Deutsche Volk."

[2] *Die Deutsche Allgemeine Zeitung*, April 1, 1898.

[3] For text of concessions, see Decharme, *op. cit., appendix*, nos. xii and xiii.

[4] For the "Scandals," see *Kolonialpolitik nicht Kolonialskandale: Ein Rückblick auf die letzten Reichstagswählen* (Berlin, 1907).

[5] *Die Urteil der Disziplinargerichte gegen Doktor Karl Peters* (Munich, 1907). Another notable case of maladministration was that of Prince Arenberg in South West Africa, discussed in the *Reichstag* February 13, 1900.

[6] Wertheimer, *op. cit.*, p. 168.

[7] Wagner, H., "Diagnose der Kolonialpolitik" in *Koloniale Zeitschrift*, August, 1902.

[8] *Supra.*, ch. iv, p. 97.

[9] *Protokoll Parteitag, Über die Verhandlungen des Parteitages der Sozialdemokratischen Partei*, 1903, 1904, 1905, 1906.

[10] *Ibid.*, 1904, p. 86.

[11] *Die Neue Zeit*, 1906, p. 617.
For the Socialists' attitude at this time, see Noske, G., *Kolonialpolitik und Sozialdemokratie* (Stuttgart, 1914).

[12] Schippel, M., *Handbuch für Sozialdemokratische Wähler* (Berlin, 1898-1903), p. 54.

[13] *Annual Register*, 1906, p. 297.

[14] These uprisings were: the Hereros and the Bondelzwarts in South West Africa, the Bane Bule and the Batchengas and other tribes in Kamerun, the Wahehes and many other uprisings of chieftains in East Africa on account of the head-tax.

[15] *Verhandlungen des Deutschen Reichstages*, 1905-1906, vol. v, pp. 4054ff.

[16] Parvus, *Die Kolonialpolitik und der Zusammenbruch* (Leipzig, 1907), p. 64.

[17] *Verhandlungen des Deutschen Reichstages*, 1905-1906, vol. v, pp. 4021ff.

[18] Parvus, *op. cit.*, p. 76.

[19] *Verhandlungen des deutschen Reichstages*, 1903-1905, vol. vi, pp. 4176, 4099, 4100. For statistics, see *Staats-Lexikon* (Freiburg, 1911), pp. 328-30.

[20] *Ibid.*, vol. v, p. 4020.

[21] Zimmermann, *op. cit.*, p. 282.

[22] Parvus, *op. cit.*, p. 112ff.
*Verhandlungen des Deutschen Reichstages*, 1903-1904, vol. iii, pp. 2401-07, 1905-6, vol. i, p. 105.

[23] *Ibid.*, 1903-1906, vol. vi, pp. 4138-4140.

[24] *Ibid.*, 1905-1906, vol. i, p. 646.

[25] *Vorwaerts*, Aug. 25, 1906.
*Verhandlungen des deutschen Reichstages*, 1905-1906, vol. v, pp. 4005, vol. iii, pp. 2257, 2236.

[26] *Ibid.*, 1905-1906, vol. iii, p. 4035ff.
For complaints of complicity of officials with this "jobbery," see *Europäische Geschichtskalender*, 1906, p. 204ff. Also, *Vorwaerts*, Aug. 23, 1906, case of Fischer.

[27] *Verhandlungen des deutschen Reichstages*, 1905-1906, vol. 1, p. 105.

[28] Parvus, *op. cit.*, p. 95ff.
*Statistisches Jahrbuch für das Deutsche Reich*, 1905, p. 98.

[29] Parvus, *op. cit.*, p. 16.

[30] *Statistisches Jahrbuch für das Deutsche Reich*, 1905, p. 321.

[31] *Verhandlungen des deutschen Reichstages*, 1905-1906, vol. v, pp. 4065ff.

[32] *Handbuch für Sozialdemokratische Wähler*, p. 62.

[32a] *Statistisches Jahrbuch*, 1906, p. 347.

[33] *Verhandlungen des deutschen Reichstages*, 1905-1906, vol. v, p. 3981ff.
*Annual Register*, 1903, p. 284.

[34] *Statistisches Jahrbuch*, 1906, p. 22, 1907, p. 23.

[35] Zimmermann, *op. cit.*, p. 242.

[36] *Verhandlungen des deutschen Reichstages*, 1903-1905, vol. v, p. 3356.

[37] *Ibid.*, p. 3357.

[38] Noske, *op. cit.*, pp. 110, 139.

[39] Compiled from *Statistisches Jahrbuch*, 1903, pp. 257, 339; 1904, p. 252; 1906, p. 201; and *Statesman's Year Book*, 1904, p. 268; 1905, p. 331; 1906, p. 339.

[40] Noske, *op. cit.*, p. 139.

[41] *Norddeutsche Allgemeine Zeitung*, Dec. 13, 1906, *Sonderausgabe.* See also Bülow's speech at dissolution of *Reichstag* 13 Dec., 1906: "The issue involves the question of our entire colonial policy and, what is more, of our position in the world." Masson, W., *Fürst Bülows Reden*, vol. 4, p. 170.

[42] *Europäische Geschichtskalender*, 1907, p. 170.

# CHAPTER IX

## SCIENTIFIC COLONIZATION

### The New Era

THE overwhelming victory of the government in the parliamentary crisis of 1906-1907 inaugurated a new era in Germany's internal colonial history. For, although the election of 1906 conveyed a national mandate to continue the vigorous prosecution of a colonial policy, which was now frankly identified with world power, it was a mandate fraught with a heavy responsibility for the administration. Criticism had been too severe and too searching, revelations of mismanagement too true and too compromising not to sound a warning and to point a moral. Henceforth, it behooved the Kaiser and his ministers, chastened by the parliamentary struggle, to direct their attention to the colonies themselves, and to cease to exploit them as mere pawns in the game of *Weltpolitik*. It had been made extremely clear that, in order to keep the colonies at all, the experimental period of mistakes, of graft, of concessions, and of individual license must be left behind and an efficient, scientific, and economic rule inaugurated in its stead, a rule which would contribute to the benefit of the whole German people and so win their hearty support.

### The First Colonial Secretary

The man to meet this situation confronting the government and to act upon it was Bernhard Dernburg, the first

246

Secretary for the Colonies. He had been originally selected by von Bülow, made cautious through the parliamentary criticism, for his business ability and his capacity to remedy those faults of bureaucracy, graft, economic inefficiency, and general maladministration which were killing the colonies abroad as well as destroying the colonial cause at home. His own past experience in the firm of Thalmann and Company of New York, in the *Deutsche Bank,* and as manager of the *Darmstädter Bank* prepared him with a knowledge of Germany's economic life and an acquaintance with financial and business groups most essential for any national colonial development; while the specific criticisms of the *Reichstag* indicated to him the mistakes to be avoided and the evils to be corrected. For Dr. Dernburg had a double task to perform: on the one hand, he was obliged to resuscitate and to popularize the colonial sentiment in Germany and, on the other, thoroughly to reconstruct the political and economic administration of the land and peoples oversea.

### A Fresh Interest in the Colonies Is Aroused

In pursuance of the former, he began early in 1907 to tour Germany, addressing meetings and lecturing upon his new colonial program, which was designed to carry a national and popular appeal to all economic classes and shades of political opinion. First and foremost, the colonies were to be henceforth, for Germany and the German people and not for the adventurer, the trader, the bureaucrat, the militarist or the commercial company; the land with its treasures was to be recovered for the national use and scientifically developed instead of exploited; commercial undertakings were to lose their speculative character and to be established on a sound business basis, and the misbehavior of officials was to be summarily punished. Finally, the natives were to be regarded as

247

the most valuable asset of the colonies; they were no longer to be destroyed but preserved and their rights guaranteed and protected, while a measure of self-government among them was to be encouraged.[1] In short, the specific grievances of the Center and of the Socialists were to be rectified as far as it was possible, so that all political parties could cooperate on this great national adventure of scientific colonization.

During his evangelizing campaign, Dr. Dernburg "discovered that the German people possessed not even a speaking knowledge of the cost or sacrifice with which the colonies had been won, and only a most superficial idea of the circumstances of their acquisition; and that, after twenty-three years of ownership." He strove, therefore, to awaken an intelligent enthusiasm and succeeded in arousing more or less general interest, especially among the business groups.[2] As a result the membership of the Colonial Society increased, investment in colonial enterprises became more universal and Hamburg created its own Colonial Institute in the year 1908. This institution flourished most successfully during the years 1908 to 1912, and became the center of information on all matters pertaining to the colonies. It directed its efforts to research and record, as well as to the dissemination of information through courses of instruction, lectures, and publications; in 1912, it numbered twenty-two professors and eighty-four assistants on the staff.[3]

But more than Dr. Dernburg's personal efforts, the discovery of diamonds in South West Africa near Lüderitz Bay boomed and advertised the colonial cause and the brilliant prospects of colonial investments, although, ultimately, the speculation to which it led proved extremely detrimental, if not in some respects disastrous. For that reason, indeed, Dr. Dernburg's policy became the subject of a great deal of adverse criticism. It was declared unsound, too speculative, and motivated entirely by the "mercantile spirit." It was charged, for instance, that out of eighty-one colonial ventures undertaken during his time, only thirty-three paid a dividend; while he himself was accused by his enemies of "juggling with figures and balancing himself with percentages." [4]

### Reorganization of the Colonial Administration

Nevertheless, the promises contained in Dr. Dernburg's colonial program, whose fulfillment constituted the second half of his task, were not made in vain. The record shows every evidence of his effort to carry out the thorough rehabilitation of the colonial system, while the state of the colonies themselves in 1914 bears witness to the effectiveness of his work.

In order more intelligently to approach his task, Dr. Dernburg journeyed to London to spend some time in the colonial office studying the British system; then to East Africa, in 1907, to South West Africa and the neighboring English colonies in 1908; and finally to the United States to study cotton culture in 1909. But, first, he reorganized the "cobwebbed" central administration at home. One of the first acts of the new *Reichstag*, elected January, 1907, had been to pass the bill which transformed the colonial department into a Cabinet ministry. [4a] As a result, the colonial office became autonomous on May 17, 1907, and as such required a new system. Besides, the needs of the internal life of the colonies themselves, if they were to be properly developed, demanded a reform of the central administration: it was necessary to provide for the different services such as the law, the army, agriculture, commerce and transportation, for which every civil state has a separate department. Consequently, the new colonial office was constituted in four divisions: the department of political affairs, general administration and justice, the department of finance, real estate, communications and technical concerns, the office for the direction of the staff and the division of military administration. It will be noted that the managerial distribution was made according to subject, and not according to the colonies themselves in contrast to the organization of the British colonial office.

Furthermore Dr. Dernburg abolished the *Kolonialrat* (colonial council) which had existed since 1891 and in its place established an agricultural and economic section with permanent officials.[5] His successor, Dr. Lindequist, carried this plan further by creating a permanent commission for the economic affairs of the colonies, drawing its members from the chambers of commerce of the important cities such as Hamburg, Bremen, Chemnitz, Cologne, and Mannheim.[6] This commission rendered valuable assistance in the development of the colonies; it made researches and surveys, regulated the credit organizations and, according to the *Norddeutsche Allgemeine Zeitung,* "promised to be of great service for colonial economics."[7] In 1913, Dr. Solf, the last colonial secretary, estimated its value so highly as to increase its membership to twenty-five.

Besides these changes in the administrative structure of the central office, Dr. Dernburg reorganized the finances of the colonies; revised and extended the colonial law, especially that part of it which related to the code of justice, so that it incorporated and synthesized the best in tribal law and custom with the German law; and reconstituted the colonial service. The reform of the latter was most urgent, demanded both by the charges of bureaucracy and of scandalous maladministration. Not only did Dr. Dernburg complete the conviction of the official culprits like von

Horn and von Puttkamer, who were degraded and cashiered in 1907, but, more fundamentally, he attacked the evil of misrule at its source and promoted the system of specialized training of colonial officials for their work, which was as yet only in its infancy. Such a system had been urged for a long time by earnest colonialists [8] and discussed in the *Kolonialrat*, but no definite plan had been adopted until the year 1905.[9] Then, a beginning was made by demanding of candidates an apprenticeship of at least one year in a bank or business; next a two-year term in Africa followed by one and a half to two years in the Seminary for Oriental Languages, University of Berlin, as well as university training in law and administration and examinations in geography, hygiene, government, and practical science.

Building upon this foundation, Dr. Dernburg both elaborated and strengthened the training course, and increased the facilities for education by promoting those institutions already started and by encouraging the establishment of others. As we have seen, the Colonial Institute at Hamburg was one outcome of his effort and the other many opportunities afforded by Germany in the year 1914 for the equipment of her colonial personnel, both official and lay, reflect the results of his work.

While Germany, it is true, possessed no single training college for colonial officials in 1914 like the one in France, the Colonial College at Harwich, England, or the Dutch School at Delft, where all phases of training are concentrated, she drew upon various institutions which specialized in diverse branches of preparation for colonial rule and settlement. Each prospective official was obliged to attend the Seminary for Oriental Languages, whose courses were extended to include other fields, such as economics, hygiene, chemistry, and administration, suitable for colonial service;

two semesters in the Colonial Institute at Hamburg, and a period of apprenticeship in the Colonial Office. There were also the *Handelshochschule* in Berlin; the Colonial Academy in Halle, connected with the University of Halle; the Colonial School at Witzenhausen for agriculture, forestry, and practical colonization; the famous Institute for Tropical Diseases at Hamburg; the Medical College at Tübingen for the special training of those concerned with such departments in the colonies. In addition, there were two schools of domestic arts for women who planned to go out to the colonies, a three-month course in the Veterinary High School in Berlin, and a Catholic Trade School, all of which received state aid.[10]

## Local Reforms

Besides the central colonial office in Berlin, the local administration was vastly improved by Dr. Dernburg and infused with a new spirit, especially in its attitude toward the natives. The military and police services were regulated, legal and judicial methods were reformed, and the civil service reconstituted and made uniform. Each colony[11] had its own governor appointed by the Kaiser with his complete staff consisting of such officials as a judge, a postmaster, a tax-collector, a doctor, a chief engineer. Directly under the governor in the larger colonies were the district chiefs (*Bezirksamtmänner*) who were assisted by smaller staffs on the model of the governor's. They served to decentralize the administration and to make it less bureaucratic, as did also the extension of the principle of legislative councils, composed of officials and citizens which had already been attached to some of the colonial governments (1903). Dr. Dernburg was especially interested in promoting self-gov. ernment, both of white settlers, especially in South West

Africa, and of natives so far as it was possible. Indeed, he encouraged an entirely different relationship in the colonies between the governors and the governed, introduced a new attitude toward the native and his rights, and attempted to win for him an equal share with the whites in the oversea territories.[12]

## A New Economic Program

But, doubtless, more fundamental than any of Dr. Dern-burg's reforms for the welfare of the colonies themselves was his economic policy. We have seen how the great companies had ravaged and exploited the oversea lands and how, during almost two decades, they had made national colonization for the universal benefit of the German people impossible. One of the most salutary effects of the crisis of 1906-1907 had been the exposition of the greed and rapaciousness of these commercial organizations, which was startlingly revealed, when the companies in South West Africa asked the *Reichstag* for national appropriations to the amount of 11,000,000 M. to indemnify their colonists who had sustained damages during the Herero revolt. So ridiculous was this made to appear and so loud was the outcry against the land policy of the companies that the imperial government appointed a commission to investigate them and to make recommendations. It advised the government, in turn, to negotiate contracts with the companies by which it could gradually purchase back their land and rights, so that they would become the property once more of the German state. Dr. Dernburg facilitated this process, which was designed ultimately to destroy the pernicious stranglehold of the concessions upon the African colonies. The commission dealt with about nine companies, but was not successful with all owing to their entrenched position. It was obliged, for instance, to restore its land to the Company of North West Kamerun. Thus the land question was not solved by 1914, but the concession policy had received its death blow and the colonial lands were slowly being recovered by the state.[13]

And how vitally essential it was for Germany to develop her oversea territories, Dr. Dernburg set out to demonstrate. His business training enabled him accurately to survey the nation's economic status and to estimate wherein the latent potentialities of the oversea territories could either supplement her strength or compensate her weakness. He was the first of all the directors of the colonial empire thoroughly to grasp the sudden and marvelous effect of the Industrial Revolution in transforming, almost overnight, an obscure agricultural country of 41,000,000 people into a strong industrialized nation of 60,000,000; he realized that Germany required as a result a vast supply of foodstuffs and of raw materials; that her productivity, furthermore, had not kept pace with her expanding industry, and that her soil was as insufficient to feed her ever-increasing population as were her natural resources to satisfy her voracious machines. Just as the Kaiser felt the struggle of his giant-like nation to burst its bonds, and sought to relieve it by more acquisitions and by gaining a "place in the sun" which coincided with his ambition for world power; so the more practical Dr. Dernburg sensed the same straining energy, but strove to release it by providing an outlet in the intensive cultivation of the already-won colonies.

His plans were comprehensive and reflected a wide study of the situation combined with a broad if sometimes too rosy vision. His idea was, on the one hand, to produce in the colonies those commodities, foodstuffs, and raw materials which Germany was obliged to import from other nations; and, on the other, so to civilize and elevate the natives that they would provide a constant market for the home industries. For Dr. Dernburg belonged to that large group who thoroughly believe in the undisputed value of colonies to the mother country as a solution for the problems of marketing surplus goods and of providing raw materials.[14] He envisaged East Africa as supplying in the future all Germany's large demand for vegetable-oil products, her hemp, and part of her immense coffee and cocoa consumption; South West Africa, a considerable share of her copper and wool; and Kamerun, Togoland, and East Africa, together, all of her rubber. He had visions of petroleum wells in New Guinea and in Kamerun, and plans for great cotton plantations in Togoland, Kamerun, and East Africa.[15] Moreover, he imagined the Bantus, the Askari, and the Buschiri, to say nothing of the Hottentots, becoming so imbued with the needs of western civilization that, within a reasonable time, they would be consuming quantities of clocks, toys, leather purses, machinery, and automobile tires all emblazoned with the trade-mark, "Made in Germany."

Nor did Dr. Dernburg neglect the problem of transportation so essential to render the vast stretches of unexplored colonial areas available and accessible. His railway program, indeed, constitutes one of his most significant contributions to scientific colonization for, prior to 1906, it had been sadly neglected. At the close of that year, Dr. Dernburg found only 1,350 kilometers of railroads in the African colonies. He more than doubled the mileage between 1906 and 1910, and gave railway construction a momentum which only ceased with the Great War.

### The Colonial Economic Committee

Of inestimable assistance to the colonial secretary and to the cause of scientific colonization were the earnest, forward-looking colonialists themselves. Indeed, they had helped prepare the way for it as private initiative always seemed to do in German colonial history. Especially active in this respect was the *Kolonial-Wirtschaftliches Komitee* (the Colonial Economic Committee). Founded in 1896 by the group in the Colonial Society who deplored the inactivity of the administration, absorbed in *Weltpolitik,* its formation was virtually a protest against the government's neglect to develop the colonies. Since the value of those territories was yet to be discovered, the Economic Committee set before itself four objectives: to ascertain Germany's need of colonial raw materials, to satisfactorily develop the economic possibilities in the colonies, to increase transportation facilities between Germany and the colonies, and to encourage and facilitate the settlement of Germans therein. By 1914, the organization had come to include princes, economic institutes, chambers of commerce, banks, cities, commercial and industrial firms, missionary societies, even workingmen's unions. It possessed in Germany a Mercantile Headquarters, a Scientific-Technical Headquarters, and many branches in the colonies. In connection with scientific institutions of the country, especially with the Royal Scientific Institute, the committee was carrying on researches in soils, seeds, plants, chemical testings of raw materials and products, diseases of plants and animals. It had sent research expeditions of experts into Central and South America and the Southern States of North America; into Mexico, North Africa, Egypt, British and Dutch India; into British and French West Africa, the Congo, Mesopotamia, and Persia. Furthermore, it cooperated with trade and industry through the dissemination of information by means of its monthly periodical, *Der Tropenpflanzer,* the *Trade Address Book,* and numerous other publications, and by means of fairs and expositions. Always working in close cooperation with the colonial office, this committee helped to focus and to perpetuate the scientific colonial policy which Secretary Dernburg so firmly established.[16]

## The Results

Perhaps the best and most graphic way to estimate Dr. Dernburg's work and the significance of the new era of colonization which he initiated is to survey the economic status of Germany's colonies in 1914, especially in their relation to the needs of the Fatherland. For Dr. Dernburg's successors in the colonial office, Dr. Lindequist (1910-1911) and Dr. Solf (1911-1918) carried forward the new colonial policy with such energy that they were enabled to witness its first fruits.

On the eve of the Great War, the economic needs of the German empire were imperious. Germany had become the third strongest industrial power in Europe, but she could support only two-thirds of her 60,000,000 people and consequently 20,000,000 were dependent upon the outside world. She was obliged, for instance, to import all of her coffee at an expense of 250,000,000 M. annually; all of her cocoa amounting to 58,000,000 M. in 1913, a large proportion of her meat, eggs, butter, milk, costing in 1913, 836,000,000 M.; vegetable fats and oils costing 721,000,-000 M. in 1913; all of her tobacco amounting to 147,000,-000 M. in 1913; and most of her fruits, for example, bananas costing 11,000,000 marks in 1913.[17]

Again for her industries, she had to import all of her

raw cotton, for which she paid 600,000,000 M. since the export of cotton goods occupied fourth place (after machinery, ironware, and coal) in her list of exports, and since she held next to England and the United States third place in the cotton manufacture of the world; all of her raw rubber, amounting to 113,000,000 M. annually, holding next to the United States second place in the rubber industry; most of her wool, estimated at 386,000,000 M.; most of her raw material for the leather industry, 453,000,000 M.; all of her raw copper, amounting to 335,000,000 M. in 1913.

By 1914, the colonies were just beginning to meet some of these enormous and pressing needs and to demonstrate the results of the sound, stable, and national colonial policy which created a great faith, whether justified or not, in their potential economic strength. For example, the oversea territories were supplying to the mother country one-twelfth of the vegetable fats and oils imported from colonial sources, one-fifth of the demand for rubber, one-fifth of the demand for cocoa, one hundred per cent of the need for sisal hemp, and a large part of the demand for phosphate.

## Increased Colonial Production

To cite some of the most striking and concrete examples of increased colonial production: The export of raw cotton from East Africa had increased ten times since 1902, while that of rubber from East Africa, Kamerun, and Togoland had quadrupled since 1908; the production of sisal hemp in East Africa had grown ten times greater between 1905 and 1914, so that it supplied all Germany's requirement and gave promise of soon supplying other countries. The output of vegetable fats and oils, so essential for soap, butter, lubricants, and food, had more than doubled since 1905; the cocoa crop had become one and one-half times greater during the five years 1909-1914; while the number of bales of hides shipped from East Africa had increased eight times and from Kamerun five times since 1910. In fact, the only serious disappointments in colonial production had been the failure of the great attempts to cultivate coffee in East Africa and tobacco in Kamerun where hopes were unfulfilled.[18]

## Colonial Research Institutes

Much of this increased production was due to the agricultural institutes, experimental and research stations established in the colonies. The Colonial Economic Committee had been largely responsible for these institutions before 1906 and had continued their cooperation after Dr. Dernburg made their support a distinct colonial policy. Each African colony posssessed these establishments: East Africa numbered four cotton and four fruit culture experimental stations, the Agricultural Experimental Station at Kibongoto (1911) and the world-famous Biological-Agricultural Research Institute of Amani (1902) The latter, situated near Tanga and comprising approximately 750 acres of grounds, was a "tropical scientific institute superior to anything in the British colonies and protectorates, and comparable with Pusa in India or the Dutch establishment at Buitenzarg in Java." [19] Kamerun contained four stock-raising stations (1901-1911), four for rubber culture, three for cocoa inspection as well as the central Agricultural School and Experimental Station at Victoria (1891); Togoland had three cotton and one agricultural station, and South West Africa supported one station for general agriculture (1911), one for sheep (1909), one for tobacco (1912), and one for ostriches (1911), besides the Imperial Agricultural Institute founded 1898. In the South Sea colonies, the economic experimental work was only in preparation; New Guinea boasted the one institute, the Experimental Garden at Raboul.

Besides maintaining these stations in the colonies, the government further fostered economic development by irrigation works, meteorological service, instruction of natives by itinerant teachers and inspectors, the payment of premiums for fighting disease. An official government personnel, consisting of experts and teachers in each colony, had charge of this work.

### Colonial Institutes and Schools in Germany

Also, at home in Germany, a number of special institutions aided and supervised by the colonial office, made colonial economic development their object. Such were the Colonial Institute in Hamburg, founded in 1908 in connection with the Hamburg University; the Colonial Academy in Halle, founded in 1908 in connection with the University of Halle and the Agricultural Institute there; the Seminary of Oriental Languages in Berlin University which of late years included courses of lectures on colonial economic development; a School for Colonial Agriculture at Leipzig founded in 1909; and the Colonial School, Wilhelmsdorf at Witzenhausen, founded in 1898 for the scientific and practical training of colonial planters and stock raisers.

This latter school is especially interesting in that it represents the reaction of the intelligent colonialists to the failure of the colonies in the nineties due to administrative neglect. They realized that to make colonization something more than an adventure and consequently useless as it then was, youthful colonizers of energy and capacity must be trained. Most picturesquely situated in the cloistered building of an ancient monastery on the Werra River near Cassel, its object, as a sort of "economic university," was to "prepare the best youth of the middle-class" for settlement in the oversea territories. It combined the humanistic studies, such as colonial history, geography, law, foreign languages, natural sciences, with the practical courses in agriculture, animal husbandry, crafts, mechanics, and boatbuilding. In 1914, it numbered six professors, thirteen visiting professors, and thirteen masters on its staff and had a registration of five hundred.[20]

## Mineral Resources of the Colonies

In addition to the scientific development of the soil, the mineral resources of the oversea territories had been also intensively cultivated since 1906, although German colonies were not rich in minerals. They were found only in South West Africa and South Sea Islands, and in East Africa to a slight degree. Nevertheless, the most was made out of little: the output of copper from South West Africa increased six times between 1907 and 1913; of tin, seventeen times; of gold, thirty-eight; and of marble, one hundred and fifty. Diamonds, discovered in South West Africa in 1908, rose from 51,180,000 M. to 58,000,000 M. value and, in 1913, their production formed one-fifth of the total African diamond output. Instead of Dr. Dernburg's petroleum wells, which had not materialized by 1913, great phosphate beds were discovered on the South Sea Islands (1910-1911), chiefly on the island of Nauru in the Marshall group and Augwar in the Pelew archipelago. Their yield was quite extraordinary, increasing to the amount of 193,125,000 kilograms in 1912.[21]

## Economic Progress in Kiao-Chow

Although Kiao-Chow was capable of no agricultural cultivation such as took place in the African and South Sea colonies, it received its own economic development suitable to its position as a naval base and trading post. Immediately after its acquisition, the *Reichstag* appropriated 14,000,000 M. to deepen the harbor, to construct a mole two miles long as well as a large floating dock capable of receiving vessels of large tonnage, which converted Kiao-Chow into a first class port, one of the most modern in the world. Private capital developed the coal mines at Poshan and Weihsen, less than one hundred miles distant from the harbor, and built two hundred and fifty miles of railroad into the interior, connecting T'singtao, where trade centered, with Chinan Fu, the capital of Shantung Province, as well as lines to Tien Tsin and other points. Industries were established, roads built, European methods introduced. General shipping increased from one hundred and eighty-two ships in 1900 to nine hundred and two in 1914, while the value of Kiao-Chow's transit trade rose from 77,000,000 M. in 1904 to 180,000,000 M. in 1912.[22]

## Slight Increase of White Settlers

The result of all this intensive economic cultivation of the colonies was, naturally, to increase the stream of white settlers going out to Africa and the South Seas which, until 1905, had been extremely thin. Although most of Germany's colonies are situated in the tropics, which renders them unsuitable for Europeans, yet constant scientific advance was making them livable and the white population tripled during the decade 1903-1913. The total number, however, amounting to about 25,000 in 1914, indicated no very great inclination on the part of the German people to leave the highly industrialized civilization of the Fatherland and try their fortunes in the highlands of East Africa, the plateaus of

South West Africa or on the plantations of Kamerun or New Guinea.

## Growth of Colonial Trade

Trade exhibited a more satisfactory growth, for the total amount of colonial trade rose in value from 71,213,000 M., in 1904, to 263,400,000 M., in 1913.

Of this total, however, less than one-half, 110,000,000 M., was with Germany and represented, in 1914, only one-half of one per cent of the nation's total foreign commerce; while the exports from Germany to the colonies slightly outbalanced the imports from the colonies to the Fatherland. Naturally, with trade and economic development, general business interests increased so that by 1914 four hundred companies and firms were active in the oversea territories. They consisted of ten banks, nine steamship lines, forty-seven mining companies, one hundred and thirty-eight plantation and stock-raising companies, forty-nine diamond concerns, and one hundred and nine miscellaneous industrial firms. The total amount of capital invested was estimated at 505,000,000 M. German and 88,900,000 M. foreign.

## Increased Transportation and Communication Facilities

Finally, the railways, shipping, and internal communications of course kept pace with awakened economic activity. Rail mileage increased about ten times, illustrating the result of Dr. Dernburg's stimulus, so that Germany operated altogether about four thousand kilometers of railroads in her colonies in 1914. On the eve of the Great War, the extension of the most important railway in German East Africa, the Tanganyika-Dar-es-Salaam line, running from Lake

Tanganyika to the seacoast, was completed and opened in March, 1914. It covers twelve hundred and fifty kilometers, the same distance as from Berlin to Milan. Shipping, likewise, employed a fleet of one hundred and thirty-eight ships of six hundred and fifty-three thousand tons register in the direct colonial merchant service to Africa and the South Seas in 1914, instead of sixty-eight vessels of two hundred and twenty-three thousand tons register in the year 1904. Colonial post offices numbered two hundred and sixty-seven in 1914, and radio stations fourteen. The direct cable connecting Kamerun and Togoland with Germany was laid during the ten years preceding the war and telegraph facilities between West and South West Africa had been lately established. Altogether, the potential economic value of the German colonial empire, based upon the beginnings of scientific colonization inaugurated during the decade prior to the war, appeared in 1914 to colonialists to be not inconsiderable.

As regards the actual economic value on the other hand, the increasing extent to which the German government made itself responsible for colonial administration and development resulted in the constant growth of expenditure and deficits which had to be met out of taxation in Germany.[23] In 1914, Togoland was the only self-supporting colony and the amount which the others were costing the nation, the accompanying table will make clear.[24]

COST OF COLONIES

| Year | Total Expense | Own Revenue | Deficit |
|------|---------------|-------------|---------|
| 1908 | 155,530,000 | 24,110,000 | 131,420,000 M |
| 1909 | 68,110,000 | 42,530,000 | 25,580,000 |
| 1910 | 82,450,000 | 48,720,000 | 33,730,000 |
| 1911 | 96,690,000 | 53,180,000 | 43,510,000 |
| 1912 | 87,630,000 | 64,520,000 | 23,110,000 |
| 1913 | 105,810,000 | 67,970,000 | 37,880,000 |

## SUMMARY
### ECONOMIC STATUS, GERMAN COLONIES, 1913-1914
### THE AFRICAN COLONIES

| | German East Africa | South West Africa | Kamerun | Togoland |
|---|---|---|---|---|
| Area—Square Miles......... | 393,500 | 322,000 | 197,498 | 34,600 |
| Native Population......... | 7,645,770 | 80,556 | 3,326,132 | 1,031,978 |
| Whites......... | 5,336 | 14,830 | 1,871 | 368 |
| Chief Products......... | Rubber, Sisal, Hides, Coffee | Live-Stock, Hides, Diamonds | Rubber, Cocoa, Palm-Oils | Palm-Oils Rubber, Cotton |
| Minerals......... | Gold, Mica | Diamonds, Copper | | |
| Chief Ports......... | Dar-es-Salaam Tanga | Swakopmund Lüderitzbucht | Victoria, Douala | Anecho, Lome |
| Railways......... | 771 miles | 1,222 miles | 193 miles | 203 miles |
| Exports......... | 31,418,000 M. | 39,000,000 M. | 23,336,000 M. | 9,958,000 M. |
| Imports......... | 50,309,000 M. | 32,500,000 M. | 34,241,000 M. | 11,427,000 M. |
| Revenue and Expenditure......... | 54,760,000 M. | 54,140,000 M. | 15,340,000 M. | 3,380,000 M. |
| Deficit or Subsidy......... | 40,940,000 M. | 38,520,000 M. | 6,940,000 M. | None |

## SUMMARY
## ECONOMIC STATUS, GERMAN COLONIES, 1913-1914
### THE PACIFIC COLONIES

| | New Guinea and Bismarck Archip. | Samoa | Caroline, Pelew, Marianne, Marschall Islands | Kiao-Chow |
|---|---|---|---|---|
| Area—Square Miles.................... | 90,000 | 10,000 | 5,160 | 220 |
| Native Population................... | 719,000 | 35,000 | 15,000 | 192,000 |
| Whites............................ | 968 | 557 | 459 | 4,470 |
| Chief Products..................... | Copra, Cocoa Cotton, Rubber | Copra, Cocoa | Copra, Phosphate | Coal, Silk |
| Minerals........................... | Mother-of-Pearl | | Phosphate | Coal |
| Chief Ports........................ | Herbertshöhe | Apia | Jaluit | Tsing-Tau |
| Railways........................... | | | | 272 miles |
| Exports............................ | 5,100,000 M. | 5,100,000 M. | 6,900,000 M. | 79,640,000 M. |
| Imports............................ | 5,871,000 M. | 4,900,000 M. | 3,400,000 M. | 6,062,700 M. |
| Revenue and Expenditure........... | 5,060,000 M. | 1,130,000 M. | Included in New Guinea | 26,470,000 M. |
| Deficit or Subsidy................. | 1,650,000 M. | 160,000 M. | Included in New Guinea | 10,340,000 M. |

266

# SCIENTIFIC COLONIZATION

## INCREASE IN BUSINESS

### The Capital of the Business Companies in the Colonies

1896: 62.000.000 M.

1904: 185.000.000 M.

1912: 505.000.000 M.

1896:   62 Million M.
1904: 185 Million M.
1912: 505 Million M.

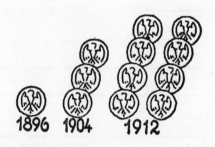

### Increase in Railroads in the Colonies
#### (Mileage in kilometers)

1896: 40 km

1904: 471 km

1912: 3867 km

1896    40 km
1904    471 "
1912  3867

1896   1904   1912

### Increase in Shipping in the Colonies

1896:   37 Ships with a total tonnage register of   94,000 tons.

1904:   68 Ships with a total tonnage register of 223,000 tons.

1912: 138 Ships with a total tonnage register of 653,000 tons.

267

# RISE AND FALL OF GERMANY'S COLONIAL EMPIRE

### INCREASE IN COLONIAL TRADE

1896: Total trade 32,500,000 M.

——————— Imports 21,000,000 M.

—————— Exports 11,500,000 M.


1904: Total trade 71,213,000 M.

——————————————— Imports 46,469,000 M.

————————————— Exports 24,744,000 M.


1912: Total trade 263,559,000 M.

Imports 142,679,000 M.

Exports 120,880,000 M.

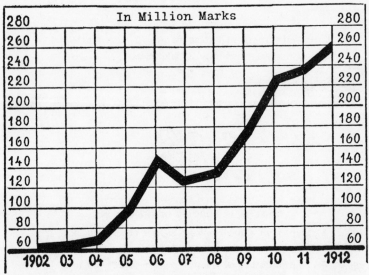

Total Colonial Trade (except Kiao-Chow)

# SCIENTIFIC COLONIZATION

## INCREASE IN AMOUNT OF LAND BROUGHT UNDER CULTIVATION

*1896: 11.000*  Hectares

*1904: 43.000.*  Hectares

*1912 · 140.000.*  Hectares

## INCREASE IN LAND UNDER CULTIVATION

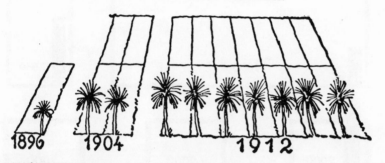

1896: 11,000 Hectares.   1904: 43,000 Hectares.   1912: 140,000 Hectares.

## INCREASE IN AMOUNT OF PRODUCTION FROM THE LAND
### (Valued in Marks)

|           | 1894      | 1896      | 1906      | 1908      | 1910       | 1912       |
|-----------|-----------|-----------|-----------|-----------|------------|------------|
| Natives.. | 4,800,000 | 4,000,000 | 8,000,000 | 5,700,000 | 10,400,000 | 13,000,000 |
| Europeans | 50,000    | 250,000   | 300,000   | 5,300,000 | 10,400,000 | 18,000,000 |

Greatest increase in East Africa.

# RISE AND FALL OF GERMANY'S COLONIAL EMPIRE

## COLONIAL POSSESSIONS IN COMPARISON TO THE HOMELAND

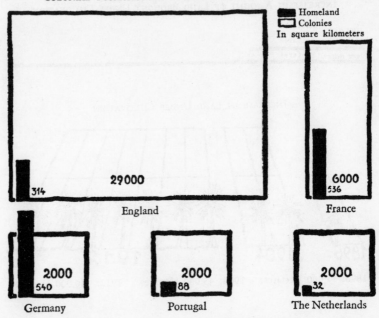

■ Homeland
□ Colonies
In square kilometers

**29000**
314

England

**6000**
536

France

**2000**
540

Germany

**2000**
88

Portugal

**2000**
32

The Netherlands

## INCREASE IN NUMBER OF WHITES IN GERMAN COLONIES

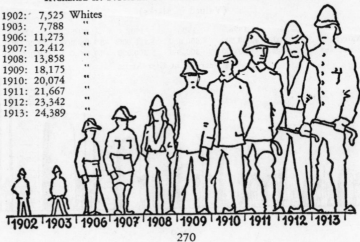

| | |
|---|---|
| 1902: | 7,525 Whites |
| 1903: | 7,788 " |
| 1906: | 11,273 " |
| 1907: | 12,412 " |
| 1908: | 13,858 " |
| 1909: | 18,175 " |
| 1910: | 20,074 " |
| 1911: | 21,667 " |
| 1912: | 23,342 " |
| 1913: | 24,389 " |

1902 1903 1906 1907 1908 1909 1910 1911 1912 1913

# SCIENTIFIC COLONIZATION

## NOTES

[1] Dernburg, B., *Zielpunkte des deutschen Kolonialwesens* (Berlin, 1907).

[2] Berliner *Tageblatt*, Jan. 9, 1910 claimed that 200 new colonial undertakings were created in the Dernburg era.

[3] Schnee, H., (Ed.), *Kolonial-Lexikon, op. cit.*, articles on *Hambürgisches Kolonialinstitut*. Also, see Rathgen, K., *Speech at Opening of Colonial Institute* at Hamburg, October 20, 1908 (Hamburg, 1908).

[4] *Deutsche Tageszeitung*, 1912, *Heft*, i, 13.
Hassell, W., *Haben Wir Eine Kolonialreform. Kolonialpolitische Betrachtungen über die Aera Dernburgs* (Stuttgart, 1909).

[4a] *Reichsgesetzblatt*, p. 239.

[5] *Ibid.*, p. 28.

[6] *Das Kolonialblatt*, p. 654.

[7] *Norddeutsche Allgemeine Zeitung*, Oct. 5, 1911.

[8] *Die Kolonialzeitschrift*, 1901, p. 88. Sharlach, Dr., "Ausbildung der Beamten."

[9] *Auswärtiges Amt. Kolonialabtheilung. Denkschrift über Ausbildung eines eigenen Beamtenstandes für die Kolonieen*, June 16, 1902.
See also, *Auswärtiges Amt. V, Sitzungperiode*, 1898, no. 16, IV *Sitzungperiode*, 1895-1898, no. 13. Zimmermann, *op. cit.*, pp. 115-116.

[10] *Kolonial-Lexikon, op. cit.*, Article, "Kolonialschulen."

[11] Except *Kiao-Chow*, which was under the ministry of marine; the Caroline, Pelew and Marianne Islands, which were under New Guinea; the Marshall, Brown and Providence Islands which were under Samoa.

[12] See *infra.*, ch. x, p. 278.

[13] *Anlagen des deutschen Reichstages*, 1909-1910. *Drucksache*, no. 196.

[14] Moon, *op. cit.*, p. 525.

[15] *Zielpunkte des d. Kolonialwesens, op. cit.*

[16] *Kolonial-Lexikon, op. cit.*, Article on Kolonial-Wirtschaftliches Komitee.
See also, *Kolonial-Wirtschaftliches Komitee, Die Arbeit des Kolonial-Wirtschaftlichen Komitees*, 1896-1911 (Hamburg, 1911), and *Verhandlungen des Kolonial-Wirtschaftliches Komitees* (Berlin, 1904).

[17] These figures compiled from:
*Statistisches Jahrbuch für das Deutsche Reich*
*Amtliche Denkschriften betr. die Schutzgebiete*
*Kolonial-Wirtschaftliches Komitee, Unsere Kolonialwirtschaft in ihrer Bedeutung für Industrie, Handel und Landwirtschaft* (Berlin, 1914).
Speech of Dernburg upon retirement, *Annual Register*, 1910, p. 312.

[18] *Ibid.*

[19] *Report East African Commission Presented to Parliament*, April, 1925, Cmd. 2387, p. 85.

[20] *Auszug aus den Berichte der Deutschen Kolonialschule Witzenhausen, Wilhelmsdorf, über das Jahr, 1907-1908, das zehnte Betriebsjahr.* E. Fabarius, Direktor.

*Nachrichten über Die Deutsche Kolonialschule* (1899).

Schantz, M., *L'Ecole Coloniale Allemande de Witzenhausen* (Brussels, 1914).

*Der Deutsche Kultur Pioneer, Zeitschrift für die Deutsche Kolonialschule.*

[21] *Supra.*, ch. ix, p. 258.

[22] *Denkschrift über Kiao-Chow, 1911, Europäische Geschichtskalender,* 1911, p. 10, 1913, p. 88.

[23] Since 1908, a considerable amount of non-recurrent expenditure for colonial purposes not always in the nature of capital investments has been covered by loans. In East Africa, Kamerun and Togoland, these were taken over by the colonies themselves—the empire meeting the interest and repayments.

| | |
|---|---|
| 1908 | 37,376,000 |
| 1909 | 33,080,000 |
| 1910 | 35,950,000 |
| 1911 | 33,280,000 |
| 1912 | 31,490,000 |
| 1913 | 52,200,000 |

Compiled from *Die deutsche Schutzgebiete, Amtliche Denkschriften.*

[24] *Ibid.*

# CHAPTER X

## NATIVE POLICY

*The Native Peoples Feel the Effect of the New Era*

"THE most valuable factor in our colonies is the native.
. . . He constitutes, in fact, our chief problem," said Dr.
Dernburg in the year 1907.[1] And the inauguration of scientific colonization witnessed the dawning of a new era also
for the indigenous peoples.

During the first twenty years of Germany's colonial history, as we have observed, the native had been most cruelly
treated and unjustly exploited. In short, he had suffered the
same fate as befalls every such population throughout those
stormy initial years which lay the foundations of all colonial
empires. Robbed of his lands, his home, his freedom and
often wantonly and cruelly of his life by the colonial adventurer, official or trading company, his continuous and fierce
revolts were but the tragic witnesses to his wretchedness and
helplessness. Nothing, indeed, is more significant of the
change for the better in the attitude of Germany's colonial
administration toward the native than the fact that there
occurred no actual native uprisings during the years 1908-
1914. Peace prevailed throughout the oversea empire. And
freed from the burden of prosecuting an almost constant and
devastating warfare in the colonies, the Colonial Office could
direct its energies and its resources toward a constructive
rather than a destructive rule.

### The Official Attitude toward the Natives

A clear definition of this new and enlightened attitude toward the native peoples may readily be found in the public utterances and programs of the colonial secretaries and other leaders of the time. "With the progress of civilization, methods of colonization have changed . . . and we can employ the most advanced theoretical and practical knowledge in all fields. . . . So that now we are able to colonize by building up instead of by tearing down, in which process the missionary and the physician play just as important a rôle as the railway and the machine," [2] asserted Dr. Dernburg who with Freiherr von Rechenberg, governor of East Africa, thoroughly believed that the colonies should be administered primarily in the interest of the natives and not of the colonial settler. Hence his attempts to equalize as far as it was possible the opportunities for whites and blacks; to protect the blacks in the possession of their own land and in their position as hired laborers on the estates of the white planters; and finally to extend to them the measures of self-government, building upon what his predecessor, Dr. Stübel, had begun.

Such an enlightened policy toward the native met with the hearty approval and support of those few colonial leaders who had been crying out, since 1890, that injustice on the part of the companies and the unscrupulous adventurers was, in their opinion, the chief cause of Germany's failure in the colonial field. They pointed out that Bismarck at the very beginning was the only one who had realized the importance of the native as an asset, and that he had laid down the principles of native welfare and of antislavery at the Berlin Congress in 1884. Now, however, such sentiments as, "The attitude towards the inhabitants

274

must change . . . we must not allow them to sink to mere chattels but must make of them independent, industrious peasants," uttered by the better class of colonizers, such as Vietor and Denhardt,[3] found an echo in official circles and, moreover, continued to determine administrative policy until the year 1918. As the last colonial secretary, Dr. Solf, expressed it in a speech to the *Reichstag* in 1913, "The natives, Gentlemen, are our wards and therefore it is the duty of the German government to consider their just interests as its own. For we do not wish to exterminate but to preserve them. . . . This is a moral duty to which we stand pledged through the act of hoisting our flag over our African and South Seas possessions." [4] And Professor Bonn repeated the same sentiments in his address before the *Royal Colonial Society* in London in 1914 when he stated: "German colonial policy is now one of development rather than of domination, of cultivation rather than of bureaucratic control. The period of iron rule and systematic exploitation has come to an end. The colonial empire is no longer to rest upon subservience and tribute. . . . The question of native treatment is a question of responsibility for all nations. It should serve to draw them all together." [5]

Also, during the last few years before the war the colonial debates in the *Reichstag* clearly exhibited in all parties, besides the Socialist and Center who had always championed native justice, a quickened conscience and a lively sense of responsibility toward the "wards of the nation." In 1912, for instance, the *Reichstag* [6] denounced Belgium's contravention of the Congo Act in regard to its provision for the protection of native production rights by her grant of an immense concession, consisting of 750,000 square miles of the best palm-oil lands, to the firm of Lever Brothers; a concession which the British parliament also condemned. Likewise, in 1914, the representatives of the German West African Planters officially stated their policy to be one of native protection and welfare.[7]

How the imperial government translated these principles into action will be the task of this chapter to describe. For so severe and so prolific have been the attacks upon Germany's colonial policy in this respect, so voluminous was the propaganda during the war and especially during the Peace Settlement,[8] that it would seem of value to read the record carefully and to assemble the facts clearly before us, so that we may draw our own conclusions from them. At the same time, it must be remembered that every one in Germany was not of the same opinion about native rule as were the official administration and the best type of colonist; that there were many both at home and in the colonies who regarded the Africans not as a responsibility, but as fair game to be exploited, or thought of him not at all so long as they received their dividends from colonial investments, and did everything in their power to block the efforts of the government in his behalf. Many of the colonial planters, for instance, highly indignant at Dernburg because of his determination to protect the native, to encourage native farming and production, became his sworn enemies and helped precipitate his withdrawal from office in 1910; others disregarded the ordinances designed to protect the blacks from abuse by the whites, and so brought down a damning and often well-deserved criticism upon the colonial administration itself.

## Political Status of the Natives

Certain aspects of every nation's colonial rule indicate its official attitude toward the primitive population in its oversea possessions. Broadly speaking these are, first, the statutes which define the legal, political, and economic status of the native; second, the laws and ordinances which aim to shield him from various abuses and injustices; and third, those measures which promote his material and moral well-being and his social progress.

In any description of the political, legal, and economic status of the native, now under discussion, it must be remembered that all Germany's colonies were located in the tropics, and that their inhabitants were at that stage of development where they could not for the most part stand by themselves so far as government was concerned. Consequently, we find in 1914 in every German colony, except in Kiao-Chow which was governed by the ministry of marine and in the Caroline and Marianne Islands which were administered from New Guinea, an imperial governor and his staff, a complete civil service, a code of native law and a judicial system. The chief officers of the civil service list consisted of a treasurer, a judge, a collector of taxes, a postmaster, a doctor, and an engineer. Directly under the governor were the district chiefs or *Bezirksamtmänner* who were assisted by smaller staffs on the model of his. This civil administration was supreme, for the military force in each colony was directly subject to the governor. However, many of the colonial administrators were or, at least, had been military officers who tended to be exceedingly strict and in some cases unduly severe and cruel. During the latter years before 1914 this situation was rapidly changing, but it had existed long enough doubtless to account for the reputation for cruelty which the German colonial rule bore in some quarters.

Besides the imperial officials, however, there were maintained, especially in the African colonies, some organs and methods of self-government, or—more correctly—of native cooperation with the alien administration. In East Africa,[9] for example, in 1901 there were created district councils to meet with the district chief on which the natives were allowed one representative and this practice was followed in the other territories. Also, the government permitted many of the original native administrative bodies to remain. In East Africa, again, which because of its great size was still in 1913 understaffed, native assistance came to be greatly relied upon and the Arab system of ruling by means of alien native officials, known as *jambes* and *akidas*, was employed.[10] As Sir Harry Johnston described it: "It is a fact that the German rule in East Africa was in no way unpopular during the decade or more before the war. The leading native chieftains were treated as we treat the rajahs in India; while the Arabs were so well satisfied with the German administration that they became their strong allies."[11]

In Togoland and in Kamerun,[12] likewise, the official machinery of the chieftains was not destroyed but, on the contrary, preserved and drawn into cooperation with the imperial rule by placing upon it the responsibility of maintaining law and order. Dr. Dernburg was especially interested in enlarging the sphere of native administrative power and did much to encourage it; while, following his example, Dr. Solf, in 1913, became very enthusiastic over increasing the semi-independent "indirect government" units in Togoland and started to install them farther in Kamerun.[13] In northern Kamerun, even native treasuries were established to receive half the taxes.

In regard to the administration of justice, this had been defined by the ordinances of 1891 and 1896 in East Africa, which recognized "mixed courts" and to some extent the judicial right of the chieftains.[14] In civil matters affecting natives the jurisdiction of the *Bezirksamtmänner* was virtually complete, but he was assisted by a native judge or assessor to whom he could assign important legal duties, especially where native law was involved. In controversies where the subject-matter exceeded 1,000 *rupees* in value the native could appeal to the governor. Also the infliction of fines exceeding 200 *rupees* (300 in Kamerun and Togoland) as well as sentences of imprisonment for more than six months required the approval of the governor, and final application of the death penalty was in his hands alone.

The same judicial practice obtained in Togoland and in Kamerun. In the latter colony a special régime existed at Douala, where an ordinance of 1892 provided that "disputes between the natives of the Doualan tribe should be settled by the native chief, if the object under dispute did not exceed one hundred marks, or if the punishment to be imposed did not exceed imprisonment for six months or a fine of three hundred marks. Appeals from the native chiefs could be taken to a native Arbitration Tribunal. This tribunal also had original jurisdiction in those cases which were beyond the jurisdiction of the native courts. The native Arbitration Tribunal could not, however, try the crimes of murder and homicide. Appeals from this tribunal could be taken to the governor." [15] How much these judicial rights were cherished by the Doualan chiefs may be seen in the bitterness provoked by their withdrawal by the French who claim that the native courts led to confusion. [16]

That the German system did lead to confusion, dissatisfaction and sometimes injustice would seem to be indicated by the petition presented by the natives in Togoland to Secretary Solf, on the occasion of his visit there in 1913, asking among other things for, "an improvement in the administration of justice . . . and the introduction of codes." [17] Since Togoland was predominantly a colony of native production where the natives were exceptionally independent, German rule was somewhat unpopular about Lome. It is of interest to note, however, that the Togo chiefs now under French rule have demanded a restoration of the native courts as they existed under the Germans. Socialist and Catholic critics likewise leveled their darts against the colonial judicial system, wherein the combined executive and judicial powers of the *Bezirksamtmänner* permitted opportunity for abuse and where a stricter definition of native law and rights, they claimed, was needed.[18] Even Dr. Dove, one of the most conspicuous colonial enthusiasts, stated in the *Reichstag* in 1914: "The whole system of justice is so undeveloped in our colonies that often the executive power and the judicial function are in the same hand. This must be altered as soon as possible." And he welcomed the establishment in 1914 of the *Kolonialgerichtshof* in Germany as, "one of the first steps towards a regulation of justice for ourselves as well as for the natives." [18a]

In the South Sea colonies, of course, there existed as yet very little evidence of self-direction, since the inhabitants were for the most part not so advanced as those in Africa, although even there the native was gradually being drawn into a very slight participation in the administrative function. The control of all the scattered possessions in the South Pacific was vested in the hands of two distinct governments: that of New Guinea with its capital at Raboul and that of Samoa with its center at Apia.

## The Economic Status

Besides the administrative and judicial measures designed to encourage self-government and to raise the native to a position of independence, was the land policy which Dr.

Dernburg especially strove to promote. As we have observed during the first decades of Germany's colonial history, the land was absolutely at the mercy of the companies to whom the government recklessly granted huge concessions and who gave no thought whatsoever to native rights. So destructive and disastrous proved this policy, however, resulting as it did in so many and such fierce native revolts, that toward the close of the century a reform set in, best expressed by the land laws of 1895 [19] in East Africa and of 1896 in Kamerun. Both of these declared all land to be "crown land" subject to the rights of private or jurisdic persons or of the chiefs and native communities. For East Africa it was stipulated that in taking possession of the "crown land" near native communities, areas should be preserved for them on the basis of future growth in population, and a Land Commission was appointed by the government including a native *jambe* or *akida* to delimit these preserves. Under a local ordinance this commission was authorized to reserve for native use four times the amount of suitable land already under cultivation by them, and was authorized to offer the natives a certain sum for withdrawing from their land. In pursuance thereof, this commission marked out 175 reserves in the northeastern highlands amounting to some 736 square miles. In Kamerun native reserves were on the basis of 6 hectares for each adult male. [20]

With this foundation of reform upon which to build, Dr. Dernburg energetically promoted a land policy in favor of native ownership and production which, in East Africa, resulted in the land law of 1907 [21] prohibiting the sale of any land to a white settler that was already occupied by a native; and, in Kamerun, led to the law of 1910 [22] restricting all land sales to the "crown lands." This legislation, together with the efforts to curtail the "concession" policy in regard to the companies and others, was aimed to insure the native in the ultimate possession of his property in these two colonies. In East Africa, the results may be judged by the material increase in the amount of land under native production,[23] although in some of the highland areas, notably in Moshi, a district capable of producing valuable crops of coffee and maize, Europeans tended to crowd the natives off the more desirable land in violation of the government policy. In Kamerun, on the other hand, the application of reform was not as successful, owing doubtless to the stranglehold of the concession policy: the natives, generally, complained that the reserves were not large enough, that the poorer land was allotted to them, and that in a number of districts no native reserves were effected.[24]

How the natives of Kamerun felt in regard to their land rights may be seen in the Doualan controversy of 1913,[25] as may also the attitude of the government toward them. In 1909 the German government pressed by the rapidly growing European population and commerce at the mouth of the Wurri River, decided to move four native villages away from the waterfront to new sites back several miles in the interior, and to build a model European city upon the land vacated. Although the government offered to reimburse the natives for their property at the rate of ninety *pfennigs* a cubic meter, which was the price of the land at the time of the German occupation, and to build for them model villages one and one-half hour's walk from the water's edge, they refused, and demanded three marks a square meter, declaring that the existence of the whole tribe was at stake. The real reason for their refusal, however, was their unwillingness to forfeit land exceptionally well situated for commerce and for speculation with European buyers. But the German government refused to pay the higher price, claiming that its enhanced value was, after all, due to European and not to Doualan activity, and forthwith it proceeded to expropriate the land on January 1, 1913, despite the strong opposition expressed by the Socialists in the *Reichstag*. For the Doualas had employed a German attorney to defend their interests and had brought the affair into the *Reichstag* and the press. An unfortunate incident of the controversy was the hanging of Chief Rudolph Bell, by order of the local administration, on the charge of plotting against the German government, an act which had serious consequences later in the Great War in that the Doualas joined the English as soon as they appeared at Douala against Germany.

Although Dr. Dernburg's land policy was extremely unpopular with the white settlers, especially in East Africa, and contributed materially to his downfall, the Colonial Office continued to protect native land ownership. In Togoland the land question did not create so sharp a struggle between blacks and whites, since that area was a fertile colony largely under well-established native production. Here too, however, in 1910 [26] "crown lands" were restricted in the same manner as in East Africa and in Kamerun, and the right of sale reserved to the government. Doubtless South West Africa, of all Germany's colonies the best suited to white settlement, afforded the worst illustration of land exploitation where, in the year 1903, only one-third of the entire area was in the possession of the natives. After the suppression of the Herero uprising largely caused by "land hunger," a new policy began after 1907 and the law of 1910 placed the control of all land sales whether for natives or whites under government control. The character of the colony, however, lends itself more to cattle raising and production on a large scale necessarily carried on by white settlers, than to small native production as in East Africa and Togoland.

## Slavery

In regard to the personal, economic freedom of the native, actual slavery as such had never existed in the German colonies with German consent. When Germany acquired her colonies in the eighties, the slave trade was flourishing in Africa but, guided by Bismarck, the government strove to enforce the provisions of the Congo Act for the suppression of slavery, especially in East Africa among the Arabs. We have already read of Bismarck's cooperation with Cardinal Lavigerie in his crusade against the slave traders in 1889 which precipitated the serious revolt in that colony.[27] After its suppression, the law of September 4, 1891,[28] forbade the sale and ownership of slaves; and this was followed by a similar law of January 15, 1893, in Togoland and of July 25, 1895, in Kamerun.[29] How successful proved to be their application may be judged from the reports of the British ambassador in Berlin to his home office. In 1894 he wrote: "It would appear that the German administration in East Africa has not interfered to any great extent with the prevailing customs in regard to domestic slavery, which is, generally speaking, of a mild form, and against which there is no movement amongst the slaves themselves. Domestic slaves are passed on from father to son. On the other hand, very stringent measures are taken to suppress slave-raiding and slave-dealing. And Arabs or natives caught, '*flagrante delecto*,' are condemned to death."[30] And later in 1900 he observed in regard to Kamerun: "Slavery has entirely disappeared in all the region immediately under German control, and it is stated that not a single case of the sale or purchase of a slave from the interior of the littoral has been noted between 1895 and 1899." [31]

To be sure there remained, as the reports indicate, so-called domestic slavery or house-peonage, inherent in native custom, which the government sought gradually to eradicate. The Colonial Congress, meeting in Berlin in 1902, passed a resolution [32] that the suppression of slavery was one of the most important duties that confronted Germany in the colonies, and a succession of laws gradually abolishing domestic slavery also followed. A statute of February 21, 1902, [33] for West Africa declared all children of domestic slaves to be half free and their children entirely free; while the law of December 24, 1904, [34] for East Africa declared children of domestic slaves born after December 31, 1905, to be free. To put a final end to the institution, the *Reichstag* passed a resolution in 1912 [35] for East Africa, that domestic peonage was to cease after 1920. The colonial office took measures for carrying out this decree and for protecting the masters and serfs; so had the World War not intervened even domestic slavery would long since have been abolished in Germany's colonies.

## Compulsory Labor

But there is another kind of slavery besides the technical sort, one which is often confused with it, and that is compulsory or forced labor. One of the favorite devices of "civilized" nations everywhere to secure in their colonies the much needed labor on plantations and on public works, it is obviously peculiarly conducive to the practice of abuses and of extreme cruelty. If the indolent native of the tropics refuses to labor, refuses to submit to the lock step of the western work-a-day routine; if he refuses to pay his tax, or if he infringes the laws of his white masters, forced labor has been the universal remedy because it serves both as a discipline and supplies a much needed commodity. This universal practice of colonizing nations is best explained perhaps by Joseph Chamberlain when colonial secretary. He stated in the House of Commons, August 6, 1901, "I believe it is good for the native to be industrious and we must bend every effort to teach him to work. . . . Under all circumstances, the progress of natives toward civilization is only secured when they shall be convinced of the necessity and dignity of labor; and, therefore, I think that everything we can reasonably do to encourage the natives to work is highly desirable." [36]

Of course, under the régime of the colonial companies with their total disregard of all responsibility, compulsory labor was universally practiced on the private plantation as well as on public works, and in its abuses brought down a well-deserved shame and contumely upon Germany's colonial administration. But Dr. Dernburg, supported by Rechenberg, the governor of East Africa, fought for the principle of free labor for private purposes in the face of bitter hostility from the planters and ultimately triumphed. Therefore, after 1907, compulsory labor [37] was made legal only for public works and was paid; the raising of the hut-tax by forced labor was forbidden, and natives were permitted to work in lieu of tax only if they were unable to pay cash. Moreover, all labor contracts, both private and public, were strictly regulated by law. These contained provisions for drawing up the agreement before a magistrate; for wages; for free transport to place of work; for overtime; for medical care; for a ten-hour day in East Africa; for licensed recruiters of labor; for living conditions of workers while building the railway in Kamerun; for food, similarity of race of workers, and so forth. [38]

As was to be expected, these rules and regulations were bitterly opposed by European planters whose economic interests were affected, and were disregarded as often as possible by the unscrupulous; so that many criticisms of the abuses due to compulsory labor in Germany's territories were as elsewhere prevalent and, in some instances, doubtless true.[39] Also, the practice inherent in native custom allowing the chieftain to requisition labor for community purposes, such as clearing the public ways and roads, was left undisturbed and was subject to frequent abuse. The administration, however, maintained and enforced so far as it was possible its principle of compulsory labor, namely, that it be employed only for public service and be paid, a system today indorsed and practiced by all the colonizing powers, even in the mandated territories with the approval of the Permanent Mandates Commission of the League of Nations.[40]

### Corporal Punishment

Closely associated with the practice of forced labor is the system of punishment and especially the use of the lash. The whip or cane is quite generally used in all colonies where there are primitive races to deal with, and in the hands of the irresponsible and uncontrolled first settlers and planters was subject to the worst kind of abuse. When Dernburg visited the colonies as one of the first acts of his administration, he reported that he "saw too many whips in the hands and on the tables of the planters and colonizers." The result was drastic regulation of both the infliction of punishment and the use of the lash.[41] Sentences of flogging could be applied as a punitive measure only, never as a disciplinary one and never legally by a private person; they had to be administered in the presence of an official and of a doctor or sanitary officer; the strokes were limited to twenty-five for a healthy, full-grown man, to be applied in two installments at least two weeks apart; and the whip was strictly prohibited for use upon Arabs, Indians, women, and children. Additional ordinances prescribed the construction and character of the lash.

These disciplinary measures of flogging were principally applied to native servants in case of desertion or failure to work properly, the alternatives being two weeks imprisonment or fines; also to natives who violated labor contracts. The latter were subject to three months imprisonment, corporal punishment or fine and, as a result, many abuses were committed by the unscrupulous companies and planters. These punitive or disciplinary powers, it may be added, were similar to those held today by the French administrative officers, except for the flogging and chaining of prisoners.

### Militarization

Still one other form of slavery, which may and often does exist in colonial territories, is the militarization of the natives. In particular was Germany's rule attacked by the Allies upon this score because of the prominence of militarism in the mother country, and because of the extremely important rôle which the military had played in the colonies during the unfortunate period of the colonial companies as well as during the first decade of imperial control. In many instances, when it was called in to suppress the native uprisings it had gained the upper hand and had subordinated the whole colony. It will be recalled, however, that Bismarck had been emphatically opposed to any military establishments being set up in the colonies as well as to the militarization of the natives. "We do not contemplate establishing garrisons in the colonies. Such a system is not suitable for us," [42] he asserted and, in accordance with his program, there were in 1914 in the African and South Seas colonies no fortified naval stations, no harbor fortifications or military garrisons. Kiao-Chow in China was the one naval base which corresponded to those of England, France, and Russia in the Far East. Had there existed such enterprises, it would have been necessary to station a considerable number of warships in African waters and in the South Pacific and this was never done.

Likewise, as Germany possessed no colonial naval system, so also did she maintain no colonial army, as the figures of the troops in the oversea territories demonstrate. According to the statute of July 18, 1896,[48] the protectorate troops were created, and supported for protection and police duty alone. Only the three largest colonies possessed protectorate troops which were organized as military troops: East Africa had, in 1914, a force of 2,500 native soldiers commanded by 152 German officers and a police force of 2,140 colored natives under 65 German officers; Kamerun supported 1,550 native troops and 1,285 native police with the corresponding number of German officers; while South West Africa was the only colony to possess a body of white protectorate troops, which numbered less than 2,000 in addition to a white police force of 600 men.[44]

The other German colonies maintained no protectorate troops at all but merely small police forces; Togoland had 500 native police, New Guinea and the islands 800, and Samoa about 30, sons of native chieftains. Everywhere the military was subordinate to the civil authority, for the governor of each colony had been placed in command of the protectorate troops and police force by the law of 1896.

It will be seen, therefore, that Germany supported no colonial army in the accepted use of the term, no colored troops outside the colonies, neither did she employ conscription of natives. Soldiers for the protectorate troops and for the police force were recruited according to the ordinary method up to the legal number; the term of service and the duties were determined by contract in accordance with the statute of 1896.

### Measures for Native Welfare—Education

More fundamental perhaps to the promotion of native welfare, than the statutes and ordinances defining his political and economic status and protecting him from various abuses, are the education system and the health service which a colonizing power maintains. Like everything else to do with the development of the German colonies, these were not taken seriously in hand by the government until the "scientific era" began. And since the rule of the colonial companies had been directed more to the exploitation and destruction of the native than to his preservation and education, there was much to be accomplished.

In the field of education the missionary societies had well prepared the way. Indeed, Germany began her educational work in Africa long before she possessed any colonies there. As a result, by 1914 missions controlled four-fifths of all the colonial schools, although they had come to be heavily subsidized and consequently supervised by the government. Each mission station, Protestant and Catholic, established an elementary school to teach the elements of the three R's in the native tongue, practical work and some gardening, but, in addition to these the missions, assisted by the government, were gradually adding higher schools and seminaries for the training of native teachers. The effect of the entrance of the government into colonial education, both by the introduction of its own schools and its supervision of the mission schools, was to broaden and to standardize the curriculum so as to include geography, nature study, the German language and literature, and to emphasize and develop vocational, manual education. By 1914 government schools were training native clerks, customs officials, telegraph operators, interpreters, carpenters, masons, and all kinds of mechanics and craftsmen, for it was becoming more and more evident that the solution of the native problem lay in practical rather than in abstract schooling.

## Schools in East Africa

Between 1902-1914 in East Africa, 99 government schools —10 higher and 89 primary—were established. Among them were six purely industrial schools and training courses for native teachers in Dar-es-Salaam and Tanga. In these schools, Swahalis, Arabs, Indians and, in fact, all colored races learned side by side and no distinction was made between them; in 1914 the number of pupils was 6,100. The staff of European teachers consisted of 24 and was soon to be increased, as 20 additional primary schools were planned. Besides these, there were, in 1914, 1,832 mission schools belonging to the 9 Protestant and 2 Catholic societies active in East Africa with 229 European workers and 108,550 children enrolled.[16] These institutions had been brought into close connection with the government schools and worked in cooperation. In 1914, the German government appropriated 381,000 M. for education with an additional 20,000 M. for the teaching of German, the use of which, however, was not compulsory in the schools.

The results of education in East Africa were evinced by the number of natives who could read and write, making it possible for the administration to send written instructions to the chiefs. Also, one could see in Dar-es-Salaam many natives acting as clerks and stenographers in the government offices. Although education had, as yet in 1914, reached only about one per cent of the huge population of 7,607,000, yet, to quote from the *Report* of the British governor of Tanganyika, the mandated territory, formerly German East Africa: "In regard to schools, the Germans have accomplished marvels. . . . Native education was drastically interrupted by the Great War. . . . Some time must elapse before education attains the standards it had reached under the Germans." [46]

## South West Africa

Of all the African colonies, South West Africa had been the most disturbed by native uprisings so that educational work there was very much retarded. Also, it is the one colony most entirely suited to European settlement, and schools had to be provided for children of the white colonists. In 1914, therefore, while there were 20 schools for white children, serving 775 scholars and including a higher school for boys and one for girls at Swakopmund, there were not, as yet, any government schools for the natives. Their education was left entirely to the Catholic and Protestant missionary societies of which there were respectively 23 and 38. Only about 5,000 children of the native population numbering 65,000 had, as yet, been reached by the 61 schools and much remained to be accomplished there. [47]

## Kamerun

Compulsory education was established by the government in 1910 in Kamerun, and in 1914 it was carried on by 4 government schools with 868 scholars. Besides, there were two manual training schools and two agricultural schools, one in connection with the Agricultural Institute at Victoria. As in East Africa, the missions bore the burden of the educational work and were subsidized by the government. The 3 Protestant missions operated 473 schools with 27,526 pupils, and the Catholic societies 158 schools with 12,591 children. There were more than 100 European teachers, and the government appropriated 266,100 M. for education in 1914 and an additional 60,000 M. for the teaching of German which was compulsory.[48] The course in the primary schools lasted four or five years, and was designed to impart Christian instruction and to train for the higher schools. In the higher schools, all instruction was given in German, and pupils were trained to become native teachers or to enter the service of Europeans. The practical schools run by the government taught the girls household work, laundry work, and farming; the boys, carpentering, boot-making, tailoring, and other crafts. Great emphasis was laid upon vocational education, and it was felt more and more that in this practical type of schooling lay the solution of the native problem, especially in Kamerun where the grade of development was not so high as in some parts of East Africa.

## Togoland

In 1891 the government founded its first school in Togoland and, in 1914, it had increased the number by only two more regular ones, an agricultural school, and a vocational school in connection with the higher school at Lome, and by one teacher-training institution. Here, as elsewhere, the mission schools far outnumbered the others; 1 Catholic and 2 Protestant societies maintained 368 schools with 14,653 scholars.[49] The methods were similar to those in Kamerun, but education here was not compulsory. Two languages were used in all the schools as Togoland is the land of the native: Ewes (the language of the coastal tribes) and German. The government appropriated 86,900 M. for education in 1914, including the amount for German. Altogether, only about 1.5 per cent of the 4,150,000 natives in Kamerun, and of the 1,030,000 in Togoland had been reached by the school system in 1914.[50]

## Kiao-Chow

Conditions similar to those in Africa prevailed in Kiao-Chow as a result of educational effort. There, besides the 15 schools of the Protestant and 8 of the Catholic missionary societies, the German government had erected, since 1900, 11 elementary schools, 2 schools for practical work, 6 higher schools, and a German-Chinese *Hochschule*. This last institution comprised departments for the study of law, science, and agriculture, and maintained also one devoted entirely to the translation of textbooks and German literature. In 1914, there were 500 scholars in the German schools, and the government appropriated 500,000 M. for education.[51]

## The South Seas

In contrast to Kiao-Chow, the government had not done so much for educational work in the other Pacific colonies, for they had provided an early and attractive field for missionary endeavor. Altogether, this area contained only three government schools in 1914: 2 in Samoa and 1 in New Guinea. But the mission societies had accomplished a great deal. They operated 320 schools in Samoa with 10,000 scholars and 424 teachers and, together with the government schools, reached 33 per cent of the 34,432 natives; while in New Guinea 5 Protestant and 4 Catholic societies maintained 425 schools with 19,000 and, with the one government school served 4 per cent of the 600,000 colored population.[52]

Altogether, on the eve of the war Germany's educational work in her colonial possessions was carried on by about 4,000 mission schools with a total of 180,000 scholars and 100 government schools with 6,500 pupils. And the government appropriated, in 1914, 1,661,000 M. to meet the educational needs of a native population of 14,000,000.[53] To the general educational service should also be added the work accomplished by the agricultural stations and traveling agents described in a former chapter.[54]

### Health Service—Research in Tropical Medicine

More important, perhaps, than education as a civilizing agency among the backward peoples of the earth, is medical service directed toward the elimination of tropical diseases, toward hospital care and preventive sanitation and toward the instruction of the natives in hygiene. Early in her colonial history German scientists and physicians recognized the importance of scientific research into the diseases of their native populations: in 1887 the *Archiv für Schiffs und Tropenhygine* was founded, in 1896 Scheube published his textbook of *Diseases in Warm Countries,* and in 1905 von Meute, the *Handbook of Tropical Disease;* but no concerted effort could be attempted under the haphazard rule of the companies. In 1901, however, the *Institute for Tropical Diseases* was founded in Hamburg and became the center of this work. As a hospital it treats only those who are victims of tropical diseases and, as such, is a laboratory of study and research in both cure and prevention as it carries on scientific investigation into proper food, clothing, and housing for hot climates. Situated on the very water's edge, high above the teeming Hamburg harbor, where the ships from Africa, the Far East, and the South Seas continually ply to and fro, it stands today as a symbol of the white man's scientific penetration of the backward lands—of the beneficent and best aspect of imperialism. All the official colonial staff of physicians and sanitary helpers were obliged to study there or at some similar institution, such as the *Medical Missionary Institute* at the University of Tübingen, opened in 1906, which was designed to train medical missionaries in the same manner as the *Livingstone Institute* in England, and the *Institute for Infectious Diseases* named for Robert Koch. It is in the laboratories of such institutions, on the journeys of physicians traveling in the tropics and in their remote clinics far from civilization, that Germany has been able to render significant service in the discovery of the cholera and pest baccili, of the germ of sleeping sickness, of yellow fever and malaria, and of preventive measures against *beriberi* and *rinderpest*.

### Robert Koch and Sleeping Sickness

Doubtless, the best known of these fighters against tropical diseases is Robert Koch who, in 1906-1907, waged successful warfare against the sleeping sickness in East Africa where its inroads were particularly severe. He was often called upon for aid by the English when a virulent epidemic swept over the borders into their territories. It was he who discovered atoxyl as a remedy for the disease, and who caused the shores of Lake Tanganyika to be deforested so that the flies carrying the infection could no longer live without the shady bushes. The work accomplished by Koch and his students, both for man and beast, in saving them from the ravages of disease is accounted even by Germany's enemies as work for civilization in the highest sense.[55]

Dr. Koch's work may be seen in the cleansing from infection of the original area of sleeping sickness around Lake

Victoria in East Africa as well as in efficient continuance
of the campaign against the disease. In 1914, Germany was
maintaining in East Africa three stations for sleeping sickness with a staff of specially selected physicians and 16 sanitary helpers besides the regular official medical corps. A
research institute had been opened in 1913 in Dar-es-Salaam
and one was planned in 1914 for Kamerun. In Kamerun
there were also three stations and a special staff of 7 physicians, 1 zoölogist, and 20 sanitary helpers engaged in the
campaign for which the government appropriated 550,000
M. in 1914.[56] Although all this work was destroyed by the
war, a new remedy for the disease was discovered by Dr.
Luter in 1923—known as *Bayer 205.* Julian Huxley, the
Oxford biologist, wrote about this in the *Daily Herald.*
"The German discovery of the chemical substance, *Bayer
205,* which heals sleeping sickness is a highly important step
in making the tropics habitable. This one discovery is of
such importance to all those nations with tropical possessions that it uncovers at one stroke how criminally stupid
it is to place a great scientific nation in such a position that
it is even more difficult for her to continue her scientific
researches." [57]

### Campaign Against Small-Pox

Similar to the campaign against sleeping sickness was the
one against the small-pox, which formerly swept in great
waves of epidemic throughout the African colonies. The
serious difficulty in the control of the disease lay in the fact
that the serum imported from Europe lost its strength and
effectiveness in transit. Finally, Drs. Krueger and Külz
solved the problem of the preparation of the serum in the
colonies and, in 1912-1913, 16 stations for its distribution

had been established in East Africa and 8 in Kamerun.[58] As a result, instead of only 4 per cent of the native population in East Africa receiving vaccination during the years 1903-1909, one-half—more than 3,000,000 persons—were vaccinated between 1909 and 1913; while in the same year, in Kamerun, 800,000 of the 3,326,132 natives, and in Togoland 25,000 of the 1,032,000 received inoculation.[59]

## Hospital Service.

In regard to general medical service for the natives there was a hospital for them connected with the hospitals for European settlers established in all the larger places as, for example, the hospitals at Dar-es-Salaam and Tanga in East Africa, at Douala in Kamerun, at Lome in Togoland, at Herbertshöhe in New Guinea and at Apia in Samoa. Besides these, there was a small hospital for the natives in every place where a government physician was stationed. The development of this medical service may be gauged by a comparison of the number of natives treated in 1903-1904— 4,516—with the number treated in 1912-1913—100,348. And these figures do not include those persons treated by missionaries who at all their stations carried on some sort of medical aid.[60]

In 1914, there were in the tropical colonies 120 physicians and 151 Europeans in the sanitary service: East Africa had a staff of 48 and treated over 60,000 native patients in 1913-1914; Kamerun, 43 and 8 European nursing sisters who treated 12,402 natives in 1913-1914; Togoland maintained 16 doctors providing, as in Kamerun, one for every 75,000 population; South West Africa only 10, New Guinea 1, and Samoa and Kiao-Chow also 1 each.[61] For the maintenance of this medical service in the colonies, the German government appropriated 1,190,000 M. in 1914.

## Preventive Medicine

In connection with all the medical centers preventive work, also, in the nature of general education in hygiene was promoted. The chieftains were personally instructed about contagious diseases and the means of fighting them. Each issue of the official *Kolonialblatt* and especially the *Amtsblätter* for the single colonies contained laws and ordinances for the sanitary protection of the natives. Beginning with the year 1903-1904, the colonial office published annually the *Medizial-Berichte über die Deutschen Schuzgebiete,*[62] whereby the results of experience in the tropics, improved methods of sanitation and of disease prevention were made public.

It is interesting to note that at a time when no one was concerned with the number of calories in one's own diet, German colonial physicians had collected some very definite data and statistics about them in regard to the diet of African native laborers. In 1907 the staff physician of South West Africa, Doctor Hans Ziemann, delivered a lecture in London, at the invitation of the *British Society for the Prevention of Tropical Diseases,* in which he presented the German program for native diet which was recognized as very new but as very essential.[63]

Just before the war, it is also significant to learn, the last expedition sent out by the colonial office was one to the South Seas to investigate the cause of the threatened extinction of so many native stems, and to discover a remedy for saving them.

## Control of Alcohol Traffic Among Native Population

Perhaps also under the heading of health service to the natives should come a brief review of the German government's effort to regulate the alcohol traffic in its oversea territories. From the time of the foundation of the German colonial empire, the missionary societies had agitated the alcohol question and the *German Society Opposed to the Misuse of Spirituous Drinks* had declared, in 1885, that the colonial trade in alcohol was "unworthy the honor of Germany." As a result, there was founded in 1896 an *Association for Opposition to the African Liquor Trade* which laid two important *Denkschriften* before the *Reichstag*.[64]

The administration cooperated with the efforts of the missionary and other private societies by imposing such a tax upon alcohol in East Africa [65] and in the South Seas,[66] that it practically eliminated its use by the native in those colonies. While in accordance with the Brussels Act of 1890, the government placed two-thirds of Kamerun and one-fourth of Togoland in prohibitory zones.[67] Liquor was thus sold in these two colonies only in specially licensed areas. In 1910, customs duties were raised in Kamerun to 1 M. *pro hectolitre* and again in 1912, in cooperation with England at the Brussels Conference, to 1.60 M. *pro hectolitre*.[68] France refused to join England and Germany, however, and so their plan for checking the liquor traffic was not realized. Nevertheless, imports into Kamerun decreased from 20,000 *hectolitres* in 1898 to 10,000 *hectolitres* in 1908-1912; and in Togoland from 16,000 *hectolitres* in 1898 to 9,680 *hectolitres* in 1908-1912.[69]

## Private Societies for Native Welfare

In addition to those measures contained in the policy of the German colonial administration, which protected the native and fostered his social and moral well-being, must also be mentioned the efforts of the numerous private societies and organizations. We have already noted the contribu-

tion of the missionary societies to education and to medical
service, but of course there were many other ways in which
they promoted native welfare through the services of the
161 Protestant and 234 Catholic stations, manned respectively with over 400 white teachers and workers and 700
priests, brothers and sisters.[70]

Besides the missionary societies, there were the *Society for
the Opposition to the Liquor Trade,* the *Society for the Protection of the Natives,* a branch of the international organization which strove to uphold the rights and to prevent the
oppression of primitive peoples generally; the *Women's
Association of the Red Cross in the Colonies* which supplied
sisters, nurses, and kindergartners; and the *German Colonial
Society* which devoted a part of its energy to the support of
native schools, hospitals, and "civilizing centers."

## NOTES

[1] Dernburg, B., *Zielpunkte des Deutschen Kolonialwesens* (Berlin,
1907), p. 6.

[2] *Ibid.,* p. 9. See also, his speech in the *Reichstag,* March, 1908,
reported in *Geschichtskalender,* 1908, p. 29ff.

[3] Giesenbrecht, F., *Die Behandlung der Eingeborenen in den deutschen
Kolonien.* (Berlin, 1898.)

Vietor, J. K., *Die nächsten Aufgaben unserer Kolonialpolitik* (Bremen,

[4] *Verhandlungen des deutschen Reichstages,* 1912-1913, vol. 285, p.
1560ff. See also his speech of March 6, 1913, in *Reichstag,* and speech in
reply to Balfour, Aug., 1918, *Hambürgischer Correspondent,* Aug. 21, 1918.

[5] Speech of Prof. Bonn before *Royal Colonial Society,* 1914. *Financial
Times* (London), July 14, 1914.

[6] *Verhandlungen des deutschen Reichstages,* 1912, vol. 285, May 12,
13, p. 2118.

[7] *Koloniale Rundschau,* 1914, *Heft* 4, p. 193.

[8] See *infra.,* ch. xii. p. 375.

[9] Hoffmann, E., *Verwaltung und Gerichsverfassung der d. Schutzgebiete*
(Leipzig, 1908), p. 56.

[10] Buell, R. L., *The Native Problem in Africa* (New York, 1928,
2 vols.), vol. i, p. 448ff.

[11] Solf, Dr., *Germany's Right to Recover Her Colonies* (Berlin, 1919),
p. 31, quoting *The Daily News.*

[12] Köbner, O., *Einführung in die Kolonialpolitik* (Jena, 1908), p. 145ff.

[13] Buell, *op. cit.,* vol. ii, pp. 307-308.

[14] *Ibid.,* vol. i, p. 448ff.

[15] *Ibid.,* vol. ii, p. 308.

[16] *Ibid.,* vol. ii, p. 311.

[17] *Ibid.,* vol. ii, p. 276.

[18] *Verhandlungen des deutschen Reichstages,* 1912-1913, vol. 285, p. 1575. Herr Müller: "With regard to the rights of native justice, *et seq.,* there exists an incredible insecurity concerning the power of administrative authority in this sphere."

[18a] *Ibid.,* 1914, vol. 295, p. 9123.

[19] *Deutsche Landesgesetzgebung,* pt. ii, pp. 200, 212, 219.

[20] *Ibid.,* pt. viii, p. 240. See also, Buell, *op. cit.,* vol. i, p. 685.

[21] *Ibid.,* pt. ii, p. 1294.

[22] *Landesgesetzgebung von Kamerun,* p. 696.

[23] See *supra.,* ch. ix, p. 269, graphic illustration.

[24] Buell, *op. cit.,* vol. i, p. 685, quoting *Report on British Sphere in Cameroons,* 1922, Cmd. 1647.

[25] Buell, *op. cit.,* vol. ii, p. 341.

See also Voight, W., *Die Entwickelung der Eingeborenenpolitik in den deutschen Kolonien* (Berlin, 1927), p. 22.

*Denkschrift,* May 5, 1914, from natives, *Geschichtskalender,* 1914, p. 279.

[26] *Landesgesetzgebung des Schutzgebietes Togo,* p. 88.

See also, *Deutsche Kolonialgesetzgebung,* pt. i, p. 279, pt. viii, p. 217.

[27] See *supra.,* ch. iv, p. 117.

[28] *Reichs-Kolonialamt,* A. VII. *Akten betr. Sklavensache,* 4, Bd. 5. *Goveneurbericht von 4, 9. 1891.*

[29] *Deutsche Kolonialgesetzgebung,* pt. i, p. 281, and pt. v, p. 847.

[30] *Foreign Office Report on German Colonies for 1894,* no. 346, cmn. 7582-7, pp. 34-44.

[31] *Ibid.,* no. 528, June, 1900, and no. 3519, for 1903-1904.

[32] *Verhandlungen des Kolonial-Kongresses,* 1902, p. 443ff.

[33] *Deutsche Kolonialgesetzgebung,* pt. vi, p. 462.

[34] *Ibid.,* II, pt. viii, p. 267.

[35] *Verhandlungen des deutschen Reichstages,* 1912-1913, vol. 284, p. 1529.

[36] Schnee, H., *German Colonization Past and Future* (London, 1926), pp. 135-136, quoting Chamberlain speaking in House of Commons, August 6, 1901, and on March 24, 1903.

[37] Schnee, H. (Ed.), *Deutsches Kolonial-Lexikon* (Leipzig, 1920), vol. i, p. 509ff., pp. 80-81.

[38] Kuhn, *Die deutsche Schutzgebiete* (Berlin, 1913).

[39] The German government was especially attacked about conditions prevailing in the building of the railway in Kamerun.

[40] Buell, *op. cit.,* vol. ii, pp. 382, 340ff.

[41] Buell, *op. ct.,* vol. i, p. 499.

*Das Kolonialgesetzblatt*, p. 274. *Kolonial-Lexikon*, vol. iii, p. 111.

[42] *Staatsarchiv*, vol. 43 (1884), p. 361ff.

[43] *Reichs*, *G. B.*, p. 643. See also, *Kolonial-Lexikon*, *op. cit.*, articles, *Schutztruppen und Polizeitruppen.*

[44] *Statesman's Year Book*, 1914, pp. 925, 927.

[45] *Deutsches-Kolonial-Lexikon*, vol. i, p. 402ff.

*Statistisches Jahrbuh für das Deutsche Reich*, 1913, 1914.

[46] Stokes Report, *Education in East Africa*, ed. by J. Jones (New York, 1925), p. 178.

[47] *Kolonial-Lexikon*, vol. i, pp. 442-443.

*Statistisches Jahrbuch für das Deutsche Reich*, 1913, 1914.

[48] *Ibid.*, vol. ii, pp. 213-214.

*Ibid.*

[49] *Ibid.*, vol. iii, p. 521.

*Ibid.*

[50] *Ibid.*

[51] *Kolonial-Lexikon*, vol. ii, pp. 289-290.

*Statistisches Jahrbuch, op. cit.*

*Geschichtskalender*, 1914, p. 175.

[52] *Ibid.*, vol. iii, p. 238.

*Ibid.*

[53] *Ibid.*, vol. iii, p. 308.

For a thorough survey of the colonial educational system shortly before the war, see Slunk, M., *Das Schulwesen in den deutschen Schutzgebieten* (Hamburg, 1914).

See also, *Süd-Deutsche Monatsheft*, August, 1915.

[54] See *supra.*, ch. ix, p. 259ff.

[55] Steudel, Prof., "Der ärzliche Dienst in den deutschen Schutzgebieten," in *Archiv für Schiffs-und-Tropen Hygiene*, 1909, *Beitrag*, 6, p. 17.

*Deutsche Kolonialzeitung*, 1910, June 11. *Article* on Dr. Koch.

[56] *Kolonial-Lexikon.*

*Verhandlungen des d. Kolonial-Kongresses*, 1924, p. 158.

Steudel, *Bedeutung der d. Tropenärzte für die Eingeborene und für die Wissenschaft. Sonderdruck aus der D. Medizinischen Wochenschrift*, No. 15.

[57] *Wirtschaftsdienst* (Hamburg), Jan., 1924, p. 22, quoting *London Daily Herald.*

[58] *Medizial-Bericht*, 1912-1913, p. 76.

See also, Kulz, L., "Grundzüge der Kolonialen Eingeborenen Hygiene," in *Kolonialzeitung*, 1912, p. 300.

[59] Steudel, *op. cit.*, pp. 3, 7.

[60] *Kolonial-Lexikon*, article on *Missions.*

[61] *Verhandlungen des d. Kolonial-Kongresses*, 1924, p. 153.

[62] *Reichs-Kolonialamt. Medizial-Berichte über die deutschen Schutzgebiete.*

[63] *Verhandlungen der Hambürgische Universität*, vol. xiii.

[64] *Denkschrift*, 26 March, 1908.

[65] *Das Kolonialblatt*, 1903, p. 254; 1905, p. 201.

[66] *Das Kolonialblatt,* 1901, p. 145; 1900, p. 535.
[67] *Ibid.,* 1907, pp. 329, 707, 556, 655; 1913, 934.
[68] *Brussels Agrement 1908, Das Kolonialblatt,* 1908, p. 991ff.
[69] *Kolonial-Lexikon.*
[70] *Reiches-Kolonialamt. Sonderdruck aus dem D. Kolonial-Kongresses,* 1924, "Kolonial Wohlfahrspflege."

# CHAPTER XI

## COLONIAL EXPANSION AND THE BALANCE OF POWER

### The Colonial Policy Is Again Subordinated to Foreign Relations

"OUR world policy is based upon the success of our European policy," wrote von Bülow in 1913; and added, after the outbreak of the war, "Unless our position in Europe be assured and strengthened, we cannot profit by the annexation of colonies." [1] These sentiments constitute, indeed, a far cry from the ruthless *Weltpolitik* which dominated Germany's Foreign Office during the "storm and stress" period of her colonial history, and which inevitably led, as we have seen, to sharp clashes with the imperialist aims of other nations, especially Great Britain.

For the Kaiser's reckless pursuit of world power, during the decade roughly defined by the years 1895-1905, had underestimated the seriousness of those international conflicts, and had not hesitated to cast diplomatic caution to the winds for the sake of acquiring a naval base or a cable station on a coral island. Indeed, since the year 1895, the German government had wished to increase its insignificant colonial possessions, not primarily for the sake of gaining rich oversea markets, tropical plantations, or places of settlement for emigrating Germans, but rather to promote Germany's prestige. And it had allowed this desire so strongly to bias its national policy that, by the year 1903, the change

305

from Bismarck's day—when caution in colonial expansion had been the slogan—was complete; the "new course" had apparently triumphed.  In other words, it was clear by that time that Germany meant to secure a share in the future apportionment of the world commensurate with her political and economic position, no matter what the consequences. How explain then the opposite point of view expressed by von Bülow, one of the keenest promoters of *Weltpolitik,* at the close of the following decade?  What had transpired to place Germany's "European policy" before her "world policy," to reinstate the cautious practice of the Iron Chancellor?

### The "Diplomatic Revolution" Interferes with the "New Course"

In the first place, Germany's clashes with other Powers, resulting from her aggressive colonial policy, were destined to become more frequent and more acute during the decade prior to the Great War for two reasons: first, because the government's victory in the crisis of 1907 strengthened and confirmed the German trend toward *Weltpolitik,* so that it secured the support of all parties save the Social Democrats and stimulated a public sentiment that was inclined to lead rather than to follow the government; and, second, because the gradual formation of the *Entente Cordiale* followed by the cementing of the *Triple Entente* created a stronger and more dangerous external opposition, which transformed what had been clashes with single nations into conflicts with united groups.  In fine, the "diplomatic revolution" among the Powers after 1904 raised the whole issue of Germany's colonial expansion into the realm of the balance of power.

In the second place, that semblance of unity which had

controlled Germany's national policy since 1895, namely, the drive for world power supported as it was so heartily by the Kaiser and his ministers, von Bülow, von Holstein, and Marschall von Bieberstein, was not destined to endure after 1904. For the formation of first the *Entente Cordiale* and then of the *Triple Entente,* with their menace of "encirclement," created an ever-growing fear in the German Foreign Office; a fear that was met by a divided rather than a united reaction on the part of its directors; a fear, indeed, which can largely be held accountable in explaining the uncertain confusion and wavering of Germany's foreign policy between the years 1904 to 1914.[2] On the one hand, von Holstein, inclined to underestimate the menace of "encirclement," was in favor of continuing the method of the "new course," namely, a steady drive toward colonial acquisition for world power in utter defiance of the "Iron Ring," a position which finally occasioned his resignation in 1906. On the other hand, the Kaiser, truly frightened by the threat of isolation and "encirclement," which were implicit in the *Entente Cordiale* and in the *Dual Alliance* after 1904, sought to combine imperialist ambition with a more favorable foreign orientation by cautious, sometimes even bold, concessions in the colonial field. While von Bülow, although at first agreeing with von Holstein at least throughout the year 1905, finally bowed to the wisdom of the Kaiser's colonial policy which, by 1911-1912, began to resemble, as we shall observe, a return to the Bismarckian subordination of Germany's expansion to her safety in the European concert. Upon this phase, then, of Germany's colonial history we must now focus all our attention, in order to trace its connection with the larger story of the maintenance of the balance of power in Europe.

### German Interests in Morocco

Morocco was, of course, the oversea area first to experience this new trend of Germany's colonial policy since it played the major rôle in the formation of the *Entente Cordiale*. By 1903, the importance of Germany's material stake in Morocco was indisputable, albeit, like everywhere else in the colonial field her interests had entered late. German travelers had taken a considerable and creditable part in the early exploration of Morocco to be sure, although at the close of the eighteen-seventies, German trade was not worth mentioning, in spite of the fact that the government maintained a representative at Fez beginning with the year 1873. During the eighties, however, it began in earnest. A commercial expedition, under the leadership of Jannarsch, went to South West Morocco and laid the foundations of what later became a scene of great activity. Germany took part in the Madrid Convention of 1880 and in 1890 gained a treaty guaranteeing commercial rights equal to the most favored nation. By 1898, German interests amounted to from eight to ten million marks and her trade constituted about fourteen per cent of all Morocco's foreign trade, ranking third after that of England and France. Her commerce concentrated at the ports of Mogador, Safi, Mazargan, and Casablanca where resided German consuls. By 1903, considerable German capital had been invested in engineering, industrial and mining enterprises, Mannesmann Brothers representing the largest interests in copper; there were at least fifty German firms along the coast; while German banks operated in several centers and two steamship lines plied regularly between the Fatherland and Morocco. Altogether about one hundred and forty Germans were resident in the country.[3]

### Germany's Policy in Morocco before 1895

In regard to Germany's policy toward Morocco prior to 1895 Bismarck is said to have remarked, "In international affairs there are three wasps' nests besides the Balkans: Morocco and the Mediterranean, the Persian Gulf, and the American Monroe Doctrine; God grant that we may never fall into one of them." That Germany ultimately fell into all three is confirmatory of the "new course." Despite Bismarck's aversion to Moroccan affairs, however, they had formed the subject of a conversation between Salisbury, Rhodes, and Eckardstein in 1889 when a plan for joint action on the part of England and Germany had been discussed; ' but it had come to nothing, Bismarck remarking, "Let sleeping dogs lie." Caprivi's administration had maintained Bismarck's indifference, although Germany continued to cooperate informally with England, whether in exploratory expeditions or in support of economic agents.

### Attitude of William II.

Despite a rising current of interest in Morocco on the part of the German colonialists, which began in the early nineties, the government, strangely enough, remained indifferent, advocating rather the "open door" but no annexations. Indeed, it definitely rejected an unusual opportunity for colonial expansion in that area. For, in 1901, as part of the attempt to establish an Anglo-German *rapprochement,* the subject of joint action in Morocco was once more revived. Again, Chamberlain and Eckardstein seem to have been the chief protagonists and they laid down the broad outlines of a cooperative policy: Great Britain to occupy Tangier and to assume control of the Mediterranean coast of Morocco; Germany to have coaling and trading stations on the Atlantic coast at Casablanca, Mogador, Rabat and, with England, to undertake a joint, peaceful penetration to be followed, if necessary, by military operations; ultimately, Great Britain and Germany to partition Morocco between them.[5] "I understood from Chamberlain," said Eckardstein, "that Salisbury agreed, only later did he begin to consider Morocco as a *quid pro quo* in a deal with France when England's efforts for a German alliance in 1901 failed."[6] Eckardstein also relates how he laid all these plans, as well as his suspicions of an Anglo-French *rapprochement,* if Germany failed to take advantage of them, before the German Foreign Office but its officials left them unanswered.[7]

Of course Germany's failure to consummate any agreement with England over Morocco in 1901 is part and parcel of the general failure of the projected Anglo-German alliance of that year, the reasons for which have been variously ascribed to the danger involved of destroying good relations with Russia, the German naval enthusiasm, and the unpopularity of England in Germany during the Boer War. But in regard to Morocco itself, there are other more specific reasons for Germany's refusal of the joint plan with England, the chief of which constitutes the Kaiser's attitude. "He was never interested in Morocco and was involved in it both by Bethmann and Kiderlen," complained Eckardstein who, with Lichnowsky, saw the whole course of Germany's foreign relations wrecked by her failure to cooperate with England, and in her insistence upon her naval and Near Eastern policies.[8]

It is indeed true that the Kaiser always and consistently maintained the Moroccan question to be relatively unimportant. In 1902 he remarked to Balfour, "A couple of

palm trees in the tropics is a matter of indifference to me";
and in March, 1904, immediately prior to the Anglo-French
treaty, he met King Alfonso of Spain on his Mediterranean
tour, and told him in the presence of the German ambassador that he was not seeking territorial conquests in Morocco,
but only endeavoring to secure free trade, railway concessions, open ports, and the participation of German capital
in the development of the country. Indeed, to him compensation for Germany in some other locality, in view of
the Anglo-French-Spanish agreements over Morocco, seemed
desirable; possibly, on the Spanish side, the transfer of Fernando Po in return for a money indemnity.[9] And, in spite
of the disagreement of his advisers, the Kaiser held to his
point of view. For they, von Holstein and von Bülow, in
accordance with the pursuit of *Weltpolitik,* would have
liked to have acquired a strip of the Atlantic seacoast, the
Sus territory, for Germany, and even wanted to send a German warship to Tangier on the very eve of the signing of
the Anglo-French treaty, for the purpose of protecting the
rights of some local German agent. But the Kaiser absolutely vetoed such an action as vitiating the sincerity of his
declarations at Vigo.[10] So emphatic, indeed, was his assertion of indifference to territorial acquisition in Morocco that
von Bülow was forced to echo his point of view as soon as
the Anglo-French treaty was published. "We have no
reason to imagine that the treaty has a point against any
other Power. . . . As to Morocco, the kernel of the treaty,
we have commercial interests which we shall and will protect. We have, however, no ground to fear that they will
be overlooked or infringed."[11] And the Kaiser reiterated
to King Edward on the occasion of his visit to Kiel in July,
1904, that Morocco had never interested him.[12]

311

## The Emperor's Policy Clashes with Public Opinion

To be sure the hostile reaction of the German colonial enthusiasts and of the Pan-Germans to the Anglo-French Moroccan Treaty give the impression that Germany at this juncture was very much interested in Morocco. And the government found itself in the anomalous situation of seeing its course strongly opposed by those very congenial groups with whom it had formerly cooperated, and whom it had indeed educated to a vigorous colonial policy during the years of "hysterical expansion," 1895-1904. For, early in May, 1904, the Pan-German League published an inflammatory pamphlet by Herr Class entitled *Marokko Verloren;* while its Annual Congress, meeting on June 3, 1904, pronounced the Fatherland to be humiliated and demanded the Atlantic coast of Morocco as its right.[13] "Morocco is a German concern," declared the *Rhenische-Westfälische Zeitung,* April 11, 1904, "owing to our increasing population and need of naval bases. If Germany does not peg out claims, she will retire empty-handed from the partition of the world. Is the German Michael to get nothing? The time has come when Germany must secure Morocco from the Atlas to the sea."

Indeed, public opinion generally had been getting a taste of world power and very naturally demanded more. In the *Reichstag,* only the parties of the Left were at all moderate in their attitude because they feared actual war. Even Maximilian Harden, that great admirer of Bismarck's restraint in colonial aggression, who had unmercifully attacked the Kaiser for his *Weltpolitik* in 1900, now went over entirely to its advocacy. He wrote in April, 1904, "We are not satiated, we need fruitful land. Our great industry thrives in a hothouse heat and we require great markets to dispose

of our wares else we will sink to a second Belgium."[14] But
the government repudiated its erstwhile friends and allies
in *Weltpolitik:* von Bülow denounced the Pan-Germans in
the *Reichstag* when closing the debate on the subject,[15]
while the *Norddeutsche Allgemeine Zeitung* reiterated that
"Germany's commercial interests are in no danger." [16]

### The Kaiser Clings to Non-Aggression in Morocco

Even when the real purpose of the Anglo-French treaty
and its hitherto secret clauses began to appear early in 1905,
with the dispatch of a French envoy to Fez, the Kaiser clung
to his original stand of non-aggression in Morocco; not
unsupported, it may be inferred, by the friendly assurances
from both the British and French Foreign Offices of no wish
to interfere with German interests.[17] And this attitude he
maintained despite von Bülow's change of front, due to the
all too obvious justification of the Pan-Germans' claim that
Germany was regarded as a *"quantité négligéable"* by
France in Morocco. For it has now been thoroughly established that the Kaiser yielded most reluctantly to his Chancellor and von Holstein, and consented actually against his
better judgment to the famous landing at Tangier and the
visit to the sultan "as an independent sovereign." [18] That
the landing was merely an *"acte de présence"* to make a
demonstration against the ignoring of German's interests,
largely to satisfy the popular clamor at home, and not a por-
tent of any intention to seize a part of Morocco may be
confirmed by several factors: first, the Kaiser's very genuine
repugnance to the theatrical journey and his eleventh-hour
reluctance to go ashore when in the very harbor of Tangier,[19]
alleging the roughness of the sea and the lack of a suitable
riding horse as excuses; second, the purport of his speech
to the German colony on landing, which stressed above

everything else the protection of German industry and commerce;[20] third, his appeal to President Roosevelt, March 6, 1905, for support of the sultan against Spain and France who, "wish to divide up Morocco and *to close her markets to the world;*"[21] and fourth and finally, von Bülow's explanation of the coming demonstration at Tangier in the *Reichstag* on March 29: "A year ago the Kaiser told the king of Spain that Germany does not strive for territory in Morocco. It is therefore useless to attribute to the Moroccan visit any selfish purposes directed against its integrity or independence. . . . We have economic interests there and, as in China, it is to our advantage to maintain the open door."[22]

*Opportunities for Annexation Afforded by the Algeciras Conference are Rejected*

This determined stand of the Kaiser against territorial annexation in Morocco, moreover, prevented Germany from taking advantage of those opportunities arising during the preliminary negotiations for the Algeciras Conference, despite the real desires of the Foreign Office, the rising tide of public opinion, and the most tempting offers from France. For Rouvier, the French premier, offered both directly and indirectly to buy off Germany's consent to a French protectorate with territory on the Atlantic coast of Morocco or in the French African colonies.[23] But von Holstein and von Bülow, although strongly inclined to acquire these significant colonial gains, were forced to refuse them because the Kaiser had committed Germany to the sultan's support and to the preservation of the integrity of Morocco.

The Kaiser, in fact, heartily disapproved of the whole principle of the Conference which was primarily due to von Holstein's *Machtpolitik,* to which he had even some difficulty in converting von Bülow. For while these ministers considered that the Congress should be carried through to assert German prestige—as Holstein expressed it, "A surrender now would rank with Olmütz and cause Fashoda to be forgotten" [24]—the Kaiser was extremely fearful of endangering Germany's European position and of irritating France. He, therefore, only reluctantly yielded to their persuasion. How divergent, indeed, was their policy from his and how firm their determination to "rap the table" at Algeciras, may be seen from the fact that they never even told him of Rouvier's second offer to effect a general clearing up of all colonial disputes between France and Germany after the pattern of the Anglo-French treaty as a bait to Germany to abandon the Conference. [25] And when the Kaiser heard of this offer later in 1907, he remarked: "That would have been very convenient and useful. Had I known of it, I would have agreed to it instantly, and the whole of this stupid Algeciras Conference would never have taken place." [26] For Rouvier's second overture did not contemplate so much annexations in Morocco, but included settlements in the Near East and in the whole colonial field.

Indeed Count Monts, German ambassador in Italy, and also Radolin in Paris strongly advised von Bülow to accept Rouvier's colonial plan, which was broached both directly and indirectly through Rome. They pointed out that mutual guarantees of territory and of interests in the Far East, delimitation of spheres of interest in Asia Minor, French support of the Bagdad Railway even against Russia and England might be secured. Count Monts declared, doubtless with some exaggeration, that it was possible to make it a veritable "Canossa" for France. [27] But von Holstein and von Bülow, mindful of the Kaiser's non-annexationist policy in Morocco, and firmly convinced by this time of the necessity

315

for Germany to humiliate France, feared to tell the Kaiser lest he cancel the Conference, and thus assumed the entire responsibility of refusal. They overreached themselves, however, in so far as colonial gains were concerned. For, having secured their main object—the Conference—von Bülow reopened the subject of a general colonial settlement, only to meet with a rebuke from France which closed the matter for that time.[28]

Thus the Algeciras Conference resulted in no territorial gains for Germany; on the contrary, it represented a decided set-back to her colonial growth. For the opportunities for annexations which it afforded were sacrificed on the one hand to the Kaiser's disinclination for aggression in Morocco, and, on the other, to his ministers' desire to pursue the old *Machtpolitik,* which no longer proved effective in Germany's new European orientation in the face of the rapidly emerging *Triple Entente.*

### Underlying Motives of the Policy of Non-Aggression in Morocco

Before proceeding to demonstrate how Germany continued this policy of colonial non-aggression in Morocco throughout the subsequent "crises" of 1907, 1909, and 1911, it would seem appropriate to pause long enough at this juncture to determine its actual and underlying motives. For it represents a complete reversal of the colonial course pursued throughout the preceding decade. As a clever Socialist pointed out, in commenting upon the Kaiser's Bremen speech of March 22, 1905, on the eve of his journey to Tangier, "His repudiation of the striving for a 'desert empire' in Africa marks a decided change from the tone of his earlier utterances such as that of July 3, 1900, when he declared, 'The trident is in our hand and there can be no decision made in the whole world without Germany's decisive word.' " [29] What was responsible for this altered viewpoint?

Everything points to the fact that the Kaiser restrained his desire for colonial annexations in Morocco, and subordinated it to the maintenance of the balance of power for two reasons: first, because he was playing for what he considered to be higher colonial stakes in the Near East; and second, because he did not wish to jeopardize his plans for the construction of a Continental League as a protection against the growing "encirclement" of Germany, in which his hitherto *Weltpolitik* had resulted and by which he was now definitely frightened. As proof for the former, we have only to remember the energy and enthusiasm with which the Kaiser had initiated the Near Eastern policy and what hopes and visions he had entertained in regard to it. To join the other Powers in the dismemberment of Morocco was flatly to abandon his pet project of an alliance with Islam, so naïvely expressed in 1898, and absolutely to destroy the Bagdad Railway plan, whose successful prosecution was dependent upon the continuance of friendship with Turkey, the foundations of which had been so carefully and laboriously laid. "It would make a bad impression on the followers of Islam if Germany gave away Morocco," wrote Marschall von Bieberstein, the Giant of the Golden Horn, advising von Bülow to refuse the French colonial offers and to support the sultan of Morocco in 1905. "If we betray Morocco in spite of Damascus and Tangier, we lose at one stroke our position in Turkey which we have won with years of hard work." [30] Thus the Oriental and the African colonial policies had crossed; they could not both be pursued with profit.

317

And William II clung to his first love and opted for the Near Eastern colonial game as holding out the greatest rewards.

In the second place, to soft pedal on colonial annexations in Morocco coincided with his larger plan to construct a Continental alliance as a means of preserving the balance of power, of which, contrary to his reckless outlook in 1895-1903, he was increasingly coming to realize the necessity. By 1903-1904, in other words, it had become clear even to William II—whose head had been slightly befuddled by the intoxication of world power—that Germany's interests everywhere, in the Near East, in the Far East, in Alsace-Lorraine, on the sea and in the colonial field, cut squarely athwart those of other states. And the concrete symbol of these conflicting aims was emerging in the *Entente Cordiale,* which spelled the beginning of "encirclement." Early in 1904, we note expressions of the uneasiness felt by the German government in regard to the unfavorable situation of world politics, in spite of official assurances for home and foreign consumption that there was no cause for alarm; that the *Entente Cordiale* was indeed a guarantee of peace.[31] For William II and von Bülow acknowledged that the *Entente* had strengthened the positions of both England and France, and that Germany could no longer count upon Italy;[32] von Bülow and the German ambassador, Monts, at Rome discussed the admitted determination of France and England to include Russia;[33] and Metternich in England confirmed von Bülow's suspicions of the secret articles in the Anglo-French treaties.[34]

To meet this situation, William II promoted his idea of maintaining the balance of power by a union of the Triple and Dual alliances and the consequent formation of a Continental bloc;[35] and how faithfully he endeavored to effect

such a combination as a guarantee against Germany's isolation, in spite of von Holstein's conflicting *Machtpolitick* and
even, at times, von Bülow's opposition, his repeated attempts
to secure a Russian alliance, especially at the Björkoe meeting, illustrate. Naturally, to facilitate this policy, extreme
caution in respect to France's position in Morocco was essential. Hence followed his reiterated disavowal of any proposed annexations, his reluctance to the demonstration at
Tangier, and his disapproval and virtual emancipation from
Bülow's and Holstein's Algeciras policy.[36] Assuredly, the
Kaiser's earnest and single-purposed endeavor from 1903-
1907 to effect a Continental League, which especially in its
alliance with Russia would have furthered Germany's colonial policy in the Near East, provides the second key to his
apparent neglect of annexationist opportunities in Morocco,
and confirms his subordination of colonial policy to the
maintenance of the balance of power.

## The Kaiser Fails to Utilize the Succeeding Moroccan Crises for Colonial Gains

As we follow the Moroccan affair through its succeeding
crises, we observe the continuance of the Kaiser's indifference to it—nay, avoidance of it—as an area for oversea
acquisition, and his increasing conciliatory attitude toward
France, in spite of the ofttimes insistent opposition of his
advisers and the rising popular clamor against the government at home. In 1906, for instance, when fresh disturbances broke out in Morocco affording France an opportunity
to send warships and to land troops, Germany, to be sure,
protested, but the Kaiser prevented the dispatching of any
military force,[37] and rejected the proposal of the German
ambassador in Tangier that the occasion afforded Germany an excellent opportunity to demand colonial com-

pensation from France.[38]   Again, in 1907, when France
utilized the assassination of a French physician at Mara-
kesch to penetrate farther into the Promised Land, and
offered Germany a colonial agreement whereby she might
acquire compensation elsewhere and renounce her claims
in Morocco, the Kaiser refused it, demanding in its stead
a higher and obviously unattainable price, a political alliance
with Germany.[39]   "France and Germany must go hand in
hand," wrote the Kaiser to von Bülow, reporting his conversation with M. Etienne, a former French Minister of the Interior in Rouvier's cabinet, "The good-will between them cannot be accomplished by such trifles as colonies. . . . Germany is a much better ally for France than England. . . I
would recognize French preponderance in Morocco after
France had concluded a firm alliance with Germany. . . .
I can no longer recognize the French policy, which consists
in giving an arm to Russia, a hand to England, a greeting
to Germany.  I now desire at least the hand, yet better the
arm. . . . For nineteen years I have stretched out a hand
to France, but she has refused it. . . . The time may come
when she will have to pay for England's broken crockery.
. . . Alliance first, then preponderance in Morocco." [40]
From which it is clear that the Kaiser was still cherishing
the dream of Björkoe and the subordination of colonial
acquisitions in Morocco to the idea of a Continental alliance.[41]

What is more, von Bülow seems to have come around to
the same point of view, for he replies to the letter: "Increasingly more does it appear that Your Majesty's policy has
been right for German interests. . . . You have hit the nail
on the head. . . . We must avoid the appearance of bar-
gaining in Morocco as if we were selling it for a mere
*Trinkgeld*.  There is too much at stake . . . our position

in the Islamic world. Only an alliance with France should make us give up our position in Turkey" [42]—which reveals again the first key, as we have termed it, to the Moroccan attitude: Germany's colonial policy in the Near East.

## The Franco-German Pact of 1909, a Blow to Colonial Hopes

The Moroccan crisis of 1908-1909, culminating in the Franco-German Pact of 1909, illustrates even more clearly the altered colonial policy of the German Foreign Office, in the respect which it was now made to pay to the balance of power. For both the dispute over the Moroccan throne between the sultan and his dynastic rival, his brother Mulay Hafid, and the quarrel over the German consul's jurisdiction at Casablanca enabled the French to be more aggressive and to land more troops. The Kaiser and von Bülow, however, maintained their conciliatory attitude: they instructed Secretary Schön that, "Germany would not look on with indifference, but to avoid all threats of war"; [43] and the Kaiser, especially, pressed for a speedy settlement in Morocco, as the intervening Bosnian crisis made it even more essential both for Germany and Austria and the Near Eastern policy to placate France. [44] "In view of these circumstances," (in Bosnia), he wrote, "this wretched Moroccan affair must be brought to a conclusion quickly and finally. Let it be French . . . and let us be done with this friction with France now that great questions are at issue. . . . Our Moroccan policy hitherto has proved a failure." [45] Besides the Bosnian crisis and the urgent appeals of the Austrian emperor, the Kaiser was influenced by his anxiety to settle the matter before the visit of King Edward to Berlin early in 1909, for he wished to avoid any suspicion that England had brought pressure upon Germany. Consequently, he hastened the signing of the Franco-German Pact of February 9, 1909.

According to this agreement, Germany promised to recognize the privileged position of the French in Morocco, provided that they again agreed to respect the integrity of the Sherifian empire and the absolute economic equality of all nations therein. In presenting the treaty to the *Reichstag,* von Bülow went so far as to say, "Why should Germany injure France?" [46] And the official *Süddeutsche Reichskorrespondenz* pointed out that the great value of the compact lay in the fact that it eliminated Morocco as an area of political discord in German-French relations. "At present, our relationship to the Western Powers has become perceptibly less tense." [47] So pleased was the Kaiser over this complete abnegation of colonial ambitions to foreign policy, that he formally congratulated Schön upon the success of his negotiations and bestowed upon Cambon, the French ambassador, the Cross of the Red Eagle! For he evidently was convinced that his attitude had led France to counsel peace to Russia in the Bosnian affair: "One can see how wise of us it was to come to an understanding with France on Morocco," [48] he wrote as a comment upon von Bülow's report.

### According to the Colonialists Germany Sells Her Colonial Birthright in Morocco for a Mess of Potage

Finally, in the Agadir crisis of 1911, the Kaiser maintained his opposition to Kiderlen-Wächter's aggressive policy as long as he was able in the face of popular clamor; and, in the last analysis, was responsible for Germany's ultimate backdown before France after the dramatic "spring of the *Panther*" in 1911. For the new secretary of state, anxious to terminate the vexatious Moroccan difficulty, to

322

satisfy public opinion and to grind an election axe, attempted a revival of von Holstein's *Machtpolitik* in order to lay the foundation of a German Central African empire. He had indeed a great plan: he visualized Africa divided into a French kingdom in the west, a British in the east and south, and a German empire in the center. Therefore he wanted territory that would connect German Kamerun with German East Africa, and thought it could be achieved first by treaties with France for the French and Belgian Congos, and then by sharing the Portuguese colonies with England.[49] If all went well, the dream of the German imperialists would be realized: a German *Mittel-Afrika* would stretch from the Atlantic to the Indian Ocean, from British South Africa to the Sudan.

But, "it seemed to me that the affair was full of explosive matter and I gave in with a heavy heart," asserts the Kaiser. "When the Foreign Office informed me of its intention to send the *Panther*, I gave expression to strong misgivings, but had to drop them in view of its strong representations."[50] These words are confirmed by the difficulty which Kiderlen encountered in gaining his Kaiser's consent to "send ships" to Morocco. For at first he wrote from Corfu,[51] opposing any intervention whatever, and continued to oppose[52] it even after he consented to the demand upon France for compensations. This he agreed to, apparently because of Kiderlen's representation that colonial gains could be obtained peacefully and easily from France with her full accord in return for her occupation of Fez, and that such an opportunity for rounding out the colonial empire should not be missed. It was only in response to the sense of alarm and fear aroused in Germany by France's attitude, and the suspicious delays in the negotiations over the compensations that the Kaiser authorized the sending of "ships." [53] And when the bellicose effect of the *"Panther's spring"* upon the *Triple Entente* became apparent, he opposed any idea of making war, and pressed Kiderlen to negotiate a settlement in the face of an almost unanimous public sentiment. [54]

Nowhere do we find that he supported Kiderlen's demand on France for the whole of the French Congo, the option on the Belgian Congo, which she had secured in 1900, and on Spanish Guinea. In fact, so urgent was his pressure to end the affair peacefully, that his foreign secretary was obliged to reject Caillaux's revival of Rouvier's offer of a general liquidation of all colonial disputed questions, such as the Bagdad Railway, the Turkish debt, and a new delimitation of seaboard territories; [55] and to negotiate the final treaty which fell far short of the original German demands. Instead of the vast territories dreamed of by the Pan-Germans, Germany added 107,000 undesirable square miles of the French Congo to German Kamerun; gained the option on Spanish Guinea; but instead of the option on Belgian Congo secured only a compromise, which left the decision of the future of that territory to a conference of the Powers, in case Belgium ever relinquished it. Germany gained, it is true, an extension to Kamerun which gave that colony a boundary on the Congo river, and also one on the Ubangi, but this territory included the entire area of three concession companies and parts of the areas of other companies, including 85 per cent of that belonging to the N'Goko Sangha Company. The agreement with France provided that Germany should respect the rights of all these companies which were carefully defined in a supplementary declaration (September 28, 1912). [55a] And upon the text of this treaty, [56] so utterly unsatisfactory as far as colonial or economic gains were concerned, the Kaiser wrote:

"Best congratulations for the termination of this delicate affair."

Certainly, all the Moroccan crises had been replete with opportunities to acquire colonial territory, but, as we have shown, the Kaiser had rejected them, one after the other, in startling opposition to public opinion at home. Perhaps a summary of popular sentiment expressed against the Kaiser's course in Morocco will provide a final illustration of the decided change in colonial policy represented by that area. For the German people, educated and stimulated during the preceding decade to a colonial drive aimed at securing a "place in the sun," gave vent to their disappointment with no uncertain voice when they observed their imperial master subordinating territorial annexation to the maintenance of the balance of power. And doubtless the measure of their disapproval indicates the extent of the altered policy.

We have already noted the popular clamor over the virtual colonial defeat sustained by Germany at the Algeciras Congress, and this rose to veritable shrieks of pain and protest from the Pan-Germans and colonialists when the Franco-German Pact of 1909 was completed, that pact whose leniency to France amazed even the French. The Colonial Society not only protested formally against the Casablanca decision, but throughout the crisis issued diatribes against the Social Democrats, the only political party which did not urge aggression in Morocco.[57] The firm of Mannesmann Brothers complained bitterly in the press and in the *Reichstag*,[58] and doubted whether economic freedom in Morocco, guaranteed by the pact, could be maintained; a doubt subsequently justified by the miscarriage of their own cooperation with the *Union of Mines* and the failure of German participation generally in railway construction, financial undertakings, and in other public works. For the German

325

interests in Morocco appeared to interpret "economic equality" to mean a German-French monopoly and the Franco-German *Société Morocaine des Travaux Publics* ran afoul British interests; while German railway ambitions encountered the usurped right of the French to control strategic lines. As Mannesmann Brothers claimed, with justification, the German Foreign Office could not urge the German capitalists' interests because of its fear, condemned by all the Nationalists, of bringing the country into conflict with the other Powers, the Powers of the *Entente*. And of the embarrassment which those capitalists caused in Germany's foreign relations we have full evidence.[59]

But popular opposition to the 1909 settlement formed merely a mild prelude to the storm of protest engendered by the Agadir crisis. The Pan-German League, which had never ceased to fret and chafe since the Algeciras Conference, now fairly "choked with rage." Herr Class published his famous pamphlet, *West Morokko Deutsch,* which ran into some five editions reaching some fifty and sixty thousand copies. But more than that, it accused Kiderlen-Wächter first of promising official support to the Pan-Germans and their territorial demands, and then traitorously betraying them by the consummation of the final treaty which fell so far short of their hopes; all of which resulted in a public controversy seriously embarrassing to the government both at home and abroad.[60]

Only slightly less vociferous and pestiferous to the administration than the Pan-Germans was the Colonial Society. Throughout the negotiations with France, it kept calling upon the government to secure the utmost in the way of compensation or else to fight. It demanded Dahomey, Sus, South and West Morocco, and poured out vials of scorn upon the territory finally secured, condemning it alternately

326

as a "swamp" and a "desert"; and it finally helped force Secretary von Lindequist to resign from the colonial office as a protest against the treaty, expressing itself as overjoyed at his action.[61]

Encouraged by the rebellious attitude of the Colonial Society, one hundred Hamburg firms joined Mannesmann Brothers in signing a formal protest[62] to the government against the treaty; while group after group of industrials passed resolutions deploring Germany's "retreat in Morocco," and sent appeals for support to authors, intellectuals, and *Gymnasium* teachers.

But the noisy colonial leaders all over the country were not alone in their opposition; practically the entire press supported them. "The world is being rapidly divided, and we are being left out. We should let the world know what we want,"[63] declared the *Rhenische Westfälische Zeitung*. Furthermore, the press identified the "surrender" in Morocco with lack of patriotism, national ambition, and even treachery—just as the government had taught it so well to do in the preceding decade of *Weltpolitik*. "If the government combats the unrighteous greed of France for power, it will have the entire people behind it," asserted the *Westfälische Zeitung*, and even the *Evangelical Church Times* asked the question, "When do we march?"[64]

At the end of July, 1911, when the government had decided that Germany would not go to war over Morocco, a cry of rage and despair shook the entire nation, which rose in higher crescendo upon the publication of the final treaty. "Have we become a generation of women?" demanded *Die Post*. "The Kaiser has become the strongest supporter of the English-French policy. . . . What is the matter with the Hohenzollerns?" The *Leipsiger Neueste Nachrichten* declared Germany's humiliation to be worse than that inflicted by Olmütz or Jena; and all the press applauded the resignation of the colonial secretary with a "Bravo, Linde-quist!" [85] Again shouts of derision from all sides greeted Bethmann-Hollweg in the *Reichstag* when he attempted to set forth the advantages of the Agadir treaty. Even the Social Democrats made fun of the "strong government," and condemned its handling of the Moroccan affair as absolutely "spineless." [86] Assuredly had the government departed from its former *Weltpolitik.*

## Full Steam Ahead in Mesopotomia

Turning now to the Near East as the second area to be affected by the altered colonial policy, we shall find that region reflecting even more clearly than North Africa the careful adjustment of expansion to foreign relations. For the Kaiser sacrificed acquisition in Morocco for imperialism in the Near East. Hence we shall find him on the one hand pressing forward with redoubled energy to the goal of his heart's desire, the completion of the Bagdad Railway and, on the other, subordinating even this cherished project to the exigencies of the balance of power, as Germany's "encirclement" grew increasingly menacing. We have already evaluated the sacrifice of the colonial "birds in the hand" in Morocco; now let us estimate the gains represented by the "birds in the bush" in Mesopotamia, and also observe how their capture was adjusted to Germany's European orientation.

## Public Opinion Now Heartily Endorses Near Eastern Imperialism

After the year 1906, the "grand design" of the Bagdad Railway and all that it implied entered upon a much more significant phase for two reasons. In the first place, the

Railway had come to be accepted and promoted as an imperialistic, and not merely as an economic, enterprise, by the German people instead of only by the governing group as formerly. So well educated to world power had been popular sentiment in Germany by the successes of the former decade that its appetite, now thoroughly whetted, could only demand further satisfaction. After 1904 the Railway came to be referred to affectionately as *"Unser Bagdad"* or, more ostentatiously as the "B. B. B."—Berlin-Byzantium-Bagdad. Publicists such as Rohrbach [67] now dilated upon its possibilities, economic, political, and imperialistic, with such exaggerated fervor that they placed it upon a plane where it was reverently regarded as an integral part of Germany's *Weltanschauung,* her mystical "manifest destiny." As the project succeeded, it was only natural that it should enlist the support of patriotic financiers, stockholders, engineers, contractors, traders, and shippers whose fervid patriotism approached one hundred per cent as potentialities for economic gain revealed themselves. And it was but natural, again, that they should clamor for the defense of their interests, which in turn coincided with the desire of professional patriots, soldiers, diplomats and consular officials who but followed the lead of their imperial master in bending the Ottoman empire to German nationalistic and imperialistic ends.

Besides the small conservative group in administrative circles, represented by Baron von Eckardstein and Prince Lichnowsky,[68] who deplored the Kaiser's Near Eastern policy as a fatal diplomatic mistake bound to precipitate a Franco-British-Russian coalition against the Central Powers, the Socialists were the only real opponents of the great scheme. True to form, they fought it, uttering many dire and prophetic warnings, as constituting solely another piece of capitalistic imperialism certain to lead to disastrous international conflicts.[69] With these exceptions, however, there can be no doubt that the preponderance of German opinion, after 1906, heartily endorsed the Bagdad Railway as an imperialistic project. Indeed, it had become "no longer a Railway but a state of mind." [70] and this support lent double strength to the Kaiser's already determined aims.

### The Entente Powers Begin to Weave Their Net of Opposition

In the second place, the period after 1906 marked a more significant era for Near Eastern expansion, because of the united instead of single opposition of the Powers to Germany's advance. It will be recalled that in 1903 Germany had secured the Konia-Mosul-Bagdad-Koweit railway concession, and by October, 1904, had opened the line as far as Konia in the face of opposition from Great Britain, Russia, and France who had each individually objected because of their separate and private interests. The next step was to extend the line through the Taurus Mountains, then beyond through desert lands to Mosul, down to Bagdad along the Tigris River; thence down the Euphrates to Basra, and finally to the ultimate goal, the Persian Gulf; a project challenging in the extreme, involving as it did extensive tunnelling through solid rock, the throwing of steel bridges across mountain chasms and rivers, and the spanning of desert stretches by far-flung railways lines. But the continuation of the Railway not only challenged imperialistic imagination; it challenged economic resource, for such an engineering project demanded immense sums. Turkey promised to furnish the funds provided the Ottoman government could raise the customs dues from eight per cent to eleven per cent. But this proposal at once encountered the opposition [71] of the Powers who were rapidly approaching each other to form the *Triple Entente;* indeed, common action against the German Bagdad enterprise was proving to be one of the bonds between Russia and England, weaning Russia away from Germany. Thus the year 1906 marked the beginning of that joint antagonism to Germany in the Near East on the part of the future *Entente* Powers which, together with their united opposition in Morocco, projected Germany's colonial policy into the realm of the balance of power.

Numerous signs of this united blocking of Germany's all-too-evident ambitions in the Near East were not wanting: in 1906 also, England and Russia had reached the decision that they would not allow the Railway to proceed unless Russia received exclusive right to a branch line to Armenia and northern Persia, while England gained control of the stretch from Basra to Bagdad;[72] Great Britain accompanied her refusal to the proposed 3 per cent raise in the customs duties with a sharp demand for reforms in Macedonia, as a prelude to which she had instigated a naval demonstration of the Great Powers (except Germany) at Mitylene in November, 1905, which had compelled the sultan to hand over to them the control of the Macedonian finances. Again, in 1907, the Kaiser met with an ominous rebuff and an effort to assemble the Powers against him when he announced during his visit to Windsor that he would "concede the Gate to India" to England, namely the corridor from Basra to the north coast of the Persian Gulf, if she would cease to block the Railway.[73] For by that time, as we have noted in the case of Morocco, he had already begun to see the wisdom of subordinating his imperial policy to his foreign relations in view of the gathering clouds of the *Triple Entente.* Although Baron von Schön and Sir Edward Grey discussed the Kaiser's proposition favorably and at length,

England in the end proposed a four-Power conference to consider it, thus definitely drawing in Russia and France, to which Germany would not consent. This was followed by the joint protest of the *Entente* Powers against Austria's concession won in January, 1908, from Turkey to construct a railroad through the Sanjak of Novi-Bazar.

The Allies also accompanied their protest with demands upon Turkey for compensation in the form of a corresponding concession for a Danube-Adriatic line running through Serbia and Albania to the sea.[74] It is significant that Italy, too, joined in this protest (foreshadowing the grouping of the Powers against Germany in the Great War) and thereby augmented the Kaiser's alarm. At the same time, also, Great Britain registered her displeasure at the establishment of a Hamburg-American-Line service from Hamburg to the Persian Gulf by a new Anglo-French demand on Turkey; namely, permission to France to build a railroad from a harbor on the Mediterranean through north Syria and along the Euphrates to the Persian Gulf; and the concession to England of the sector of the Bagdad Railway from Bagdad to the Gulf.[75] Finally, the Reval meeting between Edward VII and the Czar, in June, 1908, symbolized the completion of the *"Entente* net" woven against Germany in the Near East. For Iswolski, the Russian minister, a Pan-Slav, who wished to reverse Russia's policy in Eastern Asia, drew closer to the *Entente* Powers and, apparently, introduced at Reval plans for cooperation on the Bagdad Railway.[76]

## The Kaiser Seeks to Harmonize Near Eastern Expansion with Diplomatic Caution

The effect upon the Kaiser of this all-too-obvious opposition of the *Entente* to his expansionist ambitions in the Near East was twofold: in the first place, it stimulated his determination to pursue the completion of the Bagdad Railway, and, secondly, it increased his conviction that Germany's "encirclement," of which he was now fully aware, demanded the utmost wariness in the conduct of his colonial policy. Hence from 1907 on, where we find in Morocco a complete abnegation of colonial acquisition for the sake of the balance of power, in the Near East we observe a continual warring between expansionist ambition and diplomatic caution ending in great concessions to the latter. For, as one examines Germany's Near Eastern policy from 1907 to 1914, there can be no doubt that it was dominated, on the one hand, by that intense desire for expansion in Mesopotamia leading to economic and political control which had animated it since 1897, and for which indeed so many alluring colonial opportunities in Morocco had been sacrificed; and, on the other, by a diplomatic caution engendered primarily by fear which checked this urgent *Drang nach Osten*, and brought it into some degree of subordination to Germany's European orientation.

It was fear, indeed, of the rapidly developing *rapprochement* between Great Britain and Russia that had moved the Kaiser to offer his concession of the "Gate to India" in 1907, and it was again fear of Germany's complete isolation in Europe that induced both Marschall and himself to support Austria in her demand for the railway through the Sanjak. For, at first, both these zealous friends of Turkey's welfare were opposed to Aehrenthal's proposed railway concession as injurious to Germany's position in Turkey, and only agreed to it when they realized the imminent danger of an Anglo-Russian understanding and the consequent pressing necessity of keeping Austria as an ally. And even then von Bülow promised Germany's support to Austria only on the condition that the sultan give his voluntary consent, since "in view of our special interests in Constantinople, we cannot go against him." [77] Throughout the entire negotiations, maintenance of Turkey and alliance with Islam stand forth as primary and not secondary motives of Germany's policy. "Our commercial interests in the East are so great that they have acquired a political significance. We must defend them energetically, relying on our good cause and our strength, and not let ourselves be thrust out of the East. . . . The well-known speech of the Kaiser at Damascus still wakens a response in the Mussulman world. That is an asset we must preserve. For the day may come when it will be of service to us," wrote Marschall in the official *Report* of his Conversations with Aehrenthal over the Balkan situation in December, 1907; and the Kaiser noted upon the margin, "Very good." [78]

But if the Sanjak affair reflected the conflicting tendencies of Germany's policy in the Near East between imperialistic advance and diplomatic restraint, the Bosnian crisis of 1908 spelled it out in words of one syllable. For both the Kaiser and Marschall were beside themselves with indignation at the action of Austria in her annexation of Bosnia and Herzegovina. So fearful were they of its disastrous effect upon their relations to the Porte; and to make matters worse the Kaiser only learned of his ally's intention upon the day of the annexation. "It is simply piracy against Turkey," he raged. "Vienna will have to answer for her duplicity, they have deceived us shamefully. . . . That is the nice thanks of the Hapsburgs for our help in the Sanjak affair when we had to endure Iswolski's rage for months on end, and for our complaisance in Vienna. . . . As their (the Turks) ally I am personally wounded in my deepest feelings. . . . Our whole position in Constantinople, which we have won by twenty years of friendly policy, has been imperiled by Austria's proceedings. . . . If the sultan in his difficulty declares war and unfurls in Stamboul the green flag of the Holy War, I shall not blame him." [79]

Of course, Marschall thoroughly upheld the Kaiser's position and vehemently urged a protest against the annexation. "If we do not take up a position against the annexation every one will conclude that it has been done with our consent," he wrote.[80] And he further attacked the Foreign Office for its inability to restrain both Germany's allies, Austria and Italy, who was likewise intriguing in Tripoli, from inroads upon Turkey, warning von Bülow that some vigorous action must be taken if Germany's influence in the Near East was to be maintained, in which sentiment he was supported by Count Monts, the German ambassador in Rome.[81]

This attitude of William II and Marschall, who were always under the spell of the *Drang nach Osten,* constituted a serious problem for von Bülow, imbued as he was with the tradition of strict loyalty to Austria. Valiantly did he strive to convince his imperial master of the peril to the Fatherland which non-support of her only ally at this juncture would precipitate. Furthermore, he was obliged to instruct Marschall to be extremely reserved in expressing his opinion, and to point out in detail to William II the pressing diplomatic necessity of subordinating his expansion policy in Mesopotamia to the exigencies of the European situation.[82] Thus the Kaiser reluctantly consented to recognize the annexation, continuing to express regrets that "Aehrenthal's frightful stupidity" had brought him into this dilemma of "not being able to protect and assist the Turks, our friends, because my ally has injured them." Moreover, he feared now that, "In Turkey, German officers will be replaced by Frenchmen." [83] Nevertheless, how complete his conversion was to the necssity of diplomatic caution at this time may be guaged by remembering his coincident abnegation to France over colonial annexations in Morocco.[84]

### Germany Drives Ahead with the Railway

In the meantime, while throwing these necessary sops to diplomacy, the German government was prosecuting the Bagdad Railway with its accustomed determination, and was managing in some degree to harmonize its imperialistic expansion in Mesopotamia with its international relations. For Turkey's finances had improved by 1908 to such an extent that she found herself able to advance the required sum for the continuation of the Railway without raising the customs dues, for which the consent of the Powers was essential. In June, 1908, arrangements were made for issuing the necessary bonds and work on the Railway was again resumed after a four-year pause. By September, Medina and Mecca had been reached and German officials were to be seen everywhere in that district. But this success was short-lived, for the Young Turk revolution intervened, temporarily to postpone the continuance of the Railway and to destroy Germany's unrivaled influence in the Near East.

Eclipse both of her expansion program and her prestige, however, was of short duration, so firmly established was Ottoman confidence in her support at Constantinople, and so deeply rooted her power throughout Mesopotamia. And it was not long before the Young Turks, in spite of the apparent greater congeniality of their new régime with the Western nations, became convinced that Germany, after all, was the only great Power who did not desire their dissolution. The concrete symbol of this renewal of friendly relations and consequent revival of the *Drang nach Osten* was the loan of $30,000,000, which the *Deutsche Bank* granted the new Ottoman government in 1910, with no conditions inconsistent with the dignity of Turkey; a loan which the Young Turks had found it impossible to negotiate in Paris or London without the accompaniments of humiliating concessions which they found it impossible to grant.[85]

This significant diplomatic triumph completely restored German prestige in Turkey to the position which it had formerly occupied, and prepared the way for its final triumph in regard to the Railway, namely the Convention signed on March 21, 1911, by which Germany gained the concession for the last piece of the Railway and also a sub-line to Alexandretta. When the building of the Railway was again resumed after the delays imposed by the Young Turk Revolution and the Moroccan affairs, *Punch* published a cartoon representing Wilhelm II as Haroun-al-Raschid seated upon a locomotive bound for Constantinople, behind him Kiderlen-Wächter as the engineer—bearing the inscription, "Hearty good wishes for the success of the Bagdad R. R., from the Kaiser to Kiderlen-Wächter." [86] This picture symbolizes for us the Kaiser's driving purpose for expansion in Mesopotamia which suffered no obstacle to block it either internal or external.

### Germany Compromises with Her Rivals in Mesopotamia

For by 1910, the Kaiser had become firmly convinced of the necessity, if not of the wisdom, of shaping his colonial policy to the demands of Germany's foreign relations. And just as we have observed the culmination of his changed course in the Moroccan crisis of 1911 so do we likewise note it in the Near East after 1910. The diplomatic triumph experienced by Germany in 1909 in recovering her lost prestige in Turkey not only enabled her to drive ahead with the Railway, but prepared the way for advantageous negotiations with those Powers who sought to block her advance from without. Thus in 1910, when relations between Russia and Germany were anything but harmonious in the Near East, owing to the former's desire to weaken the Ottoman power and the latter's desire to strengthen it, the Kaiser capitalized Iswolski's resentment against England and France for their refusal of support in the Bosnian affair and invited the Czar to Potsdam for "confidential intercourse." The result was the Potsdam Agreement by which Germany recognized Russia's exceptional political position in northern Persia in return for complete equality of rights for German trade; and, further, renounced the gaining of railway concessions there upon Russia's promise no longer to oppose the construction of the Bagdad Railway.[87] So by means of diplomatic concession and restraint of expansionist ambition, one of the most formidable opponents of the great German penetration in the Near East was removed.

Meanwhile, negotiations had already been resumed with Great Britain, indeed they had never been entirely broken off. For after the conclusion of the *Triple Entente,* it is clear that the Kaiser became thoroughly convinced that he could never achieve his heart's desire in the Near East or, in fact, anywhere else in the colonial field without the cooperation of his greatest rival. Hence, after the rebuff encountered by the offer of the "Gate to India" in 1907, approaches were again made to English financiers through the agency of Albert Ballin, director of the Hamburg-American Line and close ally of the Kaiser, and Ernest Cassel, an intimate friend of Edward VII.[88] They hoped to effect cooperation in rendering financial assistance to the Young Turks. But the refusal of the French and British governments to advance a loan to Turkey without humiliating conditions, and the consequent turning back of the Young Turks to Germany for support interrupted this plan.

Again, early in 1909, just prior to his resignation, von Bülow capitalized the good feeling engendered between Germany and England, both by their cooperation for peaceful ends in the Bosnian crisis and by Germany's concessions to France in Morocco in February, 1909, by drawing up a series of tentative draft treaties of political alliance with England accompanied by contemplated colonial agreements and special arrangements about the Bagdad Railway.[89] Although these proposals reached the discussion stage, nothing came of them, because of the difficulty of reaching any naval agreement and because of the joint understanding among the *Entente* Powers that no one of them would reach any settlement on the Bagdad question without the other.[90]

In 1910, however, further efforts to reach an understanding were made both officially by Bethmann-Hollweg, who shared the Kaiser's and von Bülow's conviction that no progress could be made in the Near East or in any field without an Anglo-German *"rapprochment,"* and unofficially by von Gwinner and Cassel.[91] These two financiers hoped to remove the difficulties from the construction of the last section of the line running through the sultan of Koweit's territory which was virtually under British control. Germany was prepared to allot to English capital up to 60 per cent of the shares for this section, if England promised no longer to hinder the competition of the line to Bagdad with German capital. The temptation to England was so great that she threatened to break the joint agreement made by the *Entente* in regard to the railway, but Russia objected and the negotiations dragged on only to be again postponed by the Agadir crisis.

With the settlement of the Moroccan affair in favor of the *Entente* in 1911, Anglo-German relations materially improved and the hope of arriving at a satisfactory compromise, both in the Near East and in other colonial areas, distinctly revived. In view of the Kaiser's entire Moroccan policy, as we have analyzed it, it appears most probable that his restrained attitude during 1911, and his anxiety to bring the Agadir affair to a peaceful conclusion was due in large measure to his earnest desire to remove the difficulties blocking the German advance in Mesopotamia. What is more, the Potsdam settlement with Russia, releasing Great Britain from the *Entente* agreement regarding the Bagdad Railway, made an Anglo-German compromise essential from the point of view of both countries and, to further facilitate matters, the Bagdad Railway Company had expressed its willingness in March, 1911, to abandon its plans for the sections from Bagdad to Basra to the Persian Gulf, and to permit the construction and operation of these lines by an international syndicate.[92] Moreover, signs of British friendliness to Germany were not wanting: in the House of Commons Sir Edward Grey expressed England's willingness not to stand in the way of Germany's expansion and indicated support in developing a future colonial empire in Central Africa,[93] a promise which Count Metternich, the German ambassador, made the most of, urging the Kaiser to bargain for colonial gains from England by concessions in the proposed new navy law.[94] Thus was the stage all set for final compromise on the Bagdad Railway.

The first step toward such a *rapprochement* was taken by Cassel's visit to Berlin early in 1912, where he submitted an unofficial memorandum on behalf of Grey which suggested that Germany limit her navy construction in return for Great Britain's support of her wish for colonial expansion.[95] Germany's official announcement on February 4, 1912,[96] that she might revise her supplementary naval law, if she received satisfactory assurance of a friendly orientation of British policy, was followed by Haldane's official visit to Berlin accompanied by Ballin and by Cassel who remained behind the scenes. Here the question of a colonial settlement both in Africa and the Near East was discussed in relation to Germany's naval program. Haldane stated that Great Britain was prepared to grant her consent to the Railway if her political position in Mesopotamia was adequately safeguarded—the same position he had maintained in 1907; and he further indicated that if Germany should renounce her supplementary naval law of 1912, England would have no objection to Germany's expansion in Central Africa or, further, to the cession of Zanzibar and Pemba in case a satisfactory settlement with regard to the final section of the Bagdad Railways was reached. These proposals Haldane carried home in the form of draft treaties.[97] But all sorts of difficulties arose: the interpretation of the naval supplementary law; the British colonial secretary's objection to Haldane's unauthorized disposal of the colonies; the divided opinion in both British and German cabinets. Consequently, no agreement—either political, naval or colonial—was reached at that time.

The attempt at an understanding with England over the Bagdad Railway was not by any means abandoned, however, in spite of the intervention of the Balkan wars, which indeed made an Anglo-German approach even more desirable, and conversations over that and other disputed colonial points were continued. It is indeed highly significant of the Kaiser's keen desire to continue the Bagdad Railway only in cooperation with England, that he appointed Marschall von Bieberstein, the Giant of the Golden Horn, to the post of British ambassador left vacant by the retirement of Wolff-Metternich; and upon his untimely death in August, 1912, chose Prince Lichnowsky to replace him with the express intention of creating as good relations as possible with the English court and aristocracy.

Finally, in February, 1914, after long and tedious negotiations and the complete separation of the Bagdad question from the naval issue, an agreement was reached by which the German-Bagdad Railway Company renounced its existing right to the building of the final stretch from Basra to the Persian Gulf. It was to be constructed only after an understanding had been reached by the German, English, and Turkish governments. The harbors of Basra and Bagdad were to be built by a Turkish company, England to be allowed up to 40 per cent of the shares. Germany was to obtain neither a harbor nor a railway station on the Persian Gulf without a previous understanding with England, nor was she to have a financial interest in the construction. England pledged herself neither to build nor to finance a rival line to the Bagdad Railway and Germany recognized the rights conceded by Turkey in March, 1913, to an English company for shipping on the Euphrates and the Tigris. The Bagdad Railway Company was to be allotted 40 per cent of the share capital originally reserved for Turkey (20 per cent of the entire capital of this company). As soon as the railway to Basra was completed, the financial support guaranteed by the Turkish government to the Bagdad Railway Company was to cease.[98] The text of this treaty was initialed in London, June 14, 1914, signed by Germany on July 27 and forwarded to Lichnowsky in London on July 30, whereupon the outbreak of the Great War put an end to it.

By the agreement Germany had virtually surrendered southern Mesopotamia and the Persian Gulf as a British sphere of influence, but she had gained the cessation of British opposition to the Bagdad Railway so stubbornly maintained since 1903, and had created a community of inter-

342

est between Germany and England in Asia Minor—a make-weight against the *Triple Entente* and her consequent isolation.

Prior to the final Anglo-German Convention of June, 1914, the Bagdad Railway Company had signed an agreement with Lord Inchcape acknowledging the monopolistic privileges in Mesopotamia river navigation conferred upon his interests by Turkey, as well as another Convention protecting the British and Smyrna-Aidin Railway Company; and the German government had agreed in March, 1914, to recognize southern Mesopotamia together with central and southern Persia as exclusive oil fields of the Anglo-Persian Company.[99] Also, in February, 1914, the Franco-German Convention, initiated by French and German banking groups, was signed, whereby Germany recognized northern Anatolia and Syria as French spheres of influence.[100]

Thus it may be seen that German sacrifices in Mesopotamia were considerable and that by accommodating compromise with her rivals, instead of by blind and ruthless opposition to them, as in the decade of *Weltpolitik*, did the Kaiser finally achieve the goal of his heart's desire; a compromise, be it further noted, wherein colonial policy was attuned to the pressing exigencies of Germany's European orientation instead of, as formerly, a reckless and blustering disregard of international relations. On the eve of the Great War, then, the Bagdad Railway, that symbol of Germany's imperialistic ambition in the Near East with all that it implied of political and economic control, had reached Adana in Cilicia marking one-half of the giant stretch from Konia to Basra; westward, therefrom, lines were under construction to the Taurus Mountains, eventually to pass through the great gates to meet the tracks already laid to Burgulu; while eastward, the line was being constructed

343

through the Amanus Mountains where the costly tunnels had already been begun; a steel bridge had been thrown across the Euphrates, and the sections east of Aleppo had been completed almost to Ras-el-Ain in northern Mesopotamia. Besides this, the branch line to Alexandretta had been completed and opened to traffic, and rails had been laid north from Bagdad to Sadijeh on the Tigris. But more significant even than this great material advance, the Bagdad Railway controversy with the other nations had been all but solved in 1914, and Germany's sphere of influence in Mesopotamia well-nigh satisfactorily adjusted to the balance of power.

### The Anglo-German Rapprochement over the Portuguese Colonies

The Anglo-German Treaty drafted in 1913, dividing the Portuguese-African colonies into spheres of influence, supplies the third and final illustration of the subordination of Germany's colonial policy to international relations, which this chapter has endeavored to prove. And the story of its negotiations not only adds the last witness to the changed attitude of the Foreign Office from the days of *Weltpolitik,* but also affords an insight into the intensified desire for colonial expansion in Africa, openly expressed by public opinion and secretly supported by the government.

Since the disappointment of German hopes in Africa in 1911, the sentiment for their realization had been growing ever stronger, and had crystallized into the dream of *Mittel-Afrika-Deutsch* which gripped popular imagination almost as strongly as *"Unser Bagdad,"* inflamed as it was by the Kaiser's failure to grasp the opportunities for its fulfillment so lavishly offered by the Agadir crisis. "A later time will recognize that the Franco-German agreement of Novem-

344

ber 4, 1911, has been one of the most important crises in German colonial policy. Until then the policy had no special goal but Kiderlen-Wächter recognized the African situation and strove for a German Middle Africa. . . . He has therefore given to our African policy a great new purpose,"[101] wrote Emil Zimmermann in 1913, expressing the almost universal demand for an African colonial empire which the popular uproar in 1911 had done so much to stimulate. Consequently the government in its negotiations was obliged to restrain a blatant public sentiment, if it was not to jeopardize Germany's relations to the other Powers; a task which its own secret ambitions in Africa rendered extremely difficult.

That the German government had for some long time cherished secret plans for the extension and consolidation of its possessions in Central Africa is only too evident, although those schemes did not become part and parcel of the Moroccan policy until after 1911. Indeed, the self-imposed restraint which the Foreign Office under the Kaiser's guidance practiced in regard to Morocco, served to make it seek compensation in Central Africa. Long dissatisfied with the Anglo-Portuguese Treaty of 1898, it was always impatient to revise it and, in 1909, von Bülow definitely considered an agreement over the Portuguese colonies in Africa as forming part of his *rapprochement* with England.[102] In fact, how seriously the German official mind considered the matter is illustrated by Foreign Secretary Schön's request to Dernburg, the colonial secretary, to prepare the material for "negotiations with England over the colonial question." Dernburg, however, in his reply, advised against broaching the matter at that time as he considered the political situation not sufficiently favorable and, as we have seen in the case of the Bagdad Railway, these efforts resulted in nothing.[103] They were not even included in the final draft of the tentative proposals for an Anglo-German understanding, for fear that they might meet with England's opposition and prejudice her desire for a political alliance; a significant omission which affords another example of the subordination of colonial policy to foreign policy.

In view of the secret and thwarted desires of the German Foreign Office, it was but natural that new agreements in Africa should be mentioned in the conversations between Wolff-Metternich and Sir Edward Grey, relative to the Anglo-German *rapprochement,* after the Agadir crisis had cleared the air; and that they should proceed to specific definition during the Haldane mission to Berlin. Beth-mann-Hollweg's concrete proposals at that time indicate the extent of the German plan. For they designated for Germany all of Angola, Zanizbar, Pemba, Great Britain's support of the purchase of part of the Belgian Congo, and even the Penguin and Seal Islands; England to receive the Portuguese island of Timor and the control of the Bagdad-Basra stretch of the Bagdad Railway.[104] And, as we have seen, so anxious was Haldane to bargain with Germany for the reduction of her navy, that he stated that England had no objection to her obtaining from Portugal the larger part of Angola, the cession of Zanzibar and Pemba and possibly also a share of the Belgian Congo.[105]

But, as in the case of the proposed compromise on the Bagdad Railway which was part and parcel of the general colonial settlement, these negotiations failed mainly because of the obstacles imposed by the German naval supplementary law and by the hostility of the British colonial secretary. So great, however, was the desire of both Germany and England to effect some *rapprochement,* that discussions were continued even in spite of the interruption occasioned by the Balkan wars. With the death of Marschall, in August, 1912, von Kühlmann, secretary to the legation in London, bent every effort to bring the matter to a conclusion, in which he was ably seconded by Lichnowsky, the new ambassador, when he assumed control. "Thanks to the accommodating spirit of the British government," wrote Lichnowsky, "I succeeded in making the treaty accord with our wishes. The whole of Angola up to the 20° latitude was assigned to us so that our territory now stretched up to the Congo State. South, we also acquired valuable islands, San Thomé and Principe north of the Equator and in the French sphere. We also obtained the northern part of Mozambique, Likungo forming the boundary." [106] Thus the frontier of Angola was modified in favor of Germany, and that of Mozambique in favor of England, and the conditions for occupying the territory were altered in Germany's favor. Also, the treaty was rendered much more realizable than the treaty of 1898. [107] Whereas the latter had been based solely upon Portugal's application for loans, the present arrangement provided for occupation irrespective of Portugal's financial condition, for Article viii read:

> If in any part of the provinces of Mozambique or Angola the lives or property of British or German subjects, or the vital interests of the adjoining British or German dominions . . ., are endangered by local disturbances . . ., and the Portuguese government is not in a position to afford the necessary protection . . ., the British and German governments, after consulting together . . . shall determine the nature, duration and scope of such measures as it may be deemed necessary to take for the protection of the interests endangered.

What was more, Great Britain indirectly nullified her defensive treaty with Portugal, renewed in 1899, and promised implicitly if not explicitly in a supplementary treaty not to come to the aid of Portugal, if through financial or other mismanagement in her colonies the other Powers were obliged to interfere. It was also decided to oppose jointly any interference from a third Power, "whether this interference took the form of a loan to Portugal in return for a mortgage on the revenue of these provinces," or through the indirect acquisition of part of these territories, or by some other means. The treaty also declared that as soon as one part of the two great colonies came into possession of England or Germany, the other party would have the right of occupying the share of the territory earmarked for it.[108] "Lord Grey showed the greatest consideration for he wished to divert German development from the North Sea and Western Europe to the ocean and to Africa," concluded Lichnowsky; a consideration which had already found practical expression in the negotiations to include German capital in financing the extension of the Benguelan Railway through Belgian and Portuguese territory.[109]

On the other hand, Germany's corresponding accommodation to England in not demanding all that her colonial enthusiasts desired may be seen, first, in Kiderlen's remark that, "Marschall seems so willing to give in so much to the English that it is questionable whether the wishes of the colonial office can be met"; [110] and, later, in von Jagow's openly expressed displeasure over what he termed Lichnowsky's "too great complaisance towards the English." [111] The conflict of colonial ambition and diplomatic caution which shook the councils of the German Foreign Office stands forth only too clearly revealed in the entire negotiations. And the final triumph of the latter is further confirmed by Germany's refusal of England's secret offer to include the Belgian Congo, due to her fear of injuring Belgium's susceptibilities.

The treaty was initialed October 20, 1913, but its publication, demanded by Sir Edward Grey along with the former treaties of 1898 and 1899, was prevented by Germany. The government wished to avoid exciting again that Pan-German clamor which had already almost precipitated a war in 1911, and would very likely have arisen once more in protest against the moderation of the terms of this settlement. For German public opinion would, it was feared, interpret this moderation to negative those larger partitions making for a *Mittel-Afrika,* which by this time it had come to consider as the goal of the negotiations. "We intend to publish," wrote von Jagow, "but only at a suitable moment when the danger of hostile criticism shall be less acute and, if possible, with the simultaneous announcement of the Bagdad treaty now near completion. Our hesitation is due to the wish not to stir up fresh trouble. We also have to consider Germany's efforts to acquire economic interests in the Portuguese colonies which would have been difficult had the agreement been announced."[112] Remembering the perfect hornets' nest which the government had brought down about its ears in 1911, this explanation seems extremely plausible, although Lichnowsky bitterly ascribes the refusal to publish the treaty to jealousy of himself and his success in official circles in Berlin.

The delayed publication involved difficulties, however, and Harcourt, the British colonial secretary, pressed for a settlement in the spring of 1914. German sanction to publish was finally obtained by July, 1914, largely through the efforts of Colonial Secretary Solf, on condition that the publication did not take place until the autumn, when the outbreak of the Great War made it too late for any effect.

Just as the Bagdad agreement had divided the Near East into colonial spheres of influence, so had the treaty over the Portuguese colonies commenced to do the same in Africa.

For, although it added another foundation stone to that great structure, begun in 1911, of a Middle African colonial empire, it held in leash by its moderation that German colonial enthusiasm which brooked no spheres of influence, no compromise with rivals, but demanded outright annexation even at the point of the bayonet. These two settlements, indeed, completed on the very eve of the Great War, formed a colonial *Entente* which had been the object of the German government for several years to achieve. As the imperial chancellor stated on December 9, 1913, in summing up Germany's foreign policy to the *Reichstag*: "We have approached a solution of the Bagdad problem with England. . . . In pursuance of our *main idea* of bringing the relations of these two countries permanently back into those quiet paths which for a time they have threatened to leave, we have opened negotiations with the British government with a view to preventing the *possible appearance of economic and colonial antagonism in Africa.*" [113] Is this not an echo of Bismarck's slogan, "Safety first"? But be it noted that it was not the influence of the ripe wisdom of the Great Chancellor that made Germany's colonial policy veer around again to a position of subordination to foreign relations, but rather the threatening menace of the *Triple Entente* which had cast the "fear of God" in the shape of "encirclement" into the soul of the Kaiser and his ministers, and had converted them from their reckless pursuit of *Weltpolitik*.

## NOTES

[1] von Bülow, B., *Imperial Germany* (New York, 1914), pp. 51-52.

Beer, G. L., *African Questions at Peace Congress* (New York, 1923), p. 51, quoting Bülow.

[2] Sontag, R., "German Foreign Policy," in *American Historical Review*, vol. xxxiii, No. 2 (Jan., 1928), pp. 278-79.

See also, Dennis, A. L. P., *Adventures in American Diplomacy*, ch. xix.

[3] Kampffmeyer, G., "Die Grundlagen der Marokkofrage" in *Zeitschrift für Politik*, 1915, pp. 340ff.

See also Morel, E. D., *Ten Years of Secret Diplomacy* (London, 1915).

[4] Eckardstein, Baron, *op. cit.*, vol. iii, p. 91ff.

Kiderlen-Wächter refers to this in his speech explaining his Moroccan policy in the *Reichstag*, November 11, 1911. See *Geschichtskalender*, 1911, p. 608.

[5] *Die Grosse Politik*, vol. xvii, nos. 5152, 5153, 5159, 5162.

[6] *Ibid.*, vol. xvii, no. 5184. The German government decided to wait and "let things develop."

[7] Eckardstein, *op. cit.*, vol. i, p. 89.

[8] *Ibid.*,

Lichnowsky, Prince, *My Mission to London* (English Trans., New York, 1918), 1912-1914.

[9] *Die Grosse Politik*, vol. xx, pp. 223-224, 228.

[10] *Ibid*, vol. xvii, pp. 363-364.

[11] *Cambridge History British Foreign Policy* (Cambridge, 1922), p. 338.

[12] Eckardstein, *op. cit.*, vol. iii, p. 88.

[13] Wertheimer, *op. cit.*, pp. 170-171.

The Pan-Germans presented a *Denkschrift* to the government on the subject. *Alldeutsche Blätter*, no. 10, April 4, 1904.

[14] Friedjung, *op. cit.*, vol. i, p. 40.

[15] Gooch, G. P., *History Modern Europe* (New York, 1922), p. 350.

[16] *Norddeutsche Allgemeine Zeitung*, April 12, 13, 14, 1904.

[17] Balfour expressly controverted the idea that the treaty was incompatible with the Anglo-German agreement, but his assertion was inconsistent with its secret clauses.

[18] See his Bremen speech, March 23, 1905.

Also, on his way to Tangier, the Kaiser telegraphed that it was very doubtful whether he would land, in any case, he could only be traveling as a private tourist and begged to decline any official reception. But von Bülow replied that it was too late since the official announcement of his visit had already been made. *Die Grosse Politik*, vol. xx, pp. 262, 263, 264.

[19] In the very roadstead of Tangier, with a heavy sea running, the Kaiser hesitated about landing until von Kühlmann came on board with dispatches from Berlin. *Die Grosse Politik*, vol. xx, pp. 272-278.

Secretary von Schön's description of the landing, vol. xx, no. 6589.

[20] *The Kaiser's Memoirs*, *op. cit.*, ch. iv.

[21] *Die Grosse Politik*, vol. xx, nos. 6558ff. See also, Dennis, *op. cit.*, ch. xix.

[22] *Verhandlungen des deutschen Reichstages*, March 29, 1905, p. 5709.

[23] *Die Grosse Politik*, vol. xx, pp. 330, 334.

[24] *Ibid.*, vol. xx, pp. 304-305.

[25] *Ibid.*, vol. xx, pp. 353, 360.

[26] *Ibid.*, vol. xxiv, no. 8282, note, p. 21.

[27] *Ibid.*, vol. xx, pp. 362, 416, 425.

[28] *Ibid.*, vol. xx, pp. 593, 596.

[29] *Verhandlungen des deutschen Reichstages,* March 29, 1905, p. 5697.

[30] Friedjung, *op. cit.,* vol. ii, p. 63.

Valentin, V., *Deutschlands Aussenpolitik* (Berlin, 1921), p. 57.

This idea was distinctly confirmed by the prominent National Liberal, Basserman, in the *Reichstag* during the general discussion over the whole Moroccan policy on November 11, 1911, when he said: "Our policy in Morocco was directed by our Near Eastern policy," p. 7790.

[31] Sontag, *op. cit.,* p. 280 and *notes.*

[32] *Die Grosse Politik,* vol. xx, pp. 22-24.

[33] *Ibid.,* vol. xx, p. 26.

[34] *Ibid.,* vol. xx, pp. 27-30.

[35] See Haller, J., *Die Aera Bülows* (Stuttgart, 1922).

He states that the Kaiser was determined to make use of the opportunity afforded by Russia's entrance into the Japanese War to construct a Continental League of Russia, France, Germany, and Austria against the sea power of England and the economic rivalry of the United States.

This same idea in its relation to the Moroccan question was confirmed by the chancellor, Bethmann-Hollweg, in his explanation of the government's course in the Agadir crisis on November 11, 1911, in the *Reichstag,* when he said: "For a decade, the Moroccan policy has been so directed as to avoid placing Germany in a weak position on the Continent," p. 7709.

[36] Sontag, *op. cit.,* pp. 291, 292.

[37] *Die Grosse Politik,* vol. xxi, no. 7291.

[38] *Die Grosse Politik,* vol. xxi, no. 7300.

[39] *Ibid.,* vol. xxi, no. 7332.

[40] *Ibid.,* vol. xxi, nos. 7257, 7258.

[41] And how careful he was at the same time to subordinate colonial acquisitions to the international situation may be seen from the fact that he issued instructions, shortly after his visit to Windsor in the autumn of 1907, to "handle the Moroccan question in such a way as to prevent the English from receiving the impression that we are again trying to deal cavalierly with France, counting on our improved relations with Great Britain." Brandenburg, *op. cit.,* p. 338.

[42] *Die Grosse Politik,* vol. xxi, no. 7259.

[43] *Ibid.,* vol. xxiv, no. 8327.

[44] In this, the Kaiser was supported by his Foreign Secretary, Schön: "We were obliged to adhere to a policy of smoothing things over with France, particularly in view of the tension caused by the Bosnian crisis. At a time when all our diplomatic skill was needed in the East, it seemed very necessary that we should not be hampered with difficulties in the West." *Memoirs,* p. 93.

[45] *Die Grosse Politik,* vol. xxiv, no. 8457 and *note.*

[46] Quoted by Schultess, *Geschichtskalender,* 1909, p. 114ff.

[47] *Ibid.,* 1909, p. 57.

[48] *Die Grosse Politik,* vol. xxiv, no. 9388.

[49] Friedjung, *op. cit.,* vol. iii, p. 26.

See also, *Die Grosse Politik,* vol. xxix, no. 10702.

# EXPANSION AND THE BALANCE OF POWER

Letter of Kiderlen to Jenisch.
Jäckh, E., *Kiderlen-Wächter, der Staatsmann und Mensch* (Berlin, Leipzig, 1924), 2 vols., vol. i, chs. 11, 12.

[50] *The Kaiser's Memoirs, op. cit.,* p. 145ff.

[51] *Die Grosse Politik,* vol. xxix, nos. 10548, 10538. "We could not accomplish anything with ships, I ask you therefore to oppose it."

[52] *Ibid.,* vol. xxix, nos. 10600, 10613.

[53] *Ibid.,* vol. xxix, no. 10576. At first, German government proposed to exchange Upper Kamerun and whole of Togo in return for French Congo from Sangha to the sea.

[54] *Ibid.,* vol. xxix, no. 10608.

[55] *Ibid.,* vol. xxix, nos. 10678, 10722, 10628.

[55a] Buell, *op. cit.,* vol. ii, p. 246 and *note.*

This arrangement which complicated the decision of 1911 was the result of constant quarrels between German and French economic interests which had been in process for many years. German traders had crossed the boundaries and had poached upon the concessions of the French companies in operation there. In the case of the N'Goko Sangha Company litigation had ensued. This unsatisfactory economic situation on these boundaries helps to account for the bitter attack upon German expansion in Africa by part of the French press on the eve of the Great War, and also for France's eagerness to recover this territory in the settlement. See *supra.,* ch. xii, pp. 362, 390.

[56] *Ibid.,* no. 10771, for treaty text.

Confirming the government's position was the *Denkschrift,* published by the colonial office, Nov. 8, 1911, which stated: "The whole sense of the treaty lies in the fact that it begins a new era of understanding and of cooperation with France." *Geschichtskalender,* 1911, p. 190.

For estimation of territory gained, see Ritter, K., *Neu-Kamerun, Veröffentlichungen des Reichskolonialamts,* no. 4, 1912, Berlin, pt. iv.

[57] *Die Deutsche Kolonialzeitung,* 1907, pp. 258, 381; 1911, p. 39.

[58] *Denkschrift und Aktenstücke über deutsche Bergswerkinteressen in Marokko, Anlagen des deutschen Reichstages,* vol. 272, Nr. 189 Jan. 1910.

[59] Schön, *Memoirs,* pp. 115-118.

[60] Wertheimer, *op. cit.,* pp. 156ff., *and* 171ff.

[61] *Die Kolonialzeitung,* 1911, pp. 488, 491, 519, 667, 715, 747, 782.

[62] *Ibid.,* p. 619.

[63] *Westfälische Zeitung,* July 10, 1911.

[64] *Evangelische Kirchenzeiten,* April 26, 1911.

[65] *Die Post,* August 4, 1911.

*Leipsiger Neueste Nachrichten,* November 4, 1911.

*Die Kölnische Zeitung, Vorwaerts, Berliner Tageblatt, Vossische Zeitung, Tägliche Rundschau.*

*Zeitschrift für Kolonialpolitik,* 1912, p. 180.

"The sleeping-sickness in the new Kamerun territory has already attacked the gentlemen of the Wilhelmstrasse."

[66] *Die Verhandlungen des deutschen Reichstages,* November 9, 1911, p. 7716.

[67] Rohrbach, P., *Die Bagdadbahn* (Berlin, 1903). For a thorough discussion of German opinion at this time, see Earle, *op. cit.*, p. 123ff.

[68] Lichnowsky, Prince, *Disclosures from Germany* (Am. Assoc. Internat. Conciliation, N. Y., 1918), pp. 37-41, 127.

[69] *Verhandlungen des deutschen Reichstages*, 1911, vol. 266, p. 59840.

[70] Earle, *op. cit.*, p. 142.

[71] von Siebert, B., and Schreiner, *Entente Diplomacy and the World*, 1909-1914 (N. Y., 1922), p. 514ff.

[72] Helfferich, K., "Die Deutsche Türkenpolitik" in *Im Neuen Deutschland*, 1921, Heft 11, p. 19.

[73] *Cambridge History British Foreign Policy*, p. 386.
Schön, *Memoirs*, pp. 62-63.
Haldane, *Before the War*, p. 48.

[74] Helfferich, *op. cit.*, p. 20.

[75] Muhlmann, C., "Die deutschen Bahnunternehmungen in der Asiatiische Turkei" in *Weltwirtschaftliches Archiv*, 1926, vol. 24, p. 365ff.

[76] Siebert, *op. cit.*, p. 177. *British Documents on Origin of Great War, 1898-1914*, Gooch and Temperley, editors (London, 1928), vol. v, p. 235.

[77] *Die Grosse Politik*, vol. xxii, no. 7373.

[78] *Ibid.*, vol. xxv, no. 8688. The same opinion was expressed by Schön, "Our commercial activity both in Asiatic and European Turkey with its rich prospects necessitates our adopting the attitude of a Friend and Protector." *Memoirs*, p. 95.

[79] *Ibid.*, vol. xxvi, no. 8939.

[80] *Ibid.*, vol. xxvi, nos. 8979, 8990.

[81] *Ibid.*, vol. xxvi, no. 9150.

[82] *Ibid.*, vol. xxvi, nos. 8984, 9155.

[83] *Ibid.*, vol. xxvi, nos. 8939, 8992, and Kaiser's comments thereon.

[84] See *supra.*, ch. xi, p. 320ff.

[85] Helfferich, *op. cit.*

[86] Friedjung, *op. cit.*, vol. ii, p. 391.

[87] For agreement in full, see Earle, *op. cit.*, p. 239ff.

[88] Huldermann, B., *Albert Ballin* (English Trans., London, 1922), p. 204.

[89] *Die Grosse Politik*, vol. xxvii, no. 9961 and vol. xxviii, nos. 10302, 10303.

[90] Siebert, *op. cit.*, ch. iii, 504.

[91] Huldermann, *op. cit.*, p. 80.

[92] Brandenburg, *op. cit.*, p. 369. See also, Earle, *op. cit.*, pp. 228-229.

[93] *Die Grosse Politik*, vol. xxxi, nos. 11338, 11339.

[94] Brandenburg, *op. cit.*, p. 400.

[95] Montgelas, M., *The Case for the Central Powers* (English Trans., London, 1925), pp. 49-50.

[96] Gooch, *op. cit.*, p. 492.

[97] *Die Grosse Politik*, vol. xxxi, nos. 11360, 11361, 11362.

[98] *Die Grosse Politik*, vol. xxxvii, no. 14763, Text of Treaty.
For significance, see also, Earle, E. M., "The Secret Anglo-German Convention," in *Political Science Quarterly*, 1923, vol. xxxviii, p. 25.

[99] Earle, E. M., *Turkey, The Great Powers, etc., op. cit.*, p. 258ff.

# EXPANSION AND THE BALANCE OF POWER

[100] *Ibid.*, 244ff.

[101] Zimmermann, E., "Kiderlen-Wächter und die Deutsche Kolonial-politik," in *Der Tag*, Berlin, Jan. 4, 1913.

[102] *Die Grosse Politik*, vol. xxxl, nos. 11360, 11362.

[103] Lichnowsky, *My Mission in London* (English Trans., New York, 1918), p. 477.

[104] For discussions over the Treaty, *Die Grosse Politik*, vol. xxxvii, nos. 14656, 14662, 14664, 14671, 14673, 14676.

[105] *Ibid.*, vol. xxxvii, no. 14650.

[106] *Ibid.*, vol. xxxvii, nos. 14708, 14711, 14714.

[107] Lichnowsky, Prince, *Heading for the Abyss* (New York, 1928), pp. 270 *et seq.*

[108] *Ibid.*, p. 285 *et seq. Text of Treaty.*

[109] Buell, *op. cit.*, vol. ii, p. 473. Germany already had sent a Commission there. Lichnowsky, *op. cit.*, p. 296.

[110] *Die Grosse Politik*, vol. xxxvii, no. 14650.

[111] *Ibid.*, vol. xxxvii, nos. 14695, 14696.

[112] *Cambridge History British Foreign Policy*, p. 477.
The fact that England wished to publish with the treaty the former treaties of 1898 with Germany and of 1899 with Portugal, in order to reassure that country, increased the German objection to publication. For it was feared that the effect of these former treaties would be to arouse public opinion as they would be interpreted as nullifying the present treaty.
Lichnowsky, *Heading for the Abyss.* Correspondence of Lichnowsky and the German Foreign Office, p. 270ff.

[113] *Geschichtskalender*, 1913, p. 336. Italics mine.

# CHAPTER XII

## THE WAR IN THE COLONIES AND THE COLONIES
IN THE WAR

THE years 1914-1919 constitute the last act in the drama of Germany's colonial history. Before the close of 1915, the Allies had occupied most of her oversea territory by right of might, and the Treaty of Versailles completed her dispossession with the justification that "to the victors belong the spoils." The net loss amounted to some 1,027,000 square miles of territory, 14,000,000 population and 505,-000,000 M. invested capital.

But these figures represent only the superficial, material aspect. To appreciate the real significance of the destruction of Germany's colonial empire both to the nation itself and to her future world-relationships, we must measure the strength of the colonial sentiment on the eve of the war, the scope of her colonial aims and the character of the official and popular reaction to the colonial clauses of the Peace Settlement.

### Colonial Opinion on Eve of War

The last we heard of public opinion in Germany regarding expansion was the noisy clamor aroused by the Agadir crisis of 1911, the echoes of which had by no means died down by 1914. On the contrary, the stimulus imparted by the Moroccan affair to popular colonial sentiment had crystallized into two distinct plans to which the Great War was to give the finishing touches; namely, the *Mittel-Europa* scheme and the *Mittel-Afrika* project.

The new *Reichstag,* elected in 1912, favored even more than the *Reichstag* of 1907 the development and acquisition of colonies.[1] The debates during the years 1912, 1913, and 1914 over the colonial budget reflected the greatest enthusiasm of all parties with the exception of the Social Democrats. Irrespective of the latter, there was hardly a party which did not vote solidly for the budget. And to mere enthusiasm was added the expression of interest and of responsibility for the economic and cultural cultivation of the oversea territories. Members of the Catholic Center[2] were especially vociferous in this regard and again joined their old allies, the Social Democrats, in a sharp and ringing criticism of certain aspects of native rule. The Socialist party, however, was the only one to raise its voice in direct opposition to the colonial policy. In April, 1912, Herr Henke delivered a diatribe against "capitalistic imperialism" in the *Reichstag,* laying upon its head all the late difficulties with England, and demonstrating from his point of view what a great disappointment it had been economically.[3] In 1913 he returned to the attack, seconded by other party members, and in 1914 the Socialists generally seized the opportunity for a thorough indictment of the native policy in the discussion aroused by the Doualan land question.[4]

In spite of their continued opposition in the *Reichstag,* there were several signs in the Socialist party of a changing viewpoint regarding colonial expansion. Even concerning the criticism leveled at the administration in May, 1912, the *Frankfurter Zeitung*[5] remarked: "The opposition of the Socialists is not any too strong. Their criticism is much less sharp than formerly." The well-known Social Democrat, Dr. Quessell, published an article in the *Soziallische*

*Monatshefte* in 1912 in support of a vigorous expansion policy which, he asserted, was "absolutely necessary for our industry"; while Hildebrandt, another Revisionist, declared that, although the Socialists had always opposed colonization, they must now change their attitude, cooperate with the government, and work for the uplift of the native peoples.[6] Even Noske spoke of "the resignation" of the Socialists and of the fact that they were shifting their position. "The Social Democrats are the enemies of a brutal, capitalistic, and exploitative colonial policy, but in favor of a humane, proletarian one."[7]

On the other hand, it must be acknowledged that these were as voices crying in the wilderness of Socialist opposition, for the party as a whole was violently antagonistic. It expelled Hildebrandt for his sentiments and the *Hamburger Echo* announced: "It is falsely reported by the liberal press that the Social Democrats have changed their opinion in regard to colonial expansion and even that they are about to send some of their members out to study the colonies. This is an error. . . . The party declined the invitation of the steamship companies to transport the expedition! Their position in regard to colonization is their old one."[8]

But if the Social Democrats remained for the most part opposed, the Progressives were heartily in favor of expansion. They had abandoned their combative tactics, it will be recalled, in 1907, and since then had contributed their positive support. "There is nothing contrary to liberalism in colonialism," stated Waldstein, speaking for his party in 1912, "if it is carried on as a cultural affair. It is for that reason that we support it, to exert our influence for good upon it instead of assuming a purely negative attitude."[9]

Besides the impetus lent by such a solid party support to the colonial movement must be mentioned the accession of Dr. Solf to the colonial secrtaryship in 1912. Herr von Lindequist, who resigned on account of his disapproval of the Moroccan treaty with France in 1911, had only been in office a year and a half and had not had sufficient time to impress his personality upon the colonial policy. While he was an intelligent and efficient official, and had served well as governor of South West Africa, he was no statesman, no politician. His secretaryship had been merely an episode between that of Dr. Dernburg and of his successor, Dr. Solf. For the most part he had guarded well the heritage of Dr. Dernburg but had added little to it; although he had succeeded in overcoming some of the misunderstanding created by his predecessor between the colonial office and the planters,[10] and had improved the central administration by the creation of the Economic Council.

Dr. Solf, on the other hand, proved during his longer term of office, a positive stimulant to the entire colonial movement. Long associated with the oversea administration, he had been governor of Samoa since 1900, was well versed in the problems affecting both natives and white settlers, and at the same time possessed a statesmanlike grasp of Germany's colonial policy in its relations to other countries. Very active in the prosecution of the economic and cultural development of the colonies and largely instrumental in consummating the agreements with England in regard to Africa and Mesopotamia, he brought to the colonial office a quality of leadership which inspired national confidence and respect, best reflected perhaps in the strength and influence of the Colonial Society on the eve of the Great War. At that time it numbered more than 43,000 members, counted 435 sections in Germany, 24 abroad, and had expanded its activities to include virtually every phase of colonization from promoting the study of African dialects to preparing young women to become efficient wives of planters and settlers.[11]

## Position of the Government

With this all but universal enthusiasm for the prosecution of a vigorous colonial policy, the German government was heartily in sympathy, as we have observed in a former chapter. To recapitulate here, suffice it to say that the Foreign Office, in 1914, was doing all in its power to advance German expansion in the Near East and in Africa, and at the same time curbing both its own and the nation's ambitions in the interests of the country's international relationships, especially with Great Britain.

Consequently we find the foreign secretary, von Jagow, sounding the French ambassador in Berlin about the Belgian Congo and remarking: "With all respect to the rights of foreign nations, it must be said that Germany has not all the colonies it must have. . . . We are not an institute for lengthening the life of dying states. Those half-states which owe their existence only to the aid of foreign weapons, money or knowledge are hopelessly at the mercy of modern states. Only the Great Powers have the strength and resources needed for colonization; smaller competitors must disappear or gravitate into the orbits of the great."[12] Also, Lichnowsky tells us in his *Memorandum:* "I intended to carve the way later for further negotiations regarding other questions—for example, East Asiatic problems—when what in my opinion the most important problem, the Bagdad Railway, should be settled and an atmosphere of more confidence created."[13]

But it is very clear that whatever colonial plans the government had on foot they were to be executed only in conjunction and in compromise with England; that, in other words, the principle of "safety first" was assuredly to be the watch-word. Perhaps the anonymous brochure, which appeared in the London German embassy May, 1913, attributed by some to Under-Secretary von Kühlmann, who was so active in negotiating the Anglo-German treaty over the Portuguese colonies, may be cited as expressing the dominant opinion in the German Foreign Office. It was entitled *Deutsche Weltpolitik und Kein Krieg,*[14] *German World Power and No War,* and proposed that England should support German ambitions in Central Africa in return for German concessions in Mesopotamia; and that British and German colonial expansion should go "hand in hand."

Of course this moderation in colonial policy endorsed by the leaders of the German Foreign Office did not meet with the approval of the Pan-Germans and other over-enthusiastic colonialists, who preferred to plunge the Fatherland into war for the sake of annexation and scorned any compromise with England.[15] On the other hand the idea of "more land in Africa through diplomacy" met with the favor of such men as Rohrbach, Siebert, Singleman, and the great body of the Colonial Society.[16]

### The Foreign Press Reflects the Strength of the German Colonial Movement

Were any further proof required of the strength of the colonial movement in Germany on the eve of the Great War, the foreign press would supply it. Because of the recent agreements over African territory and the Bagdad Railway, the British press reflecting the attitude of the government was for the most part friendly to Germany's ambitions, but exhibited nevertheless a keen awareness of them. "It is very significant that lately two leading British colonialists

[John Harris and Sir Harry Johnston] have expressed their opinion that Germany's wish to extend her colonial possessions in Africa should be realized and their opinion seems to have found acceptance generally in British public sentiment," wrote the *Usambaru Post* [17] early in 1913; while the *United Empire* frankly stated: "Germany dreams of a Central Africa. That would mean a conflict of interests."[18]

## The French Press

The greatest fear and animosity, on the other hand, was exhibited by the French press especially in regard to Germany's designs in Africa. The *Dépèche Coloniale* attacked the whole system of German expansion so violently and with such animus that it called forth replies from Rohrbach and the *Kolonialzeitung;* [19] the *Annales Coloniales* went so far as to warn Belgium against the German menace in Africa, stating that: "It goes without saying that the Germans have their eyes on the Belgian share of Lake Tanganyika"; [20] and other papers worked themselves into a frenzy with articles entitled: *"L'Appetit allemande," "Le partage de l'Afrique et les ambitions allemands, "La penetration allemande dans l'Afrique centrale"*; and uttered again and again the warning: "We cannot watch with too much attention the manifestations of colonial ambition in Germany." [21]

It is indeed most significant to observe the contrast between the British and the French press in regard to Germany's colonial ambitions during the years immediately prior to 1914. But, although they differ in the attitude with which they regard her colonial plans, they are alike in confirming the existence of a deep and strong colonial movement in both government and nation. With this thought in mind, let us turn to the outbreak of the Great War and its extension into the German colonies.

## The Allies Carry the War into the Colonies

According to the Congo or Berlin Act signed by Great Britain, France, Germany, and Belgium in Berlin in 1885, those territories in the Congo basin, "its embouchures and circumjacent regions were declared in case of war to be placed 'under the rule of neutrality,' and considered as belonging to a non-belligerent state, the belligerents thenceforth abstaining from extending hostilities to the territories thus neutralized, and from using them as a base for warlike operations." [22]

Consistent with this agreement, the Belgian government on August 8, 1914, expressed its desire to the French government to neutralize the Congo basin, to which the French agreed on August 9, and stated that they had asked the Spanish ambassador to so inform Germany. On August 16, however, the Belgian ambassador in Paris reported that the French government had announced that no reply had come from the Spanish ambassador, because that government did not know the desire of England in the matter. Also, the French government expressed the opinion that, in view of existing circumstances, Germany must be met wherever she could be, and that France ought to utilize the opportunity to regain that part of the Congo which she had been obliged to relinquish in 1911. On August 17, also, the Belgian ambassador in London reported that the British government had declared that it could not accept the Belgian proposition, even if it was convinced of its political and strategic value, since German East African troops had already taken the offensive against British Central Africa, and that British troops had already seized the harbor of Dar-es-Salaam. As a matter of fact the British had laid siege to Dar-es-Salaam on August 8 and had attacked the south west boundary of East

Africa on August 13, while German troops had made their first advance (on Taveta) on August 15, 1914.

Because Germany had everything to lose in a colonial war, since her enemy, Great Britain, was in control of the seas and could cut off her oversea possessions from all communication and help from the mother country, she turned as a last resort to the United States, August 23, 1914, to persuade the other Powers to observe the neutrality of the Congo basin according to the Congo Act, a neutrality which would have included one-third of Kamerun and all of German East Africa. The United States replied, on October 7, that Germany herself had made this impossible since German troops had taken the initiative in hostilities against French and Belgian territory in West Africa. Germany, on the other hand, declared that the French had attacked the Germans at Bonga and Singa on August 6, before those border towns knew of a war and that the Belgians had seized a German official engaged upon a peaceful mission to the Belgian Congo on August 6.[23]

## The Campaign in Togoland

The German contention that it was the Allies who carried the war into the colonies against their strenuous endeavors to enforce the neutralization of the Congo basin, secured by the Congo Act, seems to be borne out by the accounts of the campaigns taken from English sources. In Togoland, for example, the acting governor, Major von Döring, proposed on August 5 that the colony remain neutral. Geographically it formed only a small island surrounded by Allied territory: the British Gold Coast colony to the west; French Dahomey and upper Senegal to the north and east; while her thirty-two miles of seacoast were at the mercy of the British fleet. It could be and was invaded at all points from all sides:

French colonial troops entered on August 6 and the British troops approached Lome, the capital, from the west. The German force, consisting of some 200 Europeans assisted by a small group of native *Askari* police, armed with rifles used in the Franco-Prussian War displayed, according to the English, a singular reluctance to offer any resistance. They did hold for a time the wireless station at Kamina, but the French and British cooperated against them. The whole campaign was rounded off within three weeks and the colony surrendered to the British and French on August 26. The rapid conquest gave great prestige to the Allies on the west coast where they could now turn their attention to Kamerun.[24]

## Kamerun

Like Togoland, Kamerun's immediate neighbors were all enemies with one exception, Muni, Spanish Guinea, which formed a neutral *enclave,* capable of being used as a supply base, together with the island of Fernando Po, until the naval power of the Allies made itself felt. The fact that the Germans were fighting not only for their original colony but in addition for those 107,000 square miles of French Congo gained in 1912, which increased Kamerun to an area of 306,000 square miles, one-third larger than the Fatherland, and which formed a considerable portion of the *Mittel-Afrika* dream, incited them to a stubborn resistance. The attack began with the Allied invasion of August 25, 1914, and a German force of 3,500 consisting of 1,800 Europeans and 7,000 natives defended the colony against 19,000 British, French, and Belgians for eighteen months. The unhealthy climate, the rough, large country, and their possession of the rivers and railways assisted the Germans who were, however, finally overpowered by numbers, a vulnerable frontier and sea power, and surrendered January 1, 1915. German West Africa was henceforth jointly occupied by British and French throughout the remainder of the war.[25]

## Campaign in South West Africa

With the subjugation of German South West Africa, more difficulty was encountered by the Allied cause, as it was first necessary to suppress a revolt in the Union of South Africa, claimed at the time to have been instigated by the Germans. Colonel Moritz, a Boer commander, sympathized with the Germans and discontent was rife throughout the colony. The rebellion was subdued by the beginning of 1915, however, and the attack against South West Africa, begun in September, 1914, by General Botha, was resumed. Both the climate and the physical conditions of the country made the campaign extremely difficult, and the Germans opposed a strong defense with a force of about 1,603 Europeans and 5,000 native soldiers against an enemy estimated at 24,000. Generals Botha and Smuts carried through the war to victory by enveloping methods and by May, 1915, had driven the Germans into the northeast corner, captured Windhoeck, and by July had rounded up all the German forces. On July 8, 1915, Governor Seitz sent the following report to the Kaiser by means of the American embassy: "We inform Your Majesty that we are obliged to surrender to Botha the residue of the troops, about 3,400 men, being surrounded by far superior forces between Otavi and Tsumbeh." [26]

## East Africa

Alone of all the colonies, the campaign in East Africa lasted from the beginning of the war until the armistice. There the Germans possessed a defense army of about 300 whites and 11,000 natives, described by the British as "a compact and efficient fighting force which operated on interior lines and was a grave danger to British East Africa and Uganda." On the other hand, the British defense forces were numerically weak and scattered over a very wide area. The first attack came from the British who bombarded Dar-es-Salaam on August 8, captured it, destroyed the wireless station, and sunk the German survey vessel, Möwe, and the floating dock by August 13. According to the German account the first German counter-attack was made at Taveta on August 15. Germany then directed the campaign during the autumn of 1914 across the British East African frontier, which resulted in a great defeat of the British at Tanga. Throughout 1915 the honors were with the Germans who held the initiative, and the British were on the defensive until 1916. In that year General Smuts took command and led the British, Indian, Boer, and native troops in a drive north and south, while the Belgians and British troops moved eastward to the lakes.

The Germans, under the very able leadership of General von Lettow-Vorbeck, offered, according to the Allies, a notable resistance, one feature of which was the great loyalty displayed by the East African natives. Von Lettow-Vorbeck had had experience in the Herero revolt and, as described by the British, was of the "very first rank." The Allied forces outnumbered the German, however, and their advance was gradual but sure. The British won Tabara in the lakes, an excellent base, and forced the Kilamanjaro Gap. By September, 1916, the German hold was reduced to the district between the Rufiji and Mgeta rivers in the northeast and to the area bounded by the Ruaha and Ulango rivers in the southwest. A colossal drive was undertaken by Generals Hoskins and Van Deventer, with the cooperation of the Belgians in 1917, against which General von Lettow-Vorbeck, whose force had shrunk to about 1,100 whites and 7,700 *Askari,* opposed the greatest resolution and endurance which won for him a place of eternal renown in the Fatherland. In the face of overwhelming numbers he did not surrender until after the signing of the armistice in 1918.[27]

### The Pacific Islands South of the Equator

In the meantime while the German African colonies, except East Africa, were falling into British and French hands during the first year of the war, the South Pacific islands were occupied with speed and completeness by New Zealand and Australia. Samoa was the first to fall. A New Zealand contingent aided by a French and an Australian battle cruiser set off on August 15, seized Apia, the capital, on August 30, and on September 1 the British flag had replaced the German.

This quick action on the part of New Zealand excited and incited Australia, so she made haste to capture all the remaining German possessions in that part of the Pacific. The British flag waved at Herbertshöhe in New Guinea on September 11 where some resistance was encountered at the wireless station, and within less than two weeks German New Guinea, Kaiser Wilhelmsland, Samoa, and the Bismarck Archipelago had disappeared from the map[28] as German possessions.

### Kiao-Chow and Pacific Islands North of Equator

Japan, meanwhile, had attended to the footholds of the enemy in the Far East. On August 23 she sent an ultimatum to Germany advising her to hand over Kiao-Chow to her but the German governor, General Meyer-Waldeck, ordered the naval base to resist to the last. A Japanese force of

22,980, assisted by one British battalion and one-half a battalion of Sikhs, landed and attacked the garrison which was defended by a small squadron, two cruisers, the *Schornhorst* and the *Gneisau,* three armed cruisers, by the forts, *Bismarck, Moltke, Iltis, and Kaiser,* and by about 5,000 to 6,000 men. Obviously the Germans could not hold out for long. By the end of October, Japan had taken possession of Kiao-Chow as well as of the Caroline, Marshall, and Marianne Islands north of the Equator. Within three months the German flag was swept from the Pacific.[29]

### German Colonial War Aims

The sudden loss of her entire oversea empire with the one exception of East Africa during the early stages of the conflict incited, of course, a deep and universal regret in Germany, and gave a prominent place to colonial acquisitions in the avowed war aims of government and people; war aims which grew more and more ambitious with the apparent victory of the Central Powers early in 1918 and the partial realization of the *Mittel-Europa* scheme.

"No one is resigned to the loss of the colonies," said Secretary Solf in his speech December 22, 1917.[30] Indeed, both official and unofficial agencies demanded not only a reconstitution of the colonial empire but substantial additions thereto. Naturally, the blockade with its accompanying suffering caused by actual privation, increased the keen desire for colonial raw materials; and the experience of losing the unprotected and small colonial empire to the Allies at once deepened the feeling that colonies depended upon a German European security, a security which it was felt was being attained as the *Mittel-Europa* dream was realized. The two great colonial objectives, *Mittel-Afrika* and *Mittel-Europa,* plus Turkey, which, as we have seen, had been rapidly crystallizing since 1911, now reached their fruition and were each supported by extremists and moderates. Emil Zimmermann was, as formerly, the leader of the *Mittel-Afrika* school,[31] closely seconded by Professors Karl Dove, Delbrück, Hettner; by Drs. Rohrbach, Kolbe; *Freiherr* von Rechenberg, Karstedt, editor of the *Kölnische Zeitung,* and by many others.[32] Articles in *Das Grössere Deutschland,* the Pan-German weekly; in *Deutsche Politik,* Rohrbach's weekly; in the liberal weekly, *Europäische Staats und Wirtschaftes Zeitung,* and especially in the *Preussische Jahrbücher* [33] urged the old stock arguments for an extensive colonial empire—the arguments of economic necessity, of power and prestige—which were now elaborated and strengthened by Germany's war experience in the colonies. "Our colonial domain should have such an extent that it would not be exposed to conquest by the other Powers," wrote *Freiherr* von Rechenberg, former governor of East Africa; and "Africa is the coming continent," wrote Professor Dove. "Its future is rich and full of hope. . . . We mean, at least, to obtain that which is our due because we need it and require it for the existence of our children." A compact empire in Africa was contemplated, "so big that it would be capable of conducting its own defense in time of war." This domain would consist of the former German colonies plus the British, French, and Portuguese possessions south of Sahara and north of the Zambesi, including the islands off the coasts such as Madagascar, the Azores, Madeira, and Cape Verde.

Zimmermann pointed out that such a territory in Africa reaching from the Atlantic to the Pacific would enable Germany to dominate some of the most important trade routes of the world: *"Mittel-Afrika* would be at the very center of

England's main arteries leading to South Africa, Australia, India and, in German hands, would contribute to crippling the British empire and would drive North American influence out of South America. . . . Then, fifty years hence, it will only be a seven days' journey to Lake Tanganyika . . . and a Berlin mercantile firm will give orders in September: 'Pack up your samples, take the Congo express, and attend the autumn fair at *Wilhelmstadt,* as Stanleyville will then be called. We shall expect your orders in two or twelve weeks, and the goods will be delivered at their destination in December.' " [34] He considered that Mesopotamia's economic and political value was overestimated and preferred to visualize the day, "fifty years hence when 500,000 Germans or more would be living besides 50,000,-000 blacks in *Mittel-Afrika.* Then, there would be an army of 100,000 men and the colony would have its own navy like Brazil." [35]

The vision of *Mittel-Afrika* seemed to be by far the most popular of the colonial war aims and counted the most adherents. For many of those who followed Naumann in the *Mittel-Europa* project, with the extension of Germany's power over Mesopotamia as their main objective, also supported the creation of a "German India" in Africa, which, furthermore, possessed the advantage of holding out the prospect of actual territorial gain instead of merely the establishment of protectorates or the promoting of economic penetration. Such promoters of both schemes were, for example, Rohrbach, Oncken, Delbrück, and a host of others. [36] These men saw great results for Germany in a thoroughgoing advance into Asia, and Rohrbach, Dewall, and Mackey went so far as to suggest a German protectorate over China. [37] A *Petition* presented to the Chancellor in

June, 1915, signed by 352 professors, 158 schoolmen and ministers, 250 authors, publishers, and others making a total of 1,341 signatures demanded Central Africa, colonies in other parts of the world, and an extension of German penetration into the realm of Islam as war objectives; while in May, 1915, six great economic organizations drew up a document known as the *Petition of the Business Man*, which defined as war aims, "the possession of a colonial empire corresponding to the many-sided economic interests of Germany, and security for Germany's colonial policy in the future." [38]

Every political party except the Socialist supported the colonial war aims especially *Mittel-Afrika*, and even it was definitely divided on the subject.[39] In 1917, a dispute raged among the Social Democrats over this issue. Dr. Quessell and those other theorists—mainly Revisionists—who on the eve of the war had declared themselves in favor of colonies, gained recruits. Many Socialists, indeed, joined the short-lived non-partisan *Gesellschaft für Kolonialen Fortschritt* (Society for Colonial Progress), formed immediately after the war.[39a] Its aim was frankly to recover the colonies, but to direct their administration wholly in the interests of native welfare, although it also emphasized the economic necessity of colonial possessions. On the other hand, the "old guard" of the Socialist party stood their ground of opposition, and absolutely declined to be influenced by the "raw materials" argument which was at that time so peculiarly potent.

Another element of opposition was to be found in the extreme group of Pan-Germans led by Count Reventlow and others. They maintained that no colonial policy could meet with success so long as England controlled the seas, and hence they preferred to concentrate upon annexations in Flanders and in northern France. In the Conservative and

Agrarian journals principally may be found the expression of their views,[40] some of which went so far as to say that the war had demonstrated the futility of colonies and that in the future naval stations would suffice.[41]

For the most part, however, the country stood solidly behind the government in favor of demanding extensive colonial acquisitions at the Peace Settlement, although the plans of the colonial office were not quite so ambitious as those of the colonial enthusiasts. Colonial Secretary Dr. Solf, for instance, was extremely moderate and temperate in his speeches. He did not employ the terms, *Mittel-Afrika,* nor "German India," but did, nevertheless, insist upon annexing additional territory in Africa. "He who desires a durable peace cannot sympathize with the present partition of Africa, since it in nowise corresponds to the colonial capabilities or to the relative strength of the nations concerned." He also stated that, "The empire intends by no means to give up its valuable colonies at the Peace Settlement. On the contrary, it will endeavor to regain what is lost and to enlarge the German colonial possessions as much as possible"; and at another time he asserted that the *Mittel-Europa* plan would not afford Germany so much control over additional territory as to preclude her from seeking acquisitions elsewhere.[42]

### An Allied Propaganda Arises Against the Return of Germany's Colonies

Just as the loss of her oversea possessions at once stimulated concrete and extensive colonial war aims in Germany, so did their easy capture incite in the Allied countries a definite and vigorous propaganda against their return to their legitimate owners. In general, this propaganda appeared in two forms: one dilated upon the menace of German

373

"world power" in colonial territory to which the demands of the extremists in Germany, just reviewed, with their iteration of the terms *"Mittel-Afrika,"* "A German India" lent an alarming reality; while the other concentrated upon casting all kinds of disrepute on the character of the German colonial administration as a conclusive argument for the nonreturn of her colonies. In the war psychology which prevailed, no scandal, atrocity, or horror in the treatment of the natives was too insignificant, ridiculous or dubious to escape the Allied muckrake, which left no stone unturned to collect sufficient material to convince the world that it was the "moral duty" of the Allies to take over the German colonies.

Consequently, we find for the most part the French playing up the "world power menace," which was but a continuation of the same tune heard so clearly and so constantly on the eve of the war. Articles entitled, *Les intrigues allemandes au Congo belge, La dernière phase rêve coloniale allemande, Le pangermanisme colonial, L'Appetit allemande,* continued to fill the French press and to terrorize and to inflame the populace with the danger of restoring Germany's colonies.[43]

## Wholesale Condemnation of Germany's Colonial Administration

The British, on the other hand, turned their attention principally to the heaping up of evidence condemnatory of German colonial rule in contrast to their own; for they had, it will be recalled, cooperated considerably with the realization of Germany's ambitions in Africa, and so found it more suitable to leave the "world power menace" to the French to elaborate. As this sort of stone-throwing, especially for those who live in glass houses, is always a dangerous pastime, it exhibits, now that passions have cooled, a certain *naïveté* which only proves that war, along with everything else, destroys a sense of humor; a *naïveté* indeed which becomes the more striking, when one compares the British propaganda with the abundant testimony of many British imperialists before the war to the excellence, in their eyes, of many aspects of the German colonial rule. The *London Daily Mail* remarked, in all seriousness, for instance: " . . . it is a great good fortune for civilization that Dar-es-Salaam has been taken by the English since the Germans were so cruel to the natives. German professors write books about their anthropology after they have murdered them." [44] Even Lord Balfour in 1918 spoke of the "God-willed" capture of the German colonies, while Lord Robert Cecil went so far as to assert that "Germany has no moral right to colonies." [45]

This sort of propaganda reached its climax in such publications as *German Colonizers in Africa,* by Evans Lewin in which he stigmatized all of them as "cruel, brutal, arrogant, and utterly unsuited for intercourse with primitive peoples, lustful and malicious in their attitude towards subject races"; [46] in the official *Handbook,* entitled *Treatment of Natives in German Colonies,* prepared by the British Commission who assembled data for the Peace Conference, which omitted any reference to the abundant, impartial testimony of British observers before the war, who had praised of their own accord much of the German colonial rule; and in the *Blue Book* regarding South West Africa submitted to the House of Commons in 1918, which Premier Hertzog characterized in 1924 as "a war pamphlet that had already or soon would go into complete oblivion." [47]

So widespread was this propaganda against Germany's colonial administration, over which it must be remembered the Allies exercised a complete censorship, that the United

States was thoroughly infected with it. President Lowell of Harvard in a speech in New York in 1917 asserted that "Germany should never be permitted again to rule over the African natives whom she has exploited and destroyed." Commenting upon this, the *Deutsche Ubersee* recommended him "to read the history of the treatment of the American Indian in his own country." [48] Echoing Lowell, the *Boston Herald,* December 2, 1918, informed its readers that: "Germany has demonstrated her unworthiness for colonial administration. It is not to be considered that her colonies should be returned. They must become the trust of all free nations united in a League of Nations." Only the New York *Nation* seemed to maintain its balance. In its *International Relations Section* it remarked on October 19, 1919: "Before the war, British imperialists praised Germany's colonial policy, her administration, and her education of the native. But during the war, they suddenly discovered the opposite." [49]

President Wilson summed up what was evidently believed by the United States government in his speech at Paris, February 14, 1919, wherein he stated:

It has been one of the many distressing revelations of recent years that the Great Power which has just been happily defeated placed intolerable burdens and injustices upon the helpless people of some of the colonies which it annexed to itself; that its interest was rather to possess their land for European purposes, and not to enjoy their confidence that mankind might be lifted to the next higher level in those places. Now the world, expressing its conscience in law, says there is an end to that. Our conscience will be applied to this thing. States will be selected which have already shown that they have a conscience in this matter, and under their tutelage the helpless peoples of the world will come into a new light and into a new hope.

Also, in his address to the Senate the following July, 1919, he asserted that, "The colonies should be taken from Germany because she used them as objects of exploitation." [50]

The Germans, on their side, met all of these attacks upon the character of their colonial rule with a smarting sense of injustice and defeat which, in turn, inspired counter-attacks upon the Allies full of the *Tu quoque* argument.[51] Like the accusations of the Allies, these lost nothing in exaggeration in the heat of the conflict; but unlike the propaganda of the Allies, they were not able to be read by the rest of the world until after the close of 1918. The net result of this "battle of lies" waged so vociferously by the presses of all parties to the conflict was, naturally, to inject an impassioned determination into the war aims of both sides. And it is with this psychology which we have attempted to describe, with its distorted and heated view of the whole question, that the victors approached the colonial settlement, one of the most important for future world peace, at the Conference of Paris.

### The Treaty of Versailles Destroys the German Colonial Empire

Before proceeding to the detailed terms of the Treaty of Versailles regarding the disposition of the German colonies, let us summarize the situation in regard to these territories as it existed early in 1919, when the Congress convened. The Allies—France, Great Britain, and Japan—had been occupying and administering all the German colonies, except East Africa, since 1915, and—it must be remembered—possession is nine points of the law. Furthermore, for the perpetuation of that occupation several definite secret treaties and understandings were in existence: on March 4, 1916, Great Britain and France had signed a Convention dividing Kamerun and Togoland between them; in the secret treaty of London (April 26, 1915) France and Great Britain had promised to Italy "compensation" if they enlarged their possessions in Africa, meaning thereby additions to the Italian colonies in that continent; and in 1917 Japan had asked Great Britain, France, Russia, and Italy to agree to support at the Peace Conference, "the claims of Japan in regard to the disposal of Germany's rights in Shantung and her possessions in the island north of the Equator." To which Great Britain agreed on condition that the Japanese "would treat in the same spirit Great Britain's claims to the German islands south of the Equator. France agreed on condition that Japan would urge China to break relations with Germany, and Russia and Italy likewise consented.

Besides these secret agreements which, it will be noted, had pretty thoroughly disposed of the German oversea possessions before the Peace Congress met, there existed a whole series of secret treaties in regard to the liquidation of the Turkish empire, where German imperialistic penetration was already so strong and where German ambitions for the extension of *Mittel-Europa* were so keen. For, by the secret agreement with Russia in 1915, Great Britain and France had secured the addition of the neutral zone in Persia to the British sphere of influence, and the right to define their claims in Turkey later by promising Russia a part of Turkey with Constantinople; and subsequent secret treaties of April, 1915, and 1916 and 1917 had defined these claims by allocating Dodekanesia, Adalia, Smyrna and the southern coast of Anatolia to Italy; Syria, Cilicia and a sphere of influence stretching eastward toward the Persian border to France; Turkish Armenia in addition to Constantinople to Russia; and finally Mesopotamia, certain parts in Palestine, and a broad sphere of influence, besides Cyprus, to Great Britain.[52]

Furthermore, in addition to all these secret, but none the less definite and binding arrangements, there existed "hopeful expectations" on the part of the British Dominions and Belgium to which the Great Powers were more or less committed. Australia and New Zealand naturally expected to profit from the part which they had so efficiently played in the capture of the South Sea islands; the Union of South Africa expected to annex German South West Africa, and Belgium had high hopes of a reward for her share in the conquest of German East Africa.

With the foregoing situation in regard to the German colonial territories before us, we can see that Clause 119 of the Treaty of Versailles merely placed a rubber stamp upon what actually had taken place. According to that brief section—and brevity was all that was needed to confirm such a *fait accompli*—"Germany renounces to the Allied and Associated Powers all rights and titles to her oversea territories."

This renunciation was elaborated and made more complete by the succeeding articles contained in Part Four of the treaty. Specifically in favor of Japan were all German rights, titles and privileges abandoned in Shantung, particularly those concerning the territory of Kiao-Chow, railways, mines, and submarine cables, which had been acquired by the treaty concluded with China in 1898; while, generally, in favor of the Allied and Associated Powers, Germany was obliged to "recognize and accept all arrangements," which the said Allies "may make with Turkey," their right to negotiate such arangements being subsequently confirmed by the Treaty of Sèvres (article 94).[53]

In addition, all German rights under the Conventions and Agreements with France of 1911 and 1912 relating to Equatorial Africa were renounced; all German rights, titles, benefits, and privileges, commercial, economic, and political were canceled in China, Liberia, Siam, Morocco, and Egypt, where the English protectorate established in 1914 was to be acknowledged; and, finally, all German movable and immovable property in the aforementioned territories, as well as in those formerly owned by Germany, was to pass without indemnification to the new governments exercising authority over them; to whom also was the right given to reserve and to liquidate all property rights and interests belonging to German nationals in the ceded areas.[53]

Thus did the Treaty of Versailles write a thoroughgoing *finis* to the German colonial empire, not only in regard to Germany's actual oversea territory, but also affecting her commercial footholds, her spheres of influence, her economic penetration, and her imperialistic ambitions.

## The Disposition of the Former German Colonies

But a more difficult task than the mere confirmation of Germany's dispossession of her colonial empire remained for the Allies, and that was the disposition of these territories already won. For several insistent, not to say inconvenient, factors seriously interfered with the apparently simple, bare-faced annexation so well outlined by the secret treaties, and so efficiently accomplished already by the *beati possidentes*.

The first of these annoying obstacles was the Fifth Point of the famous Wilsonian Fourteen Points which formed the basis of agreement upon which the Armistice had been signed; a point which was taken very seriously and was interpreted to the letter by the Germans, especially the first clause thereof. This read somewhat ambiguously, as follows:

V. A free, open-minded, and absolutely impartial adjustment of all colonial claims, based upon the strict observance of the principle that in determining all such questions of sovereignty, the interests of the populations concerned must have equal weight with the equitable claims of the government whose title is to be determined.

In the second place, there was the attitude of President Wilson himself, who fought valiantly in the face of overwhelming odds to exalt and to enforce at the Peace Conference those idealistic, non-imperialistic, and non-annexationist aims for which the war had presumably been fought. For, in addition to the general principles expressed in Point Five, President Wilson had stated specifically in his address to Congress, February 11, 1918, that, "the day of conquest has gone by"; and again at Mount Vernon, July 4, 1918, he had asserted, "Every territorial settlement must be made in the interests and for the benefit of the people concerned." Furthermore, on his way to Paris, he formally stated to his associates of the Inquiry Committee that, he thought, "the German colonies should be declared the common property of the League of Nations, and administered by small nations. Then the resources of each colony would be available to each member of the League." [54]

And, lastly, a somewhat imponderable although none the less potent barrier to the exercise of undisguised annexation existed in the more or less popular, anti-imperialistic philosophy implicit at least in the very cause of the Allies. Though this may not have amounted to anything more than a "pious wish," and a convenient war-slogan in some quarters, it was sincerely and energetically promoted by such serious and important groups as the British Labour Party, the British Round Table, the Inter-Allied Labour Conference, as well as by such eminent authorities on imperialism as E. D. Morel and J. A. Hobson.

To these sentiments, also, no less a person than Lloyd George had at least rendered lip-service when, as early as June, 1917, he stated in a speech at Glasgow: "The fate of the German colonies must be determined by the Peace Conference, and in determining the trustees of these lands the wishes, desires and interests of the peoples must be the dominant factor." And, mindful of the anti-imperialistic platform of war aims published by the British Labour Party in August, 1917, he voiced the same idea in the House of Commons on December 20, 1917, and challenged the whole system of modern imperialism on January 5, 1918, when he asserted that, "The principle of self-determination is as applicable in their [the natives] case as in those of occupied European territory," and added that the governing consideration should be "to prevent their [the natives] exploitation for the benefit of European capitalists or governments." [55]

The problem, then, which confronted the Peace Conference in regard to the disposition of Germany's colonial territories was, first, the squaring of their outright annexation, already accomplished and guaranteed for the future by the secret treaties, with these idealistic principles whose chief champion was the disinterested and powerful American Republic, and to which the Allies out of their own mouths stood committed; and, secondly, to so apportion these annexations that every one would be satisfied. In short, some formula was obliged to be discovered, some formula at once so ambiguous and elastic that it would include and preserve two contradictory principles, annexation and non-annexation, imperialism and self-determination. A compromise, to put it squarely, had to be found at Versailles in regard to the German colonies between the selfish, nationalistic, well-tried *Machtpolitik* of the old régime and the untried, altruistic internationalism of an era that had barely dawned. And such a compromise was finally achieved in the mandate system enshrined in Article XXII of the Covenant of the League of Nations.

Although an account of the origin of the mandate system is admittedly beyond the scope of this book, it would seem highly important to our story to note several significant incidents in the history of its adoption, which clearly reflect the struggle between the old and the new ideas of imperialism. In the first place, the mandate principle as set forth by General Smuts in his Plan read as follows:

> There shall be in no case any annexation of any of these territories by any State either within the League or outside it, and that in the future government of these peoples and territories the rule of self-determination or the consent of the governed to the form of government shall be fairly and reasonably applied, and all forms of administration and of economic development be based primarily on the well-considered interests of the people themselves.

In the second place, this principle was not applied by General Smuts to the German colonies at all; he evoked it for the territories of Russia, Turkey, and Austria-Hungary. It was President Wilson who, using Smuts' language, included the German colonies within the zone of the mandate principle in his First and Second Paris Drafts of the Covenant, omitting first Russia and then Austria-Hungary. And, finally, it should be noted that the Resolution of January 30, 1919, which ultimately framed Article XXII of the Covenant, and set up the mandate system for Germany's colonies and Turkey's territories, was adopted by the Council of Ten only after radical changes had been made in the Wilsonian ideas and text to suit the annexationist ambitions of the Allies.[59]

According to the mandate system then, Germany's colonies, except Kiao-Chow, and Turkey's territories in which she possessed enormous imperialist interests, were separated into three classes of so-called mandates. The "Class A" mandates, defined as those territories which "have reached a stage of development where their existence as independent nations can be provisionally recognized subject to the rendering of administrative advice and assistance by a Mandatary until such time as they are able to stand alone," included the three Arab countries of Syria, Palestine, and Mesopotamia. The "Class B" mandates, described as "Other peoples, especially those of Central Africa, at such a stage that the Mandatary must be responsible for the administration of the territory under conditions which will guarantee freedom of conscience or religion, subject only to the maintenance of public order and morals, the prohibition of abuses such as the slave trade, the arms traffic, and the liquor traffic, and the prevention of the establishment of fortifications or military and naval bases and of military training of the natives for other than police purposes and the defence of territory, and will also secure equal opportunities for the trade and commerce of other Members of the League," comprised Togoland, Kamerun, and German East Africa. While the "Class C" mandates, cleverly and inclusively classified as territories "which, owing to the sparseness of their population, or their small size, or their remoteness from the centers of civilization, or their geographical contiguity to the territory of the Mandatary as integral portions of its territory, subject to the safeguards above mentioned in the interests of the indigenous population," consisted of German South West Africa and certain of the South Pacific Islands.[57]

The most cursory examination of both the setting up of the mandate system and of its provisions reveals its character as an ambiguous and clever compromise, the citation of a few examples of which will suffice to illustrate. On the one hand, the idealistic principles of "tutelage," "sacred trust" and non-annexation were recognized by the ornate and grandiloquent rhetoric of the opening paragraph of Article XXII; by granting to the "A" mandates the exalted status of transitorial protectorates; and by placing heavy duties of "trusteeship" upon the "A" and "C" Mandataries to provide a just and beneficent native rule. While, on the other hand, the undisguised annexationist aims of the victors were all too obviously, not to say dramatically, projected at the Conference when the colonial question was suddenly and unexpectedly forced to the forefront of the discussion. According to the order of business proposed by President Wilson, it had been agreed to discuss the League of Nations first and the colonial question last. But this order was exactly reversed for, as Lloyd George succinctly remarked: "They all wanted to know what they were going to get," and so they could not wait any longer. Then, also, the old ambitions, only thinly disguised by altruistic phraseology, cropped up in the division of the colonies into different classes which, contrary to the Wilson plan, left only the "A" mandates, instead of all, subject to a provisional tutelage terminating in independence; in the failure to apply to the "A" mandates the guarantees against violations of the open door or of exploitation; in the practical annexation permitted of the "C" mandates, inserted mainly to satisfy the British Dominions; and, finally, in the vague designation of authority to allocate and to adminsister the mandates instead of definitely naming the League the sovereign authority, as Wilson intended. For, according to this latter provision, the mandate system left to the Allies themselves the right to appoint themselves as Mandataries and to exercise almost the same powers as annexation would have secured.[58]

## Germany's Reaction to the Dispossession and Disposition of Her Colonial Empire

Germany's reaction to the dispossession of her colonial empire and to the means proposed for its disposition presented to her by the Treaty of Versailles and the Covenant of the League on May 7, 1919, was an opposition that shook the nation with its violence. And we have only to recollect the strength of the colonial movement in Germany during the war and the scope of her colonial war aims not to be surprised at the force with which the German people repudiated the terms of the colonial settlement.

Indeed, as the treaty was taking shape during 1918-1919, and it became only too evident what the fate of the German colonies would be, a campaign of protest was already gaining considerable momentum in Germany. Mass meetings were held throughout the country,[59] the entire press, even the Socialist organs, were permeated with the subject, and the German National Assembly was besieged by petitions [60] from every group who was directly or indirectly interested in the colonies, one such petition containing 3,794,000 signatures.[61] The burden of the argument was ever the same: the injustice of the discrepancy between the threatening dispossession of the colonial empire and Point Five of the Fourteen Points upon which the Armistice had been signed. One *Petition* was addressed *To the American People,* and *An Open Letter* was sent to President Wilson by the Colonial Society.[62] The latter, after enumerating the American

President's various utterances in regard to "no annexations," claimed that he had allowed himself to be influenced exclusively by Allied propaganda condemning the German colonial administration, invited him to read the official publications of the colonial office in regard to native rule, reminded him once more of Point Five of his Fourteen Points, and concluded with the appeal, "We demand nothing more from you than Justice." Finally, the campaign against the threatened extinction of the colonial empire may be said to have crystallized in the official *Protest*, voted by the German National Assembly on March 1, 1919,[63] which characterized the colonial settlement as "unbearable, unrealizable, and unacceptable (*unerträglich, unerfüllbar, unannehmbar*)." This vote was unanimously supported by every party with the exception of the Socialist which was, as usual, divided on the subject of colonization, the Revisionists voting in favor of and the Independents against the *Protest*.

### The Germans Propose Another Colonial Settlement

With the force of this national opposition behind it, the German delegation at the Peace Conference did all in its power to regain—or rather from its point of view, to retain—the colonies. Dr. Bell, who had succeeded Dr. Solf as colonial secretary in 1918—by that time an office with an empty portfolio—went himself to Versailles and contributed his efforts to the *German Comments on the Conditions of the Peace*,[64] which dealt with the colonial settlement. After reiterating the injustice of the dispossession both in its contradiction of Point Five and of previous agreements such as the General Acts of Berlin and of Brussels, the Delegation claimed as Germany's right to keep her colonies, her lawful acquisition of them, recognized by all the Powers before the war; her economic need of them, especially press-

387

ing since the war; and her duty to cooperate in the civilization of backward races, justified already so amply by her record of native rule. The Germans then put forward two proposals for the colonial settlement: first, that a special committee handle the matter who would at least hear Germany's side, inasmuch as Point Five provided for an "absolutely impartial adjustment"; and, second, that Germany be allowed to administer her former colonies "according to the principle of the League of Nations—possibly as the Mandatary of the latter—if a League is formed which she can enter at once as a member state, enjoying equal privileges with other members."

### The Allies Reject the German Proposals

It is not at all surprising that the Allies rejected these proposals and refused to alter by one jot or tittle the terms of the colonial settlement which they had dictated. They could hardly have done otherwise, given the circumstances and the prevailing psychology. For the acceptance of the German plan would have entirely destroyed that carefully worked-out compromise between annexationist and non-annexationist principles—that nice balance between selfish ambition and moral responsibility; would have wrought havoc among the Allies themselves by depriving some of them of their already achieved gains; and, finally, would have wrecked that well-constructed propaganda against German native rule, upon which the whole settlement was based.

The reasons advanced by the Allies for their refusal were: ". . . the Allied and Associated Powers are satisfied that the native inhabitants of the German colonies are strongly opposed to being again brought under Germany's sway, and the record of German rule, the traditions of the German government, and the use to which these colonies were put as bases from which to prey upon the commerce of the world, make it impossible for the Allied and Associated Powers to return them to Germany, or to entrust to her the responsibility for the training and education of the inhabitants. . . .

"Germany's dereliction in the sphere of colonial civilization has been revealed too completely to admit of the Allied and Associated Powers consenting to make a second experiment and of their assuming the responsibility of again abandoning thirteen or fourteen million natives to a fate from which the war has delivered them." And accompanying the foregoing was a severe indictment of German colonial rule on the grounds of cruelty, slavery, compulsory labor, and militarization.[65]

It is obvious that these reasons contain a complete rationalization of the Allied dispossession of Germany's colonial empire. They present, indeed, the very best example to be found in history of a "defense reaction" to the application of the principle that "to the victors belong the spoils." What is more, they reflect the efficacy of that propaganda against Germany's colonial administration which was so potent that it seemed to convince even its authors of its essential truth. As a well-known British historian wrote in discussing the Allied refusal to change the colonial settlement:

Whatever concessions might be made in other fields, where the Allies themselves were assuming the risks, none could be made as regards the colonies where the burden of miscalculation would fall well-nigh exclusively upon the helpless natives.

The Allied and Associated governments were not justified in exposing thirteen million natives to such patent risks, even if the return of the colonies to Germany would have added to the stability of the European settlement. Such speculation at the expense of others is indefensible. Hence the Peace Conference refused to alter the colonial clauses.[66]

With the cooler and more dispassionate judgment evoked by the passage of seven post-war years, however, another equally famous British historian has unreservedly condemned the Allied claim that annexation of the German colonies was called for in the name of "morality" as "rash and dangerous." [67]

## The Colonial Empire Falls

Germany's enforced signing of the Treaty of Versailles on June 28, 1919, gave the Allies the legal right to carry out the last act in the destruction of the German colonial empire, which they proceeded with some delays to complete.

A Commission appointed by the Allies had already met in London, May 19, 1919, and had drafted the terms of the "B" and "C" mandates. It declared that Kamerun and Togoland should be divided between France and Great Britain in accordance with the Convention to that effect signed by the two governments, March 4, 1916. France, however, was so imbued with the annexationist principle that she interpreted the agreement to mean that the area concerned should not be governed as a mandate, but annexed. This is evident from Colonial Minister Simon's speech in the Chamber, September 7, 1919, in which he said that the "New Cameroons" had been a colonial Alsace-Lorraine, and would return to the full sovereignty of France; and in regard to the other territories, while he admitted France to be bound by Article XXII of the Covenant, he considered it sufficient to maintain the open door, to abolish the slave trade and compulsory labor, to limit the traffic in alcohol and arms, and to publish a *Yellow Book* annually, but otherwise it was purposed to administer the territory in union with the adjoining area "without a mandate, but in the spirit of the mandates." During the ensuing negotiations with the British

Foreign Office, however, this point of view was finally abandoned, and a mandate agreed to with the one significant concession that France be permitted to recruit a military force in her share of Togoland and the Cameroons not only for the "defense of the territory," but, unlike the other mandates for the defense of the territory, "outside that subject to the mandate." France had contended this right to recruit colonial troops for use outside the mandated territory from the very beginning, and the Council of Ten had accepted the principle so far as France was concerned on January 30, 1919, when it voted the Resolution which framed Article XXII of the Covenant.⁸⁸

The former German Kamerun, then, was separated into three parts: the so-called New Cameroons, consisting of 107,000 square miles and 2,800,000 natives, was reincorporated into French Equatorial Africa; nine-tenths of the Old Cameroons, 166,489 square miles and a population of 2,800,000 were given to the French government as a "B" mandate under the League; and the remaining one-tenth, with an area of 31,000 square miles and a population of 555,000, was awarded on the same terms, with the exception of the military clause, to the British government. Likewise, almost two-thirds of Togoland, containing 22,000 square miles and 747,000 population, went to France, and the rest, 12,600 square miles with 185,000 population, to Great Britain, both as "B" mandates. Great Britain also received the former German East Africa, rechristened Tanganyika territory, but later to satisfy Belgium's claims renounced a small portion of 21,255 square miles and 3,000,000 population on the northwest boundary adjoining Belgium Congo known as Ruanda-Urundi, retaining 365,000 square miles of territory with 4,125,000 population, all held as "B" mandates. According to program, former German South West Africa was awarded to the British Union of South Africa, "New Guinea" (German Kaiser Wilhelmsland, Bismarck Archipelago, and German Solomon Islands) to Australia, German Samoa to New Zealand, the valuable island of Nauru to Great Britain, and the Caroline, Marshall, Marianne, and Pelew islands to Japan, who, as we have already noted, received Kiao-Chow directly, and not as a mandate.

Owing to delays, occasioned by difficulties encountered in the delimitation of boundaries and in obtaining the consent of the United States, the "B" and "C" mandates were not actually confirmed by the Council until July 20, 1922. More than one year later, in September, 1923, the "A" mandates, designated as Palestine, Syria, and Mesopotamia, where Germany possessed, if not actual colonial territory, most important spheres of interest and extensive ambitions, were approved: Syria was awarded to France, Palestine to Great Britain. A mandate was never awarded for Mesopotamia where, instead, the Arab kingdom of Iraq was set up by Great Britain, who signed a treaty of alliance and supervision with that kingdom on October 10, 1922, and obtained the approval of the League Council thereto on September 27, 1924.

Thus the last vestige of Germany's modern colonial empire, won, organized, developed, and lost within the span of a single generation, disappeared from the map of the world.

But today, in Munich, that cultural and political center of the old imperial Germany, may be seen a tablet simply inscribed "The Colonies," set in the wall of the Hall of Generals along with many others to commemorate German territories lost in the Great War. A huge, funereal evergreen wreath conspicuously decorates it; a poignant and symbolic witness both to the completeness with which the Treaty of Versailles terminated Germany's modern colonial history, as well as to the nation's desire to keep the memory of her lost colonies fresh in the minds of the present generation and of those to come.

## NOTES

[1] See *supra.*, ch. viii, p. 243.

[2] *Verhandlungen des deutschen Reichstages,* 1912-1913, vol. 284, p. 1530 *et seq.,* April 29, 1912. Also, May 1, 1912, and March 14, 1913.

See also, *Koloniale Rundschau,* 1914, *Heft* 4, p. 193, for report of 1914 debates.

[3] *Verhandlungen des deutschen Reichstages,* 1912-1913, vol. 284, p. 1513 *et seq.*

[4] *Ibid.,* 1914, vol. 295, pp. 8876, 8892; March 12, May 13, 1914, *et seq.*

[5] *Frankfurter Zeitung,* May 29, 1914.

[6] *Report of Quessell's article in Deutsche Post,* 31 Aug., 1919. *Koloniale Rundschau,* 1911, p. 22.

[7] *Hamburger Echo,* 11 March, 1914.

See also, his speech in *Reichstag,* 30 April, 1912.

*Verhandlungen des deutschen Reichstages,* 1912-1913, vol. 285, pp. 1554, 1558, *et seq.*

"Instead of the thorough-going repudiation which we Social Democrats have always practiced towards the colonial policy, we will make it our task to cooperate with all our strength so that Justice and *Kultur* may prevail more than it formerly has done."

[8] *Hamburger Echo,* 31 May, 1914.

[9] *Verhandlungen des deutschen Reichstages,* 1912-1913, vol. 285, p. 1541, 30 April, 1912.

[10] *Jahrbücher über deutsche Kolonialpolitik,* 1913, p. 12 *et seq.*

[11] von der Heydt, A., *Kolonial-Handbuch* (Berlin), 1913.

[12] Beer, G. L., *African Questions at the Peace Conference* (New York, 1923), p. 49, citing *Belgian Correspondence Diplomatique.*

[13] Lichnowsky, *Memorandum, op. cit.,* p. 105.

[14] *Deutsche Weltpolitik und Kein Krieg* (London, 1913).

[15] *Kriegschriften der Kaiser-Wihelms Dank,* 1916, P. Leutwein, "*Koloniale Lehren des Krieges.*" Relates how Pan-Germans were not deceived by the talk of compromise with England, 1913-1914, their apprehensions having been realized by the war.

[16] *Deutsche Kolonialzeitung,* 31 May, 1913.

[17] *Usambaru Post,* 8 Jan., 1913.

[18] *United Empire,* 31 Jan., 1912.

*The Standard,* London, 23 Jan., 1912.

[19] *Dépêche Coloniale,* 20 Mar., 1913.

Reply in *Preussisches Jahrbuch,* June, 1913, *Heft* 3 in *Kolonialzeitung,* 5 April, 1913.

[20] Account in *Kolonialzeitung*, 1914, p. 230.

[21] "*L'Appetite*," *Echo Toulouse* (Toul), 27 June, 1914.

"*Le partage*," *Africaine*, Feb., 1913.

"*La pénétration*," in *Salut Public*, 12 April, 1914.

*Journal du Soir*, 11 March, 1914.

"*La rivalité anglo-allemande*," *Questions Diplomatiques et Coloniales*, Dec., 1913.

*Le Temps*, Feb. 3, 1914.

Dec. 30, 1913.

See also, *Revue Hebdomadaire*, 9 May, 1914.

[22] *The Berlin Act* (signed at Berlin, 1885), Article xi. Printed in Buell, *op. cit.*, vol. ii, pp. 897-898.

[23] *Das Kolonial Blatt*, 1920, Feb. 28, nos. 1-4, which contains German and Belgian official documents.

O'Neil, H. C., *The War in Africa and the Far East* (London, 1918), pp. 3-5.

*Denkschrift über den Krieg in Afrika, Geschichtskalender*, 25 March, 1915.

*Kolonialzeitung*, 1914, p. 555.

[24] O'Neil, *op. cit.*, ch. ii.

Lucas, C., *The Empire at War* (London, 1924), vol. iv, p. 27.

[25] *Ibid.*, ch. v.

*Ibid.*; ch. iv.

[26] *Ibid.*, ch. iv.

·Temperley, H., *History Peace Conference at Paris* (London, 1920), vol. ii, ch. v.

Von Oelhafen, H., *Der Feldzug in Südwest*, 1914-1915 (Berlin, 1923).

[27] O'Neil, *op. cit.*, ch. vi.

Temperley, *op. cit.*, vol. ii, pp. 223-225.

Lucas, *op. cit.*, p. 152 *et seq.*

von Lettow-Vorbeck, General, *My Reminiscences of East Africa* (Eng. trans., London, 1920).

Schnee, H., *Deutsch-Ostafrika im Weltkriege* (Leipsig, 1919).

Schnee, Ada, *Meine Erlebnisse während der Kriegszeit in Deutsch-Ostafrika* (Leipzig, 1918).

[28] O'Neil, *op. cit.*, ch. v.

Scott, A. P., *Introduction to the Peace Treaties* (Chicago, 1920), p. 138 *et seq.*

[29] O'Neil, *op. cit.*, ch. iii.

[30] Grumbach, S., *Das Annexionistische Deutschland: Eine Sammlung von Dokumenten* (Lausanne, 1917), p. 9.

[31] Zimmermann, E., *Das deutsche Kaiserreich Mittel-Afrika als Grundlage einer neuen deutschen Weltpolitik* (Berlin, 1917).

[32] Delbrück, H., *Bismarcks Erbe* (Berlin, 1915).

Dove, K., *Weltwirtschaft*, Nov. 1915, "Die Grossen Wirtschaftsgebiete Afrikas."

Hettner, A., "Die Ziele unserer Weltpolitik," in *Der Deutsche Krieg, Heft* 64, Berlin, 1915.

Rohrbach, P., *Zum Weltvolk Hindurch* (Stuttgart, 1915).
Kolbe, F., *Deutsche Politik* (1916), Dec. 22 (1917), Feb. 2.
Rechenberg, A., *Nord u. Süd,* Feb. 1917.
Karstedt, O., *Kölnische Zeitung,* Dec. 22, 1917.
Wiedenfeld, K., *Deutsche Kriegschriften, Heft* 6 (1915).
Mehrmann, K., *Gross-Deutschland* (Dresden, 1915).
[33] See Grumbach, *op. cit.,* pp. 183ff., 222ff., 234ff.
[34] Zimmermann, E., *Europäische Staats und Wirtschafts Zeitung,* Oct. 6, 1917, p. 948ff.
*Preussisches Jahrbuch,* Feb. 1917, p. 329ff.
[35] *Ibid., Europ. Staats. u. Wirts. Zt.,* June 23, 1917, p. 683 *et seq.*
*The New Europe,* no. 43, Aug. 9, 1917, p. 122.
[36] *Koloniale Rundschau,* Jan., Feb., 1917.
Oncken, H., *Das alte und das neue Mittel-Europa* (1917).
See Grumbach, *op. cit.,* pp. 280ff.
[37] Grumbach, *op. cit.,* pp. 303, 309.
[38] *Ibid.,* pp. 132ff., 123ff.
[39] *Koloniale Rundschau,* Jan. 1917, p. 46; 1916, pp. 126, 414.
*Kolonialzeitung,* 20 Dec., 1916.
[39a] *Gesellschaft für Kolonialen Fortschritt, Satzung u. Grundsätze* (Berlin, 1919).
[40] Grumbach, *op. cit.,* pp. 292, 56ff. Especially in *Deutsche Tageszeitung.*
[41] *Grenzboten,* Aug. 16, 1916.
[42] Solf, Colonial Secretary, *Speech* to German Col. Society, Dec. 21, 1917.
*Speech,* May 11, 1915.
*Speech,* May 3, 1916.
Grumbach, *op. cit.,* pp. 9-10.
Beer, *op. cit.,* p. 52.
[43] *L'Heure,* Aug. 5, 1916.
*L'Afrique Francaise,* March 17, 1917.
*Le Semaphore de Marsailles,* April 23, 1917.
*La Dépêche Coloniale,* May 4, 1917.
*La XXᵐ Siècle,* Havre, May 30, 1917.
France also published material attacking German colonial rule. For criticism of, see *Deutsche Ubersee,* 31 August, 1916.
[44] *Kriegsmitteilungen des Kolonial Wirtschaftlichen Kommittee,* quoting the *London Daily Mail.* Oct. 7, 1916.
[45] *Norddeutsche Allg. Zt.,* 22 August, 1918. (*Balfour.*)
*London Times,* 24 August, 1918 (Cecil). See also, *Morning Post,* 14 Dec., 1918.
[46] Lewin, E., *German Colonisers in Africa* (Pub. in German, Zurich, 1918).
[47] *Handbooks Prepared under the Direction of the Foreign Office* (London, 1920).
*Report on Natives of South West Africa and Their Treatment by Germany* (London, 1918). Issued from Government House at Windhoek.

See in regard to, Dawson, W. H., in his *Introduction* to Schnee, H., *German Colonization Past and Future, op. cit.*, p. 20.

The *African World*, 14 Sept., 1918, printed a summary of this report in which it stated: "This Report is one of Savagery, Robbery, and cruel Slavery which culminated in the Herero Rebellion."

[48] *Deutsche Ubersee*, 26 Oct., 1917.

[49] Schoenemann, F., *Die Kunst der Massenbeeinflussung in den Vereinigten Staaten von Amerika* (Berlin, Leipzig, 1924), p. 170 *et seq.*

[50] Poeschell, H., *Die Kolonialfrage im Frieden von Versailles: Dokumente Zur Ihrer Behandlung* (Berlin, 1920), pp. 1, 2.

[51] *Reichskolonialministerium, Deutsche und Französische Eingeborenenbehandlung. Eine Erwiderung auf die Journal Official de la Republique Francaise*, 8 Nov., 1918; 5 Jan., 1919.

*Die Deutsche Kolonialpolitik vor dem Gerichtshof der Welt* (Basel, 1918).

*Der Tag*, May 22, 1919.

[52] Moon, *op. cit.*, pp. 473-474.

[53] International Conciliation, *Treaty of Peace with Germany*, no. 142.

For details regarding the disposition of the private and public property in the former colonies by the Allies, see Buell, *op. cit.*, vol. i, p. 436 *et seq.*

Also *note art. 438* of *Treaty Versailles*, regarding the property of missions and of trading companies whose profits were devoted to support of missions. It provides that said property shall continue to be devoted to missionary purposes. This, the Allied governments have executed by appointing Boards of Trustees to whom they have handed over such properties. In 1928, the British restored its rights to the *Baseler* Mission on the Gold Coast.

[54] Temperley, *History Peace Conference, op. cit.*, vol. ii, p. 226.

Miller, D. H., *The Drafting of the Covenant* (New York, 1928, 2 vols.), vol. i, pp. 101-117.

[55] Temperley, *History Peace Conference, op. cit.*, vol. ii, p. 227.

[56] Miller, *op. cit.*, vol. i, ch. ix; vol. ii, *Smuts Plan*, p. 28.

*Wilson's First Draft*, p. 87.

See also, Baker, R., *Woodrow Wilson and the World Settlement* (New York, 1922), vol. i, p. 250ff.

[57] *Covenant League Nations*, Article xxii, *International Conciliation*, no. 139, p. 832.

[58] See second paragraph of Article xxii of *Covenant. Ibid.*

[59] *Frankfurter Zeitung*, 1 April, 1919.

[60] Poeschell, H., *Die Kolonialfrage im Frieden von Versailles: Dokumente Zu Ihrer Behandlung* (Berlin, 1920), pp. 113, 116, 118, 119.

[61] *Ibid.*, p. 113.

[62] *Ibid.*, quoting *Deutsche Kolonialzeitung*, August 20, 1919.

[63] *Ibid.*

[64] *International Conciliation*, Oct. 1919, no. 143, pp. 1249-1252.

[65] *Ibid.*, Nov. 1919, no. 144, pp. 1372-1374.

[66] Temperley, *op. cit.*, vol. ii, p. 228.

[67] Schnee, *German Colonization Past and Future, op. cit., Introd. by* W. H. Dawson, p. 20.

[68] Buell, *op. cit.*, vol. ii, p. 228.

Miller, *op. cit.*, vol. i, pp. 116-117.

# INDEX

399

# INDEX

Allied propaganda against return of German Colonies, 373-374
Allies, 1, 332
  carry war into Colonies, 363-364
  reject German proposals, 388-390
Alsace-Lorraine, 98, 318
Amanus mountains, 344
Ambitions, restrained, in the New World, 201-208
America, 15, 20, 26, 36, 37, 57 and *see* United States
America, Central, *see* Central America
  Latin, *see* Latin America
  North, *see* North America
  South, *see* South America
American Republic, 382
Amsterdam, 20
*Amtsblätter,* 299
Anatolia, 213, 343, 378
Anatolian Railway, 213
Anatolian Railway Company, 217
Anglo-Belgian treaty, 183
Anglo-French convention, 87
  rapprochement, 310
  treaty, 311, 312, 313
Anglo-German Accord, 198
  Agreement, 140, 191, 192
  Alliance, 310
  Colonial aims, 85
  "Colonial Honeymoon," 112-114, 183
  Convention, 343
  rapprochement, 309, 346
    on the Portuguese Colonies, 344-350
  relationships, 164
  treaty, 140, 161-165, 172, 190, 198, 344-350
    gambles on Portuguese Colonies, 189-192
  understanding, 191, 192
Anglo-Persian Company, 343
Anglo-Portuguese treaty, 87, 88, 90, 345
Angola, 90, 129, 190, 191, 340, 346, 347
Angora, 210
Angra Pequena, 88, 89, 90, 103, 107, 128, 143, 163
*Annales Coloniales,* 362
Annexation opportunities afforded by Algeciras Conference, are rejected, 314-316

Anti-German feeling in United States, 193
Anti-Polish campaign, 96
Antisocialist legislation, 96
Anti-slave-trade campaign, Catholic, 117
Antilles, 15, 30
Apia, 48, 71, 146, 280, 298, 368
Appropriations for Colonies, 240
Aquatown, 143
Arabia, 213
Arabs, 139
Arab slave-trade in East Africa, 117
Arbitration tribunal, native, 279
*Archiv für Schiffs und Tropenhygine,* 295
Areas of African Colonies, 265
  of Pacific Colonies, 266
Argentina, 39, 202, 204
Arguin Island, 15
Armed Neutrality, 103
Armenia, 378
Armstrong, 210
Arnold, Professor, 203
Asia, 208, 239
Asia Minor, 209
Asiatic trading companies, 16
Asiatic Triple Alliance, 187
Askari, 255, 365, 368
Association for Opposition to African Liquor trade, 300
  for suppression of socialism, 242
  of German merchants, 8
Attitude of William II, 309-311
Augsburg, 12
*Augsburg Allgemeine Zeitung,* 34, 209
Augwar, 261
Australia, 1, 36, 42, 63, 86, 100, 108, 146, 151, 199, 368, 379, 392
Austria, 6, 32, 51, 214, 322, 333, 334
Austrian succession, war of, 16
Axenberg, 234
Axim, 15

Bagdad, 344
Bagdad-Basra, 216
Bagdad-Basra railway, 346
Bagdad railway, 213-216, 315, 317, 324, 328, 329, 330, 340, 341, 343, 360

# INDEX

# INDEX

403

# INDEX

# INDEX

405

# INDEX

# INDEX

# INDEX

# INDEX

# INDEX

411

# INDEX

# INDEX

# INDEX

# INDEX

North West Kamerun, 254
Norway, 8, 9, 20, 22, 24
Noske, 358
Novgorod, 19
Nivo-Bazar, 332
Nubia, 34
Nuremberg, 12
Nyssa, lake, 140
Nyssaland, 140

Obstruction tactics, 97
Oceania, 48, 76
Octavi mines, 171
Oertzen, von, 146
Offenbach, 82
Official attitude toward natives, 274-276
    colonies, 124
Officialdom kills the colonies, 171-173
Officials, colonial, training of, 251
Ogrove river, 46
Old Cameroons, 391
Oncken, 371
Opolu, 70, 199, 200
Opportunist grasps the opportunity, 86-91
Opposition, 95, 96, 98, 111, 241
    and Triple Entente, 330-332
    finally vanquished, 116-118
Orange river, 89, 128
Oregon, 40
Orient, the, 15, 26
Otto, 132
Ottoman empire, 211
    government, 210
Otymbingue, 43, 47

Pacific, the, 208
    German possessions in, map of, 200
Pacific colonies, area of, 266
    chief ports of, 266
    chief products of, 266
    deficit of, 266
    economic status of, 266
    expenditure in, 266
    exports of, 266
    imports of, 266
    minerals in, 266
    native population of, 266
    railways in, 266
    revenue of, 266
    subsidy, 266

Pacific colonies, whites in, 266
Pacific islands, 146, 368-369
Palestine, 42, 378, 384, 392
Panama canal, 40, 146, 192
Pan-German League, 164, 182, 217, 231, 242, 312, 326
Pan-Germans, 203, 207, 312-313, 324, 325, 326, 361, 372
Paraguay, 13, 39
Paris, Conference of, 377
Parliamentary struggle reaches a crisis, 241
Particularism, 21
Particularists, 75
Patagonia, 56
Peace of Frankfort, 63
    of Westphalia, 24
Peace Conference, 382, 387
Peace Congress, 378
Peace Settlement, 30, 276, 373
Pelew archipelago, 261
    islands, 117, 196, 240, 392
    area of, 266
    chief ports of, 266
    chief products of, 266
    deficit in, 266
    expenditure in, 266
    exports of, 266
    imports of, 266
    minerals of, 266
    native population of, 266
    railways of, 266
    revenue of, 266
    subsidy, 266
    whites in, 266
Peltz, 81
Pemba, 135, 191, 341, 346
Penguin islands, 346
Peonage, 285
Pereira, Baron von, 39
Permanent Mandates Commission of the League of Nations, 287
Persia, 213, 256, 338, 378
    Shah of, 15
Persian Gulf, 309, 332, 340
Personnel, colonial, 172, 173
Perthes, 33
Peters, Karl, 83, 84, 115, 131, 132, 136, 137, 138, 156, 163, 166, 173, 230, 234
    founds German East Africa, 131-136
*Petition of the Business Men,* 372
Pfeil, Count, 132

417

# INDEX

Philippines, 56, 57, 191, 193, 194, 195
  neutralization of, 193
Philippsohn, 81
Phosphates, 261
Physicians in Colonies, 298
  in East Africa, 298
  in Kamerun, 298
  in Kiao-Chow, 298
  in New Guinea, 298
  in Samoa, 298
  in South West Africa, 298
  in Togoland, 298
Plantations, independent, in East Africa, 168
  in Kamerun, 168
  in Togoland, 168
Planters, German West African, 276
Podbielski, 236
Poland, 6, 22
Poles, 75, 98
Police, Askari; 365
Police force in East Africa, 289
  in Kamerun, 289
  in New Guinea, 289
  in South West Africa, 289
  in Togoland, 289
Political bureaucracy dominates the Colonies, 225-229
Political economists, 33
Political status, in African colonies, 278
  in South Sea Colonies, 280
  of natives, 276-280
Political weakness of the Hohenzollerns, 25-28
Pomerania, 14, 25
Ponape, 195
Pondicherry, 57
Population, native, of African Colonies, 265
  of Pacific Colonies, 266
Port Arthur, 188
Ports, chief, of African Colonies, 265
  of Pacific Colonies, 266
Porte, 334
Portugal, 2, 12, 37, 140, 190
  colonial possessions in, size of, 2, 270
Portuguese-African Colonies, 344
Portuguese Angola, 129
Portuguese Colonies, Anglo-German rapprochement on, 344-350

Portuguese Colonies, Anglo-German Treaty on, 189-192
Poshan, 262
*Post, die,* 327
Postl, Karl, 35
Potsdam Agreement, 338
  Settlement, 340
Pragmatic Sanction, 27
Pressel, von, 210
Preventive medicine, 299
Principe Island, 347
Private enterprise prepares the mind and the way, 30-52
Private initiative carries on alone, 17
Proclamation of a United Germany, 179
Products of African Colonies, 265
  of Pacific Colonies, 266
Progressives, 75, 95, 96, 358
Prokesch, Anton, 34
Propaganda, 81
Protectorates, 63, 125, 149
  Boer, 184-186, 190
  East African, 133, 141
  Transvaal, 184, 185
Protectorate troops, 289
  in East Africa, 289
  in Kamerun, 289
  in South West Africa, 289
Protestant National Liberals, 231
  Revolt, 18, 23, 24
  Union, 21
Protestantism, 21, 24
Providence Islands, 151
Prussia, 6, 31, 35, 50
  colonial policy of, 14-16
  economic council of, 77
  rescript, 39, 202
Prussian Rescript on emigration, 202
Prussian-British alliance, 217
Publicists, 36, 329
Puttkamer, von, 230, 234, 251

Queensland, 86
Quessell, Dr., 357, 372

Rabat, 310
Raboul, 260, 280
Radical opposition, 96
Radicals, 96, 97, 98
Radolin, 315
Railroads, 114, 140, 200, 255, 267, 263

418

# INDEX

# INDEX

# INDEX

423

# INDEX